The Economy, Liberty and the State

CALVIN B. HOOVER, one of America's most distinguished economists, has had wide experience as author, professor, and public servant.

Hoover has been professor of economics at Duke University since 1927 and in 1952–53 was president of the American Economic Association. He has been a working farmer, consultant to private business, and has served the government as researcher, adviser to military authorities and administrator.

He lived in Moscow in 1929–30 and wrote *The Economic Life of Soviet Russia.* He was in Berlin at the time Hitler came to power, and wrote *Germany Enters the Third Reich.* He continually supplements study and analysis with firsthand observation and made two trips to Russia and parts of Europe while working on *The Economy, Liberty and the State,* which he regards as the capstone of his career.

THE ECONOMY, LIBERTY AND THE STATE

CALVIN B. HOOVER

Anchor Books
Doubleday & Company, Inc.
Garden City, New York
1961

FOREWORD

This volume represents the fruit of a happy collaboration between the Twentieth Century Fund and Dr. Hoover. Inevitably more personal than the surveys with which the Fund has traditionally been associated—indeed in some sense the intellectual autobiography of this distinguished scholar and public servant—the study is the synthesis of many years and many books. Dr. Hoover has looked at the divergent economic systems of the West and Communist Russia. He has shown how often the actualities depart from the theoretical formulations by which we characterize them. He has measured the degree to which these various systems meet the basic human desire for liberty and justice.

The reader will find in these pages something more than economic analysis; he will find the reflections of a learned and widely traveled man upon some of the transformations that have shaken the twentieth century world. The Fund presents this study as part of its continuing effort to add to an understanding of this world, as well as to knowledge of its basic facts.

AUGUST HECKSCHER, *Director*
The Twentieth Century Fund

41 East 70th Street, New York
January 1959

ACKNOWLEDGMENTS

My colleagues Professors B. U. Ratchford and Don D. Humphrey have been good enough to read the manuscript of this study and I have profited greatly from their critical comments. I am also obliged for frequent exchanges of ideas with my colleague Professor Joseph Spengler. Professors Frank Hanna and Charles Ferguson have helped me with the statistical aspects of Soviet economic growth. These services by my colleagues do not imply agreement with my conclusions. Errors are mine.

I have for over thirty years given a course in Economic Systems at Duke University which, so far as I know, was the first course by that title in the United States. Its prototypes, however, were the courses in Capitalism and Socialism by the late Professor John R. Commons and Foreign Labor Movements by Professor Selig Perlman which I took as a graduate student at the University of Wisconsin in 1922. I am grateful to Professors Commons and Perlman, just as I am to the generations of students who have taken my own courses. I have profited greatly from their class discussions and term papers.

It must be recorded that the Soviet government has over the years granted six visas permitting me to enter the Soviet Union. Four of these were issued after it had become well known from my publications that I was a most severe critic of Soviet institutions and practices. I greatly appreciate the personal courtesy of Soviet officials, economists, managers of factories and of collective and state farms who gave me interviews and information within the limits of official regulations and policy.

My thanks are due to the editors of *Foreign Affairs,* the *American Economic Review, Kyklos,* the *Journal of Farm Economics* and the *Proceedings of the American Philosophical Society* for permission to reprint portions of articles of mine previously published. Similarly, my thanks are due to the editors of the *Harvard Business Review, Challenge,* and the *Virginia Quarterly Review* for permission to include portions of articles in this latest edition. All these reprinted portions have been amended and altered, however.

I am deeply indebted to the economists who made the studies of their own countries for the two volumes of *Economic Systems of the West* and particularly to Edgar Salin and Rudolf Frei, joint editors of *Kyklos,* who not only edited the volumes for the List Gesellschaft but made the arrangements for publication, and were instrumental in inducing the authors to undertake the surveys. Greatly appreciated financial aid from the Twentieth Century Fund made publication possible.

Mrs. Carolyn Thomas is due my thanks for the industry, skill and patience with which she has deciphered and typed the unconscionable number of tortured drafts through which this study has gone.

Mrs. Elizabeth Blackert has provided general editorial supervision for the study. It was fortunate that Mrs. Ruth Rocker who has so painstakingly edited the manuscript was possessed of both an unusual interest and background in the field of the study. I am grateful to both Mrs. Blackert and Mrs. Rocker.

Above all, I wish to thank the trustees and staff of the Twentieth Century Fund, whose generous support made the study possible. In particular, I am indebted to J. Frederic Dewhurst, Director of the Fund at the time the study was undertaken. The continuous and warm interest and the sympathetic support of August Heckscher, present Director of the Fund, is primarily responsible for my getting the study done at all. The encouragement of Thomas R. Carskadon, Associate Director, is also warmly acknowledged.

I wish also to express my appreciation to the Research Council of Duke University for financial aid in certain aspects of this study.

CALVIN B. HOOVER

TABLE OF CONTENTS

PROLOGUE

It would be vain to claim pure objectivity in this study. It deals with the relationships among national economies, liberty and state power, relationships which involve the ways of life and of death of all the world's inhabitants. This study is inevitably in large measure a personal appraisal. An account of my contacts as an observer of, or a participant in, the economic and political systems analyzed in this volume may facilitate the discounting of biases which the intimacy of my experiences with these systems has no doubt produced.

I had followed with avid interest and warm sympathy during my undergraduate days the news accounts of the overthrow of the tsarist government by the Russian people in the February Revolution of 1917, and had been extremely disappointed when the Kerensky Provisional Government was overthrown by the Bolsheviki. Yet later I reacted with bitterness to the rumor that my own regiment, then part of our occupational forces in the Grand Duchy of Luxembourg in the spring of 1919, might be sent to Archangel or Vladivostok to join other American troops against the Bolsheviki. While this reaction was due primarily to selfish reasons, I still had a faint hope that the Soviet state might develop into a form of democratic socialism, and I felt that it would be totally wrong to overthrow the regime with the help of foreign bayonets.

Thereafter, for years I read every history or memoir dealing with the Revolution and the Civil War which came to hand and never missed an opportunity to discuss these events with Russians in exile who had fought against the Soviets. Later, while living in Moscow, I was able to converse with those who had participated in or had endured the Revolution and Civil War. Consequently, Chapter 2, which deals with the Russian Revolution, is written with some feeling of intimacy, even though I was neither a participant nor a visual observer as in the case of most of the developments analyzed in this study. I have, nevertheless, relied upon published sources in this chapter to a somewhat greater extent than in the other chapters.

I lived in Moscow in 1929–30 during the early years of the First Five-Year Plan when the beginning of planned industrialization and the forced collectivization of the Russian peasants were taking place. I have returned to Russia for brief periods since, most recently in the late spring of 1958. On this last trip I also visited Poland, Czechoslovakia and Yugoslavia briefly.

In connection with my most recent visit to Eastern Europe it is essential to review the problem of how one obtains data in totalitarian countries from which dependable conclusions may be drawn. Assuming that an adequate background exists, it is possible to obtain most useful data from personal observation and from official interviews which one can then analyze and discount as necessary. Wherever the police state exists, however, only a substantial period of residence under circumstances in which a foreigner could develop unofficial contacts with the population might afford a chance of reaching dependable conclusions about the real feeling of the people towards a totalitarian regime. Under such conditions a few individuals might be induced to say to foreigners what they fear to say to each other, but there surely would not be many such. Moreover, in a totalitarian state, the authorities will take every precaution to see that foreigners are not permitted substantial periods of residence under circumstances in which personal relations of confidence might develop.

Thousands of American tourists, and many thousands of other nationalities, are now visiting the Soviet Union every year. A somewhat similar flow of tourists has begun to Czech-oslovakia, Yugoslavia and Poland. Visas to enter the Soviet Union are now easy to obtain. A considerable number of cities, including the principal cities in widely separated areas, are listed in the tours which can be arranged through Intourist. The limitation of tours to certain designated cities is probably motivated primarily by a shortage of suitable hotel accommodations elsewhere. Once in Moscow or in one of the other cities, one may walk about quite freely almost anywhere. Indeed, this has been generally true over the almost thirty years during which I have been visiting the Soviet Union. One is not free to barge into an office or factory without making previous arrangements, nor can the tourist ordinarily visit in the homes of individuals. But this is true in all countries.

In spite of the increasing interchange of tourists between Russia and the Western world, the success of the government in maintaining the barrier between the population and the outside world is remarkable. That this barrier is far less obtrusive than it was under Stalin reflects the very substantial diminution in the terroristic character of the Soviet regime since Stalin's day. The cultural exchange program which has been agreed upon between the United States and the Soviet Union, like similar programs with other countries, can be expected to reduce the communication barrier somewhat further. Yet even in the case of cultural exchanges it can be expected to continue.

Consider the case of a Soviet student who spends a year in the United States under such a program. Suppose that after he returns he receives a letter from an American student with whom he became friendly. Such a letter might run as follows: "I have cited many times your severe and detailed criticism of certain aspects of the Soviet system and your expression of personal distaste for Khrushchev's buffoonery to prove to Americans that there really is freedom of thought and freedom to criticize in the Soviet Union. I have often cited the case of the unjustified arrest and execution of your father under Stalin and his posthumous rehabilitation under Khrushchev as an example both of your freedom to discuss matters of this sort and of the great improvement which has taken place." The Soviet student must always guard himself against giving anyone the opportunity to write such a letter to him. Yet he must, if he can, avoid admitting to Americans that censorship exists and that he would be in serious danger if such a letter were to be written to him.

Language is an obvious barrier to appraising the feeling of the people towards any of the economic and political systems of Eastern Europe. In my own case, while I read Russian, my spoken Russian, never fluent and now rusty from disuse, did not on this most recent trip afford free and easy communication with the Soviet populace, even if this had otherwise been feasible. In Poland and in Yugoslavia, where the fear of the police was decidedly less than in Russia, I was dependent upon English, German and French, except to the extent to which reliance could be placed upon interpreters and the very limited degree to which it was possible to follow the gist of a conversation through the similarities of Czech, Serbian and Polish to Russian. In Czechoslovakia, the fear of the police state and the language barrier prevented almost all conversation in which Czechs might have wished to express criticism of the regime. On two occasions the risk was taken by Czech citizens in spite of language difficulties.

Language would have been no real barrier if the police state had not been in existence. There would have been no serious problem in communication if anyone had wished to say something like "I don't like the regime and I like Khrushchev (or Gomulka or Tito) even less," and to give his reasons for this dislike. A language would have been found to convey the basic feeling if not the precise details. The language barrier and the police state work together, however, to prevent the development of contacts between foreigners and citizens that might form the basis for at least a limited degree of mutual confidence. I was able to develop such contacts when I lived in Moscow in 1929–30 but have not been able to do so since that time. Even if there had been no language barrier at all, almost no criticism of the Soviet type of regime was to be expected. Decades during which the charge of communication with foreigners often meant imprisonment or even death have been the experience of the whole Soviet population. Though the barriers to communication with foreigners have been relaxed, there has been no general removal of the ban and the population is well aware of this. Suppose one spoke Russian fluently and without accent. Would this afford any assurance whatever to a Soviet citizen that what he might say in criticism of the regime would be kept confidential? On the contrary, if one's Russian approached perfection, a Soviet citizen might be even more likely to fear that one was an agent of the regime who was trying to entrap the careless citizen.

Patriotism and good taste do limit many United States citizens in criticizing their public officials in the presence of foreigners, yet no language barrier has prevented foreigners visiting the United States from hearing criticisms of Franklin Roosevelt or Harry Truman or Dwight Eisenhower, still less of Henry Wallace or Richard Nixon, during their terms of office. The absence of criticism of an existing regime is certain evidence of the existence of the police state. If I had traveled in Poland or in Hungary before the uprisings of 1956, I would probably have heard almost no criticism of the existing regimes. It was only these revolts which made it clear that the Polish and Hungarian people hated their rulers.

It is some measure of the undoubted but still limited relaxation of the Soviet police state since the death of Stalin that it is still substantially more difficult to have contact with Soviet citizens and conferences with Soviet officials than it was in 1929–30 when I was living in Moscow and wrote *The Economic Life of Soviet Russia*. In between these two periods of relative relaxation there stretched the Stalinist reign of active terror. Yet even in 1929–30 communication between Soviet citizens and foreigners was fraught with terror. While three or four of us were living together in a small house in Moscow during this period, we discovered that our maid had orders from the G.P.U. to deliver the contents of our wastebaskets each week. It was more serious when a minor official of the Commissariat of Foreign Affairs who sometimes used to visit us for tea and a hand of bridge, and who we assumed had been delegated to the task of keeping an eye on us, was arrested. Even though he was a member of the Party and had apparently been carrying out assigned duties, we never saw him again. We did hear that he came under suspicion because an uncle of his had tried to escape to Latvia. We used to send him parcels of food and clothing in prison, something it was probably inadvisable for us to do. We never heard from him after his arrest. According to rumor, he was eventually executed.

The most serious danger to a Soviet citizen who might communicate with foreigners was and is the utter inability of people from a free society to realize the dangers therein to Soviet citizens. At its worst this inability to understand the nature of the police state sometimes reflects a grotesque and disastrous naïveté. During this early period an American connected with a religious organization used to make periodic visits to Russia. As he was about to leave after one of these visits, he told some American newspaper correspondents how he had unmasked the Soviet claim that there was no persecution of religion. "I asked a Soviet official point-blank whether he denied that religious persecution existed. He replied that of course he denied it, whereupon I gave him the names and addresses of a number of persons who had told me that they had been the victims of such persecution." The indignation with which the American newspaper men told me of this case can be imagined.

But it is difficult oneself to avoid less obvious ways of endangering Soviet citizens. In two instances which I recall to my deep regret I merely mentioned to Soviet officials that I had talked with two Soviet economists. The mere fact of their talks with me was a minor item used against them in subsequent purge trials. Yet I tried hard never to endanger anyone with whom I came in contact. During my residence in Moscow in 1929–30 I never visited the home of my closest Russian friend; we always parted company some blocks away. My friend had reason to know the risks he ran, and he hoped that our association might not become known and that he might at least avoid involving his family in the risk.

This same friend recounted how he had once been asked by a Soviet official to serve as interpreter for an American Communist who was visiting Moscow. He was most reluctant to undertake the assignment and tried to beg off on the grounds of his insufficient command of English. The official insisted that his English was good enough. However, he said, "Do you recall the case of ——? (naming a man who was known to have been executed for alleged crimes). Do you know the real reason he was executed?" "No," said my friend. "The reason was simple," said the Soviet official. "He chattered." The Soviet official mentioned the name of another man who had been executed. Once more he repeated his question, "Do you know why he was executed?" "No," replied my friend. "He chattered," said the Soviet official. A third name was mentioned with the same question and answer. My friend was as frightened as it was intended that he should be. In serving as interpreter for the American Communist, he used all his ingenuity to explain away any critical observations about the Soviet system.

I never saw or communicated with my Russian friend after the day I left him in May 1930. I was always tempted to look him up when I returned to Russia through the years since I had a warm affection for him, but I never did. The risk to him and his family would have been too great. Only during this last trip did I learn that he had been killed during the war.

This long history of danger in almost any communication with foreigners is associated with recurrent warning signals that intimate contacts with foreigners are still sternly prohibited. The expulsion while I was most recently in Moscow of one of the secretaries in the U.S. Embassy for no other reason than that he had enrolled as a student in Moscow University and had begun to make some personal friends among Russians is a case in point. The planting of documents intended to be incriminating upon one of the personnel of our Embassy in Prague by a Czech citizen with whom he had become friendly, with the resultant expulsion of the American official, is another case in point.

I feel, nevertheless, that I always learn much of the greatest value from a visit to Soviet Russia. I learned even more from my recent visits to Poland and Yugoslavia because freedom of communication with foreigners is now greater there than in Soviet Russia. The situation in Czechoslovakia was similar to that in Russia. Yet no foreigner is now in a position to appraise with any certainty the feelings of the Russian or the Czechoslovak people towards their totalitarian states, nor, indeed, can one be sure of the feelings of the Yugoslav or even the Polish people towards their regimes. Of the Russian people one may hazard the statement "The population appears substantially less frightened of the state power than they were under Stalin," but no one can truthfully say that under present circumstances this impression is based upon free and really meaningful communication with the Russian people.

The problems of acquiring data upon which conclusions might be based were somewhat the same in the case of the Nazi system as in the Soviet case. Except during the war, however, contact with the outside world was never so restricted as in the Soviet Union. I lived in Berlin in 1932–33 during the months before and after Hitler came to power. I spent most of the summer of 1939 in Germany, and left on the day the Nazi armies marched into Poland. I returned with the American army in June 1945 to the ruins in which the Nazi regime had left Germany.

Although I have had to rely principally upon my own observation and analysis of the Soviet and Nazi totalitarian systems, I felt a need for the views of other economists with respect to the nature of the modern modified capitalistic economic systems of the United States and Western Europe despite the much greater intimacy of my contacts with the economic systems of the West. In late 1933 I became a participant in the first experiment in massive governmental intervention in the management of our own economy as economic adviser and later consumers' counsel in the Agricultural Adjustment Administration. I was closely associated at that time with Secretary Henry Wallace, with Rexford Guy Tugwell, then Assistant Secretary of Agriculture, and with the second Administrator of the A.A.A., Chester Davis. This participation in government has continued at irregular intervals down very nearly to the present time. My observation of the economic systems of Western Europe began from the very limited vantage point of a corporal of field artillery, billeted in peasant barns and cottages in 1918–19. From 1929 to the present, I have continued to observe the economies of Western Europe on various missions as a research economist or as a government official.

There is a sharp controversy among American economists with respect to the extent to which our capitalistic system has been modified. In an effort to obtain an analytical statement of conflicting views concerning the nature of the current economic system, substantially the whole of the annual meetings of the American Economic Association in 1953 were devoted to this subject and related matters. I am indebted to my fellow economists, the members of the Executive Committee and others who aided in planning the program, and to the economists who prepared papers or participated in other ways in these meetings. The papers from the 1953 meetings were published in the *Proceedings* of the American Economic Association in May of 1954. I have made use of them in Chapters 8 and 9 of this study.

With these *Proceedings* available as a background, economists from fifteen countries of Western Europe, Canada and Japan undertook to do surveys of the economic systems of their own countries. These studies, in the organization of which I participated, were published by the List Gesellschaft in two successive volumes in the fall of 1957 and the fall of 1958 under the title *Economic Systems of the West*. Their publication was in part financed by the Twentieth Century Fund. I have drawn substantially on these volumes for my chapters on the economic systems of Western Europe. Indeed, my excuse for the very limited space which I have devoted to the countries of Western Europe is that they have been covered far more adequately in these volumes. I would have felt seriously handicapped if the studies published by the List Gesellschaft had not been at my disposal. Unfortunately, only part of the galley proofs of the second volume were available in time for my use.

As recounted in the Epilogue, I was able to extend this study to a brief survey of the economic and political systems of the present or former satellite countries of Soviet Russia. So long as these systems had remained replicas of the Soviet system this had not seemed worth doing, but recent events in Yugoslavia and Poland seemed to warrant this extension of coverage.

To have attempted to cover the economic systems of countries in other parts of the world would have extended this study to unconscionable lengths. It would be highly desirable to have studies made of the economic and political systems of non-European countries by economists of these countries. I hope that some of these studies will soon be under way.

CHAPTER 1

OLD-STYLE CAPITALISM

Economic and political systems do not conform to precise and logical models. The capitalistic system was never adopted in any country as a social contract in some sort of constitutional convention. It gradually evolved in somewhat different forms in the various countries. At the peak of its development, serious vulnerabilities had become evident and it began to undergo fundamental change.

Until World War I, however, one might have maintained that the image of capitalism could be clearly visualized and that there would be near-identity between the image and the actually functioning system. Prior to 1917, capitalism could be represented by its proponents not only as the best and most efficient of economic systems which had yet evolved but as a universal system as well. There were indeed areas of the world, more or less backward, in which the capitalistic system could not yet be said to function fully. But even in these areas, it could be pointed out that development towards capitalism was being enormously accelerated by the exportation of capital and capitalistic techniques from the more advanced countries, with the developmental process steered into the most productive channels by the force of self-interest, unhampered by state controls.

The capitalistic system could logically be represented not merely as highly efficient and as universal, it could be plausibly regarded as without an alternative. Economic systems of the past had been clearly outmoded by the superior efficiency of capitalism. Critics, in talking of alternatives to capitalism, could offer only purely intellectual constructs or were reduced to drawing conclusions from the various utopian experiments like Brook Farm or such religious communities as Amana. No other actually operative economic system had appeared as a contemporary alternative to capitalism.

Just as old-style capitalism did not come into being at the same moment or in the same way in all countries in which it constituted the dominant socio-economic system, so with its ending. It was to be overthrown with violence in one major country and to undergo gradual transformation in others. Still, one can say that the foundations of capitalism were so shaken by World War I that it was never the same thereafter. In the United States and to some extent in other capitalistic countries, there was a revival of old-style capitalism which lasted until the beginning of the Great Depression in the fall of 1929. This depression brought the recrudescence to an end, and since that time the structural and functional changes in the economic systems of even those countries which did not formally repudiate capitalism have been of profound significance.

Anyone who lived for some years under old-style capitalism might wonder that such a political and economic system could have existed for an immensely important historical epoch—and equally that the system should by now have been overthrown or substantially modified throughout the world. Marx was quite logical in seeing in private property the really fundamental institution of old-style capitalism and in directing his attack upon it. Unrestricted private property, particularly when associated with the institution of unlimited private inheritance, is so vulnerable from the standpoint of social equity that one might well wonder how an economic system based upon it could exist unless originally imposed and continually maintained at bayonet point.

Private property was an absolutely necessary institution for the accumulation of capital, for its mobilization and for its operational direction, if the responsibility for production was not to be borne by the state. It is all the more remarkable that the institution of private property could have endured so long without any apparent necessity for a legal or constitutional theory or principle to justify its existence.[1] Unlike the feudal estate, capitalistic private property gave the absolute right to receive income without the obligation of service to be rendered. This property right had come to be more absolute in the United States than in any other country since it was protected by a written constitution which eventually denied the power of both the federal and state legislatures to impair private property. In all capitalistic countries, however, private property attained a high degree of inviolability. Like the concept of liberty, to which under American law it became assimilated, it was everywhere treated as a "natural" right without specific functional obligations associated with it.

To those who held little or no property, the rights of private property might appear just as hateful as the manorial obligations of the masses under a feudal system. Indeed, anticapitalistic urban riots and uprisings have historically been rooted in the same bitter sense of injustice which produced the peasant risings of Wat Tyler in England, of the Jacquerie in France or of Stenka Razin in Russia.

However, since the ownership of property under capitalism did not depend upon an unchanging personal status, the income which workers had to furnish to property owners, by comparison with manorial obligations, might well have seemed less inequitable and indeed a step towards personal liberty. Moreover, as capitalism developed, the institution of private property was essential to the separation of the exercise of political power from the exercise of economic power. Through this separation of political and economic power it became possible to reduce greatly the power of the sovereign and indeed the scope and arbitrary character of all forms of state power. Thus the state could begin to be a government of laws and

---

[1] The Supreme Court of the United States did sometimes attempt a philosophical defense of property. Thus, in the minority opinion in the first Slaughterhouse Case in 1873, which became the majority opinion in the second Slaughterhouse Case eleven years later, the doctrine of John Locke and Adam Smith of the origin of property in labor was used as a justification for the protection of private property against governmental regulation.

not of men, just as it becomes a question, now that old-style capitalism has been superseded, whether governments which must once more resume at least a large measure of control over the economy can remain governments of laws rather than of men.

Once the authority of government could be excluded from control of and responsibility for the operation of the economy, the authority of men over men, sanctioned by state power, could be set within much narrower and more inflexible limits. Again it was in the United States through the adoption of a written constitution, with the Bill of Rights, the separation of powers, the two-chamber legislature, and the division of power between state and federal governments, that this limitation upon the authority of the state reached its highest point. Yet this deliberate hampering of the powers of the state was to become in greater or less degree a characteristic of countries with fully developed capitalistic systems.

This limitation of state power was practicable only upon the assumption that the responsibilities of the state for the economic welfare of the people could be kept at a minimum. Indeed, it was assumed that the functions of the state were primarily negative: it had only to refrain from acting itself and to prohibit acts which would interfere with the freedom of individuals to carry on economic activities. So long as the state had only the function of "holding the ring" within which individuals engaged in the economic struggle, it did not much matter in peacetime how greatly the restrictions placed upon its powers interfered with the ability of government to take and carry out decisions quickly and efficiently. Unlimited priority could be accorded to whatever constitutional or other limitations might be required to protect the individual against the state.

"The executive of a modern state is but a committee for managing the common affairs of the whole bourgeoisie," says Marx in the *Communist Manifesto*. There is no doubt that the laissez-faire state, stripped of the economic powers and responsibilities which its predecessor had wielded, facilitated the development and operation of the old-style capitalistic economic system. There can also be no doubt that the bourgeois class was in the forefront of the struggle which resulted in the divestment of the economic powers of the state. But this divestment made feasible the emasculation of the arbitrary and unlimited powers of the state over the lives and liberties of men. The development of individual liberty was recognized as a good in itself. The general craving of men for personal liberty has greatly facilitated the development of capitalism as the growth of capitalism limited the power of the state over the economy. Furthermore, the weaker the power of the state, the less the power to determine the distribution of any income above subsistence levels among individuals and classes. In limiting the powers of the state, the intimacy, the frequency and the violence of the exercise of sheer coercive power in allocating income was minimized.

The record is overwhelmingly clear that the early revolutionary socialist opponents of capitalism feared and hated not only the capitalist state but any state, just as did the anarchists. The experience of the classes to which the revolutionary opponents of capitalism could appeal had always been with government as an instrument of repression, whether in feudal or in capitalistic times. It was quite logical, therefore, that Marx in appealing to the masses should advocate not an increased role for the state but instead a total "withering away of the state."

It is consequently an extraordinary paradox that both the overthrow of old-style capitalism in some countries and its transformation in others should reverse this trend towards the minimization of the role of the state. Substantially the whole complex of civil rights which characterized capitalistic society —freedom of speech, freedom of the press, habeas corpus, trial by jury, immunity from arrest by general warrant, and the like—was to disappear under the Soviet and Nazi economic and political systems.

Thus, contrary to Marx's identification of the modern state as a committee for the management of the common affairs of capitalists, the development of the laissez-faire capitalistic state afforded the most effective socio-political instrument which had ever been devised for protecting the population of a country against the coercive powers of a ruling bureaucracy.[2] The

---

[2] Thus the laissez-faire system of capitalism could quite fairly be represented as having brought as near to realization as was humanly

experience of Soviet Russia and of the other Communist states which were the successors of capitalist states was to demonstrate that a bureaucracy which, in addition to its political functions, administers the whole economy could far more accurately be described as a committee managing the common affairs of the bureaucracy in its own interests than the political bureaucracy of a capitalistic state could be said to administer the government in the interests of capitalists as a class.

When the state surrendered control over the economy, production became implicitly the responsibility of countless competing producers. They were compelled to act in the best interests of society, not by the coercive power of the state, but by the dictates of self-interest. From the beginning of the modern state and increasingly through time, this relinquishment by the state of control over the economy meant turning over production to the capitalist and eventually largely to the capitalistic corporation. Yet even so, as long as there was a substantial degree of competition, as long as numerous autonomous corporate entities existed, the denial of the coercive powers of the state to the managements of these entities meant that personal freedom was not so limited as it had been when the state had power over and responsibility for the economy.

This is not to deny that every economic and political system does indeed have its "ruling class," since a minority, not the majority, must always carry on the actual function of ruling. It has consequently been enormously important all through history to a ruling class that its "religion" be adopted by the masses of the population, even though the rule has been imposed in the first instance by the sword.[3] The task of ruling is

---

possible that "withering away of the state" which Marxists had declared to be the final and ideal stage of Communism and which they claimed could come about only by the revolutionary overthrow of capitalism.

[3] The importance of inducing acceptance of the interests of the ruling class as the duty of the ruled is comprehensively developed by Gaetano Mosca. As Arthur Livingston, who edited the 1939 translation of his *Elementi di Scienza Politica*, paraphrases Mosca: "There is always a ruling minority, but such minorities never stop at the brute fact of holding power. They justify their rule by theories or principles which are in turn based on beliefs or ethical systems which are accepted by those who are ruled." Gaetano Mosca, *The*

greatly facilitated if the ruled can be induced to find a religious or quasi-religious justification for serving the ruling class.

Thus, the ability of the capitalistic system to maintain itself without the continued necessity for the use of force against revolutionary protests has depended heavily upon the development of a general feeling that the system was morally admirable and sanctioned by the Christian religion, that its replacement was unthinkable, that it was immortal. It was the development of this charism, quite as much as the demonstrable economic efficacy of the system, which enabled capitalism to survive for so long relatively unchanged.

Yet the ruling class of the capitalistic system was a far less highly organized and exclusive class, not only than the ruling class of feudalism, but than the "New Class" in the Communist states which took over when capitalism was overthrown.[4] The fact that the management of the economy was left in the hands of numerous individual capitalists made it more unlikely that there would be a tightly knit ruling class from which the governing bureaucracy would be drawn and in whose interests the state and economy would be administered.

Moreover, the doctrine of laissez faire, so appropriate for the fullest development of capitalism, eventually was to prove incompatible with the close supervision and control of men's thoughts, speech and writings. Consequently, it became possible to dissent from the tenets of old-style capitalism without incurring the penalties exacted by other systems for nonconformity.

While it is true that the minority must always rule, it is exceedingly important from the standpoint of human liberty that the ruling bureaucracy should have its power circumscribed and that it should be responsible in some meaningful

---

Ruling Class, translated by Hannah D. Kohn, edited and revised, with an introduction by Arthur Livingston, McGraw-Hill, New York, 1939, p. xv.

[4] Milovan Djilas, himself for some years a high-ranking member of the "New Class" in Yugoslavia, Vice-President and close associate of Tito, pointed out after his break with the regime that the ruling bureaucracy in a modern Communist state, in effect, owns jointly and exploits primarily for its own benefit the property which was expropriated from the bourgeoisie. *The New Class,* Praeger, New York, 1957.

fashion to the ruled majority. The relinquishment of control over the economy under the typical capitalistic system automatically circumscribed the power of the government bureaucracy. Moreover, during the final century of old-style capitalism, popular control over the state bureaucracy, inherently extremely difficult to implement in the case of any bureaucracy, attained a substantial degree of efficacy.

The personal freedom of the worker who did not possess property was, of course, sharply limited under old-style capitalism. The possibility of loss of job was a potent limitation upon his liberty. Yet obviously this limitation upon liberty would be potentially even greater if instead of working for individual capitalists or for capitalistic corporations he were to have only one possible employer, the state, unless by some means the worker could hope effectively to limit the powers of the managing bureaucracy of the state.

However necessary the institution of private property had been as an instrument to effectuate capitalist accumulation and as a means to organize production, the inequality in the possession of property could only mean a great differential in the degree of personal freedom among individuals under capitalism. The relinquishment of control over the economy, brought about under the leadership of the bourgeois class, had been accompanied by the relaxation of the power of the governmental bureaucracy over the individual. One all-important economic responsibility and power had, however, remained in the hands of the state. This was the power to define and defend the institution of private property.

If the state could have been kept in the control of a "committee managing the affairs of the bourgeoisie," one might have expected that the institution of private property, involving a high degree of inequality in the distribution of income, would have been maintained unchanged at all costs.

In fact, all the social, political and philosophical aspects of the doctrine of personal freedom meant that it was not possible to deny representation in government to the masses of the population forever. The reluctance of property owners to permit participation of the propertyless in the election of legislators was partially overcome by the fact that the mere right of electoral participation served as at least a temporarily effective placatory device and as an alternative to the expression of revolutionary violence against the institution of private property.

During the greater part of the nineteenth century the discontent of the masses found a channel of expression in demands for the widening of political democracy through universal suffrage and associated types of parliamentary reform. Indeed, the extension of political democracy to the masses of the population could be considered a device by which their latent bitterness towards the economic system could find harmless expression in voting for or against candidates representing political parties which were in agreement that the machinery of the state should not be used to control or to intervene in the economy in any important way, much less to alter it fundamentally.

In the United States the Fifth and Fourteenth Amendments to the Constitution were to serve in this way until the New Deal period of the mid-1930s. A whole series of Supreme Court decisions under these amendments effectively barred legislation in the economic field; it was, in principle, as though a socialist regime which had once nationalized industry should change the Constitution so that thereafter it would be unconstitutional for Congress to legislate the denationalization of industry.

However, the development of political democracy based upon universal suffrage made it inevitable that the majority of the electorate should some day demand that the powers of the state be exercised in their behalf. If men were to be equal when they voted, how were they to be prevented from voting to direct the machinery of the state to function in the economic interests of the majority of the voters?

From the millions of unskilled and semiskilled workers, dependent upon a precarious daily wage, an economic system which placed no limits upon inequality in wealth and income, which provided no security against sickness and old age, which accepted no responsibility for preventing unemployment or compensating for it, or for any of the vicissitudes of life, could not be expected to receive unqualified support. It was inevitable that the granting of political democracy would eventually produce among the lower-income groups the demand for economic intervention by the state in their behalf. If this demand were to be met, the institution of private property would have to be modified.

The hatred of the have-not classes for the institution of private property has always been based largely upon the unequal distribution of income from property.[5] The unreality of the simple assumption that under capitalism one class held property while another class worked is apparent. The actual situation was, of course, far more complex.[6] Millions of small businessmen in all capitalistic societies, millions of farmers in the United States and peasants in Europe were property owners as well as workers and under the normal working of the capitalistic economic system thought of themselves as the former rather than the latter. Professional men and salaried personnel had a similar attitude. The more highly paid skilled workers owning small amounts of property did not feel instinctively that "Property is robbery."[7]

The "high visibility" of the inequity of private property as between the haves and the have-nots under capitalism served to obscure to the laborer the fact that a very large proportion of the "deductions" from the social product "withheld" from him did not in fact accrue to the property owner. Wages of management and profits as offsets to losses would have to be

[5] The development of the capitalistic corporation, which at first had the effect of increasing this inequality, was to provide a potential device for the mobilization of economic resources without the necessity for a high degree of inequality in personal wealth and income.

[6] Even during the period of greatest inequality in income distribution under old-style capitalism there was not a sharp separation between those who held property and those who worked. After the turn of the century the differentiation no longer increased but began to decrease. In 1880 the top 5 per cent of family units in England received 46 per cent of national income before direct taxes, according to Simon Kuznets. He estimates that income inequality in England was increasing from about 1780 to 1850, in the United States and in Germany from about 1840 to 1890. "Economic Growth and Income Inequality," *American Economic Review,* March 1955, pp. 1–28. See Chapters 8 and 10 for statistics on the great decline in inequality in income distribution which has characterized the United States and the United Kingdom in more recent times.

[7] The phrase is Proudhon's but it represents essentially the position of Marx as well, although he vehemently denied this in attacking Proudhon's position.

provided for in any type of economic system, apart from the necessarily large deductions for depreciation of capital equipment. If capitalists were not to receive compensation for providing new capital by refraining from consumption, the state would have to withhold a sufficient portion of the national product from consumption to provide such capital. Moreover, provision would have to be made for financing the essential functions of the state under any system. So long, however, as the capitalist did receive a return on private property for which he performed no personal service, it was easy for the propertyless to impute to him a return far beyond what he in fact received.

The vital and conceivably irreplaceable role of private property in the productive process in a free society has been pointed out. Means by which the social inequalities of private property could be mitigated without impairment of its functional uses were to be evolved under the modified forms of capitalism which now exist. The record of the capitalistic economic system with respect to the "take" of the governing, managerial and property income receivers would have to be compared with the probable "take" of the governing and managerial class in an alternative system before there could be a presumption that the abolition of private property would actually increase the income of non-property holders.

It could certainly be demonstrated that the capitalistic system of private property and laissez faire functioned not only for the profit and convenience of capitalists but that it contained within itself a built-in system of direction and control which produced a growing per capita product. Economists could show how, under the assumptions of self-interest and pure and perfect competition, a free price system allocated human, natural and capital resources to the best uses. Under such a system resources were allocated according to the dictates of consumer sovereignty. Capitalist enterprisers followed the lure of profits into those fields where the demands of consumers expanded and they retreated from those fields where diminishing demand would occasion falling profits or even losses. Under this system the amount of capital which people were willing to save would be equated by the interest rate with the amount of capital which enterprisers wished to employ. Under this system quality would also be highest and production the greatest practicable at the lowest social cost. Units of natural, human and capital resources would receive compensation according to their marginal productivity, as determined by the bidding of capitalist enterprisers on the free market. Economic resources would not remain unemployed, since at some price a profit could be made or a loss avoided by their employment.

The economists who gradually developed this model, so useful in defense of the free market economy, were quite aware that pure and perfect competition had never existed and could not exist. Yet, except during periods of economic depression, the model was a fair approximation of the capitalistic system at the turn of the century.

It is by no means certain how effective this presentation of the case for capitalism by its proponents actually was in protecting its political and economic institutions against those who wished either to modify them or to destroy them by revolution. It may be doubted in any case whether economic and political systems live or die, remain static or undergo change, by virtue of the validity of the intellectual arguments that can or cannot be made for them. Any attempt to demonstrate that an economic system which depends for its productive motivation upon the ceaseless quest for profit by each individual capitalist-entrepreneur is in fact the best possible economic system from the standpoint of society as a whole requires an inconveniently lengthy chain of logic. It may well be that such a chain of logic, even if faultless, would be too complicated to be effective as a means of securing popular support. Moreover, however "realistic" the economic system of capitalism can be made to appear in its reliance upon self-interest rather than upon ethics or the moral conscience of men, such a system by its very nature can have little emotional appeal to those who are interested in changing the organization of society for the better.

The distributive principle of this free market economic system was often inaccurately and unfairly represented by the phrase "From each according to his ability to each according to his productivity." In fact, even when it functioned perfectly, a free market economy accompanied by the institution of private property meant "From each according to his ability to each according to his productivity *and the productivity of his property.*" Because of the institution of private property, the distributive principle of old-style capitalism thus departed still further from the socialist principle "From each according to his ability to each according to his need."

It is easy to prove statistically, however, that Marx's prophecy of the increasing misery of the working class under capitalism was false as a trend from the time he made it to the present. The evidence is quite clear that the standard of living of the working class has risen tremendously during the past century. Thus, it is not surprising that, prior to the overthrow of capitalism in Russia, capitalists should have taken for granted that even the inequality in income distribution occasioned by private property would not produce sufficient discontent among the workers in capitalistic countries either to destroy the system or to bring about a fundamental change in its structure or functioning.

Under these circumstances, employers of labor felt that they were able to exercise a self-confident and even ruthless industrial discipline which in days of full employment, of unemployment compensation and of powerful labor unions has become only a memory.[8]

George Orwell, writing of England in the days immediately preceding World War I, expressed well the sense of security and complacency of the upper-income classes in capitalistic society in those days:

> The extraordinary thing was the way in which everyone took it for granted that this oozing, bulging wealth of the English upper and upper-middle classes would last

[8] This type of industrial discipline, administered by an industrial bureaucracy completely secure in its authority over the workers, was not to be revived until the Stalinist regime in Soviet Russia and was to be a continuing feature of the Soviet economic and political system thereafter. However, the Soviet managerial bureaucracy, while its authority over industrial labor is as great as that of old-style capitalism, has not had the same security of tenure that characterized old-style capitalism. The constant insecurity under the Stalinist regime reflected not only the danger of loss of position but imprisonment at forced labor and even death by the arbitrary decision of any higher echelon of authority.

forever, and was part of the order of things. After 1918 it was never quite the same again. Snobbishness and expensive habits came back again, certainly, but they were self-conscious and on the defensive. Before the war the worship of money was entirely unreflecting and untroubled by any pang of conscience. The goodness of money was as unmistakable as the goodness of health or beauty, and a glittering car, a title or a horde of servants was mixed up in people's minds with the idea of actual moral virtue.[9]

In the United States in the same period, while class differences were not so great, lavish expenditures by millionaires were to a large degree imitative of those of the English upper classes. The much larger proportion of farmers and small businessmen who had no feelings of inferiority or of servility towards the recipients of large incomes, however, actually made for a greater sense of security for capitalism in the United States than in England. Farmers and small businessmen might and generally did support antitrust legislation and other governmental action to limit the power of great corporations, but they nevertheless furnished a type of grass-roots support and guarantee for the permanency of the economic and political system which did not exist in any other capitalistic country in the world. This partially accounted for the absence of a strong socialist movement in the United States aimed at fundamentally changing the economic system. In turn, the absence of a strong socialist movement meant that the capitalistic system in the United States continued to appear unshaken and unthreatened for at least a decade longer than in Europe.

However bitter the masses of the population in the industrialized capitalistic countries may have felt about the unequal distribution of income which was inherent in the institution of private property, this, in itself, might never have culminated in the overthrow or even in the peaceful replacement of the economic system in any important capitalistic country. With the development of class-consciousness among the industrial proletariat, an increasing segment of this class

[9] "Such, Such Were the Joys," *A Collection of Essays by George Orwell*, Doubleday, Garden City, 1954, p. 41.

did, indeed, demand and cast votes for a change in the economic system which would do away with private property and thus with capitalism. So long, however, as the capitalistic economic system functioned without interruption, its record of productive efficiency and the consequent rise in real wages of the working class, even if that rise was slow, constituted a protective shield against the development of mass demands for basic economic change.

It seems probable that the development of "political democracy" through the enfranchisement of the lower-income groups, together with the development of forces within capitalistic industry itself, would have in time transformed old-style capitalism into an economic system much more serviceable to the whole of society.

It was, however, the failure of capitalism to function without interruption which was to make actual the potential vulnerability of an economic system characterized by the institution of private property. The degree of inequality in income distribution which characterized capitalism was probably within the limits of tolerance even when the development of political democracy had placed the possibility of economic change within the hands of the mass of the population. But the "built-in" susceptibility of the system to economic crises, accompanied by mass unemployment, had the effect of magnifying the sensitivity of the propertyless classes to what they regarded as the patent unfairness of the capitalistic system of income distribution.

During economic crises, the actual functioning of the capitalistic economy had little resemblance to the economist's model by which resources were efficiently allocated, factors of production proportionately compensated, and prices of goods and services set in accordance with the pertinent demand and supply schedules. Instead, unemployed laborers found that they could not sell their services at any price. In an economic crisis it was obvious that Say's Law, upon which the operation of the capitalistic economy depended so basically, was not operative. When idle factories and idle hands filled the land, Say's contention that general overproduction was impossible, since goods were the market for goods, was obviously untenable.

The capitalistic principles of reliance upon individual self-interest at such times would have meant starvation. Reliance upon private charity or upon state aid for the unemployed meant that to this extent the capitalistic economic system had failed to function. When, under such circumstances, a "critical mass" of the population became convinced that capitalism was failing to function, the state was compelled to abandon the policy of laissez faire and to take over to a greater or less degree the management of the economy.[10]

It was the inequality of distribution of income inherent in the institution of private property combined with the susceptibility of capitalism to economic depression which rendered the system vulnerable to revolutionary overthrow or to pressures for substantial changes in its fundamental institutions through legislative action. The change in the size and nature of the basic unit of production, however, had been gradually transforming the structure and functioning of the system without either a constitutional or revolutionary decision having been taken to bring this about. This change in the size and nature of the productive unit was to be reflected in the development of the corporate form of industrial organization and was to be of the greatest importance in the transformation of capitalism.

It is ironic, however, that the first complete overthrow of capitalism in a great country was brought about directly by none of these inherent disintegrative or transformational forces within capitalism. The overthrow of the tsarist government and of the semicolonial form of capitalism existing in Russia prior to the Revolution was brought about primarily by factors exogenous to capitalism considered as an economic system. The overthrow of capitalism in Russia affected in the most fundamental way the modification and transformation

---

[10] This "critical mass" which must be attained before some sort of politico-economic explosion occurs varies with circumstances. This is illustrated by the diverse cases of the Russian Revolution of 1917, the Nazi conquest of power in 1933 and the inauguration of the New Deal in the same year. Just as the minimum critical mass necessary to precipitate an atomic explosion can be changed by altering the mechanism of detonation, so the minimum critical mass necessary for a politico-economic explosion can be changed by the manipulations of leaders such as Lenin and Hitler.

of the economic system in the other major countries of the world in which the endogenous forces referred to above were also operative. The complex functioning of these endogenous and exogenous forces in bringing about the present diverse relationships between the economy, liberty and the state in different countries is the theme of succeeding chapters.

CHAPTER 2

THE OVERTHROW OF CAPITALISM IN RUSSIA

The survival value of economic systems is unfortunately not always a measure of their productive efficiency or of their contribution to "the good life." In democratically controlled countries, economic systems do undergo gradual change in the direction towards which they are impelled by the kinds and degrees of dissatisfactions felt by the electorate. Economic systems which are brought into existence by violence and drastic change, however, do not necessarily have a close relation to the kind of economic order which the majority of the population either expected or desired, or even to the type of regime which the successful revolutionary leaders originally advocated.

The contrast between the theoretical system which Marxists had championed as a superior alternative to capitalism and the actual system which the hierarchy of the Communist Party eventually chose for the Russian people is so extreme as to be almost incredible. Only by examining the historical process by which it came into being is it possible to understand how the present Soviet system could be so different from the one which had been proposed by the leaders of the Party.

World War I was to set in train forces that were not only to destroy capitalism in Russia but to deal the most severe shocks to it throughout the world. Capitalism, even though it was undergoing evolutionary changes, had never appeared stronger than in the days immediately preceding the outbreak of World War I. Already well along in its development away from individual enterprise towards the corporate form of organization, the capitalistic system before World War I was beginning to undergo gradual, if generally unrecognized, transformation in most of those countries in which it was to survive at all.

The growth of political democracy in Western Europe had permitted the development of the socialist challenge to the capitalistic economic system via the ballot box instead of the barricades. Reformist measures, adopted on the one hand by conservative governments seeking "to take the steam out of socialism" and on the other by parliamentary action of political parties seeking working-class votes, had turned Marxian Social Democrats towards the gradualism of Bernstein and the "revolution through parliamentary means" of Kautsky. The legalization of trade unions, and their rapid growth both in England and on the Continent, had produced a new element favorable to social stability and opposed to violent change. The development of capitalism in the United States, while it had not followed the European pattern exactly, had produced even less evidence of popular demand for fundamental and drastic change in the economic system, although here also the process of gradual transformation was under way.

It is striking that the destruction of a modern capitalistic economic system and its replacement by a fundamentally different economic system did not take place in one of the more advanced capitalistic countries as Marxist doctrine had forecast. On the contrary, it took place in Russia where industrial development had lagged behind that of Western Europe, from which the institutions of capitalism were imported. Russian capitalism reflected and shared the weakness and inefficiency of the tsarist government. The standard of living of the industrial proletariat was miserably low. The tsarist government had been able to prevent the organization of the industrial workers into strong, independent trade unions of the sort which were to prove so important an element of social stability and so effective an obstacle to revolutionary upheavals in Western Europe. The nominal legalization of trade unions in 1906, like the setting up of the Duma and the promulgation of the Stolypin land reforms at about the same time, might eventually have permitted the development of a modern capitalistic, parliamentary, labor-union society on the Western model if World War I had not intervened. As it was, these reforms came too late.

The Russian industrial proletariat was consequently susceptible to the agitation which had been carried on for generations by parties and groups with revolutionary goals. Whether these parties and groups were Marxist in doctrine or program, as were the Social Democrats (split into Bolsheviki and Mensheviki), or whether they advocated an indigenous form of socialism as did the Social Revolutionaries, they were agreed in their determined advocacy of a basic change in the economic and political system.

The even lower standard of living of the peasantry, with their hatred of the landlords stimulated by a fierce land hunger that was in turn exacerbated by a rapidly growing population, presented a threat to Russian capitalism from the masses of the population, who felt the absence of any institutional development which might have enabled them to believe that they had a stake in the economic system. The land reforms put into operation in 1907 and broadened in 1910 had been intended to favor the more industrious, progressive and aggressive peasants, and to enable them to leave the Russian communal village organization and become independent peasant proprietors. But these measures came too late to build up strong peasant support for Russian capitalism.

The tsarist government by its resistance to political and economic reform and by its crude attempts at censorship of intellectual life incurred the hostility of almost the entire developing urban intelligentsia. The fact that the censorship and positive control over all intellectual life was to be far more complete, uncompromising and effective under the succeeding Soviet regime than it had ever been under tsarism naturally could not mitigate this hostility.

Yet Russian capitalism on the eve of World War I was in a period of vigorous industrial expansion. Its overthrow was thus not directly connected with any weakening of capitalism as an economic system. Nor did it coincide with an economic crisis or depression of the traditional capitalistic type. It was instead the direct aftermath of war.[1] It was the incapacity of the tsarist government to wage the war successfully, and its failure to maintain internal order following the economic and administrative breakdowns resulting from the war, which allowed the February Revolution of 1917 to triumph. The catastrophic military situation, coupled with the political ineptitude of the Provisional Government formed as a result of the February Revolution, in turn enabled the armed forces at the command of Lenin and the Military Revolutionary Committee of the Petrograd Soviet to destroy the Provisional Government of Kerensky and to set up in its place the Soviet power in the October Revolution.[2] The genius of Lenin chose the moment of greatest governmental weakness to initiate the seizure of power. As Trotsky has put it, "A revolutionary situation cannot be preserved at will. If the Bolsheviks had not seized the power in October and November in all probability they would not have seized it at all."[3]

The deep yearning of the whole Russian people for liberty and the bitter dissatisfaction of the industrial workers and the majority of the peasants with the functioning of the Russian economy furnished the forces which destroyed the tsarist government. Had it not been for World War I, these forces, instead of exploding into revolution, might have produced a gradual and orderly transformation of the political and economic system. As it was, the feeble and corrupt tsarist government, shaken by military disaster and financial near-chaos, was overthrown and a new political and economic system was set

[1] Very little evidence can be found to support the contention that World War I was caused by forces inherent in capitalism. There is no substantial evidence of mounting difficulty in finding international markets for capitalistic industry during the immediate prewar period. There was, moreover, neither sharp economic crisis nor continuing economic depression on the eve of World War I.

[2] On account of the difference between the old Russian calendar and the modern calendar the "October Revolution" took place in November, just as the "February Revolution," which overthrew the tsarist regime, took place in March.

[3] Leon Trotsky, *The History of the Russian Revolution*, Simon & Schuster, New York, 1937, Vol. III, p. 154.

up after several months of a political and military vacuum.

For an instant of time there was indeed a dictatorship of the revolutionary masses. The evidence is uncontested that the mob which overthrew the tsar in the streets of Petrograd in the February Revolution of 1917 acted almost entirely without leaders. This mob for the moment expressed the fervent wish of all classes to be rid of the reigning tsar. Yet a mass dictatorship, though it can destroy, can never administer a political and economic system. Under fortunate circumstances the powers of a revolutionary mob may pass into the hands of leaders who are able both to sense the always amorphous and often contradictory wishes of the revolutionary masses and eventually to satisfy some of their aspirations.

It was the tragedy of the Russian Revolution that the momentary dictatorship of the masses which effected the February Revolution was transformed into a personal dictatorship through the military seizure of power by the Bolshevik leaders in the October Revolution. The end result was to be the extinction of even that very limited degree of representative government which the tsar had earlier been compelled to concede after the Revolution of 1905. At the same time a new economic and political system was set up, the characteristics of which were determined by the leaders of the military coup that gave it birth.

"Power lay in the streets," and the Bolshevik leaders by a military *coup d'état* picked up the power which the Provisional Government under Kerensky had proved itself unable to wield.[4] It is doubtful whether any government which attempted to conduct itself according to democratic and parliamentary principles, as the Provisional Government did, could have continued in power after the overthrow of the tsarist regime. Kerensky's effort to induce the Russian army to continue the war, and his attempt to delay the transfer of land

---

[4] Boris Souvarine has brilliantly developed this point in his "October: Myths and Realities," *The New Leader*, November 4, 1957. He quotes Julius Martov, who in the name of the Social Democrats introduced a resolution in the November 7 meeting of the all-Russian Congress of Soviets: "The *coup d'état* which has given all power in Petrograd to the Military Revolutionary Committee one day before the opening of the Congress was organized by a single party by means of a military conspiracy."

to the peasants in order that it might be done in an orderly and constitutional manner, hopelessly weakened the powers of resistance of his government.[5]

The disorder characteristic of the first days of a "dictatorship of the proletariat" would naturally prevent any orderly election of the leaders of the revolution by the proletarian masses. This is what happened in Russia. The Central Committee of the Bolshevik Party acting through its Military Revolutionary Committee[6] used the occasion of the meeting of the Second Congress of Soviets to constitute itself the general staff of the proletarian revolution.[7] The military coup, so brilliantly planned and executed by the Bolshevik Military Revo-

[5] For Kerensky's account of the factors and circumstances which made it possible for a government sincerely dedicated to political and economic reforms through parliamentary institutions to be overthrown with so little effective resistance, see Alexander Kerensky, *The Crucifixion of Liberty*, John Day, New York, 1934.

[6] The Military Revolutionary Committee was nominally a committee of the Petrograd Soviet. The Bolsheviki were, however, solely responsible for its being set up. Moreover, the representatives of other parties who were appointed to the committee resigned, with the exception of the Left Socialist Revolutionaries and the Anarchists, who at that time were cooperating with the Bolsheviki. See William Henry Chamberlin, *The Russian Revolution*, Macmillan, New York, 1935, Vol. 1, pp. 299, 300.

[7] The men who actually led the Bolshevik forces against the Kerensky government, such as Antonov-Ovseenko and the sailor Dybenko, were executed during the purges of the late thirties. The Red sailors from the Kronstadt naval base who played such a crucial role were ruthlessly put down when they revolted against the Soviet regime in 1921. None of the important Bolshevik leaders actually participated in combat or directed military units in combat. A bronze plaque on a building adjoining the Winter Palace in Leningrad which states that Lenin and Stalin directed the attack on the Kerensky government in the palace in the October Revolution could still be seen as late as the summer of 1956, even after "de-Stalinization." The plaque is an absolute falsification of history. Lenin and the other Bolshevik members of the Military Revolutionary Committee functioned in the military tradition as a general staff at the Smolny Institute, many blocks distant from the Winter Palace. As Trotsky tells us, "Those workers, sailors and soldiers who really inspired and led the operation took their places soon after at the head of the first detachments of the Red Army, and the majority laid down their lives in the various theaters of the Civil War." *History of the Russian Revolution*, Vol. III, p. 224.

lutionary Committee, could not have succeeded against a regime possessing strong leadership, a reliable military force or unquestioned political legitimacy. The Kerensky regime had none of these.

Lenin's choice of riding the revolutionary storm, instead of attempting the almost hopeless task of calming it, helped enormously to assure the success of the Bolshevik military coup. His slogan of immediate "Peace, Bread and Land" had no less propaganda value because it was to remain so long unfulfilled. The Bolshevik leaders had not indeed created the revolutionary chaos which gripped Russia at this time, but for a strategic moment they stimulated it in every possible way.

It is nevertheless a remarkable tribute to Lenin's leadership that the Bolsheviki, unlike the Jacobin terrorists in the French Revolution, did not become dependent upon the masses which they had used in seizing power for their maintenance and exercise of power. The Bolsheviki had a definite program for the transformation of the economic as well as the political system. Moreover, they had a disciplined party organization which showed itself capable both of wielding the armed forces of the state and of utilizing organized terror to carry out their plans. The fact that the economic system which the Communist Party organized after it had the state powers firmly in hand was quite different from their original goal did not hamper the effective use of that goal by the Bolsheviki in seizing and organizing power. A decade of effort was, however, required for the Bolshevik leaders to bring the Russian economy fully under a sterner and more effective discipline than had existed under the tsarist regime before this interlude of revolutionary disorder.

It is questionable whether any constituent or other type of legislative body could be considered truly representative when elected under conditions of such disorder as characterized Russia in November 1917. As Trotsky remarked, "And when a great political decision becomes unpostponable, in the course of events, that is the very moment when a referendum is impossible."[8] But the Constituent Assembly which had the mandate to provide a constitution for the new regime when

[8] *Ibid.*, p. 178.

it met in Petrograd in January 1918 was at any rate the most regularly elected body which had convened since the overthrow of the tsarist government in the February Revolution. Before their seizure of power in the October Revolution the Bolsheviki had continuously demanded the relinquishment of power by the Provisional Government and the calling of a constitutional convention. It was a fateful decision when the Bolshevik leaders repudiated their previous demands for convening the Constituent Assembly and dispersed it by force as it became evident that they did not command a majority in that body.

However, the dispersal of the elected Constituent Assembly by force was not inconsistent with Bolshevik doctrine. They considered the government which they set up a purely temporary "dictatorship of the proletariat" which would, according to Marxist doctrine, "wither away" so that after the revolution had definitely triumphed there would be no state at all.

In the meantime, the Bolshevik leaders had no respect for representative government. No one has expressed this contempt as well as Trotsky, but there is no doubt that Lenin and the other Bolshevik leaders agreed with him that "In order that the soldiers, the peasants and the oppressed nationalities, floundering in the snow-storm of elective ballot, should recognize the Bolsheviks in action it was necessary that the Bolsheviks seize the power."[9] Speaking of the Social Revolutionaries, a socialist party which all during the revolutionary period received more votes throughout Russia than did the Bolsheviki, he says, "A party for whom everybody votes, except that minority who knows what they are voting for, is no more a party than the tongue in which the babies of all countries babble is a national language."[10] He sums up the Bolshevik attitude towards representative institutions in revolutionary situations in these words: "The great stages of a revolution—that is the passing of power to new classes or layers —do not at all coincide in this process with the succession of representative institutions, which march along after the dynamic of the revolution like a belated shadow."[11]

Once possessing military and police power, and the admin-

[9] *Ibid.*, p. 179.   [10] *Ibid.*, p. 223.   [11] *Ibid.*, p. 211.

istrative apparatus of the state, the Bolsheviki could fulfill their intention of destroying the existing economic system and substituting a totally different one. They were, however, completely without guidance as to the organizational form that the new economic system should take. Marx had provided no blueprint for the operation of the political and economic system which was to succeed capitalism. He assumed that only a transitory form of the state would be required during the period of the dictatorship of the proletariat, and gave no hint of the economic structure during this period or how the leaders who wielded the dictatorship were to be selected. He apparently assumed that the economy would somehow run itself without the necessity for elaborate organization or authoritative management. He also seems to have believed that the only important function of the temporary transitional state would be to prevent the displaced bourgeoisie from regaining control.

How long were the transitional state and the transitional economic system to last? Were they to be coexistent and coterminant? Marx had indeed very sketchily indicated that there would be two stages in the development of the collectivist economy. Lenin had further developed Marx's embryonic concept of the two stages in his *State and Revolution*, written just before the October Revolution in 1917. He had called the first stage "socialism," and the second and final stage "communism." Yet even in Lenin's development of Marx's reference to the two stages there was nothing like a blueprint for the organization of the first stage of the new economy.

Indeed, it is doubtful whether Lenin would have tried to put into operation the first stage of communism (socialism) had he been free to choose the organizational form of the economy at this time. He was well aware that the Communists had been able to seize power in a country which had not gone fully through the process of capitalistic development. The exigencies of the Revolution and the Civil War with their attendant destruction and economic disorganization compelled him to acquiesce in setting up an economic system which was to be in some important respects closer at this time to the theoretical second and final stage of communism than at any later date.

The period of War Communism or Military Communism, as it has sometimes been called, followed upon the issuance of decrees nationalizing industry. These decrees were necessary in order to provide some authoritative base following the seizure of factories by workers' committees. The system of War Communism, characterized by the operation of industrial plants as part of the governmental apparatus, the equalization of wages, and the outright requisitioning of food from the peasants and its rationing in the cities, could supply only the production essential to insure the victory of the Red Army over the White armies and to provide the barest subsistence for the civil population. It was obvious at the end of the Civil War that such a system could not be depended upon either for reconstructing the economy or for producing even a minimum standard of living for the Russian people. Thus the problem of organizing the economy on some continuing basis still had to be faced.

It is ironic in the highest degree both that it was military power which gave the Bolshevik leaders the opportunity to select the type of economic organization and that this decision should have been theirs to make at all. As Marxists they could only believe that it is economic forces which are determinative and that the "political superstructure" which is the state is only the reflection of the basic economic structure of society. This economic structure itself they considered the product of deterministic, irresistible forces. Thus capitalism was supposed to collapse only after it had reached maturity and after the industrial proletariat had become the majority of the population. As capitalism developed, the numbers of peasant proprietors, artisans and small businessmen would decline as these petit bourgeois elements were pushed down into the industrial proletariat. Simultaneously with the growth of large-scale industry, capitalists would grow richer as their numbers declined. As the misery of the working class increased and economic crises became sharper, as capitalism's support became thus completely undermined, its overthrow would take place inevitably. So went the familiar Marxist timetable.

By an incredible paradox, the new Bolshevik ruling class came to power in Russia proclaiming their belief in a pattern of economic development inexorably determined by economic forces which their own success in seizing power was to prove invalid. For almost every aspect of economic and political development in Russia in 1917 was inconsistent with the Marxist pattern of capitalism's decline. Russia just prior to 1917 had indeed been in the process of rapid, large-scale, industrial development. The standard of living of the peasantry was very low, and many left the village to find employment in industry. But more than four fifths of the population were still in the village. The peasantry owned four times as much land as did the nobility. The proportion of agricultural land in the hands of the peasantry had, moreover, been increasing in the period before the Revolution.[12]

The increase in the proportion of land owned by the peasants had not diminished either their hatred of the landlord or their hatred of the tsarist government. The fact that the landlord lived far better than the peasants, that he did not work with his hands and often did not work at all, that peasants had to pay for land which they had bought from the landlords to add to their own holdings, was enough. As for the government, taxes had to be paid to it, conscripts had to be furnished for its armies, and in return for what? The peasantry had throughout Russian history seized every opportunity to rid itself of landlord and government. They were always shocked afterwards to learn that the role of government and of landlord would be played by someone and that compensation for playing these roles would always be exacted from the peasantry. Thus they were indeed a revolutionary force. It had been so since the days of the peasant revolt of Stenka Razin in the late seventeenth century and of Emilian Puga-

12 Chamberlin, *The Russian Revolution*, Vol. I, p. 245. The comparative size of the landholdings of the peasantry, of the nobility, of the state and the imperial family, and of others on the eve of the Revolution is a very complex matter, and complete and satisfactory data do not exist. However, it is quite clear that some proportion of the land in peasant hands had been increasing for some decades. See Geroid T. Robinson, *Rural Russia under the Old Regime*, Macmillan, New York, 1932, Appendix I and II, pp. 268–272, for what is probably the best analysis of the available data. The land which passed from the hands of the landlords naturally was acquired by the more energetic and relatively well-to-do peasants. Consequently, a split had begun to develop between these and the poorer peasants.

chev a century later. That there was no place for this primitive
revolutionary force in Marxist doctrine did not lessen its violence and effect.

As has been pointed out, it was inconsistent with Marxist
doctrine that the industrialization of Russia still lagged far
behind that of Great Britain, Germany and the other countries of Western Europe, as well as of the United States and
Japan, and that the urban proletariat was only a small fraction
of the total population at the moment of the Revolution.[13]
The industrial proletariat did indeed hate the tsarist government and the bourgeois capitalists at the time of the overthrow of the old system. The misery of the working class was
great, but the evidence does not indicate that it had been
increasing before the war. Russia had indeed repeatedly suffered in the past from the economic disturbances which have
always been one of the most serious defects of the capitalistic
economic system in all lands. However, as has been pointed
out, the typical capitalistic economic crisis played no role in
the revolutionary situation of 1917 in Russia. On the contrary, the immediate prewar period had been one of vigorous
industrial expansion and, of course, industry enjoyed boom
demand during the war.

The Bolshevik seizure of power in a revolutionary situation
which had not developed according to the Marxist chronologi-
cal pattern nevertheless reflected Lenin's particular choice of
one horn of the dilemma that was always inherent in Marxist
doctrine. If economic development was indeed an inevitable
process, with the political superstructure of society merely the
reflection of the economic basic structure, how could there be
a place for conscious revolutionary movements and leadership
or even for political agitation at all? If one attempted to answer this question by saying, as Marxists did, that the in-

---

[13] Lenin dealt with this inconsistency by proclaiming the doctrine
of the *smychka*, the community of interest of the peasants with that
of the urban proletariat against the landlords and the industrialists.
As a tactic this was to prove highly successful during the critical
period of the Civil War. It was, however, quite irrelevant as an argument for the validity of Marxist doctrine.

On the theoretical level, Lenin argued that capitalistic institutions
had been imported into Russia in already developed forms from the
more highly industrialized countries of Western Europe.

evitable process of economic development could be hastened and the birth pangs of the new society shortened by conscious human decisions directed toward this end, other difficult questions at once arose. If the process could be hastened, then logically it could be delayed, if only by the failure to take proper action to hasten it. If the process could be hastened or delayed, how could it be considered inevitable?

Actually all Marxists, even the Mensheviki and the followers of Bernstein or Kautsky, although they denied either the desirability or the inevitability of seizing power by revolutionary violence, were confronted by this basic conflict between depending upon the inevitable collapse or decay of capitalism and attempting to bring it about by conscious effort.

Substantially all Marxists, including Marx himself, were to accept the horn of the dilemma which logically, if not explicitly, denied the doctrine of inevitability, and to claim that the end of capitalism and the triumph of socialism could be hastened by intellectual choice between alternative courses of action, by propaganda and by deed. The difference between Lenin and the Bolsheviki, on the one hand, and the Mensheviki in Russia, as well as the Social Democratic parties outside Russia, on the other, was Lenin's conviction that the overthrow of capitalism could be brought about in Russia long before the capitalistic form of economic system had fully developed. Lenin further insisted that this could be accomplished through revolutionary violence under the leadership of the very small and tightly disciplined Central Committee of the Bolshevik Party.

Marx had conceived of the necessity for the dictatorship of the proletariat only during the period immediately after the overthrow of the capitalistic state by the revolutionary proletariat.[14] The Marxist theory of economic development, however, assumed that at this final stage of capitalistic development the proletariat would constitute the overwhelming majority of the population. Furthermore, the powers of coercion of the proletarian state were to be exercised only against

[14] It is remarkable how few are the references to the dictatorship of the proletariat in all of Marx's writings and how little content he provides for the phrase.

the former capitalistic exploiters in case they attempted to regain power. Conceptually, at least, there was not supposed to be any question of a dictatorship of an individual or of a minority over a majority of the population.[15] But Lenin's decision "to hurry the historical process" made it inevitable that the dictatorship of the proletariat would be a dictatorship of a minority, since the proletariat was itself a small minority of the population in the Russia of 1917.

In a real sense, however, the fact that the proletariat was only a minority of the population was not of decisive consequence. For, except in the case of transitory mob control, it is sheer nonsense to speak of the dictatorship of *any* large class or group of people. In a political unit of any size the management of the state power must always be delegated. That is, a minority must always do the actual ruling, even when the machinery of government is in the hands of fully elected representatives of a majority or plurality of the population.

It is striking that both Marx and Engels recognized the possibility of the existence of what they called "surplus value" under capitalism and the possibility of its expropriation by a ruling bureaucracy or class even where private property and the capitalistic system did not exist. Marx, in the preface to his *Critique of Political Economy*, states: "In broad outline we can designate the Asiatic, the ancient, the feudal and the modern bourgeois methods of production as so many epochs in the progress of the economic formation of society."[16] He elsewhere explains that surplus labor exists and is expropriated into the hands of the rulers of the state in the Asiatic system. Marx says that in India, before British rule, surplus labor, although it existed, did not depend upon private property. He thus recognizes that "from time immemorial" a portion of surplus labor has found its way into the hands of the state

[15] See Karl Kautsky, *The Dictatorship of the Proletariat*, National Labour Press, London, 1919. Marx apparently did not assume that "the dictatorship of the proletariat" would be more "dictatorial" than the bourgeois state which had been overthrown. He even assumed that the state would not "dictate" at all to the former proletarians who would constitute the majority in the new society.

[16] Karl Marx, *A Contribution to the Critique of Political Economy*, Charles H. Kerr & Co., Chicago, 1934, p. 13.

"in the shape of rent in kind."[17] In another passage Marx points out the peculiarly favorable circumstances in ancient Egypt under which surplus labor could be a large proportion of total output, with a small subsistence wage going to labor while the greater proportion of the social output was available for other purposes.[18] Stated alternatively, a relatively small proportion of the labor force could provide the minimum subsistence necessary for the existence and propagation of the working class while the larger part of the labor force could be used for building irrigation works, pyramids and the like, in addition to supporting the priesthood, the military establishment, the royal court and the nobility. Thus Marx recognized that the state and its ruling class in ancient Egypt absorbed surplus value long before bourgeois capitalism existed.

What Marx and Engels did not recognize was the possibility of a governing class of revolutionary origin appropriating for its own purposes the income which had been confiscated from the owners of private property under a previously existing capitalistic system. As Milovan Djilas points out in *The New Class*,[19] the top bureaucracy of a Communist state, although seizing power in the name of the dictatorship of the proletariat, or ruling as the successors of those who seized power, draws an income, not indeed from private property, but from state property. The producing workers have even less control over the uses to which this income is put by the "New Class" than does the worker in a capitalistic society. Marx should logically have concluded that the governing class always determines to whom the return from property goes, either within a broad institutional framework or by more or less arbitrary exercise of personal authority, whatever the economic system may be. If he had come to such a conclusion he would, of course, have been reversing the relation between what he called the political "superstructure" and the economic system and would, by so doing, have undermined his whole ideological system.

The concept of a dictatorship of the proletariat acting only

[17] Karl Marx, *Capital*, Charles H. Kerr & Co., Chicago, 1906, Vol. I, p. 392.
[18] *Ibid.*, pp. 562–563.   [19] Praeger, New York, 1957.

to resist a potential armed attack by a bourgeois minority would have been consistent with a democratically elected government exercising the minimum powers required to protect itself against violent overthrow. But the state which the leaders of the Bolshevik Party set up was not in fact to be temporary nor was it to restrict itself to the exercise of such limited coercion. The Soviet state was to become a permanent dictatorship in the most unlimited sense. As Trotsky prophetically stated at a time when he had not yet embraced the Leninist doctrine of hard centralism, "The Organization of the Party takes the place of the Party itself; the Central Committee takes the place of the organization; and finally the dictator takes the place of the Central Committee."

The astounding success of this handful of Bolshevik leaders in seizing and holding power seems to have produced a state of mind which ruled out, then or later, the question "How do we know that *we* speak for the proletariat? What procedures and mechanisms for ascertaining the will of the majority of the proletariat should we use to find out whether we retain the confidence of the proletariat? To what individuals should the state power be turned over if we do not have the confidence of the proletariat?"[20] The Bolshevik leaders sometimes spoke of the Soviets, in the name of which they had seized power, as a new and superior form of representation of the will of the proletariat. Yet Trotsky states, "The Soviet

[20] Leaders who attain power by revolutionary violence do not, of course, usually wish to ask themselves the question of how their claim to power is to be validated by the popular will. If they are to continue to hold power by any title other than brute force alone, they must, however, try to find the answer to this question.

See Edward S. Mason, *The History of the Paris Commune*, Macmillan, New York, 1930, particularly Chaps. 1 and 2, for a cogent explanation of the development of the curious concept of the "right" of a self-selected and indeterminate group of urban intellectuals to wield power in the name of the people or of the proletariat. He shows that this concept was held by the Jacobins during the French Revolution and that it was expressly put forward by Blanqui prior to the Paris Commune of 1871. In spite of the repudiation of Blanqui by Engels and by Lenin, Lenin's actual policy came very close to Blanquism. However, neither Lenin nor Stalin was ever willing to state so frankly as Blanqui had done this doctrine of dictatorship by an "elite" without sanction of popular suffrage.

form does not contain any mystic power. It is by no means free from the faults of every representative system—unavoidable so long as the system is unavoidable."

The dictatorship which seized power in the October Revolution was thus never actually a dictatorship of the proletariat. It was not even a dictatorship of the "most advanced and revolutionary" part of the proletariat. Lenin, in fact, insisted that the proletariat itself would not and could not overthrow capitalism and set up socialism without outside leadership. "The working class exclusively by its own efforts, is able to develop only trade-union consciousness. . . . Modern socialist consciousness can only be brought to them from without . . . can arise only on the basis of profound scientific knowledge. The bearers of science are not the proletariat but the bourgeois intelligentsia. It is out of the heads of the members of this stratum that modern socialism originated . . ."[21] But Lenin simply assimilated the Bolshevik leadership into the dictatorship of the proletariat and he never seems to have had the slightest doubt of his own right and ability to speak and act for and as "the proletariat."

The Bolshevik leadership was indeed to come from outside the working class. Of the original six members of the board of editors of *Iskra*, the newspaper organ by which Lenin was tortuously to build his position of dominance in the Bolshevik Party, none had ever been workers. In the so-called Unification Congress, which met in Brussels in 1903, out of some sixty delegates only four had at any time been workers.[22] At another Party Congress in London in 1905 there was only one delegate who had ever been a worker.[23] It was to be almost forty years after the Revolution before an individual who had actually done manual labor was, in the person of Khrushchev, to attain the highest power in Soviet Russia.

It was inevitable that in an illegal organization, functioning partly underground in Russia and partly in exile, there could be no orderly, constitutional system for the election of the leaders. The endless maneuverings, the formation of factions and counterfactions, the bitter recriminations among the leaders, could be overcome only by the tireless energy of

[21] Bertram Wolfe, *Three Who Made a Revolution*, Beacon, Boston, 1948, p. 159.   [22] *Ibid.*, p. 230.   [23] *Ibid.*, p. 308.

Lenin, insisting always on complete centralization of authority —while utterly refusing to submit to authority whenever he momentarily lost control—and upheld by an unquestioning confidence in his own infallibility in charting the hazardous revolutionary course.

The Bolshevik leadership was only a tiny fraction of the Russian intelligentsia, most of whom were Social Revolutionaries or Mensheviki.[24] Trotsky commonly speaks of "the radical intelligentsia" as the creators of the Provisional Government, later to be overthrown by the Bolsheviki, and as completely separate from them. Indeed, Trotsky never refers to the Bolshevik leaders as members of the intelligentsia. Instead, significantly enough, he represented them as simply the articulate and forward-looking portion of the proletariat. Almost none of the Bolshevik leaders were actually intellectual *producers* outside of their revolutionary interests. Scarcely any had written a book, painted a picture, composed music, published the results of scientific research or the like. Yet the intellectual brilliance of Lenin and Trotsky, at least, cannot be questioned. They were professional revolutionaries who worked at the job and had little time for anything else. As Trotsky further states, "The intelligentsia hardly came into the Bolshevik party at all. A broad layer of so-called 'old Bolsheviks' from among the students who had associated themselves with the Revolution of 1905 had since turned into extraordinarily successful engineers, physicians, government officials and they now unceremoniously showed the party the hostile aspect of their backs."[25]

It is almost incredible that a mere handful of nonproletarian revolutionary leaders, most of them without any other regular profession, depending to a substantial extent upon contributions from wealthy sympathizers for a meagre living,[26] could

[24] See Trotsky, *History of the Russian Revolution,* Vol. III, pp. 167, 216 *et passim.*   [25] *Ibid.,* p. 304.

[26] Although precise quantitative comparisons are obviously impossible, it is probable that as great a share of the financial support of the Bolsheviki before they attained power came from contributors among the capitalist class in Russia as in the case of the Nazis in Germany. The motivation was considerably different, however. Russian capitalists or their womenfolk who contributed to the Bolsheviki were largely neurotics, suffering from boredom or from guilt com-

overthrow even so weak a regime as the Kerensky Provisional Government. It is even more remarkable that, under the leadership of Lenin, such men could win the bitter Civil War against the White forces led by professional generals. The really astonishing feature of the dictatorship originating in men of such personalities and backgrounds was their success in utilizing largely the existing military and industrial bureaucracy to operate the state and the economy. A large proportion of the Red Army officers were former officers of the tsarist forces. That this success was to continue after the dictatorship had become completely personalized under Stalin, and after both the Bolshevik professional revolutionaries and the new bureaucracy had had to survive one massive purge after another, sets the capstone upon the pyramid of incredibility.

There is nothing in Marxist doctrine which affords a logical and consistent explanation of why the leadership for a proletarian revolution should come from among the bourgeoisie. History has proved Lenin right that it is indeed from among the bourgeois intelligentsia that the leadership for the overthrow of capitalism comes. But there is nothing in basic Marxist doctrine to account for the revolutionary and dictatorial role of this small fragment of the Russian intelligentsia who directed the Bolsheviki.

It is significant that revolutionary members of the intelligentsia undergo relatively minor risks in their attempts to overthrow capitalism. This is still true, but it is illustrated particularly by the events of the Russian Revolution. The weakness and, above all, the inefficiency of the tsarist measures of repression against those of the intelligentsia who carried on conspiratorial and revolutionary activities provide a startling contrast to those of the Soviet or of the Nazi government. For example, the works of Marx could be translated and published in tsarist Russia, although the motive was in part the strength-

---

plexes. See Wolfe, *Three Who Made a Revolution,* pp. 103–104, 376–381 *et passim.* German capitalists who contributed to the Nazis did so in the calculated expectation of economic or political advantage, much as they did when contributing to the other German parties. Trotsky notes the practice of the sons of wealthy industrialists and merchants of contributing money to the socialist parties (*History of the Russian Revolution,* Vol. III, p. 188.)

ening of the Marxian Social Democrats, who were considered
less dangerous than their rivals the Social Revolutionaries. Of
300 prisoners captured and brought to trial by the tsarist police after a raid on the Soviet Executive who had led the Revolution of 1905, 15 were condemned to life imprisonment, 2
were given short prison terms, 284 were set free. Not one was
executed.[27]

The living conditions of the revolutionary intelligentsia sent
into exile under the last tsarist regime were extremely easy in
comparison with life in Soviet forced labor camps, as the experience of Lenin in his Siberian "imprisonment" well illustrates.[28] Trotsky escaped while being sent into Siberian exile.
Stalin escaped from prison three times, perhaps with the con-
nivance of the tsarist police. By contrast, escape from Soviet
prison camps has been very rare. Members of the revolutionary intelligentsia were sometimes employed in the various
bureaus of the tsarist government and protected by their superiors at the very time that they were being sought by the
tsarist police.[29]

After the failure of a revolutionary attempt, as in 1905, the
tsarist police and army would often take the most severe re-
prisals more or less at random against the masses of workers
and peasants who had participated or were suspected of having participated in the uprisings. Hundreds, even thousands,
were sometimes shot out of hand. But very few, indeed, of the
revolutionary intelligentsia were executed, unless they were
actual participants in attempts at assassination of tsarist officials. This almost never happened among the Marxist intelligentsia, since they did not believe in the efficacy of assassination as a revolutionary weapon.

Remarkably few of the revolutionary intelligentsia were to
lose their lives in either the February or the October Revolution of 1917, whether Bolsheviki, Mensheviki or Social Revolutionaries. To a considerable extent this merely reflects the
fact that the generals of any army represent an exceedingly
favorable life insurance risk compared with the rank and file.

[27] Wolfe, *Three Who Made a Revolution*, pp. 332–334.
[28] Chamberlin, *The Russian Revolution*, Vol. I, pp. 124–125.
[29] N. N. Sukhanov, *The Russian Revolution, 1917*, translated by
Joel Carmichael, Oxford University Press, London, 1955, p. vi.

The revolutionary intelligentsia did not conceive of their role as that of riflemen at street barricades and they almost never took part in actual fighting. It was only after the Soviet government had embraced terror as an official policy that the non-Bolshevik revolutionary intelligentsia began to suffer. By that time a large proportion of the Menshevik and Social Revolutionary leaders among the intelligentsia had already escaped to live in exile. As for the comparable revolutionary leaders among the Bolsheviki, a very large proportion were to meet a violent death, but this was to be at the hands of the Stalinist secret police.

On a far smaller scale, the history of the Commune in France in 1871 had reflected a similar pattern. After the defeat of the Commune and the reoccupation of Paris by the forces of the French government, thousands of the working-class defenders were slaughtered. A large proportion of the leaders of the Commune, however, did not participate in the actual fighting and succeeded in escaping abroad.[30]

Modern capitalism, based as it is upon private property and with its insistence upon the limited power of the state over the individual, is peculiarly dependent upon court procedures and upon law and order in general. Consequently, arbitrary violence by state officials can hardly be tolerated without undermining the principles upon which the system operates. In a state of war or actual insurrection the capitalistic parliamentary state can inflict death wholesale. But, short of war or of actual insurrection, the advocates of the overthrow of the capitalistic parliamentary state can and naturally do claim the protection of the courts. Thus the risk of revolutionary agitation against the capitalistic state is not in the least comparable with the risk faced by anyone who attempted to agitate against the Soviet or the Nazi type of state. This is one reason why the resistance to such a regime is likely to be so small and so ineffective after it once has seized power.

It is, of course, easy to see why some members of the bourgeois intelligentsia might wish to promote a revolution in the name of the proletariat. They might do so out of sympathy for the miseries of the proletariat, out of indignation at the inequities, cruelties and inefficiencies of capitalism, or out of a

[30] See Mason, The History of the Paris Commune, p. 279.

sense of guilt for having shared in the benefits of the exploitation of the proletariat. Some of the intelligentsia who were failures in bourgeois society, expecting the revolution to succeed, would want to be on the winning side. Finally, it would be reasonable to suppose that some of them would join the revolutionary movement because they would expect to be members of the ruling class in the new society. But Marxist-Leninist doctrine, being materialistic and deterministic, would accept none of these reasons, whether based upon sympathy or upon self-seeking. What Lenin was asking of the proletariat in supporting his leadership of the Bolsheviki in their seizure of power was, in effect, this:

> Accept without question the leadership of us professional revolutionaries, members of the bourgeois intelligentsia who have never been workers, in the overthrow of the bourgeoisie and their economic and political system. By such a revolution you can get rid of that "surplus value" in the form of the payment of a return on property which constitutes capitalist exploitation. We offer ourselves as your leaders and you must believe that we and our successors will do a better job of running the economy and the state than did the bourgeoisie and the tsarist bureaucracy. We will do it for less pay than did the bourgeoisie so that a large part of what used to be the income from property can be divided among you workers. We will settle the matter of leadership from time to time by purges and political struggle within our ruling group. You will never have the chance to vote again, except to confirm the rule of a leadership which has already been determined, but any vote which you had under tsarism was also without meaning. We at least declare that we will manage the economy and the state solely in your interest. The tsars and the bourgeoisie never even claimed to do this.

Lenin, of course, neither used these words nor would have admitted that this was what he was offering to the Russian workers and peasants.

It was under Lenin and still more under Stalin that the doctrine of the function of the Communist Party to give guidance and leadership to the dictatorship of the proletariat was gradually formulated. Under Lenin and even more under Stalin it became evident that this did not imply that there was to be some actual periodic choice of the leadership of the Communist Party by a process of balloting.[31] Since neither the proletariat nor the Communist Party membership, much less the whole body of the Russian people, were ever to have a chance to choose whether they wished the leaders of the Communist Party to continue to exercise the dictatorship, this meant that the term "dictatorship of the proletariat" had been completely drained of its original Marxist meaning.

It might be argued, of course, that a group of proletarians who had seized power in the name of the proletariat might quite logically be expected to exercise power in the interests of their class. It might be argued that the working-class origins of such a group would guarantee that this would be so. One trouble with this argument is that the postulated proletarian origin of the group exercising power in the name of the working class is contrary to fact. The Bolshevik leaders did not, except in rare instances, have their origin in the industrial proletariat or among the poorer classes of the peasantry. This does not in the least mean that these leaders were thereby automatically less capable of interpreting the interests and desires of the proletariat than if they had been of working-class origin. It only means that a claim to the exclusive right to interpret the will of the proletariat certainly cannot be grounded on the class origin of the Bolshevik leaders.

Paradoxically enough, although the implementation of the concept of the dictatorship of the proletariat by the Bolsheviki meant the personal dictatorship of a small group of leaders and eventually the dictatorship of one man, the concept was treated as though it existed quite independently of the identity and personality of the actual wielders of the state power. The Bolshevik leaders assumed that in some esoteric sense they were the embodiment of the dictatorship of the proletariat and that consequently they had a right to take decisions and to act

---

[31] Under Stalin's immediate successors the leadership of the Communist Party was to become self-perpetuating, with the self-to-be-perpetuated determined in the last analysis by who could or could not succeed in separating whom from his armed bodyguard!

for the proletariat without the necessity for any political machinery which would permit really free elections of representatives of the proletariat.

Yet repeatedly the official wielders of the state power in the name of the dictatorship of the proletariat were to proclaim that many who had previously participated in the wielding of power as Communist leaders actually had been *at the time they were helping to wield that power* "enemies of the people," plotters with capitalistic and fascistic governments against the Soviet Union. Such members of the top bureaucracy, ranging in time from the expulsion of Trotsky from the Communist Party in 1928 to the execution of Beria in 1953, at once come to mind. The list begins long before 1928, however, and covers an unbelievable proportion of members of the Party hierarchy at almost all levels.[32]

It is one of the most extraordinary accomplishments recorded in the history of ideas or in the history of the transfer of power from one ruling class to another that Lenin shortly before the October Revolution had already prepared in his *State and Revolution* the rationalization for making his forthcoming deeds appear somehow consistent with Marxist doctrine. In so doing he performed the remarkable feat of demonstrating the necessity for the dictatorship of the proletariat while simultaneously providing an escape from the necessity of explaining how the bureaucracy were to be chosen which would govern society in the name of the proletariat after the overthrow of tsarism.

Lenin restates the doctrine of Marx and Engels that,

[32] Thus in 1912 there were six members of the Bolshevik faction in the Fourth Duma. Only after the Revolution did it become known that one of these six men was an agent of the tsarist police. Yet one of the remaining five members, Badayev, writing his memoirs in which he refers to this man's treachery, always speaks with an unquestioning retrospective faith in the social infallibility and the solidarity of the Bolshevik representatives of the working class. See A. Badayev, *The Bolsheviks in the Tsarist Duma,* International Publishers, New York, 1932. The author constantly upbraids the Menshevik delegates, of whom there were eight, for their wickedness in failing to support the program of "the working class." (The Mensheviki, of course, considered themselves to be as much entitled to be considered the representatives of the working class as the Bolsheviki.)

whereas capitalism depended upon the police power of the state to guarantee the extraction of surplus value from the labor of the proletariat, under communism there would be no state at all. The state would be unnecessary since, with no property rights and hence no surplus value, there would be no exploiting class which would need the police power of the state to enforce its will against the interests of the mass of the population. There need be no concern about constitutional means to protect the individual member of the proletariat against the power of the purely temporary state necessary during a transitory period to insure that the capitalistic exploiters could not re-establish the bourgeois state. As Lenin puts it, "The particular power of suppression of the proletariat by the capitalistic class must be replaced by a particular power of suppression of the capitalist class by the proletariat (the dictatorship of the proletariat)."

How long was this new state, embodying the dictatorship of the proletariat, to last? On the eve of the October Revolution, Lenin maintained that "the particular power of suppression of the capitalist class by the proletariat (the dictatorship of the proletariat)" was to begin to wither away on the morrow of victory; ". . . the proletariat, according to Marx, needs only a withering away State—a State, that is, so constituted that it begins to wither away immediately and cannot but wither away . . ." Lenin goes on to say in another passage, "How can we otherwise pass on to the discharge of all the functions of Government by the majority of the population and by every individual of the population?" And still further along he says, ". . . the great majority of the functions of 'the old State' have become enormously simplified and reduced, in practice, to very simple operations such as registration, filing and checking. Hence they will be quite within the reach of every literate person, and it will be possible to perform them for the usual 'working man's wage.' "[33] By the use of this amorphous phrase "dictatorship of the proletariat," and by a grotesque underestimate of the complexities and difficulties of administering a collectivist type of economy, Lenin evaded answering the problem crucial to all organized forms

[33] See Vladimir Lenin, *State and Revolution*, Vanguard, New York, 1929, p. 150.

of human society: "How is the minority of men from a given society which is to rule the majority of the population to be selected, and how can this minority be prevented from developing into a tyranny?" Lenin simply took as axiomatic the right of the Central Committee of the Bolsheviks under his leadership to wield unlimited power in the name of the dictatorship of the proletariat.

The thoroughness and ruthlessness with which the Bolsheviks destroyed the organization of industry, the civil government and the armed forces of the tsarist predecessors—by definition the instruments of the bourgeois exploiters—did not embarrass Lenin, Trotsky and their colleagues and successors at all in their task of erecting a new state power. The restoration of industrial discipline was to require decades of effort and was completed only after a decade of Stalin's rule. What was necessary and was taken in hand at once was the establishment of discipline in the Red Army.

The death penalty for infractions of discipline was reinstated and used more freely in the Red Army than it had been in the tsarist army. It had to be, since the bulk of its soldiers had to be reclaimed from the dissolved masses of the old army. No one has ever expressed more succinctly the final basis upon which the discipline of armies rests than did Trotsky, in his reference in *My Life* to the task of creating discipline in the Red Army during this period: "So long as those malicious tailless apes . . . the animals that we call men—will build armies and wage wars, the command will always be obliged to place the soldiers between possible death at the front and the inevitable one in the rear."[34] The implementation of this policy of inducing men to fight by giving them the choice between possible death at the front and certain death in the rear sometimes involved the mass execution of the rank and file of soldiers and sailors.[35]

Trotsky's success in restoring discipline in the Red Army led

[34] Leon Trotsky, *My Life,* Scribner's, New York, 1930, p. 411.
[35] For example, the commissar and commander of a regiment recruited from Petrograd workers, together with every tenth soldier, were shot on the Volga front during the Civil War in August 1918 when they were seized by panic and, commandeering a ship, tried to sail away to safety. Chamberlin, *The Russian Revolution,* Vol. II, p. 119.

him to advocate a type of militarization of labor in industry after the close of the Civil War. This idea was opposed by Tomsky, the Bolshevik head of Soviet labor unions, and by Stalin as well. Stalin nevertheless later succeeded in restoring industrial discipline by methods as stern as those which had been advocated by Trotsky. Tomsky committed suicide in despair at this loss of liberty of Russian labor under the "dictatorship of the proletariat." But this was to come about later.

It has been widely believed that Stalin perverted the dictatorship of the proletariat into the Soviet totalitarian state. Indeed, this was charged by Khrushchev when he denounced Stalin a few years after his death for setting up "the cult of personality." Yet the record is clear that the philosophy, superstructure and mechanism of the totalitarian state had already been developed by Lenin and Trotsky. Lenin did not hesitate to use the extremes of terror, not only against the adherents of the old regime, but against socialist radicals as well, even after the Civil War had ended.[36] Lenin fully acquiesced in the shooting down under the direction of Trotsky of thousands of revolutionary sailors in the Kronstadt rebellion. Neither Lenin nor Trotsky, as has been pointed out, had any respect for representative government. Instead they believed that in some esoteric fashion they were especially able to interpret and carry out the will of the proletariat. This personal capacity to interpret what the will of the proletariat should be was not limited by any system of ethics, because ethics only consisted of whatever served the cause of the proletarian revolution. "Morality is that which serves the destruction of the old exploiter's society and the union of all the toilers around the proletariat, which creates a new society of communists . . . We do not believe in eternal morality and we expose the deceit of all legends about morality."[37]

Only in Lenin's last days, when he was too ill to be able any longer to arrange the succession, did he confront the horrible reality of a man of Stalin's stature seizing this power to

---

[36] See, for example, David Shub, *Lenin: A Biography*, Doubleday, New York, 1948, pp. 377–378, and Chamberlin, *The Russian Revolution*, Vol. I, p. 138.

[37] Vladimir Lenin, *Collected Works of Lenin*, International Publishers, New York, 1927, Vol. XVII, pp. 323–324.

determine what the will of the proletariat should be. Trotsky, who during his days of power was supremely confident in the superiority of the "dynamics of the revolution" over representative government, was ruled an enemy of the people by that Soviet regime which he had played such a great role in setting up. He died with a pickaxe in his brain, assassinated by order of that same regime. Stalin, without restraint from any form of representative government, had decided what the dynamics of revolution required. It is doubtless true that Stalin had little of the intellectual brilliance of Lenin and Trotsky. He manipulated the Soviet power with greater cunning and more consciously in his own interests than had Lenin or Trotsky. Yet fundamentally the Soviet totalitarian state of Stalin could logically claim to be the legitimate descendant of the Leninist-Trotskyist revolutionary state.

CHAPTER 3

THE FULLY DEVELOPED TOTALITARIAN STATE: SOVIET RUSSIA UNDER STALIN

Under Lenin's leadership the Bolsheviki had overthrown Russian capitalism with the promise that a socialist society would be created to replace the old system of capitalistic exploitation. Lenin did not live long enough, however, to set a permanent pattern for the Soviet economic and political system. It was Stalin who, during the three decades of his power, was to build upon Lenin's unfinished work a totalitarian structure which has given evidence of permanency. Has this system which Stalin developed the right to be called socialist?

What did socialists expect of the economic system which they hoped would follow upon the end of capitalism? How has the development of the Soviet state fulfilled these hopes? Most fundamental of all to socialists was the elimination of private ownership of the means of production in the new society. From this one basic change, the most desirable consequences for society were to flow. Authority over the productive process would no longer depend upon property ownership. Administrative posts would be filled by the most talented, not simply by property owners or the favorites of property owners. Production would be carried on for use, not for profit: to supply the needs of the masses, not the luxury demands of millionaires. The wastes of competition would be avoided.

Production would be rationally planned instead of being suspended in chaos somewhere between competition and monopoly. With planning, and with the worker receiving the full value of his labor, production need never be slowed down for lack of demand. There would be no economic depressions, no poverty or starvation in the midst of plenty.

Laborers would work with enthusiasm instead of with resentment, since they would be working for themselves instead of for the profit of the capitalists. With income from property eliminated, inequality in distribution would tend to disappear. With the disappearance of the capitalist-boss, the worker would labor in freedom rather than under the stern and often arbitrary hand of authority.

Such were the expectations of socialists of all varieties, of Marxian socialists, from German Social Democrats to Russian Bolsheviki, as well as of utopian socialists. The Social Democrats and most other socialist parties believed that these ends could be attained peacefully by democratic and parliamentary means. The Bolshevik leaders, on the contrary, had insisted that the apparatus of the bourgeois state must first be broken up by violent revolution and the bourgeois administrators of capitalist society liquidated as a class; but they too believed that the complete elimination of private property would enable these expectations to be fulfilled. The Bolsheviki further maintained that after the transitional period necessary for the elimination of the power of the capitalist exploiters there would be no state at all.

The fatal defect in this reasoning was the failure to answer the obvious question: If the owner of private or corporate property or his appointee is not to direct production, then who is to do so? It is no answer at all to say that "the people" or the "working class" will do it. Responsibility is always borne and authority is always wielded by persons. How are these administrators of the economy to be selected, and what are to be the limits of their powers as between themselves and over others? Why should it be assumed that they will demand less compensation for accepting responsibility than did the former administrators? Why should they be more humane, less selfish, less authoritarian, less in need of the controls evolved by parliamentary, democratic governments than were those who owed their positions to the owners of private property? Indeed, it is obvious that the need for limitation and control of the powers of an integrated nationwide economic bureaucracy is inherently greater than where control of the economy is as fragmented and autonomous as it was under old-style capitalism. Even under present-day capitalism this fragmentation and autonomy remain infinitely greater than in the collectivized economy of Soviet Russia.

Lenin had immediately been faced by the question of collective control in an economy in which private property as an organizing principle had been effectively destroyed by the October Revolution. The overriding importance of maintaining at least the minimum industrial production essential to feed the urban population on even the lowest subsistence level and to provide for the needs of the Red Army during the Civil War shortened drastically the period of Soviet experimentation with the control of industrial plants by workers' committees or by administrative officers elected by the workers. Soon after the revolutionary seizure of factories by the workers it became evident that plants could not be managed in any such "democratic" fashion and that some form of authoritative management was going to be essential. Under the exigencies of the Civil War, Lenin did not have to debate the question whether worker control might be practicable in the future under more favorable circumstances or whether authoritarian control was consistent with Marxist doctrine.[1]

When the temporary management of industry by workers' committees in each factory had proved wholly impracticable, industrial plants were organized simply as parts of the governmental apparatus. This system was naturally extremely unwieldy and appallingly unproductive. The procedure by which one plant obtained raw materials without payment from an-

[1] The question of authoritarian control of industry was to be dealt with in terms of Marxist-Leninist doctrine by alleging that the administration of industry should be considered "the administration of things and not the administration of men." Consequently, according to Lenin, even in the second and final stage of socialism, called communism, authoritative administration of the *economy* could continue even though the "state" had "withered away," without breaking the ideological rules!

other plant in an earlier stage of production, or requisitioned agricultural products from the peasantry and delivered finished goods to state agencies, also without receiving payment, made it impossible to keep financial accounts. The provision by the government of inadequate rations for workers and the delivery of a swiftly depreciating printed currency to industrial plants to meet their payrolls completed the picture of administrative near-chaos. Consequently, the mounting food crisis that necessitated Lenin's "New Economic Policy" in agriculture actually served also as an excuse for the comprehensive reorganization of the control of industrial plants which was required.

Future experimentation and experience were to emphasize what these early efforts at a kind of primitive communist organization of industry had promptly indicated, namely, that the operation of industry most emphatically *did* involve the administration of men as well as of things. The evolution of the administrative system of Soviet industry, which was to prove far less democratic than in capitalistic Western lands, followed upon the development of the absolute, totalitarian Soviet political state. The fact that Marxist theory denied even the existence of the problem of how to administer the economy and the political state greatly facilitated the development of this absolute and totalitarian form in both realms. Instead of the state "withering away" after the overthrow of capitalism, in accordance with Marxist doctrine, it in fact became an even more powerful instrument of a dictatorship which was not that of the proletariat at all. But this did not happen all at once and abortive efforts were recurrently made to give the economic organization some semblance to that forecast by Marxist doctrine. In the meantime, the failure of the October Revolution to eliminate authority in industry could be excused by the necessity for the partial and temporary reversion to capitalistic institutions embodied in the New Economic Policy.

There can be no question but that agricultural developments following the Revolution made a radical shift in policy in this field most urgent. During the period of the Civil War and until the inauguration of NEP in 1921 a very limited effort had been made to induce the peasants who had seized land at the time of the Revolution to organize collective farms which would be operated "cooperatively." This limited effort came to nothing and the peasants were allowed to continue to operate their own holdings plus the additions of land which represented their share of the property confiscated during the Revolution.

Originally it had been intended that manufactured goods from the nationalized industries would be provided for the peasants in return for their grain, meat and other agricultural products. Since agricultural products were not voluntarily offered, they were requisitioned, with the promise that manufactured products would be provided later. Russians recalling this period of War Communism and the plan for barter between industry and agriculture used to say wryly, "The plan was fifty per cent successful. Agricultural products were taken from the peasants." Industrial production had, in truth, fallen so drastically that almost no manufactured goods were available for distribution to the peasants after the minimum needs of the Red Army and the industrial workers had been supplied. The forceful and violent means employed in requisitioning farm products during the period of almost total disorder of the Civil War were largely responsible for the peasants' hatred of the Soviet regime, which had so recently allowed their land hunger to be assuaged temporarily at the expense of the landlords. Their hatred was to express itself during the years to come in a bitter resistance to Soviet agricultural policy in all its manifestations.

The peasant reaction to the Bolshevik policy of requisitioning all "surplus" grain during the period of War Communism has been described as simply seeing to it that there would be no surplus, by restricting the sown area to the amount necessary to feed the peasant's own household. In some degree this was true, since there was little incentive for the peasant to produce more than for his own needs. However, he was to learn the hard way that one could not treat the Soviet regime so cavalierly. A "surplus" is capable of substantial expansion when the concept is defined by an authoritarian regime willing to use unlimited force. The Soviet regime merely assumed the peasant must have produced a surplus and continued to requisition very much as before. Under these circumstances, the peasant household had the alternative of reducing its consumption, using up its reserves against bad harvests, or starving. The area sown to grain shrank alarmingly. The agricultural situation was approaching the catastrophe which was actually to occur in the famine of 1921. Once more necessity enabled Lenin to make fundamental changes in the organization of the economy for which there was no provision in Marxist doctrine.

Lenin was to describe his New Economic Policy frankly as a retreat to capitalism: "A step backward in order the better to leap forward." Permitting private traders to engage in retail trade; allowing the peasants to sell their produce on the open market after the payment of a fixed tax instead of government requisitioning of the "surplus"; offering concessions on profitable terms to foreign companies in order to induce them to build plants in Russia; establishing differential wage and salary payments based upon seventeen different categories according to skill and responsibility instead of equality of compensation; re-establishing a price system in lieu of rationing; and the setting up of state-owned "Trusts," modeled on the capitalistic corporation, to carry on industrial production—this did indeed appear to be the abandonment of socialism and the return to a capitalistic economic system. It seemed all the more so when a little later the currency was gradually stabilized so that a price system of at least limited effectiveness could once more function.

Thus it was not illogical that the New Economic Policy was widely interpreted abroad as the end of any attempt to set up a truly socialist economy. This impression was strengthened when the great famine of 1921 occurred, since it demonstrated the necessity for this "retreat to capitalism." As a matter of fact, Lenin had foreseen the need for the New Economic Policy before the famine.

Belief in the permanence of the retreat from revolutionary socialism was reinforced in the immediately succeeding years by the subsidence of the terror which had been carried on by the Tcheka during and right after the Civil War. It appeared momentarily that the revolution was at an end and that Russia might soon begin to pattern its economic and political system after those of the capitalistic and democratic West.

It was, however, during this early period of the New Economic Policy that Stalin began acquiring control of the Party bureaucracy. This was to make possible that personal dictatorship which would complete the transformation of the new state into what he in 1930 correctly called "the most potent and mighty of all state authorities that have existed down to the present time."

The foundations of the absolute and totalitarian state had indeed been laid by Lenin. He had never believed in allowing disputes within the Central Committee to be referred to the membership of the Party for settlement, even before the Revolution. In fact, he did not allow his own judgment to be overruled by a majority vote within the Central Committee. Instead he tirelessly and relentlessly argued and maneuvered until his decisions were accepted. Lenin used terror without limit against the opponents of the Soviet regime,[2] and had even justified the use of the firing squad against Menshevik and other socialist critics. Yet, after he was in power he did not resort to the arrest and execution of members of the Central Committee in order to impose his will upon it as Stalin was later to do.

Lenin had justified his use of terror as a necessary instrument for the overthrow of the tsarist government and for the maintenance of the dictatorship of the proletariat during the infancy of the new regime. He did, however, begin to have most serious qualms during the last few months of his life as he saw Stalin start to use this same terror against Party comrades and national minorities. He expressed these qualms in the "testament" in which he warned the Party against Stalin.[3] The death of Lenin in January 1924 prevented him from terminating this policy of terror which he himself had inaugurated and defended.

Stalin's assumption of power was not primarily effectuated

[2] See p. 54.

[3] The authenticity of Lenin's testament, the existence of which had been known for years, was at last officially admitted by Khrushchev in his famous speech denouncing Stalin at the 20th Party Congress in February 1956.

n its early stages by the use of terror. His acquisition of au-
hority was accomplished primarily by means of staffing the
Party bureaucracy with men who knew they owed their posi-
ions to him. He followed this by intrigues within the Central
Committee of the Party by which he turned its members
against Trotsky and then turned other members against some
of those who had aided him in expelling Trotsky from the
Party. Three decades later Khrushchev used almost identical
methods in obtaining control of the Party and the state. It was,
however, not until some four years after the death of Lenin
that Stalin was able to have Trotsky expelled from the Soviet
Union and to emerge clearly as an unquestioned personal
dictator.

It is hard to imagine that anyone else could have built up a
totalitarian tyranny comparable to that for which Stalin was
to be responsible in the years to come. In terms of millions of
people sent to forced labor camps, of hundreds of thousands
executed or allowed to die of hunger, of utter disregard for
the peasant or working-class origin of those deported, imprisoned or shot, of disregard for services rendered the Soviet
regime during the Revolution and Civil War, of repression of
all freedom of speech, press and conscience, of adulation and
sycophancy required of all around him and in all organs of
propaganda, there is no modern counterpart for Stalin's
regime.[4]

The degree to which Stalin insisted upon something akin
to the status of divinity accorded the Roman emperors is unbelievable. It became customary for guides who showed foreigners newly constructed public works to refer to a large
dam, for example, as having been built by Comrade Stalin.
He insisted upon being credited with the authorship of the
official *Short Course of the History of the All-Union Communist Party (Bolsheviks)*, although he had also required ex-

[4] The writer for years had told his classes that the best account of
life in Stalinist Russia was written by a man who never lived there,
George Orwell. In this connection Howard Fast, writing in 1957,
tells how John Gates, editor of the *Daily Worker,* first read Orwell's
1984 while a prisoner in the federal penitentiary. Fast recounts how
Gates was struck by horror as he recognized in *1984* himself, the
Party and the Soviet Union. Howard Fast, *The Naked God,* Praeger,
New York, 1957, pp. 41–42.

travagant praise of himself in it. Reporting on a conference
of scientists in 1948, presided over by Trofim Lysenko, *Pravda*
referred to the ovation accorded the mention of Stalin, "the
wise leader and teacher, the greatest scholar of our epoch."
On orders from Stalin the Michurin theory of the transmis-
sion of acquired characteristics, championed by Lysenko but
rejected by almost all biologists, was officially declared correct.
Severe penalties were inflicted upon those geneticists who
failed to accept the prescribed doctrine. The paranoid character of Stalin's vanity was later used as a basis for denouncing his "cult of personality." It was claimed that this "cult of
personality," however repugnant, was not the result of the
Soviet system and had not basically altered the character of
the system. Yet there is little reason to believe that the Stalinist totalitarian state was a purely personal creation.

It is not at all clear that there would have been less terror
and more democracy if Trotsky rather than Stalin had succeeded Lenin. The defenders of Trotsky cannot rightfully
claim that he favored democracy and deplored the use of terror. He was intellectually extremely arrogant; and he clearly
favored a kind of militarization of labor immediately after
the end of the Civil War.[5] Even some of the Communist
members of the revolutionary military council of the Third
Army protested against "Trotsky's extremely light-hearted attitude toward such things as shooting." Although he referred
to the sailors of Kronstadt as "the pride and glory of the Revolution," he ordered the attack on the Kronstadt Soviet, with
the resultant slaughter of thousands of sailors, long after the
Revolution was over and the Civil War at an end.

The combination of the so-called "temporary retreat to
capitalism" of the New Economic Policy, the expulsion of
Trotsky (at that time considered more of a terrorist than
Stalin), with his advocacy of the policy of "permanent revolution," the cessation for a time of mass executions accompanied
by the relaxation of pressure against the upper and middle
strata of the peasantry, gave rise to some temporary relaxation
of tension during the early Stalinist period. This substantial
change from the revolutionary period of 1917–21 cannot,
however, be accounted the Russian equivalent of the "Reac-

[5] See pp. 53–54.

ion of Thermidor" in France in 1794 during the French
Revolution, following the fall of Robespierre. Stalin's rule was
indeed characterized by the development of absolutism in
Russia and by the establishment of hierarchical rule in the
state and the economy, together with the restoration of rank
and privilege, the prerogatives of a new ruling class. It is also
true that the great majority of the leaders of the Bolshevik
Party who had participated in the Revolution and the Civil
War were eventually liquidated by Stalin, just as a large proportion of the revolutionary terrorists had been liquidated
during the Thermidor Reaction in France. But the liquidation of the revolutionary leadership and the establishment of
the hierarchical absolute state did not bring about the resto-
ation of capitalism or the repudiation of terror as the means
by which power was to be maintained and exercised. The new
form of organization of the state and of the economy was not
socialist in nature, for socialism had always implied the operation of the economy in the interests of society. Under Stalin
a fully collectivized, authoritarian economy took shape, in
which the interests of the dictator and his "New Class" were
determinative. Concomitantly, terror as an instrument of political power was revived on a scale comparable to its use during the Civil War. This terror, now bearing most heavily on
one group, now on another, was to continue with variations
in intensity throughout Stalin's life.

Stalin not only superintended the construction of a system of
control for a fully collectivist industrial economy. He carried
through what Lenin had never been able to achieve even momentarily during the period of War Communism, the wiping
out of the system of individual peasant landholding and cultivation and its replacement by a completely collectivized
agriculture. In so doing, he eliminated the foundation upon
which a modified capitalistic system might conceivably have
been substituted in time for the Soviet economic system.[6]

[6] The Bolshevik leaders were strongly impressed by Kropotkin's
doctrine that the French peasants became resolutely conservative
as soon as the confiscated estates of the nobility were firmly in their
hands and that the French Revolution was thereby brought to an
end. See Peter Kropotkin, *The Great French Revolution, 1789–
1793,* Vanguard, New York, 1927.

Did the absolutist state which Stalin established requir
the liquidation of NEP and the setting up of a completel
collectivized economy, or did the erection and operation of
fully collectivized economy require an absolutist state? It
true that the return to terror as an instrument of power ca
be traced largely to the repercussions from the collectivizatio
of agriculture which got under way as a forcible process i
the summer of 1929. Stalin did not, however, decide upo
the agricultural program simply as the final step in the co
lectivization of the economy. He might have been perfectl
willing to continue the New Economic Policy indefinitely :
it had been feasible to do so. Indeed, he had earlier agree
to extend the agricultural policy of NEP still further by relax
ing the restrictions upon the rental of land and the employ
ment of labor by the more energetic peasants. He had bee
sharply criticized by Trotsky for this policy of "favoring th
kulaks."

The policy of encouraging individual peasants to increas
their production had not, however, paid off. The sown are
remained below prerevolutionary levels. It had proved impo
sible to resume the exports of grain with which tsarist Russi
had paid for imports. These imports were even more essentia
to the Soviet economy in connection with the grandiose plan
for industrialization than they had been to the tsarist econ
omy. Far from being able to resume these exports, food ra
tioning had had to be reinstituted in 1928. A choice had thu
to be made. Either still further concessions had to be give
to the individual peasants or a radically different solution o
the agricultural crisis had to be tried.

Additional concessions to the individual peasants woul
probably have had to be accompanied by increased conces
sions to retail tradesmen and small producers, and by cuts i
prices of manufactured goods produced by state industries i
the peasants were to receive more and cheaper manufacture
goods. This was the only concession which would have in
duced them to produce and sell more grain and meat. T
make this concession would have sharply curtailed investmen
funds for capital construction out of the profits of state in
dustry. There was, furthermore, no assurance that any con

cessions to the peasants would have solved the desperate food problem.

Stalin, of course, never considered for a moment allowing even a gradual reversion to complete capitalism in Russia. He undoubtedly realized that in such an economic and political system there would be no place for him. To Stalin, it was consequently a question of how a food supply could be obtained without abandoning the Soviet economic system. To him, the alternative to an even further retreat to capitalism was the complete collectivization of the economy.

The decision to collectivize agriculture carried with it fateful consequences. That it was the occasion for a split with what Stalin labeled the "Right Deviation" headed by Bukharin, Rykov and Tomsky, who had previously supported him against the "Left Opposition" of Trotsky, was not the most important of these consequences. These men believed that the peasantry would never agree to surrender individual ownership of their land without the maximum use of force. They were right. The bitterness of the peasant resistance to collectivization, the stirring up of "revolutionary zeal" in the Party to overcome this resistance, and the cruelty of the measures used against the peasants were to place a permanent imprint upon the Stalinist regime.

The kulaks, the so-called rich peasants, would naturally have been expected to resist collectivization, as indeed they did. But substantially the whole body of peasantry joined the kulaks in their resistance. All pretense at voluntary collectivization was abandoned. Grain requisitions were resumed and often almost all of the peasant's grain was taken. He was then told that only if he joined the kolkhoz would he be assured of sufficient grain for food for the coming year. The kulaks and others who were branded as such were denied even the right to join a collective farm, and Stalin soon announced the policy of the "liquidation of the kulaks as a class." Their houses, land, livestock and other possessions were confiscated. In an attempt to secure the support of the poorer peasants, the property of the kulaks was turned over to the collective farms to be used as part of the entrance payment of the poorer peasants. Hundreds of thousands of kulaks were rounded up and deported to the barren and unsettled areas of northern Russia or to the steppes of Central Asia.[7] Thousands were imprisoned and many were executed.

The major threat used to compel peasants to join the collective farm was that of declaring all recalcitrants to be kulaks, and this threat was often carried out. Since kulaks were deprived of civil rights, which also meant that they could not join trade unions, obtain ration cards or send their children to the higher schools, it was a powerful weapon. Nevertheless, bitter peasant resistance continued.

In the process of mobilizing party support for the collectivization of agriculture, a movement inevitably developed for the complete communization of the whole economy. Almost all Nepmen were arrested and their retail shops closed. A movement sprang up for the payment of wages according to need rather than productivity, skill and responsibility. "Communes" were organized in industrial plants in which everyone from managers and engineers to unskilled workers pooled their wages, which were then redistributed according to need. Few of the higher-paid personnel dared to resist. It soon became apparent, however, that there would be a serious decline in industrial productivity unless the equalization of wages was stopped. By the spring of 1930 it was plain that the leftward movement, which had reached the point of hysteria, would have to be halted if the economy were not to collapse.

The peasants began to show their resentment and despair by slaughtering their livestock, since they would have had to turn them into the collective farms anyhow. The government tried to prevent this by requiring the peasants to register the numbers of their livestock and by holding the peasants responsible for the delivery of this number to the collective farms. Nevertheless, the livestock population was drastically reduced. The number of hogs, for example, declined by more than one fourth within a few months. In some villages the peasants

---

[7] In May 1930, the special train on which the writer and a number of newspaper correspondents were returning from the opening of the Turkestan-Siberian Railway stopped at a small station in Kazakhstan. A string of freight cars on a siding was filled with peasant families. These peasants told us that they had been declared kulaks and were being deported to some unknown place in Central Asia.

rose against the Party managers of the collective farms and killed them. In at least one case Soviet troops sent against these peasants refused to fire upon them.[8]

Stalin, frightened at last, issued the statement known as "Dizziness from Success." He declared that success beyond all expectations had been achieved in collectivization,[9] and in consequence of the exhilaration of success many excesses had occurred in the collectivization campaign. In particular it was wrong to have used force to compel the peasants to join the collective farms. Peasants were now to be free to leave the collectives if they wished. A little later Stalin also declared that it was a mistake to have liquidated the Nepmen retail merchants. He also came out strongly against the movement for the payment of wages according to need.

Immediately upon the publication of Stalin's statement against collectivization by force, the peasants stormed out of the collectives by the millions. The percentage of collectivization was abruptly cut in half. However, Stalin did not give up his determination to collectivize agriculture. Taxes on individual farms were set at such a high rate as to be unbearable. Gradually the peasants were once more compelled to join the collectives.

The peasants, particularly those in the Ukraine, made one last desperate effort to resist collectivization in the spring and summer of 1932. Even though they had been compelled to join collectives, they sometimes tried to sabotage grain production by passive resistance. The government charged that they sowed grain on top of the ground without preparing the soil and that they made little effort to keep down weeds. Since the season turned out to be a poor crop year in the Ukraine, the harvest proved insufficient to maintain life. The peasants appealed for grain from the state grain reserves. Stalin said "No!" Hundreds of thousands in the Ukraine died from starvation or diseases of malnutrition. In the Northern Caucasus,

[8] These village uprisings were never officially admitted, yet the fact of their occurrence was well known at the time among the people of Moscow.

[9] In a sense this was true. According to the First Five-Year Plan (1928–1933) only 20 per cent of agriculture was to be collectivized at the end of the Plan. Instead some 40 per cent had been collectivized by the early months of the second year of the Plan.

punishment of peasant recalcitrance took more positive forms
Whole Cossack villages were deported en masse to the barrer
northern areas of Russia. The peasant resistance was finally
broken and collectivization of agriculture became complete
throughout the land.[10]

The form of organization which became the standard for
collective farms, the *artel*, was selected because it conformed
to the general organizational principle for the whole Stalinis
economic system. While nominally cooperative in organiza
tional form, the management of the collective farms was ir
fact appointive, just as in industry and in all sectors of the
economy. The authority of the management, moreover, was
little more limited than in industry. While major productior
was carried on as an organizational unit, peasant members
were paid according to the number of work-days, with sub
stantial adjustments for differences in skills and responsibility
Permission to cultivate private plots of land was accorded
grudgingly. The government was continually torn between the
alternatives of trying to increase output by incentives to pro
duce more on these plots and of forbidding peasants to have
them at all, since the peasants, in order to produce more on
their own plots, often neglected to work hard enough or long
enough on the land of the collective farm.

This *artel* type of collective farm had been chosen over the
commune type, a few of which had existed during the early
days of the collectivization of agriculture. In the *commune*,
an almost complete communization of production, distribu
tion and living arrangements prevailed. The choice of the
artel over the *commune* meant that the authoritarian, non-
egalitarian organizational form had been applied to agricul
ture as well as to industry and the rest of the economy.

With the end of NEP, state retail and wholesale organiza
tions took over the part of the distribution system which had
previously been in private hands. A large part of retail trade
remained in the hands of what were nominally consumers'
cooperatives. But these "cooperative" organizations were really
not that at all; in no basic sense did they differ from the state

---

[10] In February 1933, when the writer was again briefly in Moscow,
numerous peasants from the Ukraine who had fled the famine there
could be seen begging in the streets.

organizations. The organizational forms in retail and wholesale marketing were not unlike those in industry, with some
organs of state and retail trade directly under the authority
of the federal authorities and some under the "republican"
and local authorities. As in industry and in the rest of the
economy, the planning and operation were authoritative and
hierarchical. Although some changes were to take place in the
organizational forms of retail and wholesale trade during the
Stalinist period, its basic form had been achieved at the end
of NEP and gave evidence of permanency.

Even if there had been no forcible collectivization of agriculture, of course, Stalin might have carried out the deadly
and widespread purges which raged from 1934 to 1938 and
depleted the ranks of Soviet leadership. But the psychological
effect upon Stalin himself of having ordered the dragooning
of millions of peasants must have been very great. Moreover,
he had learned that by the use of unlimited force he could
compel even the sullen peasant masses to obey his will. He
had also learned that he could successfully relax pressures
when necessary and then resume them without losing control
of the situation. Yet the agricultural problem never gave him
peace, for the continuance of food shortages, which collectivization did not solve, was always a source of harassment.

The wholesale terror accompanying forcible collectivization
of agriculture thus appears to have played a decisive role in
the development of terror as a permanent institution of the
Stalinist system. It illustrates as well that when economic decisions are made by the state without the consent of the governed, this will almost inevitably be associated with personal
dictatorship accompanied by the use of terror.

The collectivization of agriculture, although carried out at a
much faster pace than planned, had been envisaged in the
First Five-Year Plan. The tempo of industrialization and capital investment provided for in the Plan could not have been
attained if the people had been free to choose between the
purchase of consumption goods and the saving of capital as
people do in a capitalistic, free market economy. Neither
could this high rate of investment have taken place if Russia
had had a freely elected parliament which decided how much

the populace would be allowed to consume and how much
they would have to save. If there had been such an institution,
the popular support of legislators favoring increased consumption goods in the present would surely have limited any national program of saving and capital investment. It would
not have been possible to enact measures which provided
for such a high proportion of investment in the heavy capital-
goods industries as did the First Five-Year Plan and the successor plans. Such a heavy concentration of investment in the
construction of mills producing pig iron and so low an investment in textile plants, for example, meant that the decision
to invest in this direction had put off an increase in the volume
of consumer goods much farther into the future than if the
investment program had placed the emphasis upon consumer
goods industries.

The speed-up of collectivization in agriculture—the result
of using force—greatly increased the strain on the economy
and demanded still greater sacrifices in the form of capital
saving from consumers. The collectivization of agriculture involved the planned mechanization of agricultural production.
The speed-up in collectivization meant that scores of thousands of additional tractors were needed beyond what had
originally been planned. Finally, when those branded as kulaks
slaughtered millions of their horses rather than turn them
over to the collective farms, the need for still more tractors
aggravated the strain on the economy enormously. Consumer
goods desperately needed at home had to be exported to pay
for increased imports of tractors and of machinery to produce
tractors. The net effect of the heavier import requirements
was to augment the use of authority divorced from popular
control and dependent upon unlimited force.

The whipping up of hatred against the kulaks, which had
been considered a necessary part of the campaign for the collectivization of agriculture, was extended not only to the Nepmen, the retail merchants, but also to the former bourgeois
managers and technicians now employed in the Soviet economic bureaucracy. Thousands were charged with the peculiar
crime of *vreditelstvo*, a word meaning "concealed sabotage."
This might include anything from planning too small a construction program to planning too large a construction pro-

gram, as well as such alleged crimes as drawing up blueprints which would result in the manufacture of defective machinery. These widespread charges were accompanied by the wholesale use of the *chistka*, or "cleaning," in which the management of industry had to undergo investigation at the hands of innumerable special commissions.

It had not been easy to re-establish labor discipline after the early revolutionary period during which the Bolsheviki had exhorted workers to strike and to hamper factory production in every way possible. Yet now, at the very time that suspicion was being directed against managerial personnel, particularly that inherited from tsarist times, any attempt at worker participation in the management of industry was ruthlessly repressed. Collective bargaining by labor unions was absolutely prohibited and the labor unions became primarily organizations to stimulate greater labor productivity and to enforce labor discipline.

In late 1929 the author attended a conference on productivity held for worker representatives by the management of the First Cotton Textile Trust at Serpukhov, a textile town not far from Moscow. At one stage of the conference, workers were allowed to hand in written questions to the "Presidium" of the meeting, seated on a platform. The Director of the Trust explained why the previous year's increase in production had not been greater. The principal cause, he said, was the activity of saboteurs. Then he unfolded one of the notes which had been handed in and declared dramatically: "We have such a saboteur in our midst at this moment!" He read aloud the question which one of the workers had handed in: "Just before the October Revolution, when the Kerensky Government was in power, the Mensheviks urged us to work hard and produce as much as possible. The Bolsheviks, however, denounced the Mensheviks and urged us to go on strike and to do everything we could to hinder production. Now you Bolsheviks are saying just what the Mensheviks did, to work hard and produce much. What is the sense of this?" The Director then said: "This shameless saboteur knows full well the answer to his question. The Mensheviks were urging the workers to produce for capitalist exploiters. We Communists demand the utmost productivity from all workers now that industry is in the hands of the toiling masses." The anonymous "saboteur" naturally did not rise from his seat and ask, as he might logi cally have done, just how the toiling masses had decided that the man who denounced him was to be the Director of the First Cotton Textile Trust. The Director, in fact, as in all such cases, had no more been elected by the workers of the plants in the Trust than the president of a corporation in a capitalistic country is elected by the laborers in the corpora tion's plants.

A little later there appeared an item in the Moscow press which illustrated the sternness of the measures which were being taken to establish industrial discipline. The workers in a plant near Sverdlovsk had got out of hand. "Hooliganism" reached such heights that workers tossed chunks of ore into the machinery just for the fun of smashing it. A Party control commission was sent into the plant and an investigation was made. As a result several of the workers were sentenced to various terms of "deprivation of freedom." The ringleader was sentenced to "the highest measure of social protection shooting."

The unlimited use of force proved successful in the re establishment of worker discipline. The frequent arrest, im prisonment and even the execution of key executive personnel in industry during the purges, which might have been ex pected to produce total lack of respect among workers for bosses who were likely to be dethroned at any time, did not operate as more than a temporary obstacle to the re-establish ment of discipline.

In a system in which the official doctrine was that industry belonged to the workers, it was no doubt inevitable that the most ruthless disciplinary measures should have been required to inculcate obedience among the workers to bosses appointed from the top down. In the complete absence at all stages of collective bargaining and of control by workers over the ap pointment of managerial personnel, they knew, of course, that the official doctrine of worker control of industry was non sense. Once the police power of the state succeeded in com pelling the workers to recognize the absolute powers of management, the matter was removed from the field of discussion.

After industrial discipline was completely restored, management no longer had to dispute with the workers the question of what elements of industry were properly a matter of joint worker-management control. Managerial personnel became entirely free of the guilt feelings that do sometimes haunt managerial personnel in capitalistic countries as the recipients of property incomes or the representatives of property owners participating in potential "exploitation of the workers." With the imposition of the doctrine that the state represented the interests of the workers and that the wisdom or justice of its acts could not be questioned, industrial managers were freed from humanitarian concern for the interests of labor, since it could be assumed that these interests were taken into account in the decisions made by higher authority.

There could not be, of course, even one articulate member of the intelligentsia, sympathetic with the workers in their relations vis-à-vis Soviet management, to champion their cause in the press, in literature, on the stage, or on radio or television. To assume a conflict of interest between the managers of state industry and the workers would have branded one an "enemy of the people," with all the deadly consequences thereof.

The severity of the measures used to maintain industrial discipline was greatly intensified by the insecurity of the managers, who lived under the constant threat of dismissal and arrest. It was not so much that they themselves were driven by a sense of insecurity to take harsh measures. The powers of the secret police were used to secure the authority of managers, who were themselves frequently the victims of the police power of the state, wielded with a frequency, severity and arbitrariness that had no counterpart elsewhere until the setting up of the Nazi state in Germany in 1933.

Stalin had wiped out the two aspects of NEP which most obviously represented a retreat to capitalism: private retail trade and individual peasant proprietorship in agriculture. He also was responsible for the liquidation of the small number of governmental concessions which had been granted to foreign capitalists. But Stalin largely retained the organization of state industry and distribution which had originated in NEP, although these had been considered no more than a form of state capitalism when they were first introduced.

The separate "Trusts," which had been set up on the assumption that they would compete with each other in very much the same way as capitalistic corporations, were indeed soon joined into "syndicates," when it was found that competition between separate Trusts in the same industry was incompatible with centralized planning and control. Moreover, the individual Trusts had shown an inability to carry out not only marketing functions, but financing, capital investment, and the provision and allocation of raw materials as well. The "syndicates," which originally were primarily marketing agencies of the individual Trusts, were transformed in 1929 into "combinations" with planning and operational authority over the Trusts in the fields of marketing, finance, raw material supply, capital construction and planning. These combinations, which existed in all major industries, were, in turn, subordinate to a Supreme Economic Council, whose director was a member of the Council of People's Commissars. *Gosplan,* the State Planning Commission, a staff organization of the Council of People's Commissars, carried out planning functions not only for industry but for the whole economy. For the less important industries a similar type of organization was set up for the constituent republics of the Soviet Union. For industries of minor importance and of purely local significance a less comprehensive and simpler type of organization was provided under the direction of the local governmental authorities.

The organization of Soviet industry was to undergo almost continuous evolution after 1930.[11] The "combination" as an organizational form did not last for more than two or three years and was gradually superseded by a proliferation of commissariats which were represented directly on the Council of

[11] For a description of the organization of the economy in 1930, see the writer's *Economic Life of Soviet Russia,* Macmillan, New York, 1931. For an excellent account of the changes which have taken place in the organization of the economy, see Harry Schwartz, *Russia's Soviet Economy,* Prentice-Hall, New York, 1954. In 1957 Khrushchev decreed a fundamental reorganization of industry intended to bring about decentralization.

People's Commissars. The Supreme Economic Council was abolished. Yet these as well as later changes were not fundamental. They simply represented experimental efforts to work out the most effective allocation of functions in a fully nationalized economy organized on an authoritative, hierarchical basis.

The development of the monetary and banking system followed a similar pattern. The *Gosbank* was the bank of issue and the bank of short-term credit for the whole economy. At the same time that industry was attaining its centralized and integrated form and agriculture was being collectivized, the *Gosbank* became the clearing agency through which the various producing, distributing and financial organs settled accounts. It also became an agency for supervision of the short-term credit operations of the annual economic plans. The *Gosbank*, with its branches throughout the Union, served as a fiscal agent for the government and a disbursing and receiving agent for the investment banks. These investment banks, the *Prombank* for industry, the *Selkhoz* Bank for agriculture, the *Torgbank* for trade, the *Tsekombank* for the financing of municipal enterprises, provided governmental grants of credits for long-term capital purposes.

The system of authoritatively planned and centrally directed state capitalism which evolved during the Stalinist era retained some of the institutions and processes which had been developed under private capitalism. The price system was retained, although it did not by any means perform all the traditional functions of a price system. During the frequent periods of acute shortages of consumer goods it was repeatedly supplemented by rationing. Prices were in general set to recover "costs of production," but in most instances a "planned profit" and a "turnover tax" were added. These were the main sources from which the state obtained funds for further capital investment and to meet the other needs of the government. The planning authorities decided how much they wished to obtain from these sources and how much from individual income taxes, and prices and wages were set accordingly. The amount of planned profits and of turnover taxes varied from industry to industry and from commodity to commodity according to the ends which the planning authorities wished to serve. A percentage of planned profits was used to provide incentive payments to managers. A much larger percentage of "unplanned profits," which were assumed to result from unusual managerial efficiency, was made available for the same purpose.[12]

Thus while both prices and profits retained some of their traditional functions, they no longer served as basic indicators in the allocation of economic resources. Production was not primarily guided into those areas where prices and profits were likely to be highest. Instead, state authority could decide what prices and profits should be, concurrently with making decisions as to the allocation of labor and capital in production, largely independently of prices and profits as causal factors.

Under the Stalinist economic system there was therefore no such "consumer sovereignty" in the pricing system as exists in a competitive, free market economy. The planning authority naturally took into account consumer preferences but gave weight to other factors, such as the judgment of the ruling hierarchy on the desired level of armaments and capital investment, and the provision of special amounts and quantities of goods and services for the new ruling class. Under the Stalinist system there was thus neither "consumer sovereignty" exercised in the market nor worker control exercised in the factory nor yet citizen control exercised at the polls or in a parliament. There was only hierarchical authority.

The centralized, authoritarian economic system which had taken definite form by the early thirties had to endure, in the period prior to World War II, the shock of repeated purges of its managerial personnel and the concomitant purges of the political bureaucracy. That it was still able to provide the armament for the huge Soviet forces which successfully resisted the Nazi attack is remarkable. That it could continue to function after the primary industrial regions of Russia had been occupied, could provide for the evacuation of labor and machinery to areas in the east, and could furnish the economic

---

12 "Unplanned profits" could thus usually be increased if the management of a plant or other economic entity could induce the planning authorities to set planned profits as low as possible. Instances of this type of "planning of unplanned profits" have been noted in the Soviet press.

support needed by the Soviet armies for their share in the final defeat of the Nazi armies almost passes human understanding.

As has been pointed out, the economic system had long before ceased to be controlled in any way by the workers. It was administered by the Communist Party, in part directly and in part through the Soviet state, itself the creature of the Communist Party. Elections of the members of the Supreme Soviet were meaningless since there was only one list of candidates, with the list determined exclusively by the Party. There was nothing resembling primary elections within the Communist Party. All positions within the Party were, in essence, appointive.

At the time Stalin first won control of the Central Committee of the Party away from Trotsky it had indeed been necessary to have majority support within the Central Committee. Eventually, Stalin simply ruled without regard for the Committee. He called it into session only when he wished, and he had enough members arrested and executed so that he was always able to obtain unanimous agreement from the surviving or newly appointed members.[13] Party Congresses, which were supposed to provide for control by the whole Party membership, were held only at long and irregular intervals.[14] Arrests and executions insured unanimity in this body also. Meetings of the Supreme Soviet could never reflect anything faintly resembling a legislative process, for death was the universally recognized sanction against dissent.[15] The Politburo, supposedly at the apex of the Soviet pyramid of power, was composed only of the most important lieutenants of Stalin whom

[13] Seventy per cent of the members of the Central Committee and candidates elected at the 17th Party Congress were declared "enemies of the people" by Stalin. They were arrested and shot. See secret speech of Khrushchev concerning the "Cult of the Individual" delivered at the 20th Party Congress of the Communist Party of the Soviet Union, February 25, 1956, p. 23 in Russian Institute of Columbia University (ed.), *The Anti-Stalin Campaign and International Communism*, Columbia University Press, New York, 1956.

[14] Thirteen years elapsed between the meeting of the 18th and the 19th Party Congress.

[15] For an excellent description of both the administrative form and the actual operation of the Stalinist political system, see the comprehensive and detailed account by Merle Fainsod, *How Russia Is Ruled*, Harvard University Press, Cambridge, 1953.

he chose at any particular moment to allow to continue to live.

The net effect of the Stalinization of the Soviet economic, political and social system was the formation of a society which had moved decisively away from the revolutionary and the egalitarian. Soviet society had become reactionary in almost all respects, including the use of violence by the state bureaucracy solely according to the arbitrary will of the dictator.

Differences in compensation paid to workers according to type of work performed had become as great as in the United States.[16] They were accentuated by the introduction of piece rates wherever possible and by the tremendous emphasis on the speed-up of workers through publicity and the payment of large bonuses to the highly productive as part of the Stakhanov movement. The large salaries paid to the bureaucracy of the state and of the Party, with even more important "fringe benefits" in the form of official cars and chauffeurs and special living quarters, the development of categories of rank paralleling those of the army, the favored treatment in assignment to vacation areas, such as those on the Black Sea and in the Caucasus, were aspects of the superior standard of living provided for the ruling class. Bonuses paid to industrial executives out of the profits of industry were an important source of income for this higher standard of living.

In the military sphere, the far higher pay of army officers than of privates, the officers' clubs, the restoration of traditional epaulettes and uniforms, the inauguration of military decorations such as the Order of Suvorov, were accompanied by ruthless discipline and the return to the traditional Russian military concept of the common soldiery as a kind of faceless mass, expendable at the will of the state bureaucracy. The evolution of this military caste system was consistent with the hierarchical developments in industry. This attitude towards the common soldier was to characterize the tactics of the Russian armies during World War II. Thus it was the standard practice of the Soviet commanders not to hold up an infantry advance until mines could be detected and cleared away but to

[16] See Abram Bergson, *The Structure of Soviet Wages: A Study in Socialist Economics,* Harvard University Press, Cambridge, 1944, for a careful statistical comparison of wage rates during particular periods.

accept instead whatever casualties might be necessary in order to get through without delay.[17]

The establishment of higher standards of living for the higher echelons in the ruling bureaucracy necessarily involved the orientation of industry towards the production of sufficient luxury-type goods to implement the incentive effect of the hierarchical incomes. When revisiting the Soviet Union in 1939 the writer was particularly impressed in both Kiev and Moscow by an advertisement on large signboards. In a style which would have done credit to *Esquire,* it depicted a lady in evening dress drinking from a champagne glass. It was advertising Soviet champagne! Ten years earlier such a sign would have been considered an intolerable blasphemy against the principles of the October Revolution.

The development of a conservative type of society was further evidenced by the return to the glorification of Russian nationalism during the Stalinist era. In part, this was necessitated by the growing danger of war represented by Hitler's coming to power in Germany. The teaching of history in Soviet schools underwent the necessary transformation. Textbooks were rewritten. Movies were produced glorifying Peter the Great and Alexander Nevsky. Ivan the Terrible was rehabilitated and given credit for his role in the expansion of Russia. Even Stalin's rejection of "modern" music and the inclusion of a greater proportion of Russian classical works in the repertoire of the opera and the ballet may be considered a part of the conservative reorientation.

The reorganization of the educational system by which "progressive education" was unceremoniously thrown out and orthodox methods resumed was carried out upon direct or-

[17] Dwight D. Eisenhower, *Crusade in Europe,* Doubleday, New York, 1952, pp. 467–468.

In 1945 when the American and Soviet forces came into contact along the Elbe in Germany, a conference was arranged between the general commanding the Soviet forces and his American opposite number, a friend of the writer. The meeting was to take place near a crossroads. As the American general waited there, a Russian soldier in a lend-lease jeep approached from another direction. The Russian military policewoman on guard duty at the crossroads called out to him to stop. When he did not, the policewoman raised her tommy gun, riddled him with bullets and directed other Russian soldiers standing by to toss the body into the ditch.

ders of Stalin. He was apparently motivated primarily by the complete failure of "progressive education" to provide the basic preparation in arithmetic necessary for the higher courses in the physical sciences and in engineering. Yet here, too, the change in philosophy was accompanied by the restoration of academic authority and discipline in place of the disorder and slackness which had been the product of the Revolution.

The conduct of the war by the Soviet government under the Stalinist dictatorship followed the pattern of the domestic exercise of power before the outbreak of the war. In spite of the defection of a million Russian soldiers to the Nazis, which reflected something of the hatred felt for Stalin by the masses, it was the national patriotism and the Russian people's capacity for enduring suffering that furnished the major force in the defeat of the Nazi armies. The deportation of the Kalmucks, the Volga Germans, the Crimean Tartars, the Esthonians, Latvians and Lithuanians, the Katyn and similar massacres of some 14,000 Polish officer prisoners, were relatively little noted in a war in which millions were being killed in battle and other millions imprisoned, tortured and executed by the Nazis throughout Europe. The halting of the Soviet armies on the outskirts of Warsaw in order to give the German armies the opportunity to wipe out the Polish underground—who had been called upon to rise by the Soviet radio—was only one more grisly incident. The offering of safe conduct to the leaders of the Polish underground and their subsequent imprisonment by the Soviet authorities was simply another piece of the same pattern.

The postwar policy of aggression and territorial expansion seems also to have been a homogeneous element in the Stalinist dictatorship. The occupation of Poland, Rumania and Bulgaria and their reduction to the role of satellites, the coup in Czechoslovakia, the Berlin blockade, the North Korean attack on South Korea, were all part of a policy motivated by the basic characteristics of an absolute dictatorship. These characteristics include suspicion of all who remain free and a frenzied drive for power which amounts to megalomania.

For a time after the war it appeared that the extension of the purges to the satellites which resulted in the execution of Slansky and his associates in Czechoslovakia, of Rajk in Hungary, of Xoxe in Albania and of Kostov in Bulgaria had replaced purges in Russia itself. Yet we now realize that the announcement of the fantastic "doctor's plot" shortly before Stalin's death was to herald the beginning of what might have been the greatest of all purges. It would apparently have included those who had been closest to Stalin and who in fact were to be his successors. The great likelihood that the high-ranking intended victims were driven by fear and desperation to do away with the dictator illustrates the striking similarity between the tyranny which had evolved out of the so-called dictatorship of the proletariat and the tyranny of the Roman emperors.[18]

Whether dictatorships must inevitably be violent cannot be answered with certainty. Some tyrannies in history have been less atrocious than others; but a tyranny or dictatorship can hardly be anything but personal and absolute. If any serious differences of policy arise within a ruling bureaucracy, the only feasible alternative to solution through at least a quasi-democratic electoral process is decision by some individual who thus becomes the chief of the bureaucracy. If such a chief will not allow himself to be voted out of office, he must, of course, rely upon his personal control of the police power of the state. The ultimate sanction upon which the police power depends is armed force.

The dictator cannot allow any judicial or other constitutional limits upon his powers if he is determined to prevent the loss of his authority. Dictators are consequently likely to be driven by an almost inescapable logic to the use of terror to maintain themselves in power. Terror reduced to its most elemental terms means the arbitrary use of the death penalty. Without the employment of the death penalty, no dictator is likely to be able to hold power.

In the beginning most dictators are probably reluctant to

[18] Khrushchev's denunciation of Stalin in 1956 included references to this new purge which only Stalin's death had prevented.

The macabre account of the death of Tiberius and the accession of Gaius Caesar, on which Suetonius in his *Lives of the Twelve Caesars* and Tacitus in his *Annals* are in substantial agreement, suggests a parallel to the death of Stalin. The parallel is not simply coincidental but reflects the major role which violence inevitably plays when absolute power passes from one ruler to another.

use the death penalty freely. But terror breeds terror. The dictator fears the friends and relatives of those whom he has killed. He comes also to despise or fear those who have been the pliant instruments of his terror: "They love not poison who do poison need." Sometimes these instruments of terror can be eliminated by charging them with having falsely accused previous victims of terror. Eventually the dictator is likely to lose his inhibitions against the killing of even those who have been closest to him.

All these stages in the growth of terror are illustrated by the history of the Stalinist dictatorship. When Stalin proclaimed the "liquidation of the kulaks as a class," the hundreds of thousands of peasants uprooted and deported, the unknown numbers of peasants who were executed, were all alike proclaimed "enemies of the people." When in 1934 Kirov, the Leningrad Party leader and close associate of Stalin, was assassinated, this incident was used as the excuse for an ever-widening series of executions in which the judges of the condemned were in turn tried and executed and finally the judges of the judges were killed. The culmination was the death of some 5,000 of the best officers of the Red Army only shortly before the outbreak of World War II.

All those to be executed were invariably charged with being "enemies of the people," the agents of international capitalism. It made no difference whether they were former Trotskyites who had long since recanted or whether they were members of the so-called "Right" of the Party, as in the case of Bukharin and Rykov. Sometimes the doomed men had been leaders in the October Revolution, like Antonov-Ovseenko, who had led the Bolshevik attack on the Kerensky Government in the Winter Palace, or like Dybenko, the Red sailor who had the cruiser Aurora brought up to shell this last holding point of the Provisional Government.

The doomed men were accorded none of the rights commonly associated with the judicial process in all Western lands. Sometimes the "trials" were public demonstrations in which the accused condemned themselves. Their children were sometimes brought into court to denounce the accused. Those arrested were often tortured, and their children as well. Sometimes the "trials" were secret, with only the sentences announced. Sometimes men were arrested and imprisoned or executed without public announcement. So in 1937 disappeared Pashukanis, the principal draftsman of the "Constitution" of 1936 which purported to give some protection to the rights of individuals against the state. It was he who had maintained that the need for criminal law would wither away with the state itself when the final stage of communism was reached and that while "certain crimes against personality and so forth will not disappear" such crimes should be regarded *"per se* as a task of medical pedagogy." One wonders whether the type of "crime" for which he presumably forfeited his life would be prevalent in the final stage of Communist society and whether its treatment would be considered a task of medical pedagogy.

So also disappeared Boris Pilnyak, second only to Sholokov as the best-known Soviet novelist.[19] Another victim was the economist Voznessensky, who perished in 1949 by mere personal order of Stalin. For several years the fact of his death was not known; it was only after the anti-Stalinist policy was undertaken that the facts became public. Meanwhile, in the terminology of George Orwell's *1984,* he had simply become, like thousands of others, an "unperson."

This growth of an absolutist, totalitarian and brutal state power during the period of Stalin's rule was, incredibly enough, facilitated by continued adherence to the Marxist myth of the "withering away of the state." In his report to the 18th Party Congress in 1939 Stalin had declared: "Since the time of the October Revolution our Socialist state has passed through two principal phases in its development: (a) the first phase is the period from the October Revolution down to the liquidation of the exploiter classes, and (b) the second phase is the period from the liquidation of the capitalist elements, urban and rural, down to the complete triumph of the Socialist system of economy and the adoption of the new Constitution." He went on to speak of the then current stage: "Ac-

---

[19] Even as late as 1956, a Soviet teacher in the higher schools of Moscow claimed never to have heard of Pilnyak. In 1958 a talented student in one of the pedagogical institutes also denied to the writer that she had ever heard of Pilnyak.

cordingly, the functions of our Socialist state have changed as well. The function of military suppression within the country has subsided and died out, for the reason that exploitation has been annihilated and exploiters have ceased to exist and there is no one to suppress."

Since these two phases had been completed, according to Marxist-Leninist doctrine, the state should have finished its process of withering away and a Communist society should have been in existence. But Stalin added that even under communism the state would continue to exist and to carry out the function of military defense, so long as the dangers of "capitalist encirclement" existed. Since this statement practically coincided with the outbreak of World War II, this reservation of the function of military defense was certainly realistic. But Stalin's statement that the function of military suppression *within the country* had subsided and died out was, of course, utterly contrary to fact. The powers and functions of the Stalinist state, uninhibited by any representation of the popular will, had been constantly expanding, quite apart from those associated with the needs of national defense.

Yet the continued formal adherence to the doctrine of the eventual withering away of the state afforded a cloak to conceal the current existence of the Stalinist absolutist and totalitarian state. The doctrine of the withering away of the state was rigidly maintained down to the time of Stalin's death.[20] This was of small importance domestically. The Russian people, including Party members, naturally had no illusions about the nature of the Stalinist state since they could never escape from the daily manifestations of its power.

Party sympathizers abroad, however, pointed out that this doctrine was still upheld by Stalin, and they argued that any dictatorial aspects of the Stalinist state were only temporary manifestations of the still necessary "dictatorship of the proletariat." Thus they claimed that it was quite unnecessary to

[20] In an authoritative article in *Izvestia* of October 12, 1951, for example, G. Glaeserman quotes Stalin's previous statements and justifies the continued delay in the withering away of the state in the following words, "The frontiers of the capitalist world have been pushed further away from the Soviet Union, but this world still exists and consequently the threat of an attack on the U.S.S.R. still exists."

provide for limitations upon the powers of the Stalinist state or for protection of the liberty of the individual against the state, since that state was eventually to wither away. They conveniently overlooked Stalin's statement that the preconditions for the abolition of the internal powers of suppression of the state had already been fulfilled.

Such a line of argument was of course fantastically unreal. It would have been greeted with contempt if it had been advanced by anyone in a free society. Its validity obviously did not depend upon the logic of an individual philosopher. It was developed under the shield of the Soviet state power, and this gave it a totally different status. The doctrine was apparently accepted within a realm of almost two hundred million inhabitants. It bore the official seal of a ruler who had over two hundred infantry and armored divisions at his command. The incredible doctrine of the "withering away of the state" applied to "the most potent and mighty of all state authorities that have existed down to this time" literally depended in the last analysis upon these infantry and armored divisions. They gave a terrible and grisly demirespectability to a completely contradictory and intellectually totally disreputable doctrine.

It was not until Stalin's death that the intellectual bankruptcy of the argument was to be nakedly exposed. The decision by the new rulers to dethrone Stalin posthumously simply meant that the Stalinist economic and political system as it had existed in his lifetime was now officially admitted to have been the totalitarian tyranny that it actually was.

The horror of life in the Stalinist totalitarian state in the absence of all popular control over government, with the power of torture and death exercised not only at the whim of Stalin but by thousands of underlings, will forever raise the question of how it could possibly have existed for three decades. It has, indeed, been almost impossible for the non-Communist world to believe that such terror could have existed at all. Only the people of Russia and the satellite countries could fully believe it because they lived through it. But even they could not dare to let the horrors become part of their stream of consciousness, for by consciously admitting their existence a person would almost certainly at some time betray himself. When, however, three years after the death of Stalin the crimes of his regime were officially proclaimed by Khrushchev, they could no longer be denied. The horrors of the Stalinist totalitarian state were inherent in the false "dictatorship of the proletariat." That dictatorship was always a personal one, and personal dictatorship can only be maintained by terror.

CHAPTER 4

THE SOVIET TOTALITARIAN
SYSTEM AFTER STALIN

There could be nothing constitutional, parliamentary or democratic about the assumption of power by Stalin's successors. The Central Committee of the Party, which nominally determined the succession, had been appointed by Stalin after he had killed most of their predecessors. There was no provision in the Soviet Constitution for the dictatorship which Stalin had wielded. Thus there could be no procedures in that Constitution for the transfer of dictatorial power or for the withdrawal of that power from the dictator and its resumption by representatives of the people, even if one had been disposed to take the Constitution seriously. If a democratic, constitutional, parliamentary regime had ever existed previously, then the procedures of such a regime might have been resumed upon the death of the dictator. But there had never been such a government in Russia.

Until the official revelations connected with de-Stalinization three years after the death of Stalin, there had never been an admission that the Soviet dictatorship was less than fully democratic with respect to the workers. According to Soviet dogma, the dictatorship form of the state, falsely referred to as a dictatorship of the proletariat, had been justified during the first twenty years of the Soviet regime by the alleged necessity for protecting the new society against the counterrevolutionary efforts of the dispossessed capitalistic exploiters.[1] It was admitted as part of the process of de-Stalinization that, after the dictatorship could no longer be justified according to Soviet doctrine, Stalin had perverted the so-called dictatorship of the proletariat into the personal dictatorship which his successors were to denounce as the "cult of personality."

The Stalin dictatorship had not always been absolute even though it had never been democratic. During the period when the illness of Lenin had forced him gradually to relinquish power, Stalin had played faction against faction in the Central Committee of the Party in order to gain power, but there never had been even an indirect electoral process by which Stalin's dictatorial position received some sort of popular mandate even within the Party. After Lenin's death Stalin had to maneuver further within the Central Committee to consolidate his power until in 1928 he achieved the expulsion of Trotsky from Russia.

During the last decade and a half of Stalin's regime, however, he had ruled without being limited by the will of the Central Committee. He simply imprisoned or killed whomever he wished in that body and ordered whomever he wished "elected" as the successors.[2] It is doubtful whether even a

---

[1] See the resolutions of the Central Committee of the Communist Party of the Soviet Union, June 30, 1956 (published in *Pravda,* July 2, 1956). Strictly speaking, according to Marxist doctrine, there should have been no problem concerning the degree of democratic control of the state under communism for the state would not exist: it would have "withered away."

[2] In Khrushchev's denunciation of Stalin at the 20th Party Congress he states: "As facts prove, Stalin, using his unlimited power, allowed himself many abuses, acting in the name of the Central Committee, not asking for the opinion of the Committee members nor even of the members of the Central Committee's Political Bureau; often he did not inform them about his personal decisions concerning very important Party and government matters. . . . It was determined that of the 139 members and candidates of the Party's Central Committee who were elected at the XVIIth Congress, 98 persons, *i.e.,* 70 percent, were arrested and shot (mostly in 1937–38). . . . The same fate met not only the Central Committee membership but also the majority of the delegates to the XVIIth Party Congress. Of 1,966 delegates with either voting or advisory rights,

nominal process of election took place. Consequently, the members of the Central Committee could have no claim to represent the membership of the Communist Party, much less the whole population of the Soviet Union.

It was nominally, however, this purged and repurged Central Committee which chose the successor to Stalin for ratification by the Supreme Soviet. Presumably some form of vote did take place in the Central Committee which reflected a decision made and presented to it. It is certain, however, that there was no process by which alternative names were placed in nomination and voted upon. Under the circumstances there could not have been any such process. The terror machine of Beria was at that time still unimpaired, and no candidate could have come to power without Beria's acquiescence, unless by the exercise of superior force against him. Since the transfer of power took place at this stage with his acquiescence it appears that the Soviet personages in a position to wield power—Beria, Malenkov, Khrushchev, Molotov and Zhukov—agreed upon the first stage of the transfer. With the supreme power as well as the lives of this small group at stake, it would have made no kind of sense to allow the succession to be determined by vote in a body whose membership was in no way representative of the people as a whole, of the Party, of particular economic interests, or even of powerful political forces.

To the Soviet public, as well as to outside observers, it appeared momentarily that Stalin's power had been transferred to Malenkov. In a series of rather bewildering reorganizations of the Soviet and Party apparatus, however, the control of the Party passed primarily into the hands of Khrushchev even though the premiership was for a time retained by Malenkov. Only gradually did it become apparent that the power of Stalin had not as yet come securely into the grasp of anyone.

The arrest of Beria in July 1953 and his subsequent execution was to underline the conspiratorial character of the struggle for power which had been going on in the Kremlin since Stalin's death in March. Not only were Beria and a number of his henchmen executed without public trial; but it seems certain that he would never have allowed himself to be arrested

---

1,108 persons were arrested on charges of anti-revolutionary crimes, *i.e.,* decidedly more than a majority."

without resistance, and he was probably killed some time before the officially announced date of his execution. It is rumored that he was shot at the meeting of the Central Committee at which he was first denounced as having plotted the seizure of power. In line with what had become routine procedure in such cases, he was charged with having been a spy and counterrevolutionary agent of the imperialistic powers, even from the days of the Civil War in 1919, and was also charged with having tried to seize power.[3]

While the charge that Beria had all along been a secret spy and agent of imperialistic governments is patently ridiculous, there is no doubt at all of the truth of the charges that he was guilty of a mass of false accusations and executions while head of the secret police. After his execution, these crimes were ascribed to him, with Stalin in the position of having been innocently deceived by him.

In the speeches by Khrushchev and Mikoyan at the 20th Congress of the Party in February 1956, when the process of de-Stalinization was undertaken, this previously maintained separation of Stalin from the guilt of Beria disappeared. Now the false arrests and executions were ascribed as much to Stalin as to Beria. The earlier arrests and executions of Trotsky, Bukharin, Rykov and others were still presented, not as miscarriages of justice, but as legitimate punishment of men who had actually been traitors to the Soviet regime. The primary reason for this seems to have been that Khrushchev, Molotov and Malenkov were so deeply implicated that it was not feasible to admit that the charges against these victims were false.

Yagoda, the head of the secret police at the time of the great purge which had resulted in the execution of Bukharin, Rykov and other Soviet leaders as well as thousands less well known, had later been denounced by Stalin and executed on the ground that he, Yagoda, had falsely accused his victims. His successor, Yezhov, had in turn carried out mass arrests and

---

[3] Following the announcement of the execution of Beria it was publicly recommended that owners of sets of the Great Soviet Encyclopedia should cut out the pages containing his eulogistic biography. Substitute pages containing an article on the Bering Sea were to be furnished for insertion where the pages dealing with Beria had been excised.

executions and had then disappeared in mysterious circumstances. Now Beria, the last head of Stalin's terror machine, was officially proclaimed a traitor.

Consequently, there can be no possible basis for claiming that Stalin's regime had ever been representative of the Russian people, or had embodied the dictatorship of the proletariat or had been anything but a highly organized tyranny which ruled by extreme physical and psychological coercion. The self-proclaimed "collective leadership" which succeeded Stalin's rule could thus have originated in no other source of power than this same physical and psychological coercion. The evidence available to the outside world had long ago made this perfectly plain. The Russian people too had all along been quite aware of these circumstances. Yet so long as there existed a monolithic and unchallengeable authority which could arrogantly deny fact and reality, they could be compelled to cooperate in a gigantic conspiracy of affirmation of falsehood.

The results of the official admission as to the real nature of the Stalinist regime were to affect profoundly the ability of the new "collective leadership" to maintain itself in power. Until the proclamation of de-Stalinization in February 1956 there had been a regular succession of authority to establish the Marxist orthodoxy of Soviet policy. The immense prestige which accrued to Lenin as the leader of the Russian Communist Party with the success of the Bolshevik Revolution had placed him in a position to promulgate doctrine so long as he was alive. Outside of Russia the very success of economic reformist measures in the Western world had taken the revolutionary wind out of the sails of the Social Democratic parties of the West that were following the more moderate Marxist doctrines of Bernstein and Kautsky. The Communist parties were the only ones left that could represent themselves as really revolutionist either in program or in tactics.

It was thus inevitable that Lenin should have been accepted as the infallible leader of the revolutionary Communist parties throughout the world, and Stalin was able to take over this "papal position." Even the purges and executions of so many of the Bolshevik leaders by Stalin did not break the "apostolic succession." After Stalin died or was assassinated, there was no longer a single unquestioned ruler but instead a self-proclaimed collective leadership. With the execution of Beria and the subsequent denunciation of Stalin, the chain of infallibility was fatally impaired.

The record of the Soviet regime under Stalin had demonstrated that it is possible for a totalitarian system not only to maintain itself in power, even though it is hated by the majority of the population, but also to succeed in extracting from the whole population positive expressions of loyalty. Moreover, the regime was able to secure workable obedience from the peasants and from the industrial workers. In spite of and, of course, partly because of continued purges of the bureaucracy, the essential functions of the economy and of the government could be maintained. The prostitution of literature and the other arts, of philosophy, history and economics, in the service of the totalitarian regime could also be successfully induced.

This ability of the Stalin regime to impose its will on the people, not merely negatively but positively, required much more than physical coercion to achieve its ends. If a regime which depends upon purely military force once allows the hatred of the people to crystallize and to manifest itself, it is then likely to require such wholesale and violent means of repression that the functioning of the economic and political system becomes virtually impossible. It is this crystallization of hatred around any sort of leadership which must be prevented at all costs.

The Stalin regime did indeed approach the limits beyond which the scale of physical repression required to maintain the tyranny in power would have prevented the functioning of the system. One has only to recall the great purges followed by thousands of executions, the sentencing of hundreds of thousands of citizens to slave labor camps, and the deportations of entire populations which Stalin's control of the army and secret police made possible. But the very intensiveness, the detail and the comprehensiveness of the system of terror prevented crystallization and public manifestation of the popular hatred of the regime from taking place.

When the writer was living in Moscow in 1929–30, among the small group of Americans there the question was once raised, "What would happen if thousands of workers were organized for a march on the Kremlin, entreating from Stalin the redress of grievances and an improvement of living standards, as was done by the workers of St. Petersburg on Bloody Sunday. Would Stalin order the troops to fire on the marchers as the tsarist officials did January 22, 1905?" The question was really rhetorical, for the answer was unanimous. Such a march never could have got under way. As soon as the workers began to grumble, the more articulate would have been arrested at once upon denunciation by police spies who permeated their ranks and these potential leaders would have disappeared. After several such arrests the workers would have assumed the omnipresence of police spies and would not have had the courage to grumble further.

A factor of immense importance in the maintenance of the total domination of the population by the Stalinist state was the feeling of each individual that he was utterly alone in any opposition to the regime. This feeling of isolation was created and maintained not only through the negative censorship of every possible form of public expression and information but above all by the power of the regime to induce or compel an immense and continuous volume of laudatory statements about Stalin personally and about every phase of the Soviet regime. All scholarly, professional and artistic media of expression were required to show that they were based upon the current Stalinist line. The expression of any idea which might be in conflict with what was currently orthodox carried with it not merely the danger of arrest, imprisonment and possibly execution but the certainty that such a person would be denounced by his colleagues as an enemy of the people or an ignoramus, or both.

Voting by the population in elections was a useful psychological device for requiring the voter as an individual periodically to make an act of submission and homage to the regime and affording each individual unmistakable evidence that everyone else could be compelled to do likewise. Under this one-candidate-per-office system the "counting of votes" was of course meaningless. At each election the authorities doubtless decided what the minimum number of absent voters and of voters who did not cast ballots for the candidates should be, and announced these figures. It is quite possible that occasionally the announced figures of absent voters and of dissident voters, always almost infinitesimal, were higher than the real figures.

The result of all this was what might be called a dual level of consciousness among the Soviet population. Loyalty and support of the regime had to be something far beyond mere lip service. It was dangerous merely to mouth loyalty and support while consciously harboring hatred for the regime. The individual had to try to find at least some arguments to justify in his own mind his loyalty to the state, since he might otherwise betray himself by the ostensible spuriousness of his publicly proclaimed allegiance.

Simultaneously, on a deeper level of consciousness, the effect of the overwhelming pressure of a totalitarian regime upon the individual's freedom of thought was to produce a total skepticism about anything and everything which appeared in the official organs of information, even when true or partially true. This is not meant to imply that an individual can construct in detail an entire alternative world for himself, different from that presented to him through the organs of information controlled by a totalitarian regime. That is beyond the capacity of any human being. Nevertheless, the "citizen" of the totalitarian state is always conscious that there are two worlds—the world of lies and "information" which is provided in detail by the totalitarian state, and a world of truth and reality which he is sure exists but about which he has painfully little detailed knowledge. This is a major reason why, in the case of Hungary and Poland, an apparently wholly submissive and even loyal population could shake off en masse the bonds of the first level of consciousness and revert instantly to its more basic feelings.

Why was it several years after the death of Stalin, and only when some amelioration of the repressive character of the totalitarian regime had taken place, that the true character of the Stalinist regime was definitively established? Why was it that, in spite of a considerable relaxation of the oppressive aspects of the Soviet regime under Stalin's successors, popular opposition to the regime began to manifest itself in the satellite countries and later to a lesser extent in Soviet Russia itself? Why did this opposition in Poland and particularly in Hungary take violent forms which it never had in Stalin's day?

It is altogether likely that de-Stalinization was primarily motivated by the fears of Khrushchev, Malenkov, Bulganin and Molotov that they might otherwise sometime be accused of having planned the death of the great Stalin and would thus become vulnerable to denunciation as "enemies of the people" by an ambitious competitor for power. Only by destroying the false legend of Stalin as the great leader could the "collective leadership" protect itself against this grave danger. In Khrushchev's speech denouncing Stalin at the 20th Party Congress, February 25, 1956, he is reported to have said that if Stalin had not died Molotov would not still be alive.[4] By implication and strongest probability this would have been true of the other members of the "collective leadership" as well. The whole tenor and content of Khrushchev's speech confirmed other substantial evidence that Stalin at the moment of his death had been on the verge of the greatest of all purges, one which would have eliminated all important figures.

It had at first been thought that any resistance to the regime which might follow the announcement of de-Stalinization would come from those who had revered Stalin and who might be shocked by this "downgrading." The riots which broke out in Tiflis, Georgia, on the occasion of the anniversary of Stalin's death in March 1956 seemed to confirm this. In retrospect, however, these disorders seem to have reflected as much the hostility of the inhabitants of Tiflis to the Soviet system as their affection for the memory of Stalin.

It required the bloody uprising in Poznan and later in Buda-

[4] This speech was never publicly released by the Soviet authorities although it was reportedly read at meetings of officials of the Party throughout Russia and copies were sent to officials of Communist parties abroad. A version of the speech came into the possession of our State Department and was released on June 4, 1956, without guarantee as to its literal accuracy. It was published in the *New York Times* and in a number of other places. The reported substance of the speech was not denied at the time by Soviet sources. About a year later Khrushchev spoke disparagingly of the version released by the State Department to a correspondent of the *New York Times*. Communist circles outside Russia have never denied the essential validity of the version. It is apparently not a complete account of everything Khrushchev said. Some of the worst atrocities committed by Stalin were toned down or omitted.

pest to demonstrate that the main danger of revolt was not from admirers of Stalin but on the contrary from those who had most detested the Stalinist system. What needs to be explained is how the very "loosening" of the regime of oppression brought about a revolt which had not taken place when the Soviet regime was functioning with unmitigated severity. These outbreaks in Poland and Hungary, and the mounting unrest in the Soviet Union, were the logical consequences of the decision of Stalin's successors to expose him as the tyrant that he was.

The shock of de-Stalinization to the monolithic character of the Soviet regime was terrific. The effect was all the greater because in a real sense all that Khrushchev "disclosed" was already quite well known. The whole of Soviet society had, however, been successfully coerced into pretending to believe for three years after his death that Stalin had indeed been the benevolent leader of a democratic and socialistic society. Only now could there emerge from the second and basic level of consciousness of the Russian people the recognition of reality which had been there all along.

The reaction to de-Stalinization within Communist parties abroad was violent. For example, the Italian Communist leader Togliatti, in his report to the Central Committee of the Italian Communist Party on June 24, 1956, stated:

> The question arises as to what made such serious errors possible and above all the fact that around these errors there arose an atmosphere of consent and connivance reaching as far as the co-responsibility of those who today denounce those errors.[5]

Appalled by this reaction, the "collective leadership" attempted to quiet the storm, maintaining that even the enormity of Stalin's crimes had not changed the fundamentally socialistic and democratic nature of the Soviet economic and political system.

> Indisputably the personality cult has seriously harmed the cause of the Communist Party and Soviet society. It

---

[5] Russian Institute of Columbia University (ed.), *The Anti-Stalin Campaign and International Communism,* Columbia University Press, New York, 1956, p. 231.

would, however, be a serious mistake to deduce from the fact of the existence in the past of the personality cult some kind of changes in the social system in the USSR, or to look for the source of this cult in the nature of the Soviet social system. Both alternatives are absolutely wrong, as they are not in accord with reality and contradict the facts.

In spite of all the evil which the personality cult of Stalin brought to the Party and the people, it could not change and has not changed the nature of our social system. No personality cult could change the nature of the socialist state, based on public ownership of the means of production, the alliance of working class and the peasantry, and the friendship of peoples, even though this cult did inflict serious damage on the development of socialist democracy and the upsurge of the creative initiative of millions.

To imagine that an individual, even such a major one as Stalin, could change our social-political system is to enter into profound contradiction with the facts, with Marxism, with truth, and to sink into idealism. This would be attributing to an individual such excessive and super-natural powers as the ability to change the system of society, even a social system in which many millions of working people are the decisive force.

As is known, the nature of the social-political system is determined by the nature of the means of production, to whom in society the means of production belong, and what class holds the political power. The entire world knows that in our country, as a result of the October Revolution and the victory of socialism, the socialist method of production was established, and that for nearly 40 years powers had been in the hands of the working class and peasantry. Thanks to this, the Soviet social system is gaining in strength from year to year, and its production forces are growing. This is a fact even those who wish us ill must admit.[6]

[6] Resolution of the Central Committee of the Communist Party of the Soviet Union, June 30, 1956 (published in *ibid.*, pp. 293–294).

But the protests continued. Marshal Tito of Yugoslavia declared:

> From the very beginning, we said that here it was not merely the question of the cult of personality but rather the question of a system which made the creation of the cult of personality possible, that it was necessary to strike at the roots unceasingly and persistently.[7]

Following Khrushchev's disclosures, all the authoritarian, ruthless, inegalitarian and bureaucratic characteristics of the Stalinist regime which had always been evident could for the moment be freely discussed. Men could now admit to each other that they had known this all the time. Thereafter it was going to be difficult to maintain with any sort of logic that manifestations of these traits which still existed under the successor regime were actually nonexistent.

The evidence indicates that the so-called collective leadership which wielded precarious power after Stalin's death and after the liquidation of Beria really wished to modify the repressive character of the regime domestically, to avoid a desperate struggle for power among themselves and to relieve tension in foreign affairs. These men who had participated during most of their lives in the killing of so many thousands had come to live in constant fear of death. Now they evidently would have liked to escape from this unrelieved fear, to bask in the gratitude of a people whose bonds had been partially loosened, to enjoy life a little, "to live it up" as Khrushchev and Bulganin phrased it.[8] Yet they were to find it impossible to live in peace with each other.

[7] *New York Times*, December 2, 1956.

[8] This judgment is based not only upon conclusions drawn from the events of this period but upon impressions which the writer received from a variety of sources during a month in Russia in the summer of 1956, including a very brief meeting with Bulganin, Khrushchev, Malenkov and Molotov.

The relaxation of terror when a new emperor succeeded a notorious tyrant, and the joyous relief and adulation of the Roman populace, was a major element of the recurring cycle depicted in Suetonious' *Lives of the Twelve Caesars*. Yet the possession of absolute power and the necessity for the use of terror to maintain this power produced repeatedly the other elements of the cycle—repression, fear and popular hatred. Thus, Suetonious recounts the joy of the

It is striking that the ameliorative measures which the collective leadership endeavored to put into effect were at least slightly in the direction of a more socialistic type of economic and political system, as the term socialistic had been understood prior to the advent of the Soviet regime. These changes were also somewhat in the direction of an economic and political system such as exists under modern Western capitalism. This was not merely coincidental. It reflected the closer identity of humanitarian socialism with modern capitalism than with Soviet totalitarianism.

Criminal prosecution for absence from work and for quitting the job was abolished. Violations of the principle of "collective leadership" in trade union organizations, evidenced in the failure to convene plenary sessions regularly and in the practice of settling questions by individuals instead of by collective discussion, were deplored. Similarly, past violations of collective farm democracy by local Party, Soviet and agricultural agencies were viewed with regret. Compulsory delivery of produce at low fixed prices from the individual plots of peasants on the collectives was abolished in 1957.

Hours of work were somewhat shortened, old-age pensions were increased, minimum wages were set so as to raise the average wage. There began to be criticism in the press of excessively high bonus payments to industrial executives. Income tax exemptions were raised and tax rates on low earnings reduced. Price changes which included higher prices for luxury-type goods, particularly automobiles, announced at the beginning of 1958, reflected this same slightly egalitarian trend. The repudiation of billions of rubles in Soviet bonds which citizens had been compelled to buy was also a greater disadvantage to the upper classes.

The decentralization of industry announced by Khrushchev in 1957 reflected some personal hostility to "soft-living bureaucrats." An effort was made to move thousands of these out of

---

Roman people at the death of Tiberius. He tells how his successor, Caligula, recalled exiles from banishment, dismissed informers, lowered taxes and constructed public works in the most assiduous pursuit of popularity. Suetonious, as he turns to an account of the infamous crimes of the emperor later in his reign, says, "So much for Caligula as emperor. We must now tell of his career as a monster."

Moscow and to retrain thousands in "productive labor." As a former manual laborer, almost without formal education, Khrushchev rejoiced in the discomfiture of these bureaucrats. Yet it is doubtful whether the privileges of the "New Class" were seriously impaired. All these changes came about at irregular intervals following de-Stalinization. Sometimes they were important enough to be proclaimed by the collective leadership; sometimes they took place by administrative action at the lower echelons of power.

Soon after the death of Stalin a great shift in agricultural policy was instituted by Khrushchev. In 1953 he called attention to the nearly catastrophic shortage of meat and dairy products which was evidenced by a smaller livestock population in the Soviet Union in 1952 than had existed in 1916. To remedy the situation a number of changes were made for the purpose of offering incentives to individual peasants to increase their production of meat and dairy products. Past arrearages of compulsory deliveries were wiped out. Annual norms of compulsory deliveries were reduced. Payments for meat and dairy deliveries were very sharply increased. The net effect was to encourage peasants on the collective farms to devote even more time to their individual plots of land and to their own livestock than before, although the decrees implementing the new policy were designed to avoid deleterious effects upon the production of the collective farms.[9]

Malenkov, for his part, had been responsible for reducing somewhat the emphasis upon the production of capital goods in industry and for increasing the production of consumer goods. Though this policy was officially abandoned later and Malenkov was compelled to relinquish the premiership, the net effect was a slowly rising standard of living which, along

---

[9] As one result of the new decrees, many persons living in the suburbs of Russian cities acquired cows in one way or another and began to make large sums by selling milk. In the summer of 1956 new decrees were issued designed to compel such persons to sell to the collective farms the more than one million head of cows which they had acquired under the new policy. The final straw requiring the partial reversal of policy was the practice of these so-called "milk millionaires" of buying bread at the low fixed price and feeding it to their cattle. This bread could be bought at about half the cost per pound of grain on the free market.

with partial relaxation of the ironhandedness of the state, probably did improve the popularity of the new rulers.

The power of the secret police to make wholesale arbitrary arrests was curtailed. The secret police were no longer to be permitted to exercise the combined roles of investigator, prosecutor, judge and penal administrator. It was announced that public trials would be required before persons accused of crimes could be sentenced. In such trials, defendants were supposed to be chargeable only with crimes which existed on the statute books, not with crimes "by analogy." Hundreds of thousands of persons were released from forced labor camps. Some few surviving "Old Bolsheviks" who had been falsely accused by Stalin were now released from prison. Of the much larger number who had been executed or had died in prison, some were posthumously "rehabilitated." There was widespread discussion of a comprehensive revision of the criminal code with the intention of preventing these things from happening again. However, by the end of 1957 the proposed revision was still in the discussion stage.[10]

Nevertheless, the collective leadership apparently retained the right to disregard these new rules whenever it seemed desirable, for there continued to be announcements of the execution of officials charged with having been part of the "Beria conspiracy." Eventually some of these executions were preceded by public trials. What other essentials of a judicial process, if any, were permitted in these trials remains unknown. The defendants continued to confess their treasonable deeds and to be executed as in Stalinist days.[11]

In the foreign field, the new rulers as part of their announced policy of coexistence with capitalistic countries withdrew the Soviet occupational forces from Austria. They gave up a Finnish port which they had the right to garrison under the terms of the Finnish capitulation near the end of World War II. A reduction in manpower of the Soviet armed forces was announced. Eventually there occurred the "summit" meeting at

[10] See John N. Hazard, "Laws and Men in Soviet Society," *Foreign Affairs*, January 1958, pp. 267–277.
[11] See the account of the trial and execution of M. D. Bagirov and others in *Bakinsky rabochy*, May 2, 1956 (translated in the *Current Digest of the Soviet Press*, July 4, 1956, p. 12).

Geneva with President Eisenhower in the summer of 1955 at which the wish to maintain peace was strongly proclaimed. Once de-Stalinization had been embarked upon, it was possible also for the new rulers to blame Stalin for any overaggressiveness in Soviet foreign policy in the past.

It seems probable that the ruling directorate did indeed wish to reduce the possibility of general war. This reflected not only the deterrent effect of wholesale destruction in an atomic war. It probably reflected as well the sense of domestic insecurity of power of the directorate, who no doubt dreaded the additional threat to their hold which might be associated with war. Furthermore, it probably reflected a somewhat lesser degree of greed for the extension of personal power over ever greater areas which had become so characteristic of Stalin.

Even during Stalin's regime it would not be exact to speak, as had sometimes been done, of his devotion to the principle of "World Revolution." It is perfectly true that Marxist phraseology was still used in promoting revolutionary activities against non-Communist governments. But "World Revolution" to Stalin had become merely an instrument in his policy of Soviet expansion in power throughout the world. The top Soviet bureaucracy had long since ceased to be revolutionists. After the death of Stalin, for a time at least, his successors were more interested in consolidating their power than in extending it geographically. Paradoxically enough, it was the revolts in the satellites, accompanying a policy of some slight relaxation of Soviet control, which brought to an end this particular period of relaxation on the international front.

As noted earlier, Stalin had succeeded in compelling a kind of positive collaboration by the Russian people in the myth of the Soviet state as a "people's democracy." But as soon as de-Stalinization permitted the mutual and articulate recognition by the people of their complicity, the consequent feeling of shame, until then submerged by fear, began to express itself in a distaste for Stalin's successors. This happened in spite of the indisputable fact that the Russian people were not only somewhat less repressed than under Stalin but were also better off materially.

When the Russian people were told in the course of de-Stalinization that democracy and freedom had been repressed by Stalin, but that now all was changed, they began cautiously to press against the massive limitations on freedom and democracy which still existed. In the fields of art and literature men were quick to attack the continuing rigid controls and stultifying censorship on the ground that these perversions of a socialist society were attributable to Stalin. For a while there was vigorous discussion in the press. But the authorities quickly became alarmed and asserted the necessity for continued leadership and authority by the Party.[12] The minor relaxations which had occurred did not obscure the fact that the character of the successor regime continued to be much like that of Stalin's. It quickly became apparent, moreover, that the new rulers were not going to permit uncontrolled popular criticism of those continuing aspects of the regime which they had denounced as Stalinism.

The whole structure of totalitarian repression which Stalin had built up had been badly shaken when Beria was eliminated. Until then, officials of the secret police could be relied upon to carry out the orders of their superiors, however atrocious, secure in the knowledge that they would not be called to account for acts of terror performed on orders from the head of the security organs of the state. But now scores of high officials were executed because they had followed Beria's orders. Thereafter an officer of the secret police naturally could not be counted upon with certainty to obey an order to eliminate, for example, a prominent Party official simply at the personal command of Khrushchev, lest the police officer himself be held accountable if Khrushchev were later liquidated. This structure of repression, of which the organs of internal security[13] were the core, had come to be the real administrative machine through which decisions were passed down from Stalin to the lower echelons. After the prestige and authority of the terror apparatus had been gravely shaken by

[12] Admitting that "The harmful consequences of the cult of the individual left a deep trace on literature and art," *Pravda* denounced "the false idea that art does not need any guidance on the part of the state and the Party." (November 25, 1956.) *Izvestia* of the same date agreed. (Both translated in the *Current Digest of the Soviet Press,* December 19, 1956.)

[13] Known successively as the Cheka, G.P.U., O.G.P.U., N.K.V.D. and M.V.D.

the execution of Beria, and the populace told by post-Stalinist rulers that its repressive and atrocious acts were no longer to be allowed, there was for a time no other effective administrative organization to maintain the kind of intimate and comprehensive control over the thought and actions of the people which had existed under Stalin.

The disappointment of Stalin's successors with their attempt at a relaxation of repressive measures on the domestic scene and a slight loosening of controls over the satellites serves to point up the difficulties inherent in such an effort. Stalin had maintained himself in power by the employment of unlimited terror inherent in a dictatorship and in the organization of the Communist Party.[14] It is possible that in the beginning he had employed terroristic methods with reluctance. Eventually he developed sadistic characteristics and apparently sometimes employed terror for its own sake.[15] The universal fear which Stalin's use of terror had induced in the Russian people had brought with it bitter respect. The victorious outcome of World War II had added a dimension to the respect compelled by fear.

After Stalin's death there was no procedure by which the charism which had become attached to Stalin could be transmitted to his successors. No one of them, nor all of them together, had been designated by Stalin to succeed him. The conflict for power among Malenkov, Beria and Khrushchev

[14] Curiously enough the inherent organizational and ideological propensity of the Communist Party toward murderous purges can be seen not only in those countries where the death sentence can be inflicted at will by the Party hierarchy but even in countries where the Party does not control the state. Thus, Howard Fast, *The Naked God*, Praeger, New York, 1957, p. 51, relates that, during the period of temporary upheaval in the American Communist Party in 1956 following publication of Khrushchev's speech denouncing Stalin, he asked a small group of dissident Communists, of which he was one, whether anyone among them believed that they would still be alive if the leaders of the American Communist Party had the power to inflict the death penalty. No one did.

[15] This is substantiated by the disclosures in Khrushchev's speech before the 20th Party Congress. This development seems to be almost inevitable since dictators to whom terror remains repugnant are not likely to be able to endure the strain involved in carrying out such procedures.

made it perfectly plain that conspiratorial methods alone, and not selection by any representative body, had determined the succession and that the succession was still insecure. After the execution of Beria there was no one who could wield the power of life and death with certainty that his orders would be obeyed. Until some one individual could establish this certainty, in the absence of representative government, there was bound to be at best an unstable equilibrium of power.

In this connection, the writer witnessed a curious reaction in a movie theatre in Leningrad in June 1956. The movie about to be shown to a packed audience was *Bezsmertnyi Garnison* (The Immortal Garrison). A part of the de-Stalinization campaign, the movie showed the unpreparedness of the Soviet border troops (blamed by implication on Stalin) for the Nazi attack. Before the feature film began, a newsreel of the current visit of Marshal Tito of Yugoslavia to Leningrad was shown. Tito was accompanied by Khrushchev, Bulganin and other Soviet dignitaries. At one point in the newsreel the narrator announced, "And now Comrade Khrushchev comes forward." Khrushchev, a rather fat man, walked into the center of the picture, with a slightly clowning sort of strut, and a look of jocular good humor. There came a half chuckle, half snicker from the movie audience. Twenty-seven years earlier when the writer had first lived in Russia there had been a few surviving "anecdotes" told about Stalin; but for at least twenty-five years the writer had never seen or heard of a Russian laughing at or with Stalin. He had been too greatly feared for that. It flashed across the writer's mind that if Khrushchev were going to try to continue to rule without the legitimacy supplied by some sort of popular electoral process, he would feel the need to make himself feared by much the same sort of terror that Stalin had wielded.[16]

The anti-Soviet disorders which broke out in Poznan, Poland, in July 1956 climaxed the official disclosures of de-

---

[16] Nevertheless, it cannot be gainsaid that there have been instances in which terrorists such as Khrushchev have later taken a leading role in the elimination of terrorism. Thus, Tallien, when he felt his own life endangered, turned against Robespierre and set in motion the "Reaction of Thermidor." Although Tallien in fact had shared responsibility for the deaths of countless victims of revolutionary terror, he took a leading role in bringing about the execution

Stalinization as a final demonstration of the utter falsity of the claim of any of the Soviet countries to be socialist societies founded upon a dictatorship of the proletariat. Industrial workers and students led the riots in Poznan. Workers and students later furnished mass support for Gomulka, the new head of the Communist Party in Poland, in obtaining a degree of independence for Poland in the face of Soviet troop movements by which Khrushchev threatened to eject the new leadership. Gomulka forced Khrushchev to back down. Khrushchev simply did not have the nerve to oust Gomulka from power at the probable cost of scores of thousands of casualties in a struggle in which even the majority of the Polish Communist Party would have joined the rest of the population in fighting the Soviet occupying forces.

The pattern of events in Poland was to be repeated, up to a point, in the revolution in Hungary in October. Once more the revolt was led by the industrial workers and the students. In its early stages, it was successful, in spite of the intervention of Soviet troops and tanks. But when Khrushchev and the upper hierarchy of the Russian Communist Party decided that the disintegration of the Soviet empire must be stopped at all costs, the intervention of massive Soviet forces was bound to succeed in crushing the revolt. Resistance continued in the form of repeated strikes under the leadership of workers' councils which were set up throughout industry. Eventually the Soviet puppet regime of Janos Kadar, in an effort to stamp out opposition, dissolved these councils and decreed the death penalty for striking.

The thousands of dead in the Hungarian revolution, both among the Hungarian workers and among the Soviet occupational forces, definitively established that the Hungarian Communist regime had represented neither the Hungarian people as a whole nor the Hungarian proletariat. The revolt in Hungary emphatically corroborated the situation in Poland. Ironically enough, the training in street fighting which had been given by Russian Communists to Hungarian Communist Youth

---

of Robespierre and numbers of lesser-known terrorists and thus brought the terrorism of the French Revolution to an eventual end. A somewhat similar statement with reference to Barras might be made.

organizations, to be used against "capitalistic invaders," had proved very effective in destroying Soviet tanks in the streets of Budapest. Apparently the majority of the members of the Hungarian Communist Party joined the resistance to the Soviet-installed regime.

Both the Polish and Hungarian revolts demonstrated that it was entirely possible for authoritarian and totalitarian regimes of the Soviet type to rule for a decade without evidence observable by the outside world of the bitter hatred felt by their subjects. The seeming docility of the population of the satellite countries could no longer be cited as definitive evidence of their acceptance of the Soviet regime. It is true that the demonstrated popular hatred of the Soviet-dominated regimes in Poland and Hungary would not of itself prove the existence of a similar hatred of the Soviet regime on the part of the Russian people. There can be no doubt that nationalism played a major and critical role in the Polish and Hungarian uprisings. Revolution aimed at emancipation from the hated foreign rule, enforced by the bayonets of Russian soldiers, was a goal consistent with all past Polish and Hungarian history.

It was, indeed, this element of nationalism which provided the unifying spark and made possible a spontaneous mass uprising. Just such a spark could not, in all probability, be generated in the same way in Russia. Yet the nationalist element in these revolts drives another nail in the coffin of the Marxist doctrine of the inevitable evolution of society toward two antagonistic classes, the proletariat and the bourgeoisie, in which only economic interests are important. In Poland and in Hungary, a decade after the elimination of the capitalist state, after the nationalization of all large-scale and medium-scale industry and the collectivization of a large part of agriculture, after the confiscation of the wealth of the former bourgeoisie which deprived them of significant economic resources, revolutions occurred which could not possibly be explained in Marxist-Leninist-Stalinist terms. The workers rose en masse against a state which had arrogated to its own bureaucracy the right to rule the workers.

The Soviet-installed regime nevertheless continued to use the old Marxist phraseology. The Hungarian government stated over the Budapest radio:

The successes of the Government are causing the hatred and the fury of the counterrevolutionaries and of the international imperialists. Their fury is based on the fact that the Government is not a government of the capitalists and dollar millionaires but a government of the workers and peasants. After the armed defeat of the counterrevolutionaries they undertook an attack on freedom and democracy. But the Government has unmistakably stated that there is a dictatorship of the proletariat in Hungary.

It (the Government) could only achieve its success by an open and consistent fight. In a dictatorship of the proletariat every citizen enjoys the democratic rights and freedom. The counterrevolutionaries and persons who attack the legal order and the basic principles of the people's democracy have no freedom even if they mask their counterrevolutionary efforts by democratic slogans. The law will always punish them severely . . .

The anti-Leninist methods of the Rakosi and Gero clique must never return. Among these we count the cult of the individual and the disregarding of the interests of the masses.[17]

It could not, however, be concealed that only massive armed intervention had made it possible to maintain a Soviet-dominated regime in power against what was obviously the willingness of the masses, especially the industrial workers, to fight to the death for freedom. What a commentary upon the feelings of the population towards a regime which was alleged to have come into power as the dictatorship of the proletariat! To the extent that nationalism had played a critical role in the revolution, what a commentary on the Marxist doctrine of the disappearance of nationalism with the rise of working-class consciousness!

The disclosures of Khrushchev which accompanied the process of de-Stalinization, together with the evidence furnished by the revolts in Poland and Hungary, gave the final proof that the overthrow of capitalism and the dispossession of the bourgeoisie did not in the least alter the fundamental problem of how men are to be governed. While substantially

[17] *New York Times,* January 7, 1957.

all of Stalin's crimes had been known before these disclosures were made, the fact of their occurrence had either been denied by the Communist press throughout the world or they had been excused on the grounds of justified and necessary punishment of "enemies of the people." Even the Communist Party leadership in the United States, split wide open by the disclosures of Khrushchev and the events in Poland and Hungary, now confessed in the *Daily Worker*:

> We were wrong, terribly wrong. We . . . [were guilty of] stupid and arrogant condemnation of those who told the truth about the violations of justice in the Soviet Union. We did not want to believe these crimes could occur in a socialist state, and so we refused to believe. What was unforgivable and inexcusable was the manner in which we passed judgment—harsh and sometimes vindictive in tone—on many of our fellow Americans based solely on their criticism of the Stalin rule.[18]

Many intellectuals throughout the world had found it impossible to believe that the head of a so-called socialist state could have committed the sort of crimes which Stalin had been charged with all along and which were now verified. Even the intellectual who prided himself on knowing the "facts of life" about the Soviet regime had felt that the criminal charges against Stalin must have been exaggerated and that at least some of his victims must have really been counterrevolutionary "enemies of the people."

Similarly, in spite of the obvious lack of democratic processes under Stalin's rule, Communists had maintained that the system was unqualifiedly "democratic" and that this term reflected reality as used in the official titles designating the postwar Communist states. In the main, this unqualified claim to be democratic (now officially admitted to have been false) had never been supported by the evidence, as indeed it could not have been. The Soviet state was somehow supposed to have been automatically democratic simply because the regime claimed to have originated in a dictatorship of the proletariat.

[18] Quoted from an article by Louis Herman in *The New Leader*, January 21, 1957, p. 8.

The same type of one-party-list elections with the inevitable 95 per cent-plus affirmative vote which had characterized the Nazi regime in Germany was supposed somehow to confirm the acquiescence of the population in Soviet rule. There had been some feeble talk for foreign consumption about pre-election processes which would choose among alternative candidates before they were placed on the single official list, but this line of possible justification was never developed with any seriousness. The talk of "democratic centralism" within the Communist Party had been proved meaningless by the disclosures of de-Stalinization.

Most intellectuals outside the Communist countries had realized that the Hitler-Stalin type of elections were not free elections in the Western sense. Many had, however, felt that the apparent acquiescence of over 90 per cent of the voters reflected the success of governmental propaganda appeals rather than the actual use of repression and terror to force a vote of affirmation.

Long before the death of Stalin there had been overwhelming evidence that the Soviet dictator and the ruling class which he had created had no better title to represent the Russian people than Hitler and his ruling class in Germany or Mussolini and his ruling class in Italy had to represent their peoples. As Milovan Djilas, himself once a leading member of Tito's Communist ruling class in Yugoslavia, put it after his disillusionment, "Totalitarianism is a mere excuse for the exploitation of the workers by bureaucracy and a new ruling class." This exploitation of the workers by the new ruling class has been characteristic of all modern totalitarian regimes, whether Soviet, Fascist, Nazi, Yugoslav or Red Chinese.

Yet these regimes had a crucial propaganda advantage in claiming to rule in the interests of their respective peoples. The political system of tsarist Russia had been based, not on the tsar's duty to rule in the popular interest, but simply on the stated and enforced duty of the people to obey him and his officials. In democratic and capitalistic countries the political system is indeed based upon the doctrine of the control of the state by the people and for the people. However, the economic system of capitalistic countries, founded upon the inviolability of private property, did not legally recognize the concept that private property must serve the people, although the whole trend of legislation and court decisions in the United States and other capitalistic countries in the twentieth century has in fact recognized this in principle. In capitalistic tsarist Russia both the political and the economic system lacked the propaganda base later exploited by the Bolsheviki that their system was by and for the people. With respect to their economic systems, capitalistic countries have been under somewhat the same handicap as was tsarism in both its political and economic aspects.

It could indeed be logically argued that in a capitalistic country like the United States, under a system of laissez faire and private property, capitalists were compelled even before the passage of reformist legislation to furnish consumer goods at competitive prices and to pay laborers competitive wages. One could further point out that in a country with a democratic and parliamentary political system the people could change the economic system by amending or reinterpreting the Constitution if they were seriously dissatisfied with it. It could be further argued that if the citizens of a democratic, capitalistic country had not, as consumers or workers, attained satisfactory standards of living they would already have voted for the elimination of capitalism. But this required a chain of reasoning which was a handicap in terms of simple propaganda.

The whole history of the Stalin regime, with its fictitious representative government, its refusal to permit free elections or alternative political parties, its countless executions of revolutionary leaders, its wholesale deportations of peasants, its statized labor unions, its establishment of a centralized and uninhibited authoritarian bureaucracy, proved that the Soviet government was far more tyrannical than the tsarist government and that the people had far less control of both the political and economic system than in capitalistic countries of the West.

So long as the authority and ideology of the regime remained monolithic, however, the utter absurdity of its claim to represent the Russian people had been by no means universally recognized. It was the official disclosures by the Soviet "collective leadership" after Stalin's death that his regime had in fact been a personal tyranny, accompanied by the atrocities associated with the great tyrants of history, which shook the monolith and destroyed the myth of a people's democracy.

It is hard, in retrospect, to understand the extent to which the Stalinist defense had been accepted by segments of the intelligentsia outside Russia, the size of the segment and the completeness of the acceptance largely depending upon how recently the Stalinist crimes had been committed. It is true that whenever incidents occurred like the suppression of the uprising of the revolutionary sailors of Kronstadt, the purging and subsequent assassination of Trotsky, the liquidation of the kulaks, the execution of hundreds of old Bolsheviki and thousands of ordinary peasants, workers and members of the bureaucracy by the secret police, the signing of the Nazi-Soviet Pact in 1939, those intelligentsia who had previously been sympathetic were repelled by these events. Some of them lost sympathy for the regime permanently.

In the case of many, their indignation faded as time passed and as the Soviet government persisted in its insistence that these crimes had in fact never happened or that the alleged crimes were not in the least crimes. Even the fact that the offenses with which the purgees were charged were later proclaimed to have been fabricated and the accuser, as in the case of Yagoda, later executed for having falsely accused his victims of being "enemies of the people" did not fully prevent the eventual and at least partial acceptance of the Stalinist defense by many of the international intelligentsia. Nor did the fact that men who until their arrest had been lauded as revolutionary leaders were immediately thereafter denounced as long-time agents of the capitalist-imperialist powers suffice to produce complete skepticism of the Stalinist defense. Furthermore, even the intelligentsia could not be expected to remember the details of one atrocity after another. Who nowadays recalls the suppression of the Kronstadt rebellion or the liquidation of the kulaks?

In part this was due to the intelligentsia's traditional position of being "impartial." It was simply not possible that the Stalinist regime could be so wicked, and consequently the crimes which the regime had committed could not really be crimes. To understand is to excuse, and it was felt that there must be a "good" side to the case.

Above all, the intelligentsia have, almost by definition, identified themselves with the "progressive" cause, and have traditionally sympathized with revolutions, opposed conservatism and fought "reaction." The Soviet regime, so long as it remained monolithic, had great success in maintaining its status as a proletarian, revolutionary regime. Intellectuals might and generally did condemn wholeheartedly the violent repression of the Stalinist regime even when it was exercised against "enemies of the people," but that this was a proletarian, revolutionary regime defending itself by understandable, if deplorable, violence against reaction was widely accepted. Daniel Bell's explanation of the support of Stalinist communism by French intellectuals is essentially true for many intellectuals throughout the world:

> What brought these intellectuals to Communism was the *mystique* of revolution, for what French workers could not accomplish in 1848 or 1871 the Russian workers had accomplished in 1917. This was the compelling myth —the proletariat, bare-handed, tearing up the cobbled streets, defending themselves against tanks and guns; and this myth had sustained Sartre and other French intellectuals in their allegiance to Russia despite all the rational evidence of betrayal which had become apparent five, ten, twenty, twenty-five years ago.
>
> Now the Hungarian workers have risen in the very same heroic posture and with the same lack of arms, but against the Russians; and the Russians, in the classic answer of oppressors, have coldly shot them down. A French intellectual can withstand anything but the destruction of his myth, so the break has finally come. And it seems complete.[19]

It was not recognized that the proclaimed adherence to Marxism, the self-identification of the Stalinist dictatorship with the dictatorship of the proletariat, and the coming to power by revolutionary violence had constituted no guarantee at all against the regime's becoming totally reactionary. To

[19] *The New Leader*, January 21, 1957, p. 19.

the intelligentsia of the West, the absence in Soviet Russia of any strikes, of any voices of protest, of any revolutionary leaflets, of any references in contemporary literature or drama to labor unrest or dissatisfaction, seemed conclusive evidence that, whatever its repressive character, Russian labor considered the Soviet regime its own. To the Western intelligentsia it had been simply unthinkable that human beings could be repressed en masse, with no signs of revolt except for the melancholy record of multitudes condemned for crimes never committed. The official disclosures of de-Stalinization and the revolts in Poland and Hungary finally made it plain for all time that a regime which claimed to rule in the name of the proletariat could repress laborers individually and in mass as ruthlessly as any "Fascist" regime.[20]

The Soviet leadership had been appalled at the results of de-Stalinization and at the response of the peoples of the Soviet empire to their policy of relaxing controls. The concession to Tito that there were "many roads to socialism" had not prevented but had evidently encouraged the progress of the revolts in Poland and Hungary. Indeed, while Tito had at first looked with favor on the Hungarian revolution since it meant the final repudiation of his enemies, Rakosi and Gero, even he became alarmed as it became evident that the revolt was not only anti-Russian but anti-Communist.

Even Gomulka, who had led the nationalist revolution in Poland, became alarmed by its developing an anti-Communist character. Faced by possible repudiation in the elections of January 20, 1957, he announced defiantly that the Communist Party would not allow itself to be voted out of power and

[20] Despite the evidence which had been accumulating for decades, some Communists outside Russia had apparently still believed in the proletarian character of the Soviet regime. The effects of de-Stalinization and of the repressive measures against Hungarian workers were shattering for such individuals. Thus, John Steuben, a former union organizer and leading Communist theorist whose books had been translated and published in Russia and the satellite countries, finally broke with Moscow after the Kadar regime in Hungary decreed the death penalty for strikers. He said that any government which decreed death for strikers was "morally bankrupt." He urged American Communists to "repudiate everything which smacks of Stalinism." *New York Times,* January 19, 1957.

reaffirmed his loyalty to Soviet Russia. The Polish elections of January 20, 1957, which were originally supposed to have been free, turned out to be in effect "one-list" elections on the familiar totalitarian model.

The unrest among students and workers in Russia itself and the revolutionary events in Hungary and Poland were effective in bringing about an attempt to reverse or at least halt the policy of de-Stalinization. In early January 1957, Khrushchev was once more referring to Stalin as a great leader and a great Marxist. He declared that in carrying out a foreign policy in opposition to capitalistic imperialism "We are all Stalinists." On January 27, at a reception in Moscow for China's Premier Chou En-lai, Khrushchev went even further. He declared that Stalin was "an example of a good Communist" when it came to "fighting for the interests of the working class." Although Stalin had made mistakes, Khrushchev now claimed that these had not been essential and asked that "God grant that every Communist should be able to fight like Stalin."[21]

Khrushchev's return to something like the state of admiration which he had always professed during Stalin's lifetime could not in the least obscure the official record of Stalin's crimes against the Russian people. Khrushchev's second *volte-face* only meant that he had now learned that Stalinist terror was a functional characteristic of a totalitarian system. He was able to resist the efforts of Malenkov, Molotov, Kaganovich and Shepilov in July of 1957 to remove him from power, and to succeed in ousting them instead, primarily because of the military power of Marshal Zhukov. Three months later, taking advantage of his absence in the Balkans, Khrushchev moved against Zhukov and demoted him prior to consolidating his own position.

In the July 1957 purge of Malenkov, Molotov, Kaganovich and Shepilov, the official announcement issued in Moscow stated that the action of the Central Committee was unanimous, including all of the accused, except Molotov, who abstained! This unanimity was supposed to prove that there was no opposition whatever to Khrushchev in the Central Committee. It is now generally believed that the majority of the Presidium of the Central Committee of the Party at first voted

21 *New York Times*, January 18, 1957.

against Khrushchev. Since the members of the Presidium were also members of the Central Committee, it is clear that the unanimity claimed was due to pressure which no one save Molotov dared resist. When Zhukov was later removed from office he himself signed the Central Committee's official criticism of him. There had apparently been a bitter fight in the Central Committee, but this "unanimity" is supposed to illustrate in some esoteric fashion that the succession to the dictatorship of the proletariat remains unquestioned. The official statement says, "The Party is not a debating society." Interestingly enough, the *Daily Worker* commented that perhaps all this would not have happened if there *had* been public debate.

All "the discussion" in the lower ranks of the Party came about *after* the action of the Central Committee. The Russian people were allowed only the pretext of expressing themselves with respect to these successive shifts in power—the execution of Beria, the ousting of Malenkov, Molotov, Shepilov, Kaganovich and later Zhukov, and the elevation of Khrushchev to supremacy—in the meetings called by trade unions, collective farms and every sort of organization to denounce those who had been deposed. Similar meetings had regularly been called by Stalin after his purges of important figures. These meetings always greeted the winners in the struggle for power with fulsome praise and denounced the losers with loathing. Such meetings were always stage-managed. The resolutions of denunciation were obviously prepared in advance and were always unanimously approved. Yet in a totalitarian state ruled by terror, the enthusiasm manifested for these resolutions of denunciation has a certain reality. Those denounced are invariably men who have held great power and have been involved in the denunciation and death of others before them. It is little wonder that the downfall of these men who have inspired fear and compelled adulation is greeted with glee almost regardless of the identity of the winners or losers in the endless struggle for power.

The Soviet success in the race with the United States for space satellites and intercontinental ballistic missiles has powerfully strengthened the prestige of Khrushchev and the Soviet regime not only abroad but at home as well. The final wiping out of the age-old Russian sense of inferiority in relation to the West must be accounted of major importance.[22]

What is the likelihood that the present Soviet totalitarian system will somehow evolve into a free, democratic parliamentary regime? The short period of "collective leadership" after the death of Stalin led some non-Russians to believe that this represented progress away from personal dictatorship and might even evolve into representative government. It is now apparent that "collective leadership" was only a temporary designation which camouflaged the struggle for personal power at the top of the hierarchy of Party and state. The restoration of one-man rule under Khrushchev did not, indeed, automatically mean a return to a Stalinist regime. After the execution of Beria and many of his associates, neither death nor imprisonment was to be the immediate fate of those whom Khrushchev eliminated from power.[23] But this is no guarantee that the rest of the Stalinist pattern will not be duplicated. In the absence of representative government it is extremely doubtful whether a dictator can hold the power in a great country like Russia without the use of massive terror.

Khrushchev's age makes it certain that he will not rule for many years. There is little reason to believe, however, that a successor who seizes power in the way that Khrushchev did can hold it without terror. This does not completely rule out the possibility that, during another interim such as that following the death of Stalin, a temporary successor to Khrushchev might permit representative government to be revived, somewhat as General Monk finally permitted King Charles II and Parliament to resume an altered power relation after the death of Cromwell. But the Communist Party with its control from the top affords an instrument for the propagation of personal power which will always tempt an ambitious man. Indeed, the knowledge that this is so is likely to impel anyone

[22] Even as late as a decade and a half after the Revolution the author occasionally used to hear what Russians in tsarist times commonly remarked to foreigners, "We are a dark people."

[23] In the new edition of the *Great Soviet Encyclopedia*, which appeared late in 1957, Malenkov is not referred to as a former Premier, or party leader or even Minister of Electric Power Stations, but only as an anti-Party plotter. Dispatch from Moscow by Max Frankel, *New York Times*, December 21, 1957.

near the top to seize power as his only sure guarantee against its seizure by another.

Finally, the control and direction of a completely collectivized and centralized economy by a parliamentary, democratic government presents almost insoluble difficulties.[24] It is, indeed, not impossible that the present giant industrial combines in the Soviet Union might somehow evolve towards a form more like that of capitalistic corporations and that new small-scale businesses might be permitted to operate privately at some time in the future. The essence of any such evolution of Soviet industrial organization would have to be a great increase in the autonomy of the managements of such industrial entities, and provision for some sort of social control in their selection. At this point the problem of the choice of industrial managements approaches that of the modified form of capitalism in Western countries. A development of this sort, however, could not happen without the emergence of some form of representative political government, of which there is as yet no sign.

[24] See Chapter 12.

CHAPTER 5

SOVIET ECONOMIC GROWTH

The defenders of capitalism have always claimed that the degree of individual liberty inherent in the system is one of its principal virtues. The weight of the argument made in the past by these opponents of a collectivist economic system was, however, generally directed at proving that it would be far less productive than capitalism, if it could function for any substantial length of time at all. The belief that personal liberty was a fundamental factor in productive efficiency and that such liberty would be decisively curtailed in a collectivist economy was implicit in this contention. That the Soviet economic system is inimical to personal liberty is now indisputable from the record. The survival values of the rival economic systems may, however, be determined directly by their comparative productivity instead of by the degree of personal liberty inherent in them.

What is the record with regard to the productivity of the Soviet economic system? Has the almost complete repression of liberty kept production at an intolerably low level, or has it been increasing at a rate as high as or higher than that in capitalistic countries? An analysis of the economic data set forth in the Sixth Five-Year Plan which began in 1956 affords a means of answering these questions, even though this plan was set aside in 1957 and a new Seven-Year Plan was announced.

The Sixth Five-Year Plan was proclaimed at the 20th Congress of the Communist Party, where Stalin was first publicly denounced by Khrushchev as a murderous tyrant. It embodied the economic policies and expectations of the temporarily stabilized "collective leadership" after the execution of Beria and the deposition of Malenkov as Premier by Khrushchev. The economic growth rates set forth in the Plan were impressive. National income in 1960 was expected to be 160 per cent of 1955 income, an increase of about 10.5 per cent a year. This figure is far above that for the United States, where the average annual rate of increase in national income during the past eighty years has been on the order of 3.5 per cent. Yet this rate of increase in national income projected in the Sixth Five-Year Plan was slightly lower than that claimed by Soviet authorities for the recently ended Fifth Five-Year Plan when national income in 1955 was said to have been 168 per cent of 1950 income.[1]

Real wages in the entire national economy were planned to increase to 130 per cent of the 1955 level by 1960, compared with 139 per cent of the 1950 level in 1955. This rate of increase in real wages, while lower than that planned for national income as a whole, is still much above the rate in most Western capitalistic countries. If the rates of increase in national income and its components claimed under past economic plans and proposed for the future reflect reality, the consequences for the capitalistic countries either in terms of

[1] As is pointed out later, the rate of increase planned for the year 1957 was later radically reduced to 7.1 per cent. This rate was announced at the sixth session of the Supreme Soviet, February 5, 1957. (*Pravda*, February 6, as translated in the *Current Digest of the Soviet Press*, March 20, 1957.) However, it was abandoned later and the whole Sixth Five-Year Plan as well. It was claimed at the end of 1957 that a rate of increase of 10 per cent for 1957 had been achieved. A new Seven-Year Plan was announced, with planning data to be set forth later. On December 20 the planned rate of growth in gross industrial production for 1958 was announced as 7.6 per cent, which would probably indicate a rate of increase in national income somewhat below this. (For example, during 1950–55 a rate of growth in industrial production of 135 per cent was claimed compared with a rate of 168 per cent for national income.)

military potential or in terms of economic supremacy would be fateful. But are these rates attainable? Have the even higher rates of increase claimed in the past been realized?

It is not feasible in a brief space to discuss adequately the complex problem of the validity of Soviet statistics. However, the publication in 1956 of a statistical abstract for the Soviet Union raised again the whole question of the validity of Soviet statistics.[2] The Central Statistical Administration stated in a foreword that "this statistical compilation contains the most important data which reflect the development of the U.S.S.R. national economy by comparison with the years 1928, pre-war 1940 and pre-revolutionary 1913." It stated further that "some of the indexes contained in the compilation illustrate the goals of the Sixth Five Year Plan as specified by the Directive of the XX Congress of the C.P.S.U. and are compared with the results of previous five-year plans." It was announced that additional statistical data would be published from time to time.[3]

Far more data were published in the new statistical abstract than had been available since before World War II. Furthermore, numerous data previously given only in percentages of uncertain base were now stated in terms of absolute figures. Consequently, non-Soviet economists and statisticians are no longer dependent upon figures derived from a composite of general percentages and references to actual quantities that occasionally appeared in some obscure technical journal which escaped the eye of the censor. Examination indicates a rather close correspondence between the figures published in the new statistical abstract and those built up by statisticians in the United States through the laborious process of compiling data gleaned from a variety of Soviet sources, including statements by Soviet officials appearing in the press from time to time.[4]

[2] *Narodnoe Khoziaistvo SSSR (The National Economy of the U.S.S.R.)*, Central Statistical Administration, Moscow, 1956 (hereinafter referred to as "the new statistical abstract").

[3] This promise has to a considerable extent been fulfilled. For example, in 1957 *Promyshlennost' SSSR*, giving some additional data on industry, was published. Additional breakdowns of data on foreign trade were published in the November 1957 issue of *Vneshnyaya Torgovlya*. There have been other examples as well.

[4] The estimate of the population of the Soviet Union as approximately 200 million is a conspicuous exception. It is in conflict with

This only proves that figures now published are generally consistent with those previously derived from heterogeneous sources; it does not prove that the earlier data were correct. The new statistical abstract does little to correct the almost fantastically upward bias in the statistics of past economic performance, but there is evidence that statistics of more recent years come somewhat closer to reality.

The publication of the new statistical abstract seemed to strengthen the convictions of those economists and statisticians who accept substantially at face value Soviet claims of annual rates of increase in industrial production and in national income three or four times as great as those of the United States. For example, the *Economic Survey of Europe in 1955* and the *World Economic Survey, 1955,* published by the United Nations, accept current Soviet statistics at their face value. There has been an increasing tendency to do this in European bank letters and other publications.[5]

Almost none of the specialists who have worked in this field have indeed ever believed, as have many non-specialists, that Soviet statistics were either completely falsified for propaganda reasons or were totally unusable. They have, however, differed as to the accuracy of some of the data and the extent to which the national income estimates would have to be adjusted in order to reflect reality. These statistics were considered sufficiently valid, nevertheless, to warrant their use as the basis for corrected estimates.

One of the best analyses of Soviet statistics is the symposium entitled *Soviet Economic Growth,*[6] in which the past efforts by various specialists in the field such as Colin Clark, Jasny and Wyler were reviewed. Beyond this, the symposium made new efforts to reduce the past strong upward bias in Soviet statistics and to subject them to reanalysis. Thus Greg-

---

the estimate of about 220 million people based on previous Soviet sources.

[5] For example, A. Nove, writing on "The Pace of Soviet Economic Development" in *Lloyd's Bank Review,* April 1956, accepts the Soviet claim of an annual growth rate of industrial production of almost 13 per cent for the period 1951–55 as approximately correct.

[6] Abram Bergson (ed.), Row, Peterson and Company, Evanston, Ill., 1953. Most of the American specialists in the field participated in this symposium.

ory Grossman, who deals with national income in the symposium, arrived at an annual rate of growth for 1928–37 and for 1928–50 of 6.5 to 7 per cent, compared with official Soviet statistics of 16 per cent and 19 per cent for the two periods. Grossman's figure is quite close to the revised goals proposed for the year 1957 by the Soviet planning authorities.[7]

The complete skepticism about the truth of Soviet statistics on the part of non-specialists is easy to understand. The disclosures of Khrushchev with regard to Stalin's regime confirmed what had been generally believed, that what purported to be a dictatorship of the proletariat and a system of socialism was in fact a tyranny without any sort of democratic control. It became indisputably clear that the Stalinist charges against innumerable "enemies of the people," which led to their death, were without foundation and based upon complete fabrication of evidence. It is natural that this general skepticism about any statement of fact made by the Soviet authorities during Stalin's regime should carry over to the statistics of that period.

It would obviously not be feasible to test directly the accuracy of Soviet statistics on any really comprehensive scale. The very idea of a count by some impartial statistical body of the actual annual production of, say, steel, compared with official estimates, is, of course, absurd. Soviet statistics of steel production, to the extent that these are available, may, however, be examined to see whether they are internally consistent and consistent with other official data, such as statistics for the end uses of steel. Until the new statistical abstract was published, statisticians and economists outside the U.S.S.R. had to rely in

[7] Substantially all specialists in the field agree that Soviet official statistics of economic growth have shown much higher rates of increase in industrial production and in national income than could be derived from any reasonable relation between these aggregates and their basic components, such as labor inputs, steel consumption, fuel consumption and the like. There is general agreement that recent statistical aggregates reflecting economic growth are more realistic than the early figures, and that even after revision the rate of economic growth shown is impressive. See also Donald R. Hodgman, *Soviet Industrial Production, 1928–1951,* Harvard University Press, Cambridge, 1954; F. Seton, *The Tempo of Soviet Industrial Expansion,* Manchester Statistical Society, Manchester, 1957; and Naum Jasny, "The Rates of Soviet Economic Growth," *American Statistician,* June 1958, pp. 21–24.

the main upon this kind of checking of the limited data available during the last couple of decades, with results which always left a substantial margin for doubt.

The principal reason why non-Soviet economists and statisticians have generally ruled out wholesale, deliberate fabrication and falsification is the insuperable difficulty involved in trying to keep "two sets of books," one for the general public, including foreigners, and another for those Soviet officials who must use statistics in running the economy. With the issuance of the new statistical abstract of 1956 in an edition of 100,000 copies, and another large edition planned, it became obvious that hopeless confusion would be entailed in maintaining another comprehensive set of "true" statistics in contrast to the published ones.[8] This does not, of course, rule out the possibility that the statistics in the new abstract are inaccurate, conceivably on a large scale. As pointed out above, past official estimates of the annual increase in national income have probably been from two to three times too high. It is now admitted that agricultural statistics were defective. The method of using "biological yield" instead of actual "barn yield" led to a serious overstatement of grain production. Although "barn yield" was later substituted, it is now admitted that the correction was not large enough. Consequently, statistics of grain production published in the past have been much too high and require further correction.

It is certain that aggregate figures which purport to show changes through time in the output of consumer goods have been greatly exaggerated. Thus, according to the new statistical abstract the physical volume of production of consumer goods by industry at the end of 1955 was nine times that of 1928.[9] The claimed increase for producer goods during the

---

[8] The National Bureau of Economic Research has been carrying out under the direction of Warren Nutter a critical analysis of Soviet statistics of economic growth. This study should afford us as definitive a test of their validity as can be obtained from internal analysis of the data. Preliminary results of Nutter's findings have been published in the *Papers and Proceedings of the American Economic Association* in 1956 and 1957.

[9] This estimate on pp. 46–47 of the abstract appears inconsistent with an estimate of a 14-fold increase from 1928 to 1960 on pp. 48–49.

same period was 39 times, and for consumer and producer goods combined, 21 times. By way of comparison, during the same period in the United States industrial production increased threefold.

The claimed increase of 900 per cent in the industrial output of consumer goods by 1955 needs to be considered in connection with Khrushchev's statement in 1953, confirmed by the new statistical abstract, that the total number of cattle of all types on Soviet farms in 1952 was no greater than in 1916 and was actually smaller than in 1928. Taking into account hogs, sheep and goats as well as cattle, meat production in 1952 showed little or no increase over either 1916 or 1928. Thus, after allowing for population increase, per capita consumption of meat was lower in 1952 than it had been in 1916. Even though the number of cattle and cows had by 1955 reached the 1928 figure, while the number of hogs had almost doubled from 1952 to 1955 (thereby almost doubling the level of 1928), in terms of meat consumption per capita the Soviet people were little, if any, better off in 1956 than in 1928 at the beginning of the First Five-Year Plan. The meat and dairy situation has been only the most extreme aspect of the generally unfavorable agricultural situation, which must have been a constantly limiting factor in the supply of raw materials for the production of consumer goods by industry. Food production has increased substantially since 1953, but this could not have influenced the output of consumer goods during most of the period for which such high rates were claimed.

It would be possible theoretically for the total output of consumer goods to increase 900 per cent from 1928 to 1955 on the basis of some weighted average while the consumption of meat did not increase at all, but this is not likely and is not in accordance with the writer's personal observation, as will be pointed out later. Furthermore, as a measure of consumer well-being, a rise in the consumer goods index in which an important and scarce food component did not increase would be basically different from a similar rise in which such a food component did increase.

The inaccuracy of Soviet statistics is reflected also in claimed rates of increase in national income. For example, national income in 1955 according to the new statistical abstract was more than 14 times as large as in 1928. By comparison, during the same period in the United States real national income roughly doubled. It is not feasible to check this estimate of Soviet national income with anything like precision, but an almost 14-fold increase in national income is certainly far beyond observed reality.[10]

The apparent paradox of the observable low standard of living in the Soviet Union and the stated high rates of economic growth has sometimes been explained in terms of the high rates of saving and investment and the much greater rate of increase in the output of producer goods as compared with consumer goods. While Soviet statistics have indeed shown high rates of saving and investment and higher rates of production of producer goods than consumer goods, they also indicate very high rates of increase in the production of consumer goods. Observation does not confirm anything like the claims that are made for consumer goods output, although substantial increases have taken place.

Skepticism with respect to production claims in the Soviet Union or in its satellites is underlined by the Polish experience. An annual average rate of increase in industrial production of 23 per cent for the years 1949–52 had been claimed, made up of a 25 per cent annual increase for producer goods and an 18 per cent increase for consumer goods. A combined rate of 18 per cent was claimed for 1953 and 11 per cent for 1954.[11] Even the 11 per cent rate for 1954, made up of a claimed 11 per cent for both producer and consumer goods, is of course a very high rate.

Yet the Poznan uprising of the summer of 1956 was caused

[10] It is generally agreed by specialists in the field that the claimed rates of increase for the earlier periods are not to be taken seriously. Nutter notes that Khrushchev continues to refer to Soviet industrial production as having increased thirty-odd times since 1913 and compares this with growth in Western countries, especially the United States. He comments, "One thing is clear: the myth of industrial output that is embodied in the official Soviet index of industrial production should be revealed and dispelled, once and for all." *Papers and Proceedings of the American Economic Association,* May 1958, p. 410.

[11] United Nations, *World Economic Survey, 1955,* New York, 1956, p. 99.

in large measure by the workers' bitter dissatisfaction with the supply of consumer goods, which was getting worse instead of better. It is obviously impossible to reconcile the statistical data on consumer goods production with the facts as they were disclosed after the Gomulka regime took over. In a speech before the Plenum of the Central Committee of the Communist Party on October 22, 1956, Gomulka stated: "Generally speaking, after the conclusion of the Six Year Plan, which according to its premises was meant to raise high the standard of living of the working class and of the entire nation, we are faced today in the first year of the Five Year Plan, with immense difficulties which are growing from day to day. . . . The juggling with figures which showed a 27 per cent rise in real wages during the Six Year Plan proved a failure." He goes on to speak of the low productivity per man-hour in the coal industry, of the great lag in housing construction, of the low productivity and high costs of production on the state and collective farms compared with the individual peasant farms. Yet it is obvious that Gomulka was puzzled, for he also says: "I have no grounds to doubt the given indices of increase of industrial production. I accept them as true. There are, however, certain 'buts' which force me to make a reappraisal of the evaluation of our economic achievements during the past Six Year Plan."

There are some facts in Gomulka's speech which do help to explain why the alleged percentage increases in production were illusory. He points out that "At the cost of tremendous investment we built an automobile factory in Zeran," and that the factory produced only limited numbers of automobiles, at high production costs, of types so obsolete that they are produced nowhere else in the world. Referring to capital investment he further states: "In the meantime a considerable part of these credits *in the shape of machines and installations has so far found no application in production and will not find any such application for years to come, and part of it must be considered irretrievably lost.*" (Italics supplied.) In other words, there had been included in the statistics of industrial production of producer goods very large amounts which represented little or no addition to real national income. The steel, coal, man-hours and other elements in the cost of production of these erroneously planned investments had been practically thrown away. There are almost no statistical devices for making appropriate discounts for bad planning. If investments so badly planned as to be almost worthless were made in a capitalistic economy, these could also appear in statistics of production and investment;[12] but the complex system of pricing, resource allocation and decision-making in a capitalistic economy ordinarily results in fewer badly planned investments which get embodied in the statistics.

These disclosures by Gomulka help to explain the unreliability of the statistics which showed high rates of output of producer goods. They do not directly explain the discrepancy between the claimed large increase in real wages and the miserable condition of the workers.[13] This may be partially explained by the fact that even official statistics claimed that agricultural production in 1954 was no more than 98 per cent of the prewar 1937 level.[14] In the main, however, it must be concluded that the claimed figures on output of consumer goods and increases in real wages were statistically false. As Gomulka put it, "It only exasperated the people even more and it was necessary to withdraw from the position taken by poor statisticians."[15]

---

[12] For example, the very large expenditures on the British government-sponsored groundnuts scheme in East Africa appear in the statistical accounts as capital investment although they were abortive. P. T. Bauer and B. S. Yamey, *The Economics of Underdeveloped Countries*, University of Chicago Press, Chicago, 1957, p. 37.

[13] After the Poznan outbreak it was admitted by the then Premier Ochab that there were considerable numbers of workers who were no better off than in 1949 and that the position of some groups of workers was in fact worse. This was a reversal of previous claims of large increases in real wages during that period. Ochab placed the blame on military expenditures. Nicholas Spulber, *The Economics of Communist Eastern Europe*, Wiley and Technology Press, New York, 1957, p. 480. However, Stefan Jedrychowski, in charge of economic affairs in the Politburo of the Polish Communist Party, denied the validity of this explanation in a lecture in February 1957, since he claimed that defense expenditures in 1956 amounted to only 2 per cent of industrial production.

[14] *World Economic Survey, 1955*, p. 101.

[15] The planned rate of growth of industrial production announced by the Gomulka government for 1958 appears much more realistic.

It has been pointed out that Soviet statistics claim greater increases in the production of consumer goods than do capitalistic countries. The evidence indicates that these claimed rates of increase in consumer goods and in real wages are certainly far too high. Janet Chapman in a careful reanalysis of Soviet statistics[16] shows that real wages in Soviet Russia declined substantially between 1928 and 1952. The considerable reductions in consumer goods prices which took place after 1948 had not by 1952 restored real wages to their 1928 level. Price reductions since 1952 have, however, raised the level of real wages above those of 1952, and indeed above the 1928 level.

If, then, the validity of Soviet statistics is to be judged by such past estimates as rates of increase in national income or annual improvement in the standard of living, Soviet statistics would have to be accorded a very low rating. Soviet statisticians who translated absolute figures into aggregates showing annual rates of increase knew quite well that high rates would be far more acceptable to the Soviet hierarchy than low rates. Under the Stalinist regime rewards were high and punishments severe for obeying or disobeying the wishes of the ruling hierarchy. The cumulative effect of this pressure, operating at all levels of statistical compilation and aggregation, could be expected to be very important, even without actual falsification of component data.

There is, unfortunately, some recent evidence that the forces which were at work to impair the validity of Soviet statistics in Stalin's day may again become fully operative now that "collective leadership" has been displaced by Khrushchev's personal ascendancy. Shortly before his ousting of Malenkov, Molotov, Kaganovich and Shepilov, Khrushchev made a speech at a conference of farm personnel of the provinces and autonomous republics of the northwestern part of the Russian Republic in Leningrad on May 22, 1957.[17] Declaring that

---

The average rate of increase planned is 5.5 per cent and the rate for consumer goods is 8.4 per cent.

[16] "Real Wages in the Soviet Union, 1928–1952," *Review of Economics and Statistics*, May 1954, pp. 134–156.

[17] It was reported in *Izvestia* and *Pravda* of May 24 and translated in the *Current Digest of the Soviet Press*, July 3, 1957.

Khrushchev's dissatisfaction with the reduced rates of growth

Soviet Russia can and must surpass per capita meat production in the U.S.A. by 1960, he stated that this will require

> a volume which is 250% more than the actual 1956 level.
> . . . I asked the economists to present estimates of when
> we could catch up to America in the production of these
> items. I shall tell you a secret. They handed me a signed
> paper. . . . On that piece of paper was written: We can
> increase meat production by 220% and catch up with the
> U.S.A. in 1975. (Laughter) Excuse me, Comrade econo-
> mists, if I rub a little salt in your wounds. . . . How did
> our economists approach this matter? As is usual, they
> took their pencils and computed the increase and then
> projected it over the number of years, that is, they used
> data stretching over many years. From the arithmetical
> point of view there is no mistake here, everything is
> proven. But, Comrades, it is necessary to take into ac-
> count the capacity that our people have built up on our
> collective and state farms. . . . How can all this be reck-
> oned in an arithmetical calculation? This is policy, this
> is a political phenomenon, the result of many years of
> work by our party and the entire people. The comrades
> I spoke of are not bad people. I shall not mention their
> names here but I hope they are blushing. Then they will
> be more critical of the way they use their pencils, they
> will address themselves more to the people, study the
> state of the economy and feel the people's pulse and
> heartbeat. (Applause)

There seems little doubt that the next time Soviet economists use their pencils to forecast annual increases in meat
production they will pay less attention to past data and more
to the "people's pulse and heartbeat." Moreover, if Khrushchev is still in power in 1960 and Soviet economists have to
estimate meat production for that year, they will have to decide what weight to give to Khrushchev's estimate as against
the actual data.

---

planned by Soviet economists is reflected in his decision to return to
rates more nearly like the very high rates claimed in the past for
the new Seven-Year Plan, as reported in dispatches from Moscow in
late October 1958.

The means for translating absolute figures into large percentage increases lay readily to hand during the period of Soviet industrialization. Percentage increases in the early stages of mass production of new goods will naturally be quite large. The possibility of allowing such percentage increases to inflate aggregates while omitting statistics for industries of slow growth is obvious. Furthermore, the prices assigned to new products based upon their early production costs are likely to inflate the importance of new products in the aggregate production indices. There are indications that this occurred. Similarly, the inclusion in statistics of national income of commodities and services previously produced and consumed by peasant households and not reported as a component of national income constituted another of many possible sources of inflation of economic growth rates.

Nevertheless, there is evidence that the quality of current Soviet statistics has been improving. Serious distortions due to the use of an obsolete pricing basis were corrected some years ago. In general, however, past statistical exaggerations were not corrected in the new statistical abstract, though an effort is apparently being made to place current statistics on a more realistic basis. The Soviet ruling directorate, as constituted at the time that the new statistical abstract was published, was apparently more willing to allow statisticians and economists to produce and publish objective statistical data than was true under Stalin. Many new figures on production are appearing in the Soviet press, not merely percentages but some absolute figures as well. The very fact that much more data are being published may make it easier to arrive at more accurate statistics. How long this apparent improvement in quantity and quality will continue is uncertain.

The absurdity of any attempt at a direct and independent check of Soviet statistics of production has been pointed out. Some sort of test of the reality of Soviet claims with respect to the rate of increase through time of the production of consumer goods, of real wages, and of the standard of living in general may, however, be made through actual observation. Though it would not have been feasible for a foreigner to observe and record prices of commodities in the Soviet Union in the recent past, and such pricing of goods by means of actual "shopping" would have meant the danger of arrest for economic espionage, this was no longer true during the summer of 1956. Prices of consumer goods and their availability could be ascertained in this way, as had been possible at times in the more distant past. Unfortunately the same process is not as feasible when applied to wages. One can obtain from the managers of Soviet industrial plants statements concerning wage rates, and even test these statements after a fashion by asking individual workmen about their wages. Obviously, this is not a very precise method of determining actual wages and is not at all comparable to ascertaining retail prices by "shopping." Very rough estimates of changes in the standard of living over a period of years can nevertheless be made. The margin of error in any purely individual observation is of course great, particularly in the absence of time and facilities for the construction of actual index numbers of prices and wages.

It was with this objective that the author revisited Soviet Russia in the summer of 1956, seventeen years after his last extended visit to that country. By coincidence, personal observations of prices and wages were made during the same month in 1939 and in 1956, namely, July. Economic conditions in the Soviet Union were better than anticipated. This meant that statistics of rates of economic growth had been too greatly discounted. On the other hand, the composite evidence from all available sources, including personal observation, does not support claims of improvement in the standard of living at anything like the stated rates.

There had been some increase in the standard of living since 1939. Although people were still not nearly so well clothed as in Western Europe or the United States, improvement was noticeable. General rationing of consumer goods no longer existed, although some degree of limitation on purchases by each customer was enforced. Queues for milk were frequently in evidence, and supplies of particular goods were often sold out. In view of the unimpressive improvement observed by the writer in agricultural efficiency compared with 1939, it was surprising that the food situation was as good as it was. The government had succeeded in keeping the price of black bread of excellent quality at 1 ruble 25 kopecks per kilo.[18] In terms of an average wage of urban workers in the summer of 1956 of around 700 rubles, with the lowest wage a little under 300 rubles a month, this is not an exorbitant price for bread.[19] The price of black bread was, however, maintained at a price relatively far below that of other foods, largely through the operation of a system of compulsory deliveries of a large portion of the grain crop at low prices. This produced such anomalies as a price for grain per kilo on the free market double that of the fixed price for black bread, and resulted in many peasants feeding bread to their cows in spite of severe penalties for so doing.

Although the price of black bread was not exorbitant in terms of current wages, the same could hardly be said of beef at 12.50 rubles per kilo in state stores (usually not available) and at 22 to 24 rubles per kilo in the free kolkhoz market, pork at 18.50 rubles per kilo in state stores and at 23 rubles per kilo on the free market, butter at 26 rubles per kilo in state stores, sugar at 9 rubles per kilo in state stores for the cheapest grade, cheese at from 26 to 32 rubles per kilo in state stores, eggs at approximately a ruble each in state stores and a ruble 40 kopecks on the free market. Cabbage could be purchased at 1 ruble per kilo in state stores when available, while the price went to 6 rubles per kilo in the free market when it was not available in state stores. Potatoes were selling at 60 kopecks per kilo, when available, in state stores, and at 1 ruble 25 kopecks on the free market. The price of a 100-gram chocolate bar was from 12 to 16 rubles in state stores, depending upon quality.

Men's leather shoes sold at from 180 to 400 rubles, depending upon quality. A man's worsted suit of standard quality

[18] At the official rate of exchange the ruble is worth 25 cents. American residents in Moscow generally estimated it to be worth about 7 or 8 cents.
[19] The writer's estimates. They may have been too high in view of the announcement in the Soviet press on September 8, 1956 establishing minimum wages as of January 1, 1957 at 270 rubles monthly in nonurban areas and 300 rubles in urban industry. It was stated that this would increase the compensation of workers affected by 33 per cent and that the total Soviet wage bill would be increased by 8 billion rubles.

cost 1,500 rubles. What appeared to be a good quality woman's rayon dress which might have sold for $15.00 in the United States was priced at 582 rubles. Another, of summer weight, was priced at 319 rubles. A woman's rayon slip which might have cost $3.00 in the United States was priced at 280 rubles. A small, rather crudely made, electric refrigerator cost 680 rubles, an electric washing machine 2,250 rubles.

These prices of consumer goods, observed at random, when compared with the minimum wage and average wage referred to above afford some means of judging the current standard of living. It should be added that rental costs, particularly for old housing, are quite low and medical services are free. In comparison with 1939, the price of black bread had gone up 46 per cent, pork 85 per cent, butter 25 per cent, eggs 33 per cent, chocolate bars 100 per cent, sugar 137 per cent, milk 29 per cent, to name a few foodstuffs of reasonably standard quality available in state stores in both periods. Comparison of vegetable prices for the two periods is very difficult because vegetables were often available only on the free market, where the price fluctuated widely from season to season. Roughly, one might estimate that food prices were some 60 per cent higher than in 1939. Prices of shoes had apparently increased much less, probably no more than 20 per cent, although variations in quality made comparisons difficult. Prices of men's worsted suits had increased by some 60 per cent, although here also differences in quality made comparison difficult. In 1939 almost no electrical appliances had been on sale. Assuming the importance of food in the cost of living in relation to all other goods and services at 50 per cent and assuming an increase of 30 per cent in the prices of all goods and services other than food, one could estimate that the cost of living had increased some 45 per cent in comparison with 1939.

In 1939 the average wage of urban workers, according to the best available information, was around 350 rubles a month. Thus from 1939 to 1956 the cost of living had increased some 45 per cent while the money wage had doubled. This meant that real wages of urban workers had by the summer of 1956 increased by somewhat less than 40 per cent over those of the immediate prewar period. This should be regarded, however, primarily as a subjective estimate rather than as a statistical calculation.

This estimate of an increase in real wages of Soviet urban workers of about 40 per cent between 1939 and 1956 is in contrast with the official calculation in the new statistical abstract of a 90 per cent increase in the real wages of industrial workers from 1940 to 1955.[20] It might be compared with an increase in the average real hourly earnings of industrial workers in the United States during roughly the same period of some 50 per cent.

Housing continued to be exceedingly bad in spite of huge new apartment house construction programs for urban workers. The low quality of Soviet housing reflects not only the lag of housing construction behind the growth in urban population but also the almost unbelievably low standards in the inside and outside finishing of housing and in maintenance after construction. Yet improvement in maintenance in other fields, such as railroads and rolling stock, which had taken place since the writer's 1939 visit did indicate that standards of maintenance even in housing might well improve in the future.

There were a substantial number of private automobiles, although per capita ownership was still insignificant compared with the United States. Television sets were on sale in addition to radios. Electrical appliances, rather crudely made, were available in increasing numbers. Because of the marked inequality in compensation, and the low average wage, these luxury products were purchased primarily by members of the political, military and economic bureaucracy, by those with higher scientific and technical training, by the more highly paid workers, and by some peasants from the more productive collective farms who managed to sell considerable produce from their individual plots while putting in the minimum number of work-days on the collective farm. Yet there were signs

[20] A subsequent look at prices and wages in May 1958 disclosed a slight lowering of prices of basic consumer goods, and a small increase in the prices of nonessential consumer goods. Some improvement could be observed in the availability of consumer goods since 1956. There had also been a slight increase in the minimum wage. A substantial amount of housing had been constructed in Moscow since 1956.

of a large increase in what might be called the Soviet upper middle class, so that a higher standard of living is gradually being made available to a widening number of citizens.

A sizable share of Soviet national income has gone into monumental and grandiose projects such as the Leningrad and Moscow subways, new railway passenger stations and airports, the new Moscow University, and the hundreds of costly, ornate and even luxurious sanatoria, particularly in the Black Sea area. These expensive projects never have to meet the test of consumer sovereignty in the market place. Neither do they depend upon public approval through voting on bond issues nor upon the appropriating of funds and levying of taxes through parliamentary processes. Nevertheless, a substantial part of the population does benefit from these monuments. The quality of their construction demonstrates, as does the quality of armament, that low standards are not characteristic of Soviet industrial production in areas of highest priority.

An improved system of old-age pensions was announced during the summer of 1956 providing for a minimum payment at retirement age of 300 rubles a month. This particular measure was of relatively greater benefit to the lower-income classes since the pension payments are proportionately higher for those with lower income and there are maximum limits upon payments. The virtual repudiation during 1957 of all previously floated compulsory bond issues later offset somewhat this improvement in old-age pensions. Probably the net effect was more painful to those who received large incomes than to small-income receivers.

A minimum wage of 300 rubles a month in cities and 270 rubles a month in nonurban areas was to go into effect in January 1957. A reduction in working hours in industry from 48 to 46 hours was also announced. A substantial reduction in taxes on incomes of less than 450 rubles a month was decreed by the Presidium of the Supreme Soviet in April 1957. This reduction amounted to 80 per cent for those receiving less than 380 rubles a month. There also began to be some references in the press to the desirability of reducing excessively large bonus and other "incentive payments" to industrial executives. The quality of consumer goods in 1956 was still very low although somewhat better than in 1939. The food situation was still unsatisfactory, with meat and dairy products in short supply. Nevertheless, measured in calories, the food supply did not appear to be so low as to limit labor productivity appreciably, except to the extent that agricultural raw materials were themselves a directly limiting factor in industrial production.

One reason why the food situation, and the meat situation in particular, was not as bad as might have been expected in view of Khrushchev's statement that the number of cattle was smaller in 1952 than in 1916 or in 1928 was that the population had not increased during this period to the extent indicated by official figures prior to the publication of the new statistical abstract. According to the new figures, about 10 per cent fewer people had to be provided for out of the available supply of meat than the writer had previously supposed. Moreover, the supply of pork had increased substantially since the time of Khrushchev's speech, and the supply of fish products had also improved.

Agricultural production showed evidence of continuing to be a weak element in the Soviet economy, and this was officially admitted to be true. The number of agricultural workers on collective and state farms in relation to output is by American standards unbelievably large. This is true in spite of substantial increases during recent years in the output of agricultural machinery. Great numbers of horses and even oxen were still in evidence on some collective farms, in addition to the large tractors furnished by the machine tractor stations and the small tractors which some of the collective farms themselves maintain. Despite the large numbers of laborers and the use of both agricultural machines and animal draft power, there is a shortage of both men and machines in terms of adequate tillage and harvesting of crops. This was reflected in the weedy condition of the fields newly planted to corn which the writer observed during the summer of 1956 and also in the efforts of the government to induce young men and women from the cities to take up agricultural work in the "new lands" in the arid regions of Central Asia.

The immediate future of Soviet agriculture depends upon the success or failure of Khrushchev's grandiose program for the expansion of production in these "new lands" in Central

Asia. The area of these lands, estimated by the government in 1957 at more than 85 million acres, is substantially greater than that of the total area planted to wheat in the United States. Whether or not grain can be successfully grown in a region of such low rainfall is uncertain. Soviet officials believe that they can produce wheat by large-scale methods of production even if the yield per acre is no more than seven or eight bushels instead of the ten bushels which is roughly the limit of feasible production in the United States. After a very bad harvest on the "new lands" in 1955, the 1956 harvest was excellent and grain production in the Soviet Union was the highest on record. The harvest in 1957 was much below that of 1956 although substantially above the bad year of 1953. The harvest for 1958 has been reported to be good.

If it should prove feasible to grow grain in this area while still providing an adequate supply of manpower, machinery and fertilizer to other areas, the long-standing agricultural problem would be well on the way to solution. A shift out of wheat production in the Ukraine, the Kuban and similar areas to general farming, including the growing of more corn and the feeding of livestock, is also planned. A tremendous effort to expand corn-growing is being made under the direct patronage of Khrushchev. It is uncertain whether the "new lands" can be continuously cultivated without producing something like the "dust bowls" in the wheat-growing area of the United States in 1934–36. If this should eventuate, the Soviet agricultural situation would become desperate.

Great strides have been made in the transformation of collective farms into state farms. More than a fourth of the total area in cultivation in 1957 was in state farms as compared with 10 per cent in 1953. The state farms produce at lower cost and employ fewer laborers per unit of output. State farms are the main reliance in the "new lands" program. A recent plan for adding substantially to the area of irrigated land available for cotton production could relieve the shortage of textile fibers materially. In addition, the announced intention of partially reversing the flow of the Pechora River from north to south in order to stabilize the flow of water in the Volga would materially improve the possibilities of irrigation. Such a grandiose project, matching in capital investment some of the more costly and ornate expenditures for public buildings, is not likely to pay off for some years to come even if it is successful.

The release of peasants on the collective farms from compulsory delivery of products grown on their small individual plots, announced in July 1957, apparently reflects confidence in the agricultural outlook, even though it was probably done for political reasons to coincide with the ouster of Malenkov, Molotov, Kaganovich and Shepilov.

Great as are the limitations upon testing the rates of improvement in the standard of living by personal observation, under the circumstances previously noted, they are even greater when an attempt is made to estimate the likelihood that Soviet targets of economic growth for the Sixth Five-Year Plan might be attained. It is more useful to compare the planned rates of economic growth with those attained in capitalistic countries and then consider whether there are particular characteristics which might enable the Soviet system greatly to surpass the rates of economic growth achieved by the quasi-capitalistic countries of the West. Personal observation plus one's judgment of the validity of current Soviet statistics must then determine the extent to which the differences in structure and functioning of the Soviet economic system can be expected to be more or less effective in making attainable the projected high rates of growth.

It has been pointed out that the projected rate of annual increase in national income for the Sixth Five-Year Plan was roughly 10.5 per cent, or about 60 per cent for the five-year period. This is somewhat lower than the 68 per cent claimed to have been achieved during the Fifth Five-Year Plan ending in 1955. On February 5, 1957, M. V. Pervukhin, then Chairman of the State Planning Commission, announced to the Supreme Soviet an additional and far more radical reduction in the planned rate of increase in production in 1957. The rate was cut from 10.5 per cent to 7.1 per cent. Though this revised program was later repudiated and a rate of increase of 10 per cent was claimed to have been achieved in 1957, it is reasonable to suppose that the 7.1 per cent rate was closer to reality. This conclusion is confirmed by the announcement of a 7.6 per cent planned rate of increase in industrial production for 1958.[21]

Apart from the increase in labor force, labor productivity in industry during the five-year period was originally planned to increase to 150 per cent of 1955. This would have been an increase over the 144 per cent claimed for the period 1950–55. It may be compared with an annual rate of increase in per capita labor productivity in the United States of some 2 per cent a year during the past eighty years. According to the Sixth Five-Year Plan, the increase in labor productivity was to account for more than 80 per cent of the increase in industrial production as compared with 68 per cent during the Fifth Five-Year Plan.

If one were to discount the originally planned rate of increase in national income for the Sixth Five-Year Plan by the amount of probable exaggeration in the claimed rate of increase in Soviet real national income from either 1913 or 1928 to date, the rate would have to be cut by more than half. There is reason to believe, however, that the greatest overestimates in claimed rates of economic growth were in the earlier periods and that the upward bias is being reduced in current statistics. Whether this improvement in statistical reporting would survive any pressure in the future to show results more favorable than the actual ones is doubtful.

The rate of some 10.5 per cent of annual growth originally planned for the Sixth Five-Year Plan was twice as high as that attained by any important capitalistic country over any long period.[22] The Soviet claimed rate is three times as high as the average annual rate of increase in national income in the United States during the past eighty years. There are,

[21] However, as indicated in note 17, press dispatches from Moscow in late October 1958 refer to a decision by Khrushchev in favor of more grandiose future rates of economic growth for the new Seven-Year Plan, the final form of which is to be approved by the 21st Party Congress in January 1959.

[22] However, rates of increase as high as 10 per cent a year have been reached for several years in some Western countries, for example in France during 1953–56. In the United States the rate of increase for one year has been as high as 15 per cent, but this has happened only when there was a sharp recovery from an abnormally low level.

indeed, some reasons why Soviet rates of economic growth might be expected to be higher than those of capitalistic countries. A collectivistic, authoritatively directed economy does not have to fear that its average economic growth will be reduced by recurrent economic depressions, and Soviet economic growth has not been limited in this way. When all the important elements of an economy are centrally directed, an economic depression of the type experienced by capitalistic countries in the thirties is out of the question. The evidence indicates in addition, however, that the Soviet economy is not even characterized by recurrent brief interruptions in the rate of growth of industrial production like those in the United States in 1938, 1949, 1954 and 1957. The management of Soviet industry apparently does not have to reduce production in order to prevent excess inventories due to temporary slackening in demand. This is partly because there is such a short supply of virtually all types of commodities that almost everything which can be produced is taken off the market without much question of price or quality.

It may be that if production per capita were as high in the Soviet Union as in the United States, this situation would change. However, in the nature of the Soviet economic system, industrial managers do not have to compete with each other in satisfying the consumer's needs, preferences or whims. Moreover, neither research effort nor advertising and promotion cost are incurred in developing new products or new styles in products simply in order to entice additional dollars from consumers. There is some evidence that if excess inventories in certain industries pile up temporarily, current production is not reduced, although further investment and employment of manpower may be reduced during the next planned period until increased demand restores equilibrium in inventories.

There is still another reason why it is difficult to compare given percentage increases in quantities produced under the Soviet system with those of the current capitalistic system. A given percentage increase in production under the Soviet system inherently possesses less consumer-satisfying qualities than a similar increase under the capitalistic system where "consumer sovereignty" is far more the rule. Furthermore, as pointed out in the case of Polish statistics, Soviet statistics probably contain an element which embodies badly planned investment that would usually be reduced by the operation of the price mechanism in a capitalistic economy. However, the crude quantitative advantage in terms of annual economic growth in not having to adjust production and inventories closely to consumer preferences is considerable.

Associated with the above is the circumstance that there is no tendency under the Soviet system for the volume of saving to be limited by the volume of investment. Indeed, saving has been largely compulsory, and the volume of investment is sharply limited by the amount of saving which the Soviet government feels it can require of the population. This means, on the one hand, that the percentage of national income saved can be much higher than in a democratic, capitalistic economy and, on the other, that there is never any problem of national income being limited through failure of investment to take place because of unfavorable managerial expectations. The contrary is true, in fact, and the Soviet planning authorities have to try continually to resist pressures from industrial management which would cause overinvestment if acceded to.[23]

The high rate of investment made possible in an authoritarian regime which can restrict the supply of consumer goods and withhold consumer purchasing power, while devoting correspondingly large proportions of national income to the construction of capital equipment, means that as long as this continues a relatively larger stream of goods can be expected in the future if the investment is properly planned and executed. Since the production of consumer services is so little developed in the Soviet Union, relatively little has to be devoted out of national saving to provide necessary capital equipment for the service industries. Consequently, a higher national income is possible in the future as the ratio of capital equipment to labor rises.

Furthermore, a substantially higher proportion of saving in the Soviet Union goes into capital goods used in increasing further production rather than into "saving" in the form of

[23] In an interview with the writer in July 1956, a Deputy Chairman of the State Planning Commission spoke with obvious feeling of the pressures of this nature.

durable consumer goods such as housing and automobiles as in the United States. This is accentuated by the concurrent ability of an authoritarian regime to insure that investment in industries producing capital equipment is relatively greater than investment in industries producing either durable or nondurable consumer goods. For these reasons a given "unit" of saving in the Soviet Union results in a larger construction of capital goods used for further production than in the United States.[24]

This pushes increases in national income further into the future but magnifies future rates of growth, provided, of course, the investment is efficiently planned and administered. There are some indications that the length of time required to construct plant and equipment is probably substantially longer than in capitalistic countries, in addition to evidence of inefficient planning of such investment. This may substantially limit the advantages of a high rate of capital saving and investment.

A collectivist authoritarian economic system also has an advantage in carrying out new industrial construction in that the managers of expanding enterprises do not need to fear that competitors might simultaneously build new plants with resulting excess capacity in a particular industry. Paradoxically, this can mean that the Soviet economic system may push new plant construction more continuously up to the limits of economic resources than a corporate "free enterprise" capitalistic economy would do. Whether the decentralization of control of the economy attempted in 1957 will nullify any advantage which a centralized economy might have in this respect is as yet uncertain.

An obvious advantage purely in terms of productivity is the complete absence of legal strikes. Unauthorized strikes almost never happen. There is no collective bargaining in Soviet industry. Consequently, there is no organized pressure for raising wages or changing work norms. Increases in real wages depend primarily upon lowering the prices of consumer goods

[24] For a statistical analysis of Soviet capital formation in comparison with that of the United States, see "Capital Formation and Allocation" by Norman M. Kaplan, in *Soviet Economic Growth*, pp. 37–100.

rather than upon increasing wage rates. In spite of this, there has been some tendency for wage rates to creep upward during the complicated process of setting piece rates, and this tendency has had to be sharply rebuffed by the planning authorities.

The advantage which any less developed economy has in importing the techniques of more advanced countries has influenced the rate of growth of Soviet industry favorably in the past. This advantage, however, has largely been exploited and is unlikely to affect future rates of growth greatly. But the end of the "catching up" period during which the Soviet rate of economic growth may have been abnormally raised by importation of advanced techniques from abroad is not likely to produce a decline in the future rate of growth. On the contrary, the evidence indicates that the levels of scientific research and industrial technique in the Soviet Union are advancing more rapidly in relation to those of the industrialized Western countries than in the past. Indeed, Soviet progress as evidenced by space satellites and ballistic missiles raises the grave possibility that the Western level may even be surpassed in the future. A survey of the Soviet educational system supports this view.

The decade and a half following the Revolution represented almost a total loss to the Soviet educational system. Formal education, in the Western European sense, was largely junked. In the lower grades, "progressive" education and the "project method" took over. Discipline was abandoned, and teachers were badgered and treated with little respect. Communist indoctrination was considered more important than rigorous instruction. The deterioration of scientific and engineering education in institutions of higher learning during this post revolutionary period was never so great as in the rest of the educational system. By the middle thirties, however, students were coming up for entrance into the scientific and engineering schools with totally inadequate preparation, particularly in mathematics. Stalin, disgusted and enraged, ordered a drastic reorganization of the curriculum and methods of instruction. As a result, the educational system swung sharply away from near-anarchy and laxness towards authority, disciplined behavior, and the restoration of a formal educational curriculum and methods of instruction largely on the model of Western Europe.

A far greater amount of time is now devoted to mathematics and the physical sciences in the lower levels of the Soviet educational system than in the United States, and much less time to the humanities and social sciences. The study of a foreign language is required in the secondary schools. There are no elective courses in these schools. A much larger proportion of students at the higher levels specialize in physical sciences and in engineering than in the United States.

The Soviet educational system demands of the student more hours per day and more days per year than is true in the United States. The system of higher education is not a system of mass education; it is more exclusive than in the United States. Only one-third to one-half as many of the students of college age are in educational institutions in Soviet Russia.[25] Lack of finances is not a major factor in limiting the number of students, since free tuition is provided for those who pass the entrance examination and stipends are given in addition to those with superior qualifications. (There have been reports, however, that the children of persons prominent in the bureaucracy sometimes receive favored treatment.) The less qualified are eliminated by a much more rigid system than in the United States. An important result of this exclusion of the less qualified is the conservation of teaching and research personnel and of physical facilities.

The repression and regimentation of thought which characterizes Soviet society and which has been so manifest in literature, art, music, the social sciences and biology has not been exercised on a decisive scale in research in physics, chemistry and engineering. Consequently, in these fields the curtailment of liberty has apparently not served as yet as a net limiting factor on the rate of Soviet economic growth. As long as Soviet physicists, chemists and engineers are not interfered with in their own work, and as long as they are generously provided with laboratory facilities and high living standards,

[25] Within the past two years an effort has been made to broaden opportunities for higher education by facilitating the entrance of industrial workers into universities and technical schools.

the absence of civil liberties and representative government does not seem a major deterrent to productive effort.

The whole educational setup is thus consistent with the economic and political system of the Soviet Union. It is authoritative. It emphasizes the training of an elite rather than the masses. It emphasizes the objective rather than the subjective aspects of culture. It tends to be routinized and to provide relatively little scope for imagination and for discussion and argument. The incentives for success are high and the penalty for failure is to be left behind in the prospect for social advancement. The opportunities for those who do not succeed in reaching the upper levels of the educational system are relatively fewer than in a society where opportunities for small business exist. Whatever the effects of such an educational system upon the general culture of a society and upon the development of the good life for free men, the immediate effect upon the rate of Soviet economic growth is likely to be positive.

The primary purpose of the Labor Reserve System for vocational and on-the-job training of boys and girls is the large-scale mobilization of young people for industrial work. While its compulsory features are repugnant, the system is effective in salvaging for productive work a large portion of those boys and girls who are unwilling to do, or intellectually incapable of doing, satisfactory work in the secondary schools. There is no sharp separation between vocational training and on-the-job training in the system. The costs of the program are largely covered by the earnings of the trainees in industry. The potentialities of such a system for reducing the problem of the "Blackboard Jungle" in secondary schools while integrating these young people into industrial society should not be underestimated.[26]

[26] For an account of the organization of the Soviet educational system, see U.S. Department of Health, Education and Welfare, Office of Education, *Education in the U.S.S.R.*, 1957. See also Alexander G. Korol, *Soviet Education for Science and Technology*, Technology Press, Cambridge, 1957. For an interesting comparison from the Soviet point of view of the larger role of mathematicians and physicists in research institutes and in the training of scientific personnel, see D. Panov, "Science and Socialism," *Kommunist*, No. 1, pp. 11–25 (condensed text in *Current Digest of the Soviet Press*, April 2, 1958).

It is true that these advantages of the Soviet economic system may be offset or more than offset by some of the well-known advantages of an economic system such as that of the United States. The competitive spur which functions even under corporate capitalism is, of course, missing in the Soviet economy and the resource allocation function of the price system is almost entirely absent as well. The cumbersomeness of a centrally planned and directed economy is evidenced by the efforts to reduce this through repeated reorganizations of the Soviet economy.[27] The attempts to create incentives for the Soviet industrial bureaucracy in lieu of the profit motivation of capitalism have indeed put a high premium on the fulfillment of the yearly plan. A premium as high as the standard 30 per cent bonus to management for plan fulfillment operates, however, as a penalty against risk-taking through experimentation with new methods and processes which may pay off only in later years.[28] The general advantages in productive efficiency of both labor and management working in a system of personal freedom might be expected of themselves to offset some or all of the economic advantages of a directed economy and an authoritarian society.

It has been pointed out that the Soviet economic system has the advantage in terms of continuity of production and construction of new capital facilities and in the ratio of savings-investment to national income, although apparently not in the rate at which construction takes place or in the efficiency of choice among investment alternatives. This clearly leaves the advantage in terms of improvement in quality and, on balance, in terms of the development of new products, new methods

---

[27] A deputy chairman of the State Planning Commission described to the writer in July 1956 a reorganization of the Commission which had just taken place. Within a few months Khrushchev announced still another reorganization. Still later, in early 1957, Khrushchev's scheme for an even more grandiose reorganization of planning and of industrial organizations was announced.

[28] It also operates as an incentive to formal fulfillment of the plan, regardless of other results. Thus in a plant producing nails, if the goal is stated in value units, more small nails are produced, if in physical units, such as pounds, more large nails. A plant producing machines may fulfill its quota at the expense of spare parts. Minute regulations are required to prevent this sort of thing.

and new processes with the quasi-capitalistic economies of the West.

In terms of economic growth, measured quantitatively, i' would be reasonable to expect a Soviet rate of growth around that attained in capitalistic countries during the most favorable periods of uninterrupted production. Such an annual rate o' increase might be put at some 6 per cent, or not much more than half that originally projected in the Sixth Five-Year Plan

The reason alleged for the drastic reduction in the planned rate of increase in national income announced by Pervukhir in February 1957 was the excessive capital investmen' planned, which would have added to production only afte' many years. There can be no doubt that the total amount o' capital investment which had been planned was excessive and that capital investment in producer goods industries was very high in comparison with capital investment in consumer good industries. There were a number of references in the press also to the slowness of capital construction in many cases, to the shipping of machinery to places where it was not needed, and to general inefficiency in the capital construction program.[2]

The correction of an excessive capital investment progran could have come about, however, primarily by reducing the output of producer goods and increasing the output of consumer goods. The rate of increase in production might thereby have been reduced somewhat, but hardly by one-third as wa

---

[29] In an interview with the author in Moscow in July 1956, one o' the deputy chairmen of the State Planning Commission referred with noticeable feeling to the practice by each of the various economic ministries and organs of pressing for much larger capital invest ments than the resources of the national economy warranted. In an article by I. A. Kulev, "O Dallneishem Sovershenstvovanii Planiro vania i Rukovodstva Narodnym Khoziaistvom," Seriia III, No. 11 Izdatelstvo-Znanie, Moscow, 1957, reference is made to total re quests for 70 billion rubles more capital investment for the year 195' than the 170 billion rubles programmed by the state planning com mittee. Kulev points out how the inability to provide these addi tional sums necessarily limits the rate of economic growth. He point out also how programs of capital investment greater than can be sus tained by potential labor and raw material resources have length ened the time required for capital construction because of shortage in numerous cases. Such delays in the completion of industrial facili ties limit the rate of growth in production even more.

actually announced. Furthermore, the announced reduction did not provide for an increase in the planned rate of production of consumer goods. Instead, the rates of increase for both producer and consumer goods were reduced. It would have been highly embarrassing politically to have announced a cutback in producer goods and an increase in consumer goods, for this was the very issue which Khrushchev had claimed as the reason for his ouster of Malenkov. Nevertheless, the fact that the rates of increase in both consumer and producer goods were reduced suggests that one reason for the change probably was an effort to bring statistics closer to reality. This would confirm the conclusion that rates of 11 to 12 per cent which had been claimed for recent years, though much below previously claimed rates, were still unreal.[30] In part, at least, this reflected an overvaluation, in terms of their discounted future product, of the capital goods embodying the portion of national income invested in capital facilities.

The extremely radical reorganization and decentralization of industry announced by Khrushchev during the first half of 1957, by which the Union and Republican economic ministries were abolished for most industries and over one hundred regional economic councils substituted for them, reflected great dissatisfaction with the cumbersome bureaucracy which had developed. In the process of arguing for the reorganization, Khrushchev and his supporters cited many instances of failure of the planned economy to function as had been intended. These included freight "crosshauls" by which plants in the Caucasus, for example, ordered goods from suppliers in Siberia while identical goods were being shipped from the Caucasus to Siberia. This kind of "crosshaul" was one of the oldest examples of the inefficiencies charged against competitive capitalism which a planned economy would supposedly eliminate. Instances were also cited of the failure of adjoining plants under different managers to cooperate. In one instance a plant manager spent thousands of rubles constructing a cement wall to separate his plant from another in order to pre-

---

[30] If this is so, Soviet statistics are likely to show a "jog" in the production curve for the year 1957, since it is unlikely on the basis of experience that past statistics will be corrected so as to be consistent with current and future statistics.

serve his autonomous authority. These examples were intended to show that decentralization of the control and direction of industry was a crying need.

Probably no such radical plan of reorganization would have been instituted if conditions had not become almost intolerable. These confessions of inefficiency are an interesting commentary on the doctrine that a centrally planned and directed economy is superior to the "planless chaos" of private capitalism. The hundreds of thousands of bureaucrats in Moscow and the other capital cities of the republic could, of course, be expected to oppose the reorganization. Many of them are having to undergo retraining in the effort to change them from "bureaucrats" to "workers in production." Apparently their dissatisfaction was a factor in the great split in the collective leadership in July 1957 which ended in the ousting of Malenkov, Molotov, Kaganovich and Shepilov and the demotion of Saburov and Pervukhin, the two preceding heads of the State Planning Commission. Momentarily at least the "bureaucratic faction" lost out.

It is possible that efficiency will indeed be promoted by this decentralization of the control of the economy. At present, however, it is uncertain what the relation will be between these regional councils and the industries under their control, on the one hand, and between the local economic councils and the central planning apparatus in Moscow on the other. The uncertainty prevailing while such a large part of the economic bureaucracy of the capital cities is being transferred to posts with the regional councils is also bound to be great. How the economic system can function without either centralized control or market price as a directing mechanism seems to have been inadequately considered. The immediate effects upon productivity are not likely to be favorable.

It is only fair to say that the writer's estimate of an annual economic growth rate of 6 per cent instead of the 10.5 per cent originally planned probably represents a greater discount of Soviet potentialities than would be acceptable to many specialists in the field.[31] By coincidence, it is fairly close to the

---

[31] Such a rate would, however, not be far from the 6 to 7 per cent estimated by Grossman. As noted above, Grossman derives his estimate from a reanalysis of Soviet statistics and considers this esti-

revised 7.1 per cent rate set for 1957 when the planned rates of increase in industrial production were radically reduced and to the 7.6 per cent rate announced for 1958. This rate would, however, be higher than the writer would have considered as probable before revisiting the Soviet Union in 1956 and 1958. The personal subjectivity of any estimate of the rate of economic growth in the Soviet economy, based upon a combination of personal observation and statistical analysis, is, of course, undeniable.

In summary, the Soviet economy in 1956 certainly did not appear to be one in which the rate of increase had been proceeding at twice that of capitalistic countries during periods of full employment. It did appear to have a growth rate which might conceivably be as great as that in capitalistic countries under conditions of full employment when measures to control inflation do not have to be taken.

The level of production of the Soviet economy at the present time, as distinct from its rate of growth, might be estimated at some 40 to 45 per cent of that of the United States.[32] The average standard of living would, on the other hand, probably be only one-fifth that of the United States, to the limited extent that valid quantitative comparison of the standards of living of the two countries can be made.[33] If considered, how-

---

mate as the probable real rate of growth during "normal" periods of the past and as a rate which might be attained during the next decade or so.

[32] However, the comparison with Soviet production would be much more unfavorable to the United States if made, say, in mid-1958 when industrial production had fallen sharply owing to the recession which began in 1957.

[33] This personal estimate is generally consistent with the excellent analysis of the subject prepared for the subcommittee on Foreign Economic Policy of the Joint Economic Committee by the Legislative Reference Service of the Library of Congress, *Soviet Economic Growth: A Comparison with the United States*, 1957.

A. Arzumanyan, Corresponding Member of the U.S.S.R. Academy of Sciences, estimates in *Pravda*, July 9, 1958, that total industrial output of the Soviet Union was at that time approximately half that of the United States, while per capita industrial output in the United States was two and one half times greater. He estimates per capita agricultural output of the United States to be approximately double that of the Soviet Union. *Current Digest of the Soviet Press*, August 13, 1958.

ever, as an estimate of Soviet industrial war-making potential, this would be a serious understatement since the proportion of Soviet income capable of being embodied in armament production is relatively so much larger. In terms of heavy industry in general, Soviet industrial production is probably around 45 per cent of that of the United States. A rate of economic growth of some 6 per cent is not higher than that physically attainable by the economic systems of the United States and Western Europe for short periods, at least.[34] It is almost double the rate at which national income in the United States seems to increase so long as it is recurrently necessary to put brakes on business expansion to prevent inflation.

The comparative rates of economic growth will, of course, be affected by the percentage of the national income which is devoted to armament in the two countries. However, these proportions are not independent variables, since the rate of expenditures of one country influences that of the other. If, in the future, the Soviet populace should begin to exercise control over the proportion of national income devoted to consumption as compared to investment, this might reduce future rates of Soviet economic growth. While the rulers of Soviet Russia, of course, take into account both the actual and potential resistance of the populace to capital saving reflected in reduced consumption at various levels, there is as yet no parliamentary

[34] For the years 1953, 1954 and 1955, for example, the gross national products of the Western European member countries of the Organization for European Economic Cooperation increased at a rate of between 5 and 6 per cent. The rate of increase for 1956, however, was only about 4 per cent. Organization for European Economic Cooperation, *Europe Today and in 1960*, Paris, 1957, Vol. I, "Europe Today," p. 17.

After a sharp increase in the rate of economic growth in the United States during some of the postwar years, the rate of increase for 1956 and 1957 seems to have fallen to hardly enough to provide for the population increase of some 1.7 per cent. Industrial production was at the same level at the end of 1957 as at the end of 1955, although a higher level had been reached in between these dates. The other components of gross national product did not show the same failure to increase as did industrial production, but even so the increase during the last two years has been no more than enough to keep per capita income unchanged. For a further analysis of rates of economic growth in the United States, see p. 283, and for Western Europe, p. 322.

or market mechanism by which the people can express this resistance directly. Consequently, Soviet rates of economic growth are not likely to be limited by this factor in the foreseeable future.

It is not out of the question that in our Western modified systems of capitalism new techniques of monetary and credit control may be developed in the future which will permit the control of inflation without substantially limiting the physical productivity of the economy. In this case there would be little reason to expect the rate of Soviet economic growth to be greater than that of modern capitalistic countries after allowance for the much higher production of services in proportion to goods in Western countries as compared with the Soviet Union.[35] However, the recurrence of economic recession in the United States in 1957 carrying over into 1958 demonstrates that the control of inflation and the prevention of depression are still unsolved problems in capitalistic countries.

In the meantime a Soviet rate of economic growth almost twice the past rate in the United States, if the writer's crude estimates were assumed to represent reality, would represent a factor of great force in the present world conflict. This is particularly true with respect to the underdeveloped countries of the world, which are bound to be impressed by the Soviet example. If the interruption of economic growth which developed into an economic recession in the United States in late 1957 had continued for several years, the contrast with the Soviet rate of growth would have indeed become dramatic. Whether the resumption of economic growth following the end of the recession in 1958 can be maintained at a satisfactory

[35] Although the diminution in the rate of growth in the last two years is certainly temporary, the rate of increase in the production of physical quantities of goods in Western countries is damped down by the shift of consumers' preferences toward services. Productivity increases are likely to be smaller in services than goods. Indeed, it is conceptually difficult to measure increases in the value of the output of personal services at all.

In general, statistics of production in capitalistic countries make no allowances for improvement in the quality of goods and services, while there is some evidence that Soviet statistics do. On the other hand, much that is included as services and added into Western statistics of national income, such as the services of government, is not so treated by Soviet statisticians.

rate without an unacceptable degree of inflation will be a major factor in world-wide appraisal of the comparative success of the Soviet and the modern capitalistic economic systems.

CHAPTER 6

THE NAZI TOTALITARIAN SYSTEM

There was never any dispute about the totalitarian nature of the Fascist and Nazi economic and political systems. Their critics and enemies charged them with totalitarianism, while Fascists and Nazis gloried in the designation. The Soviet regime, by contrast, has repudiated the charge of totalitarianism and, largely through the manipulation of Marxist dogma, continues to deny the charge against all the evidence. Yet in estimating the prospect for the survival of the kind of personal liberty which modern capitalism makes possible, the Soviet type of totalitarianism offers a living alternative to capitalism while Italian fascism and Nazism are dead. A brief analysis of these defunct systems seems justified, however, since some of the basic characteristics of totalitarianism may be observed, somewhat as a student of anatomy examines cadavers in the medical laboratory.

There is a clear distinction between capitalistic, democratic and parliamentary systems on the one hand and totalitarian systems on the other. In the one type of system the individual as such is considered of importance and as possessed of some inherent rights vis-à-vis the state, while this is not true in the other. In the one type of system there is reasonably effective machinery for the control of the state power by the population, while in the other type the machinery works almost wholly in reverse. There is generally a separation between the operation of the economic system and the exercise of the political power of the state in the capitalistic type, while in the other no form of human activity is immune from the exercise of state power. In the one type the principle of constitutionality and of a government of laws and not of men is recognized, while there is no such recognition by the totalitarian state. The capitalistic, democratic and parliamentary type has not assumed the exclusive function of massive indoctrination of the population in its behalf, while this has been one of the most fundamental of the functions exercised by the totalitarian state. It is always associated in the totalitarian state with the one-party monopoly under the dictator, from which all power-wielding members of the bureaucratic hierarchy are drawn. Finally, the totalitarian state, except for interludes in which the struggle for power is temporarily undecided, is always headed by a dictator who has no legal limits upon his power.

It will be seen that the Nazi, Fascist and Soviet states meet all these tests of totalitarianism. It might well be asked, however, whether totalitarian states should not be subdivided into Soviet and Fascist types. They can, indeed, be so subdivided, but the differences between them are not nearly so sharp as those between the capitalistic, democratic, parliamentary type and the totalitarian type.

The Soviet totalitarian state was claimed by its founders to have been based upon Marxist doctrine, and this claim is still maintained by the present ruling bureaucracy. As has been pointed out in previous chapters, however, the circumstances under which the Soviet state was created were not consistent with Marxist doctrine, and the economic and political system which developed was basically different from the kind of society which Marx envisaged as the successor to capitalism.

In spite of these departures from Marxism, the claim to be Marxist sets the Soviet type of economic and social system somewhat apart from the Nazi, Fascist and other non-Marxian systems. This claim means that when a system of the Soviet type is set up it will be accompanied by the violent despoilment of private property and the killing of a substantial portion of the capitalist class. By contrast, although the Nazi, Fascist or similar types of totalitarian state may be set up over the opposition of a majority of capitalists, capitalists as such are not liquidated. Neither is their property usually confiscated, although its ultimate control passes into the hands of the state bureaucracy.[1]

Although there is eventually re-created in the Soviet type of totalitarian state a bureaucracy with some of the characteristics and many of the perquisites of the liquidated capitalists, relatively few of the former capitalists will have positions of importance in it. In the Nazi or Fascist type of totalitarian society, on the other hand, the greater part of the top economic bureaucracy will normally consist of former capitalists or influential members of the capitalistic bureaucracy. Thus there can be no doubt that if capitalists in general were confronted by the choice between the Soviet and the Nazi or Fascist type of totalitarian system, it would be in their interests to choose the Nazi or Fascist system.

Nevertheless, the ruling bureaucracy of the Nazi economic and political system came to be fundamentally different from that of capitalism under the Weimar Republic. It was not merely that thousands of Nazi Party leaders now took over positions in the government, in the army and to a lesser extent in the economy. These Nazi members of the bureaucracy represented a "New Class" with a basically different psychology and set of values from those of the former bureaucracy. Although the older members of the bureaucracy inherited from the pre-Nazi era outnumbered the new, the old bureaucracy itself increasingly took on Nazi characteristics. Different criteria now determined advancement in the political, military and even in the economic hierarchy. It is impossible to say how far this process would have gone had the Nazi regime not been destroyed. The final arbiter in setting goals and in distributing the benefits which the economic system produced for the "New Class" in Germany was Hitler, just as it was

[1] The modern corporate form of capitalism enormously facilitates the take-over of the economic system by a totalitarian regime either by outright confiscation, as in the Soviet type, or by control over the boards of directors of corporations, as in the Nazi type. The modern corporate form also facilitates the process of nationalization of industry by peaceful, parliamentary means as in Britain.

Stalin in Soviet Russia. Nevertheless, as in the Soviet system, the Nazi state was to be directed and managed by the "New Class" in their own interests and in the furtherance of their own goals.

There is indeed greater likelihood that under the Soviet type of system more members of the working class will become part of the administrative bureaucracy immediately after the destruction of capitalism than under the Nazi or Fascist type. Since this proportion of the working class will in any case be small, it is not clear how much difference it might make to the majority of workers. After the revolutionary period has passed and a new generation has grown up, the process of selection of the "New Class" and the type of person selected are not likely to differ greatly as between the Soviet and the Nazi and Fascist states.

The Marxist origins of Soviet totalitarianism account for some other differences as well. Weirdly enough, the Marxist doctrine that under Communism there would be no state at all proved useful as a means of escape from the necessity for justifying the repressive nature of the all-powerful Soviet state, on the grounds of the state's allegedly temporary character. Similarly, the phrase "dictatorship of the proletariat" provided excellent cover for the development of personal dictatorship.

At one time it could have been said that the Soviet type of totalitarian state was much less militaristic and nationalistic than the Nazi or Fascist types. The sharpness of this distinction obviously became blurred as the Soviet military machine was developed and as the glorification of Russian nationalism was resumed. Even so, the glorification of war and of the military tradition remained a more striking characteristic of Nazism and Fascism than of the Soviet system. The anti-Semitic character of Nazism sets it apart even though some anti-Semitism has developed under the Soviet system too.

While it is possible to differentiate between the Nazi and Fascist systems on the one hand and the Soviet system on the other, there is considerable heterogeneity about the non-Soviet totalitarian states. The Nazi system was far more anti-Semitic than the Fascist system in Italy, or than Franco's regime in Spain or Peron's regime in Argentina. The Nazi regime was far more racist, warlike, fanatical and brutal than the others.

The ideology and psychology of the Party leaders and masses were anti-intellectual, anti-urban and anti-bourgeois, shot through with nostalgia for a more primitive, rural and warlike kind of society. Control over the economy was much greater.

The Peronista regime in Argentina was more directly based upon the working class than the other regimes. It never developed a body of doctrine like Marxism-Leninism-Stalinism or a fanatical "thinking with the blood" creed like the Nazis. Partly as a consequence of this, the Peronista regime never possessed a fully developed propaganda line or an effective mechanism for the integrated direction of literature, drama, newspapers and radio.

The Franco regime has been more closely connected with the historic, conservative institutions of Spain, such as the Church and the army, than have the other regimes. Unlike the others, it came to power only after a bitter civil war.

There were many other heterogeneous aspects of the various regimes. The sharpest distinctions between the Nazi state and the others were due largely to the fact that it came to power in a large, highly industrialized country, with important natural resources, a well-educated population and an advanced technology. Consequently, the defunct Nazi state is much more significant as a case history of a totalitarian economic and political system than any of the others. In spite, then, of the substantial differences which separated the Nazi system from Italian fascism and from other totalitarian states in the "Fascist" subdivision, it is worth analyzing the forces which gave rise to National Socialism and determined its operation until the nightmare regime was finally brought to ruin.

The most widely believed stereotype concerning the origin and nature of the Nazi totalitarian system is that it was simply the creation of the reactionary German industrialists and Junker landlords. According to this stereotype, Hitler was the demagogic figurehead chosen by the industrialists to enable them to maintain and extend the cartels which had become the characteristic form of business organization in the final monopoly stage of German capitalism. The industrialists and reactionary aristocracy were driven to place this demagogue in power, the stereotype continues, because they felt themselves threatened by an imminent Communist revolution. After Hitler had been placed in power, the same economic system continued to operate; only the political system was drastically altered. This was and is the official Communist doctrine of the origin and nature of the Nazi political and economic system.

This explanation has been far more widely accepted than simply by Communists. It is still largely regarded as historical truth even among industrialists in the United States and in the rest of the world. Yet in essence it is false and was bound to be false. The inevitable hostility between an aristocracy and a tyrant was recognized in the days of classical Greece and Rome. This hostility and distaste was characteristic of the established upper classes in Germany towards Hitler. Tocqueville in his *The Old Regime and the French Revolution* noted that the existence of a powerful aristocracy is an almost insuperable barrier to the attainment of power by a dictator. The modern dictator knows that he must not allow either a powerful aristocracy or a powerful plutocracy to exist. When a new totalitarian system is set up, the modern dictator molds his own "New Class," from the apex of which he rules.

Unfortunately the historical facts are much more complex than the false stereotype. It is no wonder, therefore, that the stereotype has survived while the complicated patterns of actual forces and events are either forgotten or are remembered only as they can be fitted into it. It is certainly true that the severe economic depression which held Germany as well as the greater part of the capitalist world in its grip from 1929 onward was the all-important factor which brought National Socialism to power in January 1933. The evidence is clear that the ultranationalistic, xenophobic, anti-Semitic characteristics of National Socialism never had sufficient voter appeal in the absence of the economic depression to win for the Nazis anything like the plurality of seats in the Reichstag which they were able to obtain in July 1932, some months before Hitler became Chancellor. The record shows that popular support for the Nazis waxed and waned with changes in the economic climate.

If there had been no Hitler and no National Socialist movement, the Communist party in Germany, in spite of the unbelievable ineptitude of its political strategy and tactics, might just possibly have constituted a serious threat to German capitalism during a depression of such length and severity as that which gripped the country. In this limited sense, Hitler might be said to have "saved Germany from communism"— and to have provided an alternative route to destruction. Yet during the months preceding Hitler's take-over almost no one in Germany considered a Communist revolution a serious possibility.[2]

German industrialists at this time were particularly contemptuous of the idea of a Communist revolution, or of any serious prospects of trouble from the Communists. The complacency of German conservatives with respect to any "Communist danger" largely reflected the experience of the immediate postwar period in 1918–19 when the embryonic Reichswehr formed by a handful of regular army officers had, upon the invitation of the Social Democrats who were in power at the time, put down with such ease the attempted Communist revolt of those days. The resulting bitterness that persisted between the Communists and the nominally Marxist Social Democrats, who controlled the majority of the trade union membership, was one of the reasons for this complacency towards any "Communist danger."[3] The bankruptcy of Communist leadership in Germany, which had produced nothing but hopeless strikes and abortive revolts, accentuated the weakness of the Communist Party and increased the contempt in which it was held by substantially all conservatives.

By contrast, it was the Nazis whom the majority of German industrialists considered a potential threat to the established order at a time when there were some seven to eight million unemployed due to the economic depression.[4] In the election

---

[2] For a detailed analysis of the situation in Germany during the months before, during and after Hitler's advent to power and the economic and social forces responsible for the events of this period, see the writer's *Germany Enters the Third Reich*, Macmillan, New York, 1933. See also John Wheeler-Bennett, *Wooden Titan*, Morrow, New York, 1936.

[3] Their hatred for the Social Democrats even led the Communists at times to collaborate with the Nazis, as in the case of the transport strike in Berlin in the fall of 1932.

[4] Conservatives often insisted to the writer that National Socialism, if allowed complete power, would be in essence national com-

of July 31, 1932, the Nazis succeeded in securing 230 seats in the Reichstag out of a total of 608, almost twice as many as those of any other party. The conservative government of von Papen had been installed by von Hindenburg in late May 1932 under the emergency powers conferred on the President by virtue of Article 48 of the Weimar Constitution. It had for its primary purpose the use of the military power of the Reichswehr to prevent a Nazi *coup d'état.*[5] This same purpose was carried out by von Papen's successor as Chancellor, von Schleicher, until he lost the support of von Hindenburg and was compelled to resign, to be followed in the Chancellorship by Hitler.

It is perhaps inexact to say that German conservatives feared Hitler. Certainly whatever fear they had was mingled with contempt. Almost none of them favored the ideology and proposed program of Hitler, and hardly any believed that he could come to power under circumstances that would permit him to carry out his proclaimed policies. Most industrialists were convinced that he could and should be prevented from coming to power at all, and their confidence was reinforced by the momentary success of the von Papen and von Schleicher governments in preventing his accession even after the great

---

munism. At an earlier date a small fragment of the Nazis had split off under the leadership of Otto Strasser. This tiny independent group published a newspaper called *The Black Front* and advocated national communism outright. *Germany Enters the Third Reich,* p. 56. This attitude of German industrialists toward Hitler just before he came to power was common both to those industrialists who feared National Socialism and to those who held it in contempt.

[5] Article 48 of the Constitution of the former German Republic provided that if public safety and order were menaced in the Reich the President might take the necessary measures to restore them. President Ebert had established the precedent of using the authority of Article 48 in order to avoid asking for legislation from the Reichstag. Brüning had carried on his government by favor of von Hindenburg's frequent exercise of this power. Every kind of decree imaginable was put in force by virtue of its authority. The von Schleicher cabinet at a later time even proposed to compel the admixture of butter in oleomargarine by a decree under the authority of Article 48! Von Papen in the heyday of his power intended to amend the Constitution itself under cover of this famous Article 48. *Germany Enters the Third Reich,* p. 57.

increase in popular votes and in Reichstag seats won by the Nazis in the July 1932 election.

Still other conservatives were so confident of themselves that they favored bringing Hitler into the government under circumstances such that they would be insured against violent action or change and that his popular support could be utilized to keep a conservative government in power. As part of the effort to influence and control him, Hitler received substantial financial support from some of the leaders of heavy industry. German industrialists made large financial contributions to a number of different parties simultaneously, however.

It was the Junkers of the German Nationalist Party and a small group of industrialists who induced President von Hindenburg to appoint Hitler Chancellor on January 30, 1933. Hitler drove a hard bargain with these men. This he could do since their popular support was almost negligible. This German Nationalist Party could count upon only some 40 seats in the Reichstag out of a total of 608, by comparison with the 230 deputies elected by the Nazis the previous July. Indeed, the German Nationalist Party was opposed at this time by the tiny People's Party, which was the particular party of the industrialists and which was strongly opposed to this deal with Hitler.

The conservative factions which had made the deal with Hitler believed they had "brought him to power with his hands tied." All the cabinet posts which they considered of strategic importance were put in the hands of men on whose conservatism they believed they could count. These included the Ministries of Foreign Affairs, Economics, Finance, Labor and Agriculture. The new Minister of Defense was a regular army general of aristocratic family but with close personal ties to the Nazis.[6] Actually Hitler had held out for the barest minimum

---

[6] This appointment neutralized the Reichswehr at this critical moment, removing it from the control of General von Schleicher, the previous Chancellor, who had been in effect the political boss of the Reichswehr before he became Chancellor. With the Reichswehr neutralized, the Nazi S.S. and S.A., together with the Prussian state police, who had now passed under the control of Goering as Minister of the Interior for Prussia, gave Hitler the decisive military strength which was to enable him to consolidate absolute power, including power over the Reichswehr.

which would assure him complete power without civil war. His bargain was a perfect one: he had obtained all that was necessary while allowing the conservative group to believe that they had outwitted him. By acquiring the immense prestige of the Chancellorship for himself, by neutralizing the Reichswehr, by obtaining for the Nazis the cabinet posts of Minister of the Interior for the Reich and for Prussia, he was able later to eliminate step by step those conservatives in the cabinet whom he considered an obstacle to attainment of the supreme power. He was able almost immediately to get a cowed Reichstag to pass the Enabling Act which freed him from reliance upon President von Hindenburg for continuance in office.

Once Hitler was in power both those industrialists who had held him in patronizing contempt and those who had feared him as a man of violence collaborated with him completely. So indeed did almost everyone in Germany in a position of any prominence at all who did not emigrate or who was not thrown into a concentration camp.[7] A very few withdrew from public life to avoid collaboration. This alternative was not open to most, however, for the Nazis, like the Communists in Russia, never recognized any right of the individual to neutrality.

No nationalization of German industry such as the Bolsheviks had carried out in Russia was necessary. Industry did not, however, escape the process of *gleichschaltung*, or "coordination," by which almost every organization was compelled to accept intimate Nazi domination. The exceptions were the Catholic and Protestant churches, where the attempt at domination was unsuccessful. The expulsion of the Jews from the

[7] Fritz Thyssen was almost the only prominent German industrialist who favored a full-fledged Nazi government for Germany. His sympathy for the Nazis was apparently based upon a complete misunderstanding of the real nature of the movement. After his later disillusionment, he was allowed by them to escape to Switzerland during the war. Among the Junkers who collaborated with Hitler even before he came to power was Hermann Rauschning, who actually joined the Nazi Party and became President of the Danzig Senate. He escaped from the Danzig Free State in 1935 after his disillusionment and fled abroad, where he wrote *The Revolution of Nihilism*, Longmans, Green, New York, 1939. In this book he records his awakening to the realization that the driving force of the Nazi movement was destructiveness, both domestically and in the foreign field.

directorates of all corporations and from all managerial positions in the economy afforded the opportunity for putting pro-Nazis in their positions. As a rule, no additional purging was necessary, for German industrialists were unable to oppose Nazi economic policies, and indeed generally did not find it in their own self-interest to do so.

The vigorous full-employment policy of the Nazis, implemented by make-work schemes at first and by armament orders as soon as these could be planned and put into production, brought to industry a prosperity which it had not enjoyed since before the depression in 1929. Nevertheless, since most industrialists were intelligent men of the world, they were not happy. They did not like the enormous increase in governmental control to which they were subjected.[8] They were uneasy in the realization that, however important an industrialist might be, a Nazi official might summarily dismiss him from his post and perhaps throw him into a concentration camp. That this did not often happen and was quite unlikely to happen so long as the industrialist collaborated did not fully reassure him. Above all, industrialists feared the war which they hoped would not come but which they saw was in fact imminent. Substantially all of them realized that Germany could not win another war, and the prospect filled them with gloom even while their order books were bulging.[9]

Hitler's popular support had come from a wide variety of sources. Primarily it had come from the lower middle class, who were frightened by the depression and the fact or pros-

[8] For an analytical description of the organization and functioning of the German economy under the Nazis, see Otto Nathan's *The Nazi Economic System,* Duke University Press, Durham, 1944. See also Ludwig Hamburger, *How Nazi Germany Has Controlled Business,* Brookings Institution, Washington, 1943.

[9] The writer was living in Berlin during July and August 1939. As it became evident that the policies and acts of Hitler were making war inevitable and even an immediate prospect, the gloom of the upper middle class increased. Their efforts when talking to foreigners to disassociate themselves from the Nazi Party were, with some few exceptions, quite striking. On the other hand, persons in the lower income classes, such as servant girls, newspaper venders, taxi drivers, army noncoms and the like, showed enthusiasm for Hitler together with some anti-foreign suspicion and even hostility, which the writer had never before experienced in Germany.

pect of losing their jobs or small businesses. Hitler in his own experience personified this abhorrence of the respectable lower middle class to being reduced to the level of the jobless proletariat. This class resisted to the utmost their identification with the proletariat and welcomed the radical demands of the Nazis for action which would bring an end to "starvation in the midst of plenty." They resented deeply the lack of any protection of their interests in the existing economic system. Most of them were not and could not be members of trade unions. The social security laws did not make provision for unemployment insurance for the self-employed or for those dependent upon investments which no longer paid dividends or interest.

Small peasants who had lost their farms or were afraid of losing them on account of the fall in agricultural prices, students who had graduated, or were about to graduate, with little prospect for the kind of position for which they had trained or indeed for any position, young unemployed workers, particularly those who had never held a job, and unemployed veterans of World War I swelled the Nazi ranks.

Thus it was a party of the masses, though not to any major degree a party of the industrial workers. The industrial workers continued to vote largely for the Social Democratic Party and for the Communist Party. However, in the July 1932 election, which was their high-water mark before Hitler became Chancellor, the Nazis had a popular vote high enough, even in an electoral system of proportional representation, to win 230 seats in the Reichstag against a total of 222 won by the Social Democrats and Communists, the mutually antagonistic parties claiming to be Marxist. It is true that there were perhaps a million voters who swung back and forth between the Nazis and the Communists, or remained away from the polls at one election and came back the next, according to whether or not the Nazis seemed likely to be able to take power. If the prospects for the Nazis were poor at the moment, these people sometimes expressed their fierce hatred of the existing system and their desperate longing for some sort of violent change by voting for the Communists. If the prospects for a Nazi victory seemed good, many of them voted for the Nazis. They were mainly unemployed workers who were not eligible for unemployment insurance payments or who had exhausted their claims for benefits.

In spite of this fragment of the proletariat which sometimes voted Nazi, the significance of the Nazi vote being larger than those of the Social Democrats and the Communists was in the declining numerical importance in the total population of workers who were employed in manufacturing and who looked upon themselves as members of the proletariat. This development tends to be characteristic of modern industrialized countries and is a fact of major sociological importance. It means, among other things, that during a crisis such as a severe economic depression, numerically speaking, "the masses" susceptible to demagogic appeals may not be primarily the industrial workers but a much more heterogeneous group with a quite different social outlook.

It is small wonder that Hitler, once in power, was successful in winning a large, although probably not the major, portion of German industrial workers to his support. He had succeeded in eliminating unemployment in Germany some time before World War II. By 1939 it was estimated that there were some two million jobs available which could not be filled because of lack of manpower. He had accomplished this without causing serious inflation, and had placed only a very limited number of consumer goods under rationing.[10]

Industrial production in Germany in 1938, prior to the outbreak of the war, was more than double what it had been in 1932, the year before Hitler came to power, and about one-fourth larger than in 1928 at about the peak of predepression prosperity. Agricultural production was about 10 per cent higher in 1938 than in 1929. On the average, real wages were by 1938 substantially the same as in 1929 before the depression. Total employment of wage and salary earners had increased from 12,680,000 in 1932 to 20,360,000 in 1938, or some 7.6 million. Their total income, measured in reichsmarks of constant purchasing power, increased from 21,905,000,000 RM in 1932 to 40,997,000,000 RM in 1938, almost doubling.

[10] For an account of how German rearmament and the general expansion of the German economy was financed, see Samuel Lurie, *Private Investment in a Controlled Economy: Germany, 1933–1939*, Columbia University Press, New York, 1947.

The increase in the production of capital goods was much greater than the increase in the production of consumer goods. Armament production was the dynamic element which sparked the increase in production, yet the statistical evidence is clear that the population of Germany substantially improved their status as consumers prior to World War II compared with the pre-Hitler year 1932. This improvement included food as well as other consumer goods.

The proportion of national income going to wage and salary earners, however, fell from 68.8 per cent in 1929 to 63.1 per cent in 1938[11]—a decline which was accompanied by an increase in the size of the labor force. The decline in the share of a greatly increased national income going to wage and salary receivers reflected to a large extent the reinvestment of increased corporate profits in capital goods and armament industries.

Under Hitler, a country with severe unemployment had become a country of full employment, with the effects on national income which could be expected. Somewhat the same process took place in the United States under the New Deal, although full employment was not attained until after the country entered World War II. The ability to achieve full employment was no monopoly of the Nazi economic system. Real national income increased in West Germany after World War II, beginning with the currency reform of 1948, until in 1955 it was some 50 per cent above what it had ever been under the Nazis. In contrast with the immediate pre-Hitler period when, owing to the failure to understand Keynesian economics, the measures of the Brüning government to deal

[11] The larger decline from the abnormally high figure of 77.6 per cent in 1932 to the level of 63.1 in 1938 was a phenomenon which commonly characterizes changes in the business cycle in all industrialized countries. The statistical decline in the percentage of national income going to wage and salary earners in the United States between the same dates was similar, although the data are not strictly comparable. See Chapter 10, "The Effect of the Military Economy on Civilian Consumption" in *The Nazi Economic System*. The statistical conclusions of Dr. Nathan with respect to real income, standard of living and the availability of consumer goods are consistent in a general way with the observations of the writer in Berlin in July and August 1939.

with unemployment proved wholly abortive, the record under the Nazis could not fail to be impressive. Those workers who had previously been unemployed were not the least impressed portion of the German population.

Concurrently with the steadily improving economic situation, however, went the development of a totalitarian state of unlimited terror and unrestricted violence, of official corruption and license, of concentration camps for scores of thousands of the population, of unspeakable atrocities, of wholesale repression of personal liberty.[12] An aggressive and expansionist foreign policy is apparently inherent in the totalitarian form of the state. Supernationalism and militarism was, of course, from the very beginning a basic element of Nazi doctrine. Whereas it might be said of Stalin's later foreign policy that he was determined to expand his conquests even at substantial risk of war, he preferred to get as much as he could without war. With Hitler this was not quite the case. He wanted as much territory as could be got without a war in which Germany ran a risk of being defeated. He would have been disappointed, however, if he could have secured all the territory he wished without even little wars, since war in itself was desirable.

The war for which Hitler prepared, and for which he was as personally responsible as any man in history has ever been, probably brought more complete destruction to the Nazi totalitarian state than if it had been destroyed by revolution. At no time, even after the military position was hopeless, was there a mass uprising or even a mass movement against the Nazi regime. This absence of overt resistance did not reflect popular support for the Nazi regime; it simply reflected the helplessness of a population controlled by a monolithic totalitarian regime where all instruments of coercion and propaganda are in the exclusive control of the state.

The conspiracy of July 20, 1944 which almost succeeded in

[12] Some two weeks after Hitler became Chancellor, the writer left Germany for a brief trip to Soviet Russia and was astonished to discover upon his return how rapidly the conditions of terror in Russia were being duplicated in Germany by the Nazis. *Germany Enters the Third Reich*, pp. 109–10. A Russian refugee, a friend of the writer then living in Berlin, remarked, "The Nazis are certainly not Communists but they are Bolsheviki!"

assassinating Hitler and overthrowing the regime was primarily a military plot of the upper classes in which there was some participation by Social Democratic and trade union leaders. Although a conspiratorial resistance movement among the generals had waxed and waned since 1938, it was only the prospect of complete military defeat that brought the conspiracy to the point where a series of assassination attempts could be made. In spite of some Soviet success in espionage through the so-called *Rote Kapelle*, there was not at any time a significant Communist underground resistance movement among the industrial population of Germany. The Communists had almost no part in the assassination attempt of July 1944, primarily because the conspirators had learned by hard experience that the Communists could not be trusted.[13]

The antagonism which Hitler had always felt for the aristocratic and plutocratic elements in German society, even when he had succeeded in tricking them into collaboration, found full expression after the attempt upon his life. Thousands of participants in the plot were hunted down and executed.[14] The generals and other army officers who had participated were singled out for insult and disgrace before execution.

Force had been the substitute for any sort of morality or ethics as the basis for the Nazi regime. Now force had destroyed Germany in total war, spiritually and physically. The evidence of wartime destruction and the consequent misery of the German population were seen and experienced by everyone. The gangster quality of Nazi officialdom, the horrors of the murder

[13] See Allen W. Dulles, *Germany's Underground*, Macmillan, New York, 1947, for an account of the German opposition to Hitler during the war. See also Hans Rothfels, *Die Deutsche Opposition Gegen Hitler*, Im Scherpe-Verlag, Krefeld, 1951; Rudolf Pechtel, *Deutscher Widerstand*, Erlenbach, Zurich, 1947; and Fabian von Schlabrendorff, *Offiziere Gegen Hitler*, Europa Verlag, Zurich, 1951.

[14] Dulles states: "Later Hitler came to regret his 'leniency' in dealing with the upper strata of society. Otto Meissner, who was State Secretary in the office of the Presidency from the end of World War I through World War II, quotes Hitler as saying that Lenin and Stalin had been right in annihilating the upper classes in Russia and that he, Hitler, had made a mistake in not doing likewise. After July 20, 1944 Hitler tried to correct his 'mistake.'" *Germany's Underground*, p. 14, note.

concentration camps such as Buchenwald, Dachau and Belsen, were now made public by the victors, a kind of foretaste of de-Stalinization in Soviet Russia more than a decade later. But when these disclosures[15] were made in Germany, the Nazi regime could no longer override their effect by the exercise of state power. Not only the evils of the system had been revealed but also its utter defeat in the trial of strength which it had brought upon itself and upon Germany.

It is perhaps unprofitable to speculate whether the Nazi economic and political system would have survived if it had not been destroyed by war, since war was inherent in the nature of the system. There is no evidence, however, that the regime would have collapsed at any early date were it not for the war. The considerable degree of economic success attained before the war had greatly facilitated the maintenance of Hitler's unlimited power, directly based though it was upon monopoly of the means of coercion and propaganda.

Whether the Nazi system could have survived the death of its first dictator if that had happened during peacetime is another matter. The transfer of power from one dictator to another is one of the most difficult of processes to accomplish without wholesale violence. The one modern case where it was done successfully, though eventually at the cost of many lives, was the transfer of power from Lenin to Stalin. The most favorable circumstances existed in this instance. Lenin's long illness before his death enabled Stalin to build his personal machine under the aegis of Lenin's prestige but under circumstances in which Lenin was not aware of what was going on until it was too late. Hitler had used the prestige of the aging President von Hindenburg to build up his power in somewhat the same way. But there could, of course, be no assurance that a hypothetical successor to Hitler would have found so propitious a set of circumstances for transferring dictatorial power to himself, as indeed the successors of Stalin have not.

A totalitarian regime like that of the Nazis might survive

[15] Actually, as in the case of de-Stalinization, there were no real disclosures, since the events "disclosed" were known to many people, even if in detail to only a few. But in both cases, in a different way, disclosures became more complete, they were made public, and it became "legal" to admit that these events had occurred.

even large-scale bloodletting at the top in the process of transferring power upon the death of the dictator, were it not for the fact that such a state depends importantly upon a monolithic ideology to sanction its personal autocracy. This ideology may be illogical, confused and mystical and still retain its efficacy as an indispensable adjunct to that monopoly of coercion which is the fundament of the modern totalitarian state. Once it becomes necessary to admit in the course of internal struggle for power that the "infallible" ruler has been the source of false doctrine, fissures appear in the totalitarian monolith. Thereafter, power may be transferred and maintained for a time by pistol, poniard or poison, but the charism of such a regime is likely to be seriously impaired.

Is the Nazi type of totalitarian state now a closed chapter in the annals of history, or is there a continuing danger that a similar regime might come to power? To answer this question another may be asked: Could the Nazi regime have been prevented from taking over on January 30, 1933? A meaningless answer would be that since it did come to power the forces which brought it to power were stronger than those operating to prevent it. If this fruitless approach is abandoned, the answer is certainly, "Yes, it could have been prevented."

The last really parliamentary government of Germany was that of Brüning, which was supplanted by the von Papen government in May 1932. If France had been willing to give some assurance to Brüning of French disarmament in return for the continuance of German disarmament, and of a reduction in and final settlement of reparations payments, this success in foreign relations might have enabled Brüning to survive.[16] His survival would have been only momentary, it is true, in the absence of economic recovery, since the desperate economic situation was the real source of popular support for the Nazis. By the early fall of 1932, however, there had occurred the beginnings of an economic upturn in Germany—at least unemployment did not increase after that time. The New Deal was to come to power in the United States in March 1933, and thereafter economic recovery in the United States and in the rest of the world got well under way. So great is the weight of the United States in the demand for international commodi-

[16] See Wheeler-Bennett, *Wooden Titan*, pp. 378–383.

ties that German economic recovery might have followed in the wake of that of the United States. If this had happened, the Nazi movement probably would have disintegrated as a major factor on the German political scene, as did the movement of Boulanger in France in the late 1880s and the recent movement of Poujade.

If, indeed, the Brüning government or some other parliamentary regime had been willing to put into effect a massive public works program by means of deficit financing, as the New Deal administration in the United States was to do, there can be little doubt that Hitler could have been kept out of power. But with the memories of inflation so sharp in the minds of the people, no parliamentary government in Germany was willing to take this risk. Hitler took the risk and the Nazi regime got the credit.

It is significant that the destruction of personal freedom in Germany did not come about by the gradual extinction of individual rights through the expansion of the police power of the state. In retrospect, indeed, it appears that the republican government would have been well advised to have pursued a much more repressive policy towards both the Nazis and the Communists, neither of whom concealed their intention of seizing power when they could do so. Furthermore, it was always quite clear that personal liberty would be completely crushed if either the Nazis or the Communists came to power. The republican government of Germany was confronted by the dilemma of every democratic and parliamentary regime when faced with the threat of a totalitarian movement. How far can such a government make use of the repressive measures of a totalitarian government in protecting itself against a totalitarian threat?

After Hitler had become Chancellor it is most doubtful whether even a court with powers such as those of the United States Supreme Court could have prevented the destruction of liberty which was carried out by the Nazis. A Supreme Court with such powers would have limited the power of the parliamentary, republican government to act against the Nazis before Hitler consolidated his power. Once the police and the army were in Nazi control, an attempt by such a court to render an unfavorable decision would no doubt have meant the suppression of the decision, and the concentration camp for the judges. Such "courts" as continue to exist under a totalitarian regime do not serve as protectors of the rights of individuals; the courts become only one of many instruments of repression and coercion.

On the other hand, even Article 48 of the Weimar Constitution, though it provided the widest possible base for emergency action by the President without the necessity for legislative sanction, did not avail to protect parliamentary government. After Hitler's accession Article 48 actually facilitated the consolidation of his power.

The record is thus clear that the threat of disaster to parliamentary government and personal liberty in Germany could have been avoided if the economic organization of the country had been such that the Great Depression would not have happened or if the government had taken measures to deal with it adequately after it did happen. But this means that a government while stopping short of the permanent acceptance of full responsibility for the operation of the economy must take the minimum responsibility necessary for the prevention or cure of economic depressions. This is indeed a tightrope to balance upon.

Two quite different types of economic systems came into being in Germany upon the collapse of Nazi totalitarianism, each imposed by the occupying powers in their particular areas of occupation. The Russian occupying power installed the Soviet type of totalitarian system in East Germany. The Western allies installed the capitalistic, parliamentary, democratic system in West Germany. The system installed by the victors in the West represented in general the preference of the population, while the system in East Germany was installed contrary to the wishes of the population.[17] The economic system which developed in West Germany turned out to be a less cartelized and more "liberal" type of economy than had existed even prior to Hitler. This was due at first to the insistence of the American occupying power, but it was continued

[17] The historical record confirms this conclusion. It is also supported by the observation of the writer in 1945 as economic adviser with the American armed forces in Germany during the early months of the occupation.

by the free will of the Adenauer government after the occupation had come to an end and German sovereignty had been restored.

The disastrous consequences of the Nazi regime in Germany and of the Fascist regime in Italy render it unlikely that these particular types of regimes will be reinstituted in either country or that they will be duplicated elsewhere. The destruction of German cities, the millions of war dead, the countless victims of the Nazi gas chambers, have left indelible memories. Yet if a severe and prolonged economic depression should occur, or if the conflict between economic groups and classes should become irreconcilable in any important country, it is likely that some sort of totalitarian government would again take over, whether of the Soviet type or of some different type, accompanied by new trappings and a new propaganda mystique but equally destructive of human liberty.

CHAPTER 7

THE TRANSFORMATION OF CAPITALISM IN THE UNITED STATES: THE NEW DEAL AS EFFECT AND CAUSE

When capitalism has been overthrown by violence with the revolutionary leadership proclaiming the establishment of a new order, the fact of a drastic change in the economic and political system is self-evident. This is so even if the system turns out to be utterly different from that advocated by the revolutionary leadership before the overthrow, as happened in Russia. Similarly, the nationalization of individual industries by parliamentary methods, as in the United Kingdom, is recognized as a deliberate and indisputable, if piecemeal, departure from capitalism in the direction of socialism. This is true even though there may be some question of just how the functioning of an industry thus nationalized differs from its functioning under modern corporate capitalism.

Even a fundamental change is often not seen in clear focus, however, where basic alterations in the capitalistic system take place which are not recognizable either as nationalization or as a form of socialism and indeed cannot logically be so designated. Thus, it was not until the comprehensive program of the New Deal that a change in the character of the economic system of the United States was generally recognized as having taken place. Thereafter, there was general agreement up to about the time of the entry of the United States into World

War II that momentous changes had occurred. But even during this period there was violent disagreement as to the nature of those changes and later there was no longer unanimity that a fundamental change had taken place at all. Different groups and economic classes were in sharp disagreement as to the nature of the changes, and why and when they took place. But these groups and classes were to change their positions often on these matters over a period of time.

Thus, after the enactment of the New Deal legislative program, businessmen and other conservatives were agreed for a time that fundamental, not to say catastrophic, changes in the economic system had occurred. They thought of these changes as having been brought about by the Roosevelt New Deal and regarded them as the unfortunate product of demagogic political pressures during a temporary economic crisis. There was little realization that the economic system had already undergone substantial transformation prior to the first Roosevelt administration, that this transformation was largely responsible for the New Deal's coming into existence and that it determined the character of the economic program enacted under the Roosevelt regime. With economic recovery, businessmen hoped for the elimination of almost all New Deal measures, though this hope faded with succeeding Democratic victories at the polls. As these conservatives saw it, the elimination of New Deal economic legislation would have restored a substantially unimpaired capitalism. This attitude reflected in part a time lag in the thinking of businessmen and in part a failure to understand a complex historical evolution. Outside the community of business leadership, a realization of the nature of the transformation had long been growing. It did not, however, develop at the same speed among different groups and economic classes nor was the understanding of it precise or uniform.

Socialist critics of capitalism had quite logically always considered private property to be the most characteristic institution of the capitalistic economic system and had concentrated their attack upon it. Capitalists themselves agreed with this appraisal and, so long as the rights of private property seemed unimpaired, both socialist critics and capitalistic defenders of the economic system generally refused to recognize any substantial change in it.

On account of the development of constitutional law peculiar to the United States, private property before the New Deal was more inviolable than in any other country. A series of Supreme Court decisions had established the rights of property against the executive or legislative powers of the states or the federal government.[1] This meant that, even if a majority of the population should wish to have legislation enacted which would affect property rights and should elect representatives pledged to such legislation, the will of the majority could not prevail: these rights were constitutionally inviolable. American courts conceded that this inviolability could be infringed upon if the judiciary found a need for the exercise of the vaguely defined "police power of the state." If the popular majority were great enough and determined enough, of course, the Constitution might be amended; but the cumbersomeness of the amendment procedure made its utilization generally impracticable. The net result was that, until the Court reversed itself under the New Deal, the legislative avenues to state regulation and control of the economy, to the redistribution of wealth and income and to even partial socialization of the economy were largely blocked.

The preservation of the institution of private property is closely tied up, nevertheless, with the maintenance of the two other basic institutions, competition and a policy of laissez faire. The maintenance of competition is essential to the control of income flows from private property if these income flows are to be socially defensible. Laissez faire could be successfully defended only so long as these income flows from private property could be represented as effectuating some currently tolerable size and distribution of national income. In spite of this close relation of competition and laissez faire to private property, preoccupation with private property as the

[1] For example, in *Adair v. U.S.,* 208 U.S. 161 (1908) the Supreme Court held that Congress had no authority to protect the rights of workers to belong to labor organizations, as this would deprive persons of liberty and property without due process of law contrary to the Fifth Amendment. In *Coppage v. Kansas,* 236 U.S. 1 (1915) the Supreme Court held that state legislation of similar purpose was contrary to the Fourteenth Amendment.

one basic institution of capitalism served to disguise fundamental changes affecting competition and laissez faire which had taken place long before the New Deal.

Even among economists who might be expected to have a professional comprehension of the transformation of the economy, understanding developed slowly and not always with unanimity. It is a confusing and inconvenient paradox that the maintenance or the restoration of competition is inconsistent with a policy of complete laissez faire although the maintenance of a policy of laissez faire depends upon the maintenance of individual enterprise and competition. While this conflict between complete laissez faire and state intervention to guarantee the maintenance of competition is fundamental, it is also true that without a large measure of laissez faire the concept of competition would be meaningless. If the state abandons the principle of laissez faire and takes responsibility for the control of prices and production, the function of competition automatically disappears. If the doctrine of nonintervention by the state is strictly adhered to, however, there is nothing to prevent monopolistic agreements in restraint of trade or mergers and combinations in which independent producers might be swallowed up.

The necessity for anti-monopoly legislation if an economic system is to remain effectively competitive is now so universally accepted in the United States that it is easy to forget that state intervention to preserve competition was by no means unanimously supported by American economists at the time when measures such as the Sherman Antitrust Act of 1890 were being considered.[2] In the early days of the controversy, some economists, both in the United States and in Europe, took the extreme position that laissez faire included even the freedom of individuals to make contracts with each other limiting competition and of producers to merge their produc-

[2] In Europe, the necessity for state intervention against agreements in restraint of trade and in support of competition never was generally accepted. The German government actually facilitated the formation of cartels. Even in the United Kingdom the government did not in general attempt to enforce competition by statute. Legislation such as our Sherman Antitrust Act, for example, was never enacted. Only in 1956 was a limited form of anti-monopoly legislation adopted in the United Kingdom.

ing or selling operations through the formation of trusts, cartels or other forms of corporate organization. They believed that competition tended to reassert itself so long as governments did not enforce monopolistic agreements. These economists held that the constant temptation to members of a cartel to violate the agreement plus the incentive provided by monopoly profits to the entry of new competitors into a temporarily cartelized market insured this.[3] The possibility that internal erosion of a cartel agreement could be prevented by complete merger or by outright purchase of one concern by another was largely disregarded in advancing the extreme laissez-faire argument.

When the choice eventually had to be made in the United States between laissez faire and the maintenance of competition the decision, in principle at least, was unequivocal. The passage of the Sherman Antitrust Act in 1890 meant that competition had been judged to be more important than unbridled laissez faire. The Clayton Act of 1914 and subsequent legislation reflected the permanence of this judgment. This antitrust legislation had some effect in impeding the development of monopoly and in preserving some degrees and kinds of competition. The further development of a large-scale corporate type of economy was not, however, seriously impeded by the judgment that competition must be maintained even at the cost of a partial abandonment of pure laissez faire. Indeed, there was for a long time no thought of interfering with the formation of corporations or their growth through the purchase of assets of other corporations, or still less with their expansion through internal growth. Even growth through merger was limited only if such mergers contributed to monopoly, and this limitation was tempered by the adoption of the "rule of reason" by the courts.

Actually, the first and really decisive step away from an individual-enterprise economy had taken place much earlier when the courts accorded to corporations the status of legal persons. The courts had then accorded to corporations the same protection and immunities against the exercise of legis-

[3] The view that monopoly is inherently degenerative is apparently a factor in the current revival among American economists of the belief that our contemporary economy is still essentially competitive.

lative control or executive intervention by state or federal government that were given to individuals under the Fifth and Fourteenth Amendments. Since the corporation was an association of many persons and possessed much greater economic and political power than an individual, this meant that individuals who were not organized into some collective form were thereafter likely to be at a relative disadvantage when buying or selling goods or services. This legal protection of the corporation served to limit narrowly the powers of the state to control and regulate the corporate economy until the Supreme Court reversed this policy during the New Deal.

Prior to the New Deal the courts did not extend this kind of protection to labor unions. Indeed, efforts to facilitate union organization through legislation either by the states or by the federal government were usually knocked down by the courts right up to the New Deal period. The courts had even legalized the use of the injunction against efforts of labor organizers to induce employees to join labor organizations.[4] The Norris-La Guardia Act (1932) outlawing the use of injunctions against labor unions and, above all, the National Labor Relations (Wagner) Act (1935) affirming the right to organize and bargain collectively—a manifestation of the vastly increased political power of labor unions during the New Deal —eventually reversed the balance of power.[5]

While eventually American economists came to support almost unanimously the series of legislative enactments intended to protect the competitive system and to prevent monopoly, competition could not in fact be preserved by legislation which simply forbade monopolistic practices. Thus in the very process of providing protection for competition it became necessary to enact legislation which forbade some forms of competition which large producers might use to drive smaller producers out of business. Here was a double paradox. In the effort to maintain a competitive, laissez-faire

---

[4] See *Adair v. U.S.* and *Coppage v. Kansas* referred to above. See also *Hitchman Coal and Coke Co. v. Mitchell*, 245 U.S. 233, 268 (1917). The exclusion of labor unions from regulation under anti-trust legislation was a partial offset, however.

[5] See Chapter 8 for an account of the backward swing of the pendulum reflected in the passage of the Taft-Hartley Act.

economy it had come to be considered necessary to limit both competition and laissez faire.

It also became apparent that a court decision holding a particular corporate organization in an industry to constitute an illegal monopoly was essentially meaningless unless the court assumed the additional power to prescribe an alternative corporate structure designed to restore a competitive market in the industry and thus meet the test of legality. To establish such a test was not easy, and to set up an alternative corporate structure in a particular industry might, and in practice sometimes did, require years. In any event, such an undertaking obviously involved a further breach of the principle of laissez faire.

American economists, even before the depression of the thirties, had consequently reached a consensus that the economic system had been undergoing substantial modification through a decline in competition and the development of quasi-monopoly and monopsony, oligopoly, imperfect and monopolistic competition, price leadership and the like.[6] Economists almost universally came to recognize the necessity for the modification of the policy of laissez faire. This was reflected both in the statutory attempts to maintain competition and in the enactment of detailed governmental regulation in the case of public utilities where it had become obvious that regulation through competition was not feasible. Thus the typical economics textbook of the pre-New Deal decade of the twenties usually pointed out the tendency towards "cutthroat competition" followed by monopolistic agreements in industries characterized by decreasing costs of production.

In spite of the failure of business leaders to recognize basic change, and doubtless quite independently of the scholarly research and analysis of the economists, this transformation of the economy from a system of individual enterprise to one of corporate organization was probably recognized instinctively, if amorphously, by the majority of the population. It was quite clear that there had been a significant change in the scale of production, in the degree of concentration in industry, and

---

[6] This consensus on the part of economists that competition had been seriously impaired was broken in the post-World War II period. See Chapter 9.

in the nature of the pricing process. There had been concomitant changes in the process of saving and capital formation, and in the proportion of the population who worked as
hired employees of corporate industry instead of for themselves or for some other individual. It would have been strange
if a transformation so comprehensive had not been popularly
recognized.

These fundamental changes in the structure and functioning of American capitalism were of course an inevitable part
of the development of large-scale industrial production. This
had come to mean, in a real sense, the supplanting of individual enterprise by corporate organization of industry. The man
in the street saw this simply as the replacement of the small
manufacturer by "Big Business." Popular antagonism to "Big
Business" therefore was largely synonymous with hostility to
corporations and to the various devices and organizational
forms by which corporations grew in size and economic power.

Farmers and industrial workers as a whole had not, of
course, suffered economically with the development of large-
scale corporate enterprise. The concentration of industrial
production in fewer and larger-scale productive units meant
that prices measured in human costs were far lower, or, alternatively, that real labor income was far higher, than if the
system of small-scale individual enterprise had continued unchanged. Thus the development of the corporate economy did
not in the least reflect any Marxist "increasing misery of the
working class." On the contrary, real wage rates proceeded to
climb, interrupted only momentarily by recurring economic
depressions. This climb in real wages continued not only as
the individual-enterprise economy was undergoing transformation but even after corporate enterprise came under a heavy
measure of state control during the New Deal.[7] It did mean
that the pricing process under the corporate organization of
industry was different from that under small-scale individual
enterprise, that it had become even less an approximation of
the pure and perfect competition of the economists' abstract
model. A corporation which produced a significant proportion

7 Sumner Slichter has estimated that real wages increased nine-
fold from 1840 to 1953. See *Papers and Proceedings of the American Economic Association,* May 1954, p. 32.

of a particular product or products, even though the amount was far short of monopoly, no longer had to choose between accepting a price set in a free market over which it had no control or not producing. Instead both production and pricing by the typical corporate producer were now carried out with an eye both to the effect of his production upon the market price and to the probable reaction of other producers to his price and production policies.[8] Furthermore, it could mean more remunerative returns to manufacturers of commodities where monopolistic competition or price leadership by a major producer was the rule than to small-scale and numerous producers in a fully competitive market such as that in which farmers bought and sold. In some economic conjunctures this meant that the "terms of trade" in the national economy moved in favor of large-scale corporate industry. It could also mean that the management of a large-scale corporate industry having superior bargaining power to that of its unorganized workers, could use that power to buy the services of labor at a lower price than it would otherwise have had to pay.[9]

The hostility of millions of farmers and industrial workers who felt themselves vulnerable to the growing power of corporate industry did not express itself against the economic system of capitalism as such. Neither of the twin institutions of the economic system particularly dear to the capitalist, private property or laissez faire, was ever in serious danger. It was only in periods of abnormally low farm prices and industrial unemployment that popular discontent expressed itself in political form at all. Even during recurrent economic crises substantial popular sentiment for the overthrow of capitalism and its replacement by an alternative system never gained force; there existed only a nostalgic wish to restore the position of the small independent producer.

[8] See, for example, Edward H. Chamberlin's development of this point in the section "On the Origin of 'Oligopoly,'" in his *Toward a More General Theory of Value,* Oxford University Press, New York, 1957, pp. 38–42.

[9] Economists are, however, sharply divided on the question of whether and to what extent either wage rates or the total wage bill has been or is likely to be affected by the kind and degree of collective organization of employers and employees involved in wage bargaining. See pp. 203–208.

The reactions of farmers and of industrial workers to the growth of large-scale corporate industry had taken different forms. Apart from some limited and largely abortive attempts to deal on equal terms with large-scale corporate industry through marketing cooperatives, the infeasibility of centralized economic action by millions of isolated individual farmers induced them, unlike industrial workers, to rely upon political rather than organized economic power in attempting to maintain their economic status. The political power of farmers, up to the twenties, was, however, directed primarily at the restoration of individual enterprise through governmental enforcement of competition rather than at governmental control of prices and production in their behalf.[10] It was largely the political power of the farmers that had been responsible for the antitrust policy of the government.

By the time industrial workers were able to develop effective forms of labor organization in some industries, their union leaders had generally accepted the fact of the corporate organization of large-scale industry. It was natural that industrial labor, unlike the farmers, should come to rely primarily upon economic action expressed in collective bargaining through labor unions to maintain its countervailing power vis-à-vis corporate industry. As Selig Perlman states:

> Early in the present century, while almost the whole nation was insisting that the government should break up the trusts, or at least regulate them with most stringent legislation, many going so far as to demand price fixing by government, the American Federation of Labor declared unequivocally that the "trusts" were an inevitable economic development before which the law was com-

[10] Following the short-lived depression of 1921 agitation began among farmers for some form of government support of agricultural prices. The McNary-Haugen bill, first proposed in 1924, finally passed in 1927 and quickly vetoed by President Coolidge, was one of the products of the developing agrarian demand for governmental action. The Hoover administration found itself compelled to begin using government credit on a large scale in an effort to "stabilize" farm prices under the direction of the Federal Farm Board. Nevertheless, it was not until the election of President Roosevelt that sentiment among farmers crystallized in favor of comprehensive and permanent intervention in agriculture by the government.

pletely helpless, but the power of which could be controlled by another economic power, the organized trade union movement.[11]

If there had been no severe depression it seems altogether unlikely that there would have been an effective demand by farmers, industrial laborers or the lower-income classes in general for substantial and comprehensive intervention by government in the operation of the economic system. However, with millions of industrial workers unable to find employment, hundreds of thousands of farmers losing their farms through foreclosure, other thousands of householders losing their homes by the same process, thousands of small businessmen going into bankruptcy and finally even the largest corporations threatened with the collapse of their financial structures, the continuance of a policy of laissez faire was manifestly no longer possible.

In a country obviously possessing adequate natural, capital and human resources it had become politically unacceptable to tell millions of desperately worried people that nothing could be done since economic matters were not the concern of government. Men were not willing to wait until "natural forces" had somehow brought about an upturn in the business cycle which would restore prosperity. The long-term upward trends in real wages and in the standard of living were not now of crucial importance. At the moment, the catch phrase of "starvation in the midst of plenty" expressed a real threat to millions of Americans.

Concurrently, a similar threat of starvation in the midst of potential plenty, under a different economic and political situation, brought Hitler to power in Germany in the same year in which Roosevelt was inaugurated as President in the United States. It is almost a certainty that, if the economic depression had continued and if the government had failed to undertake comprehensive measures to grapple with the desperate economic situation, a revolutionary situation would also have developed in the United States. A government relying upon armed force to maintain itself in power would have been a

[11] *A Theory of the Labor Movement*, Macmillan, New York, 1928, p. 200.

probable outcome. As a result of experience with the depression of the thirties, the political handbook in all countries now contains the rule "No serious economic depression can be allowed to continue without economic intervention by government."

It was, then, the widespread unemployment of the depression of the thirties which swung the American labor movement away from almost sole reliance upon its economic power exercised through collective bargaining towards reliance upon its political power to compel intervention by the state in its behalf. It was this same economic depression which deflected the political power of farmers away from generalized efforts to eliminate monopoly towards demands for governmental control of prices and production. The specific legislative goals and the political strategy which reflected these shifts were worked out by the leaders of farm organizations and labor unions. The labor movement's switch to greater reliance upon political power and the farmers' shift in political goals were responsible not only for the Democratic victory in 1932 but also for the continuance of these policies beyond the tenure of Democratic administrations.

These shifts in the attitude of farmers and industrial workers proved all the more effective because they coincided with a moment of extreme vulnerability in the defenses of industrialists against governmental intervention in the economy. The collapse of the price level and the credit structure, which was both cause and effect of the failure of thousands of banks, induced and exposed defalcations by many bankers. These and the other disclosures in 1933–34 by the Senate Committee on Banking and Currency, with Ferdinand Pecora as counsel, of flagrant despoilment of hundreds of thousands of stockholders by corporation managements shattered the charism of old-style capitalism and almost destroyed the unrivaled prestige which its ruling class had hitherto enjoyed in American society. The bankruptcy, actual or threatened, of countless firms, the desperate and eventually successful pleas for financial rescue through massive governmental aid, and the further pleas for governmentally sanctioned production controls and price supports which businessmen felt it necessary to make, undermined the confidence of American businessmen in themselves.

The doctrine of nonintervention by government in the economy had already been substantially breached by the Hoover administration, with, of course, the greatest reluctance. Now, however, the Roosevelt administration could intervene massively and over the widest areas, secure in the knowledge that public opinion would tolerate anything but inaction. It was inevitable that its first measures should be directed at propping up the collapsing price and credit structure, extending relief to the unemployed, creating employment and building up mass purchasing power, without any great concern for the consistency of these measures, one with another.

The New Deal needed, however, a philosophical justification for its developing programs that would be understandable to the economic groups and classes which had given and could be appealed to for further political support. Both a policy and a program as well as their theoretical justification had to be made up as the New Deal administration went along, for events would not wait. The necessary elements for such an amalgam of policy, program and theory lay ready to hand and were gradually put together. To begin with, there was among the political leaders of the New Deal not much more than an attitude: that the government should no longer restrict itself to its historic laissez-faire role but should do whatever was necessary to combat the depression and bring about economic recovery. It was not even clear whether such action was to deal only with the existing emergency or was to extend to possible future depressions as well, or whether permanent legislation designed to prevent future depressions would be feasible and necessary.

The onset of the depression of the thirties had added a new element to the economist's analysis of the character of the economic system. Some economists, indeed, viewed the depression only as an unusually violent and protracted manifestation of the convolutions of the business cycle, doubtless inherent in the economy, but largely independent of any changes in the competitive or non-competitive character of the economic system. Others, however, considered the decline in the competitive character of the economy an integral cause of the depression. They believed that the prices of manufactured products were no longer "flexible" as under old-style competition, but were now "administered" by corporate executives. These prices no longer reacted to a falling off in demand by declining to the point where the quantity of goods offered on the market and the quantity taken would be equal. Instead, under current conditions of "administered prices," a fall in demand was ordinarily met by a reduction in output in order to maintain price. Such reductions in output could not have happened under the assumptions of a fully competitive economy; that they had taken place was accepted as evidence that the economic system was no longer characterized by competition of the traditional type.[12]

As a result of these general reductions in output, the demand for consumer goods had fallen and new investment had declined. This had happened for three reasons, it was argued. Unemployed industrial workers could not purchase as much consumer goods as when they were employed. Farmers, who could not reduce their production in order to maintain prices but had to sell in a competitive market at lower prices, could not maintain their former purchases of manufactured goods. Finally, industrialists, because of reduced demand for their products, had not undertaken new plant construction, and had even failed to replace depreciated plant and equipment.

This linking of the claimed decline in competition with the

---

[12] These concepts of "flexible prices" versus inflexible "administered prices" were developed primarily by Gardiner Means, one of the economic advisers in the Agricultural Adjustment Administration during the early days of the New Deal; similar theories were held by other economic advisers. Means published his ideas in a report to the Secretary of Agriculture, "Industrial Prices and Their Relative Flexibility," 74th Cong., 1st sess., S. Doc. 13, 1935. These ideas were developed in more general form in *The Modern Economy in Action*, written with Caroline F. Ware, Harcourt, Brace, New York, 1936.

The theory that the prices of manufactured goods had been growing more inflexible as the result of a decline in competition accompanying increased concentration in industry has been challenged on statistical grounds by Don Humphrey, Alfred Neal, Richard Ruggles and others. Some support for it has been recently advanced, also on statistical grounds, by John R. Moore, Lester S. Levy and John M. Blair.

causes of the economic depression conveniently fitted the popular agrarian demand for the employment of the powers of
government to raise agricultural prices to their former "parity"
with those of manufactured goods. Farmers bitterly resented
the fact that prices of industrial products had not fallen during the depression nearly so much as had the prices of farm
products. They pointed out that agricultural production had
fallen hardly at all while industrial production had been cut
almost in half.[13] The whole concept of "parity prices" embodied in the New Deal's Agricultural Adjustment Act
whereby the prices of products which the farmer sold were to
be brought into balance with the prices of the goods he
bought, was tied in with this belief of farmers that the power
of the state should be used to do for the prices of their products what industry through corporate organization had been
able to do for itself. Simultaneously, labor leaders were demanding that their power to organize and bargain collectively
should be strengthened through measures like those which
later eventuated in the Wagner Act. They maintained that the
power to bargain collectively was only the counterpart of the
collective bargaining power possessed by corporate industry in
both the wage bargain and the pricing process.

Industrialists could not well counter this line of argumen
on the part of farm leaders and labor leaders. They were at
the same time begging the government to grant them improved organizational powers to control production through
legalized collective action so that *their* prices could be prevented from falling further. As the culmination of the economic crisis approached at the moment of President Roosevelt's inauguration in 1933, American businessmen desperately
importuned the federal government for drastic action, by
which they meant primarily sanction of the "right of self-

[13] Farmers contended that manufacturers had been able to maintain their accustomed level of profits through this reduction in output. The reduction in industrial output was a fact; the maintenance
of industrial profits certainly was not. While under conditions of falling demand and imperfect competition each manufacturer suffered
smaller losses by reducing his output than he would have if he had
maintained his output unchanged, corporate industrial profits in the
aggregate declined to zero by the time the bottom of the depression
had been reached.

government in industry" in addition to some sort of emergency extension of credit. This self-government in industry was intended to prevent, through governmentally enforced price-maintenance agreements, so-called "cutthroat competition" which industrialists alleged was demoralizing business and preventing economic recovery.

Businessmen were, however, quickly disillusioned with the limited form of self-government in industry which they actually obtained under the Code Authorities set up under the National Industrial Recovery Act. Far more governmental control and intervention were embodied in the N.I.R.A.—and it was more galling and frustrating—than they had expected. They soon became appalled at the size of the administrative apparatus involved, and at the amount of time which they had to spend in dealing with governmental agencies. They also resented the right to collective bargaining which they had had to concede to labor as a *quid pro quo* for what businessmen, and particularly "Big Business," now found a quite unsatisfactory form of "self-government in industry."[14]

If substantial economic recovery had not occurred, industrialists would probably have supported the continuation of N.I.R.A., although certainly without enthusiasm. It gradually became apparent, however, that the sort of tripartite arrangement by which agricultural prices, prices of manufactured goods and industrial wages were to be supported by collective agreements sanctioned by government would not be effective in the absence of large additions to the money supply by government. The increased level of governmental expenditures accompanying New Deal legislative measures had, indeed, made a deficit inevitable in any event. Pressure from all sides for a more rapid restoration of the price level and for an expansion in employment was effective, however, in removing lingering inhibitions about the already unbalanced budget. When progress in restoring farm prices to parity through reductions in farm production proved to be disappointingly slow, increased reliance upon the evolving New Deal policy of deficit financing was a logical consequence. If additional

14 This was so in spite of the dissatisfaction of labor with the collective bargaining provisions of the N.I.R.A. as set forth in Section 7a.

money were pumped into the economy it could be expected to have a greater effect upon "flexible" farm prices than upon the more rigid "administered" prices of manufactured goods. The stimulus to expansion of employment in industry could likewise be expected to be greater than the upward pressure on costs of manufactured goods.

A new ingredient was added to the mixture of ideas which gave direction to the economic policy of the New Deal in the form of the Keynesian theories on the causes and cure of economic depressions. While the theory that the depression resulted from a decline in old-style competition was by no means wholly consistent with the economic theories of J. M. Keynes, there were significant points of agreement.[15] Above all, reliance upon deficit financing as a major remedial measure provided a bridge between the two. Out of the mixture of popular sentiment for equalizing the economic power of farmers and industrial labor with that of corporate "Big Business," the recognition of a transformation in the nature of competition and the Keynesian policy of deficit financing there evolved a new doctrine justifying the expanded role of the state in the economy.

The economic recovery which got under way as the new economic doctrine came into operation induced very different reactions among farmers and industrial workers on the one hand and industrialists on the other. With the demand for goods experiencing a sharp expansion, with the credit structure of the economy no longer at the point of collapse, and with the price level showing some recovery, industrialists came to believe that the aid of government to sustain "self-government in industry" could be dispensed with. The majority of industrialists consequently hailed with the greatest relief the Supreme Court decision declaring the N.I.R.A. unconstitutional,

[15] Though Keynes' *General Theory of Employment, Interest and Money* did not appear until 1936 his ideas were well known to the economists who were advisers in the Roosevelt administration during the earliest New Deal days. Keynes was in personal touch with these men and with President Roosevelt early in 1934. Of these advisers, Rexford Guy Tugwell had the most intimate contact with the President and was influential in propagating Keynesian ideas. The present writer was one of this group of economic advisers in the Department of Agriculture.

and the later decision invalidating the Agricultural Adjustment Act.

Industrialists and businessmen in general vehemently denied that the monetary and credit policies of the New Deal had been responsible for underpinning the credit structure of the economy, or for the recovery in the price level or the expansion in the volume of industrial production. While the extension of governmental credit through the Reconstruction Finance Corporation, the Farm Credit Administration and the Home Owners' Loan Corporation had been received with relief if not with enthusiasm, most industrialists regarded the monetary policy of the New Deal, including deficit financing and the abandonment of the conventional gold standard, as undermining the very foundations of a sound capitalistic economy. They quite correctly viewed these policies as inflationary, without recognizing that inflationary measures were inevitable if the purpose was to reverse deflation. The escape from bankruptcy which the reversal of the downward spiral of deflation brought to many industrialists did not entirely console them. They realized uneasily that the freedom of action which an economically successful program of deficit financing afforded a radical governing group introduced a new factor into the politico-economic balance of power.

Following the declaration of unconstitutionality of the N.I.R.A. and the A.A.A., businessmen began to assure themselves that an "economic upturn due to natural forces" had already begun before the advent of the Roosevelt administration and that the governmental intervention and control involved in the remaining New Deal legislation was now delaying rather than expediting recovery. It was argued that the policy of deficit financing had been proved unworkable by the alleged failure of "pump-priming" and that a return to hard money was consequently essential.[16] But the hopes engendered by these Supreme Court decisions were soon dashed. The Wagner Act, its constitutionality upheld by the Court,

[16] The reduction of governmental deficit financing in 1937 followed by the sharp depression of 1938 followed in turn by further deficit financing was cited to prove that "pump-priming" had failed. At most it only proved that "pump-priming" could never be permanently dispensed with.

served to increase immensely the bargaining power of organ
ized labor.[17] The revival of a governmental agricultural pro
gram in forms designed to circumvent the Court's declaration
of unconstitutionality also meant that this particular form o
governmental intervention was likely to be permanent. Fa
more significant than any legislative act was the Suprem
Court's reversal of its position with respect to the inviolabilit
of private property. The action of the Court in upholding th
Washington State Minimum Wage Act in 1937 and affirmin
the constitutionality of the Wagner Act immediately thereafte
opened the way to fundamental changes in the economic func
tions of the state through legislation at both the state and th
federal level. No longer would the Court stand as an inflexibl
bulwark against intervention by the state in the corporat
economy or as a guarantor of the absolute inviolability of pri
vate property.

The provision of financial aid to home owners through th
H.O.L.C., to home builders through the F.H.A., to farmer
burdened with mortgages through the F.C.A., the enactmen
of social security legislation, added to the price-support legis
lation for farmers and the Wagner Act for industrial worker
meant that the government had now "done something fo
everybody," with the ensuing gains in popular support. Indus
trialists and businessmen in general had believed that th
Roosevelt administration's need for billions of dollars to carr
out these programs would in itself set a limit and eventuall
bring them to an end. They reasoned along the following lines
Government programs "to aid everybody" would require eithe
heavy taxes or greatly increased governmental bond issue
Heavier taxes would mean less money available for the pur
chase of consumption goods or for investment. More govern
mental borrowing for public works construction or for othe
public expenditures would mean less funds available for in
vestment in private industry. If the government tried to obtai
funds via the printing press, inflation would cancel out an
additional purchasing power in the economy. Business leader

[17] The Wagner Act was, of course, far more obnoxious than Sectio
7a of the N.I.R.A., which had been accepted by industrialists a
an unavoidable condition of getting price-maintenance legislatio
adopted.

were confident that any government that wished to maintain its credit and borrow at a reasonable rate of interest could not afford to carry on an economic policy and program repugnant to conservative financiers.

It was a profound shock to conservatives to find that this prognosis turned out to be false. The Roosevelt administration was able to borrow billions of dollars and to devote these vast sums to its economic programs without diminishing the funds available for the purchase of consumption goods or for investment in private business. Instead, the funds available for these purposes were, of course, greatly increased as the total of bank deposits was built up by deficit financing. Simultaneously, total national income increased substantially from the lowest depression level. Nor were these merely dollar increases, for not only total national income but funds for consumption and for private investment measured in real terms increased substantially over what had been available at the bottom of the depression. While the policy of deficit financing in depression has now become so much a matter of course that it seems incredible that it could have caused astonishment, it is hardly an exaggeration to say that to conservatives in general and to financiers in particular it seemed at the time like inducing water to run up hill.

The popular effect of the success of deficit financing in stimulating economic recovery was enormous. The degree of inequality in the distribution of wealth and income which had characterized the United States economy prior to the New Deal was able to exist without any serious demands from the lower classes for governmental intervention in their behalf largely because it was thought that the government could not successfully intervene. Now, however, it had been demonstrated that governmental action could increase employment and improve the economic position of particular groups and classes.

In the period of extensive unemployment of resources following the depression, deficit financing made possible great expansion in production and improvement in the economic well-being of almost all groups and classes. It appeared to each recipient group except businessmen, however, that the principal factor which had determined how well it fared was what and how much the government had done for the particular group or class. In a certain sense this was quite true. How well each group fared under the new regime of governmental intervention depended importantly upon what the government had done for it, in comparison with what the government had done for other potential recipients sharing in the distribution of national income. Under conditions of full employment, however, governmental intervention which directly gives a larger share of the national income to one group or class than it has previously been getting, or which does this indirectly by increasing the bargaining power of one economic group or class will ordinarily diminish the share of the national income going to some other group or class.[18] Even so, once the practice of intervention has become established, each group feels the need for pressing the government to take action in its behalf regardless of the effect upon the others. There might appear to be a countertendency for each group to try to prevent action favorable to the others, thereby damping down or even canceling the effect of pressure by special interest groups. This tendency is much weaker, however, since the specific gain to a particular economic group or class usually appears to come not so much by opposing governmental aid to every other special group or class as by obtaining positive action for itself.[19]

Never again would governing officials be able to resist the

[18] It is possible, however, that the maintenance of full employment in the major sectors of the economy may depend upon the maintenance of demand for the products of any one of these sectors. For example, it is not certain that agricultural income could be allowed to fall precipitously without producing eventually a decline in the demand for manufactured products. If one assumed that the lowered prices for agricultural products enabled consumers to buy greater amounts either of these products or of manufactured goods and that consumers actually did so, no fall in employment would be thus induced. However, in practice the fall in agricultural prices does not always cause the compensatory effects necessary to maintain employment levels.

[19] For example, a lobbyist for a higher price support for a particular farm product could not be expected to receive much approbation from his clients if he were to help prevent a higher tariff on manufactured goods or a raise in wages in the steel industry by a governmental arbitration board.

clamor for action in behalf of particular economic interests commanding substantial popular support by declaring that economic matters were not the responsibility of government and that government could not intervene in or control the economy effectively. The policy and practice of state intervention in response to political pressures had become permanently rooted in our economy.

Consequently, after something like a decade of the economic and political policies of the New Deal and up to the outbreak of World War II, most businessmen felt that laissez-faire capitalism had been seriously if not fatally impaired. They believed that only by the elimination of the New Deal economic measures could a full-fledged, dynamic, laissez-faire capitalism be restored. The economic system had, however, undergone fundamental changes. Some of these changes had been responsible for the New Deal's existence; others the New Deal itself brought about. It is somewhat ironic that within a decade businessmen were to begin either to accept or to disregard these changes, and to think of the greatly altered economic system as "American capitalism."

CHAPTER 8

THE WAR AND POSTWAR
AMERICAN ECONOMY:
THE CHANGED ECONOMIC SYSTEM
ASSUMES PERMANENT FORM

The outbreak of the war in Europe was a milestone in the transformation of the American economy. The further extension of the powers of government over the economy ceased to have the purposes which had previously motivated the Roosevelt administration. Thereafter, until the end of the war in 1945, there was to be no New Deal-type legislation designed to prevent or overcome depressions or to redistribute the national income or to provide economic security for lower-income groups. Scarcely any of the New Deal legislation was repealed, however, though some of it was reversed in purpose. Governmental support prices for farm products were employed during the war to stimulate production, rather than to restrict it in order to help sustain prices. Governmental control of the prices of manufactured goods in wartime was designed to keep prices from rising rather than to keep them from falling as in the days of N.I.R.A. Wage controls were similarly reversed in intent.

Yet the effect of United States participation in the war was to increase greatly the area and the intimacy of governmental control. Such a network of controls is of course an inevitable concomitant of waging modern wars, as the experience of World War I had demonstrated. Experience under the New

Deal, by accustoming industrialists, farm leaders and labor leaders to operate under a network of governmental controls, greatly facilitated the transition to a highly regulated wartime economy. The experience of industrialists in the war economy, many of whom served as governmental administrators, in turn conditioned them to accept a degree of governmental intervention and control after the war which they had deeply resented prior to it. Thus the removal of wartime controls, even though it meant no more than a reversion to the level of controls and intervention in the prewar New Deal economy, was to seem like a return to old-style, laissez-faire capitalism. Further, the combined experience of operating the Code Authorities of the National Recovery Administration in the early New Deal days, even though these had been unpopular with most industrialists, and of operating sections of the W.P.B. and similar agencies during the war was significant psychologically in habituating industrialists to thinking in industry-wide terms rather than in terms of their own particular corporations. This wartime experience thus became a factor in the further evolution of the American economy away from old-style competition, just as experience with the N.R.A. Code Authorities had left behind a legacy of cooperation among the executives of corporate industry even after the act had been declared unconstitutional.

After the death of President Roosevelt and the end of the war, some effort was made through the "Fair Deal" of President Truman to expand the legislative program of the New Deal concurrently with the gradual dismantling of wartime controls.[1] In essence, however, the "Fair Deal" consisted in adapting the economic and political policies and legislation of the New Deal to the postwar economic situation.

In the field of labor legislation the Truman administration carried out a defensive rather than an offensive operation. President Truman's veto of the Taft-Hartley Act was an effort to continue governmental sanction of the superior bargaining position which labor unions had acquired under the Wagner Act. Though it failed to prevent the passage of the Taft-Hartley Act, the Truman administration employed the powers of gov-

[1] For instance, the proposal for a system of health insurance.

ernment to maintain a continuous upward pressure upon wage rates. This was accomplished in the first instance by refusal to invoke the act in order to deal with strikes. Secondly, labor leaders could generally count upon governmental appointment of a "fact-finding board" which would recommend an increase in wages when it proved impossible to obtain acceptable increases by striking. Indeed, when strikes occurred in industries as endowed with public interest as steel, for example, there could hardly be a feasible alternative to some sort of governmental intervention. The influence of the Truman administration was consistently used to raise wage rates.

Before the advent of the New Deal the large proportion of the labor force which was unorganized had been at a disadvantage when bargaining individually with corporate industry. The employees of a particular concern had had to depend primarily upon the competition of corporations for the service of laborers as the determinant of their wages.[2] Under the assumptions of pure and perfect competition and of full employment of resources, wages so determined would represent the workers' marginal productivity and the wage rate would increase in commensuration with the trend of improvement in techniques of production in the economy.

The passage of the Wagner Act under the New Deal reflected the increased political power of labor organizations. Labor leaders believed that neither wages nor prices were being determined by the forces of competition as they would have been in an individual-enterprise economy, and that in wage bargaining within the modern corporate economy labor had suffered from its lack of comprehensive organization.

Although the weight of evidence supports the conviction of labor leaders that industrial workers were in an unfavorable bargining position vis-à-vis the management of corporate industries, economists are by no means in agreement about this. Many would deny that unorganized farmers or unorganized industrial workers had less bargaining power because of the alleged decline in the degree of competitiveness in the economy. Further, American economists have differed sharply

[2] The employing corporation under these conditions could be assumed to compete for the supply of labor and to offer the wage which would enable it to maximize its profits.

with respect to the extent to which laborers have profited from their increased organizational power. Some have maintained that the effect of unions upon wages has been and is almost bound to be negligible. There is evidence which shows that wages have not invariably been higher in unionized plants or industries than in nonunionized industries,[3] and evidence is conflicting as to whether wages have regularly been higher after unionization than before. Some economists have argued that union leaders are helpless to obtain higher wages than unorganized workers would obtain, since the penalty would be unemployment. Others have maintained, on the contrary, that a union protecting a monopoly position by limiting its membership can secure higher wages for its members. It has been argued that this would be at the expense of less organized workers, whose real wages would be lowered by the payment of higher prices for goods produced by higher-priced labor or whose actual wages would be lowered by the competition of surplus workers pushed out of employment where wages had been raised. Still other economists have claimed that the bargaining power of labor unions may be used only to the extent necessary to counterbalance the monopsony power of corporations as buyers of labor and their monopoly power as sellers of goods and services.[4] Some have argued that labor unions may increase money wages but not real wages, since induced inflation tends to wipe out any increases beyond those reflect-

[3] In this connection, see H. M. Levinson, *Unionism, Wage Trends and Income Distribution, 1914–1947*, University of Michigan Press, Ann Arbor, 1951, and A. M. Ross, *Trade Union Policy*, University of California Press, Berkeley, 1948. For a most useful cross section of the views of American economists on this and closely related matters, see the section devoted to "Wage Determination in the American Economy," in *Papers and Proceedings of the American Economic Association*, May 1954, pp. 279–366. See also Clark Kerr, "Labor's Share and the Labor Movement," Reprint No. 93, Institute of Industrial Relations, Berkeley, California, 1957. Kerr believes that the effect of labor unions on labor's share in national income is minimal.

[4] It is indeed doubtful whether in the absence of labor unions going wage rates would be much closer to the "free market" equilibrium rates than they are now. See Lloyd G. Reynolds and Cynthia H. Taft, *The Evolution of Wage Structure*, Yale University Press, New Haven, 1956.

ing gains in labor productivity. There can be no doubt that industry-wide collective bargaining does facilitate increasing prices to offset wage increases. After weighing these arguments and counterarguments, however, it seems thoroughly untenable to deny that labor unions may and often do exert some degree and kinds of monopoly power.[5]

Finally, many economists have maintained that labor's share in national income has remained substantially unchanged through time and that consequently the increased unionization of labor cannot have enlarged the return to labor as a factor of production although particular groups of workers may have gained.[6] But even supposing that the share of national income going to labor has shown no important change over time, this would not prove absolutely that labor unions have been unable to affect the relative size of distributive shares in national income. It might be that the growing power of labor unions had largely offset the increased monopoly-monopsony power of industrial corporations, apart from temporary fluctuations.

Contrary to what is perhaps the position of most American economists, however, the evidence does not support the conclusion that the share of national income going to labor has in fact remained unchanged. At the bottom of the depression in 1931, 1932 and 1933 corporate profits disappeared and indeed were negative, and consequently the share of national income received as compensation of employees increased from 58.2 per cent in 1929 to 73.4 per cent in 1933. This does show that wage rates were far less flexible than profits during the depression and perhaps indicates that labor unions did have some

---

[5] Edward H. Chamberlin, *The Economic Analysis of Labor Union Power*, American Enterprise Association, Washington, 1958, and Fritz Machlup, *The Political Economy of Monopoly*, Johns Hopkins Press, Baltimore, 1952, particularly Part IV, Labor Policies. See also "Labor Monopoly and All That," in Edward S. Mason, *Economic Concentration and the Monopoly Problem*, Harvard University Press, Cambridge, 1957, pp. 196–223, and Charles E. Lindblom, *Unions and Capitalism*, Yale University Press, New Haven, 1949.

[6] For example, Kenneth Boulding concludes that increased organization has apparently not enlarged materially the relative size of shares of industrial workers or of farmers in the national income. *The Organizational Revolution*, Harper, New York, 1953, p. 208.

influence in keeping up wage rates. Parenthetically, this short period when the labor share in national income was so high coincided with a period of high unemployment and certainly was not one which workers in general would prefer to other periods in which the share of workers was smaller. Apart from this extreme but temporary shift in the relative size of distributive shares of employees' compensation and corporate profits, it is quite plain that the share of employees' compensation in national income has increased substantially over the past several decades while the share of national income going to corporate profits after taxes has declined. Thus, out of total national income in 1929, compensation of employees amounted to 58.2 per cent, corporate profits before taxes to 11 per cent, and corporate profits after taxes to about 9.5 per cent. By 1957 compensation of employees had increased to 70 per cent and corporate profits before taxes had increased to about 12 per cent, but profits after taxes had declined to 6.3 per cent. During the same period the share of net interest, a property return, declined from 7.3 per cent to 3.4 per cent and proprietors' and rental income, a mixture of property and labor income which includes the income of farm operators, declined from 17 per cent to 12 per cent. Rental income of persons declined from 6.2 per cent to 3.4 per cent.[7]

This evidence is confirmed by other data which are on a somewhat different statistical basis. Since 1929 there has been a substantial increase in the percentage that wages and salaries and transfer payments constitute of total personal income flowing to families and unattached individuals. Together these payments accounted for 61 per cent of total personal income in 1929, 67 per cent in 1937 and 73 per cent in 1950–55. In contrast, there was a marked reduction in the shares of dividends and interest—types of income that are heavily concentrated in the upper end of the family income scale.[8]

Another effort to separate the shares of labor and property shows labor's share increasing from 71.7 per cent in 1920–29 to 74.5 per cent in 1947–52. If corporate income taxes are

[7] These data are computed from the *Survey of Current Business,* July 1958, pp. 4–5.

[8] Selma F. Goldsmith, "Changes in the Size Distribution of Income," *American Economic Review,* May 1957, pp. 508–509.

deducted from national income and government interest is added, the share of labor increases from 69.9 per cent in 1920–29 to 75.8 per cent in 1947–52.[9] This would represent an increase of somewhat more than 8 per cent in labor's share and a decrease of somewhat more than 19 per cent in the non-labor or property share of national income.

A substantial portion of the increase in the share represented by compensation of employees can, it is true, be accounted for by the shift of persons out of self-employment in farming, out of unpaid household work and out of self-employment in non-farm unincorporated enterprises into activities such that their incomes became included in statistics of employees' compensation.[10] Some of the increase in the share going to employees can also probably be accounted for by the increase during this period in the proportion of workers employed in relatively higher-paid employment. Still another part can be accounted for by increased employment in government, where there is no property counterpart to labor income. Nevertheless, after correcting to allow for this shift in employment, the increase in the share represented by compensation of employees is substantial.[11] It would be necessary to assume that corporate taxes should not be deducted from corporate profits in order to be able to claim that the share of salaries and wages in

[9] Gale Johnson, "The Functional Distribution of Income in the United States, 1850–1952," *Review of Economics and Statistics*, May 1954.

[10] For example, Professor William Fellner believes that the increase in the share of labor is due almost wholly to what he calls "changes in the relative significance of various sectors in the economy." *Trends and Cycles in Economic Activity*, Holt, New York, 1956, p. 261.

[11] Stated in another way, and confining the analysis to distributive shares originating within corporate business, compensation of employees increased from 75 per cent in 1929 to 79.5 per cent in 1957. (Compensation of employees includes wages, salaries and supplements to wages and salaries.) The share of profits *before taxes* changed very slightly from about 21 per cent to about 19.5 per cent during the same period. The share of profits *after taxes* declined from about 18 per cent to about 10 per cent. Net interest fell from 3 per cent almost to zero. Data from *Productivity, Prices and Incomes*, Materials Prepared for the Joint Economic Committee by the Committee Staff, 1957, p. 29, and computed from the *Survey of Current Business*, October 1958, p. 9.

national income did not increase—an assumption which seems quite illogical.

The conclusion that the share of labor in national income has increased substantially from 1929 to the mid-1950s is strengthened if the matter is stated in terms of *disposable* income, i.e., income available to persons after taxes. Based upon a study of Klein and Frane, the staff of the Joint Economic Committee[12] have estimated that the share of wages and salaries after taxes increased from 62 per cent in 1929 to 77 per cent in 1956, while the share of farm income (which is a mixture of labor and property income) declined from 6.7 per cent to 3.7 per cent, and the remainder of national income (which might roughly be taken to represent the income of property) declined from 31.4 per cent to 19.6 per cent.

No pronounced change took place in the relative size of distributive shares when the Eisenhower administration succeeded the Truman administration after the election of 1952. In particular, there has apparently been no noticeable upward trend in the size of the property share, as might perhaps have been expected with the inauguration of an administration generally considered to be more conservative than its immediate predecessors.

The evidence that in the past several decades labor's share in national income has shown an upward trend, while the property share has declined, does not, of course, prove that it was the increased economic power of labor unions which brought about this change. In fact, it is impossible to allocate causation among shifts in economic and political power, monetary and fiscal policy, changes in the volume of employment, changes in the progressiveness of taxation, and other factors which probably carried weight. Increased taxation of corporate profits apparently played a major role. However, the evidence does appear strongly to support the belief that economic and political power can affect the distribution of national income. Assuredly the leaders of economic pressure groups are going to assume that this is so and act accordingly.

The possibility of increasing the share of labor in the na-

[12] *Ibid.*, pp. 39 and 123, and Lenore Frane and L. R. Klein, "The Estimation of Disposable Income by Distributive Shares," *Review of Economics and Statistics*, November 1953, pp. 333–337.

tional income is, naturally, not without limits. The process of squeezing the property share cannot proceed indefinitely. This is true, in the first instance, because the share of property is relatively so much smaller than that of labor.[13] In the second place, sharply squeezing the return on capital and the premium for risk may lead in the short run to restriction of output from existing facilities and in the long run would certainly inhibit capital investment. There is, however, in the modern capitalistic economy apparently a zone of indeterminateness in which the property share can be substantially compressed without bringing these limiting forces at once into play. There begins to be evidence that the pressure of labor unions to compress still further the property return may already have confronted the economy with the choice of growing unemployment or inflation. This dilemma, too, was to be left to the Eisenhower administration.

The normal resistance to legislation strengthening the power of organized labor which might have been expected of Congressmen from agricultural areas was undermined by the similar conviction of farmers that they had to sell *their* products and buy *their* supplies at a disadvantage in an economy dominated by large corporations. Having succeeded under the New Deal in invoking the powers of government to redress the balance, farmers became conditioned to similar efforts by other economic interests. The amending of the Wagner Act by the Taft-Hartley Act did diminish the bargaining power of labor unions vis-à-vis corporate industry, although it is impossible to say with certainty on which side the balance lay thereafter. But the day of bilateral or unilateral individual wage bargaining was now gone. Even if a theoretical balance of power could have been determined and achieved, this would not have assured the settlement of wage disputes without the intervention of government. Equality of bargaining power between large collective groupings of economic power is at least as likely to mean more and longer strikes as is recognized inequality.

---

[13] Simon Kuznets estimates that property incomes constitute 15.8 per cent of the total income receipts of individuals in the United States. *Shares of Upper Income Groups in Income and Savings,* National Bureau of Economic Research, New York, 1953, p. 29.

The shift in favor of what the general public thought of as the economic and political power of "labor" meant in actuality a shift in favor of the power of the managements of labor unions. There had already developed the same kind of potential divergence of interest between the managements of labor unions and the rank and file as had developed between the managements of corporations and the stockholders. It generally proved almost as difficult to induce the membership of local unions to attend meetings and participate actively as to induce the majority of stockholders of corporations to do so, even when local labor leaders made most earnest efforts in this direction.[14] This apathy sometimes afforded an opportunity for hoodlums or for a small but disciplined Communist minority to capture control of locals. Sometimes this could be prevented only by strenuous action upon the part of the higher union officials, which, in turn, meant that control from the top down became almost inevitable. Democratic control of nationally organized unions was often rendered more difficult by the failure to hold annual meetings for the election of officers—partly because there often was not enough business to be transacted to justify them. Once entrenched, the management of a national labor union customarily perpetuated itself; members of the managerial hierarchy almost never became ordinary workers again. Thus, labor unions were acted upon by the same forces that tend to perpetuate the power of managerial groups in almost all organizations, including cooperatives and farm organizations.[15] It is as unrealistic to expect the managers of labor unions to alternate between, say, working on the assembly line in an automobile plant and running the affairs of the United Auto Workers as to expect the President of the United

[14] For a penetrating analysis of the forces and circumstances involved in the existence of one-party oligarchy in the American labor movement, see Seymour M. Lipset, "The Political Process in Trade Unions: A Theoretical Statement," Reprint No. 171, Bureau of Applied Social Research, Columbia University, New York, 1954.

[15] Political power in democratically controlled countries is a partial exception to this generalization. But a most elaborate system of publicly controlled elections, primaries and other machinery is required to prevent perpetuation of a ruling oligarchy. Such elaborate machinery can with difficulty be provided to police the election of the managements of corporations and labor unions.

States to return like Cincinnatus to his plow after he completes his term in office.

Since the election of managements of labor unions depends upon masses of workers who are at least potential voters in union locals, the attainment of power by a managerial group or by an individual leader does not depend primarily upon the advocacy of alternative union policies by rival candidates. It depends rather upon techniques of psychological appeal, upon the organization of personal "machines" or even upon the employment of physical force. The process is, indeed, analogous to the struggle of rival political leaders for state power. Thus a kind of "police power" on the part of union management determines maintenance of succession in office as is not ordinarily the case with corporation managements, although there is even less reality in their election by the stockholders than in the election of union management by union members.

This does not mean that the interests of the rank and file of labor unions and their managements must always diverge, although there is impressive evidence that this often happens. The disclosures of the McClellan Committee (Select Committee on Improper Activities in the Labor or Management Field) in 1957 and 1958 of flagrant examples of corruption in the management of the Teamsters Union, the Bakers Union, the United Textile Workers, the Union of Operating Engineers and others are strikingly comparable to the revelations of the Pecora Committee of the U.S. Senate in 1933–34 with respect to the exploitation of the stockholders of corporations by their managements. The evidence of bribery, fraud and violence employed against union members in the election and perpetuation of union managements, the wholesale use of union funds for personal investment and speculation by managers of these unions, their extravagant and often illegal use of expense accounts for luxurious living, the payment of large sums to hoodlums out of union funds, were perhaps less significant than the evidence of personal profit by union managements from dealings with corporate managements. The widespread evidence of "sweetheart contracts," whereby employers obtained the privilege of paying substandard wages in return for various favors to union managements, involved as much moral turpitude on the part of the employers as on the part of the labor leaders. The role of "paper locals," both in "unionizing" workers who were often unaware that they even belonged to these locals and in determining the control of national unions, sheds further light on the divergence of interests between "labor" and the managements of labor unions, even though the hearings did not establish the extent to which these practices were common among unions.

The conflict of interests between the workers and the managements of labor unions was also reflected in the continuous rise in the number of complaints of unfair labor practices brought against unions by workers. It has been generally assumed that such complaints are brought almost exclusively by employers, but by 1957 almost one-half of all complaints of unfair labor practices filed against labor unions before the National Labor Relations Board were brought by employees.

Just as the revelations of the Pecora Committee led to the enactment of corrective legislation which was administered eventually by the Securities and Exchange Commission, it may be that somewhat similar corrective legislation will follow the revelations of the McClellan Committee. Within the labor movement itself, the A.F.L.-C.I.O. began at once to take energetic action including the expulsion of offending unions which failed to rid themselves of corrupt managements. However, the conclusion is inescapable that under current organizational forms of modern capitalism neither the managements of corporations nor the managements of labor unions can be assumed to be dedicated representatives of "capital" or of "labor." At times both types of management may be in mutual agreement to further their own interests rather than those of either stockholders or laborers.

So long as Democratic administrations were in power, labor union leaders were able to use the threat of a strike more effectively than they could under a Republican administration in which the political power of labor managements was much weaker.[16] The "area of maneuver" for the managements of

[16] This did not mean that under a Republican administration the managements of labor unions did not obtain wage increases. Corporate industry had still to balance off the costs of enduring a strike with consequent loss of current income and bad public relations against wage increases which often could in large part be added to

labor unions in collective bargaining is naturally substantially larger under an administration which considers itself under obligation to "labor's" political power. Conversely, under an administration less obligated to labor, the "area of maneuver" of corporate management is extended. The amount of wage increase had thus come to vary both with the kind of labor laws and institutions under which wage bargaining took place and with the relative power of labor unions and corporate industry in influencing the government.

The necessity for some form of governmental intervention in wage setting by means of "fact finding" or arbitration was not obviated by shifts in the bargaining power of either side of the conflict. Labor union leaders were more likely than corporations, however, to invoke some form of governmental arbitration if they could not attain their ends by striking, and they were doubly likely to do so if an administration favorable to unions was in power. There was thus evolving a pattern of relations between corporate industry, labor unions and the government. This pattern was to vary with changes in administration and with the state of economic conjuncture, but it differed basically from that which would exist under the assumptions of old-style competition and laissez faire and which had to a considerable extent existed in the past.

The pattern could be more easily discerned when price controls were in existence, as, for example, after the outbreak of the Korean war. When the United Steel Workers in late 1951 asked for a wage increase, what were the motives of the managements of the various steel companies in resisting this demand? Of course, the profits of the industry would be reduced if an advance in steel prices was not permitted by the government as an offset to a wage increase. The managements of the different steel companies could not, however, hope to be allowed to advance steel prices unless they put up what appeared to be a "respectable" resistance to a wage increase. The managements of the steel companies had, consequently, to "make their case" for advancing prices by making a case against increasing wages. They did resist the demands for

the sales price of the product. Further, the Republican administration realized that to secure the necessary labor vote real wages had to rise as fast as under the previous Democratic administration.

wage increases and a strike resulted. The Truman administration, in effect, imposed a settlement of the strike which compelled a "package" wage increase of slightly more than 21 cents an hour. The steel companies were allowed to advance the price of steel $5.20 per ton.

Undoubtedly the managements of the steel companies would have preferred no advance in wages and no advance in prices just as they claimed in the public statement of their position. There obviously had been some risk that they would not be allowed to pass on the full amount of the wage increase in price increases. Even if this had not been true, however, the steel companies would no doubt have preferred to retain the lower wage-price relation for reasons other than immediate profit maximization. Wage-price increases in steel could be expected either to push steel wage-prices above their previous relation to the general level of wages and prices or to result in a round of wage-price increases in the rest of the economy. In the one case, this might impair somewhat the competitive position of steel versus other metals after the removal of price controls. In the other case, a general round of wage-price increases would constitute an inflationary force in the economy which the corporate managements in the steel industry in their concern for economic, political and social stability would presumably have found distasteful. To the extent that these motivations had effect, however, they were outside the area of concern of managers of independent corporations if they had been acting within the assumptions of old-style, free-enterprise competition.

Even during periods when neither price nor wage controls were in force, the behavior of prices and wages in highly concentrated industries characterized by administered prices and price leadership did not follow the pattern of competitive pricing. Thus on May 1, 1948 the U.S. Steel Corporation announced a reduction in the price of steel which amounted to around $1.25 per ton. At the same time the Corporation resisted the union's demand for an increase in wages. According to Roger M. Blough, Chairman of the Board of the Steel Corporation, this lowering of prices was not intended to increase the demand for steel generally or to take business away from competitors, for neither was necessary. These would have been normal motives under the assumptions of competition. Instead, the motive alleged for the cut in prices and the refusal to raise wages was to help in stopping the current inflationary movement of the general price level.[17] There is reason to believe that the alleged motive was the actual one. But, in spite of the fact that the whole industry apparently followed the price leadership of U.S. Steel, the action was unsuccessful in halting the general inflationary spiral. Three months later the price reduction was rescinded and wage increases were granted.

The management of the Steel Corporation in this episode appears to have been in some degree motivated by concern for the public interest. Yet the whole sequence of events did not reflect the operation of the price and cost system under old-style competition. Indeed, in neither the steel industry nor the automobile industry, during periods when their products were in short supply, for example, were prices set by the managements of the producing corporations at the point where profits would have been maximized.[18] Instead, during a number of years after World War II prices were kept so low relative to what they would have been had profits been maximized that the phenomena of "black markets" and "gray markets" were often in evidence, even when official price regulation was not in force. On the other hand, where a situation closer to that of the traditional competitive market existed, as in the textile industry, the managements of the small corporations in the industry generally set prices high enough to more nearly maximize the profits of each individual company. In such industries "rationing through market price" largely eliminated black and gray markets. Because of the difference in pricing policies between the more and the less competitive industries, during periods of short supply prices tended to rise more in

[17] See Blough's statement before the Subcommittee on Antitrust and Monopoly of the Senate Committee on the Judiciary, August 8, 1957.

[18] In other words, the quantity demanded and the quantity offered were not brought to identity through "rationing by market price" as would have been true under the assumptions of a free, competitive market but instead by outright rationing by corporate managements to customers.

competitive industries than in those characterized by some form of oligopoly or imperfect competition.[19]

As might be expected, during periods when prices were advancing more rapidly in the more competitive industries, wages sometimes temporarily rose more rapidly in these light industries than in the less competitive heavy industries.[20] Managements of small independent corporations naturally felt much freer to compete for a short supply of labor by bidding up wage rates than did their counterparts in large corporations. Managements of large corporations realized that they could not usually get labor away from other corporations in the same industry by offering higher wages, since wage setting would generally be industry-wide, with little even temporary advantage to the corporation initiating the increase in wage rates. The management of a small corporation which was only one of many could feel that selling its products at the highest price obtainable and offering higher wages than the other companies would not immediately affect the general level of prices or wages in the industry and would provide at least a momentary profit advantage. It would also reason that neither public opinion nor government would hold it responsible for price or wage changes.

Not so, for example, with the management of the United States Steel Corporation. To raise prices to the point where profits would be maximized would have meant that the rela-

[19] This was the reverse of the price-production policies of the two types of industry during the depression of the 1930s. At such times, industries that have relatively few corporate producing units or in which one or a few large corporate producers are dominant, and that are characterized by "administered prices," reduce production in order to limit price declines in the expectation that a similar policy will be followed by the limited number of other producers in the industry. The managements of corporations in industries with a large number of independent producing units, such as the textile industry, do not reduce production to the same extent to protect prices since it would not maximize the profits of an independent producer to do so and common action among a large number of independent producers is more difficult to attain.

[20] The reverse has been true during periods of depression. At such times wages in industries characterized by heavy corporate concentration did not fall as much in response to a fall in demand as did wages in industries characterized by lesser degrees of corporate concentration.

tively few other producers of steel could raise their prices as well. In consequence, labor unions in the steel industry would have insisted on at least a proportionate wage increase. This in turn would, as has been pointed out, either bring steel wages and prices out of line with other wages and prices or induce an inflationary price-wage spiral in the economy. Thus, when prices and wages were not under governmental control, the management of U.S. Steel could not escape responsibility in the eyes of the public for price increases,[21] if they were initiated in order to maximize profits in the way in which entrepreneurs were assumed to act under a competitive, laissez-faire system.

In those special circumstances, the temporarily more rapid rise of wages in industries more nearly characterized by old-style competition naturally did not occur *because* of the lower degree of unionization of labor. It occurred *in spite* of the lower degree of unionization. Unionization tends to be strongest in industries characterized by concentration of production in relatively large corporations where, for the reasons explained, price rises are sometimes partially limited by the self-restraint of corporate managements. Labor union leaders are likely to have greater difficulty during periods of strong inflationary pressure and a sellers' market in obtaining wage increases in industries where price rises are kept under some control by corporate management than in industries with large numbers of competing producers where prices can be allowed to advance without restraint. Under the present organization of labor and corporate industry, *reductions* in wage rates are likely to be extremely rare in either type of industry, and indeed nonexistent in large-scale corporate industry even during periods of reduced business activity. Governments no longer dare allow severe or prolonged depressions to occur. If necessary, massive "reflationary" measures must be taken to prevent them. Furthermore, governments do not dare to allow the level of money wages in any industry to be materially

[21] To a lesser extent the management of the relatively few other steel companies could not, of course, have avoided acceptance of some responsibility also. This contrasts with the anonymity of the managements of textile plants which charged higher prices and paid higher wages than before.

reduced during temporary "recessions." Stated more briefly, money wage rates no longer decline.

As a trend, the resistance of corporate managements to wage increases has been diminishing steadily. With rare exceptions, they no longer attempt to operate plants when a strike sanctioned by a labor union has been called. Confronted by a strike or the threat of a strike for higher wages by a labor union with industry-wide organization, corporate managements know that public opinion and governmental pressure will almost always insist upon settlement of the strike by whatever concessions from management are necessary to get production going again. Since all major producers will normally have to grant the same wage increases and since some or all of the increased wage cost can be recovered from price increases, the burden of blame for these price increases is likely to be less onerous than for refusing to make wage increases which would prevent a strike. Further, even if price increases do not fully compensate stockholders for the loss of earnings, it is unlikely that stockholders will either attempt to or be able to punish managements for making too liberal wage settlements. There is thus little danger that the compensation of corporate managements will be diminished by the wage increases granted; in fact, there are no cases on record where this has happened.

Wage agreements which during periods of full employment provide for increases in annual earnings larger than the increases in productivity for the whole economy are, of course, inflationary in their effect. Since productivity is likely to increase at a higher rate in large-scale industries than in the remainder of the economy, and particularly in the production of services, wage increases which no more than equal the increases in productivity in those industries will also produce inflationary effects. In practice, wage increases are likely to be larger than productivity increases even in the large-scale industry. This is true first of all simply because a 2 per cent annual increase in wages and fringe benefits, which has in the recent past been the amount of the average annual rate of increase in productivity for the national economy, seems so niggardly that the managements of labor unions would hardly expect the union membership to allow them to settle for it.

Second, once an inflationary movement is under way, the managements of labor unions naturally feel that they must obtain a settlement which compensates for past and even prospective increases in the cost of living in addition to whatever real increase in wages they might otherwise be able to obtain.[22] Third, it is extremely difficult at any particular moment to prove that a rise in the general price level has been caused by an increase in wages. It has often been caused in whole or in part by other factors and forces. In any event, the management of the labor union in the steel industry, for example, is not likely to limit its demands for a wage increase on account of the possible effect of such an increase on the general cost of living, any more than the managements of the various steel companies are likely to renounce compensatory price increases for that reason. Finally, the managements of corporate industries *might*, indeed, either lower prices or raise wages sufficiently to provide purchasing power in the economy to take off the market the results of increased productivity even in the absence of bargaining pressure from labor unions, either because the existing kind and degree of competition compelled them to do so or because of concern for the public interest. The managements of labor unions can, however, hardly be expected to have confidence that this will inevitably happen, and of course they do not believe it will.

During periods when inflationary pressures are not being initiated from the monetary side, the higher the degree of corporate organization of industry the more feasible it is for such wage increases to be passed on through price increases. These increases may require monetary expansion through deficit financing and related measures if a general fall in demand is to be avoided. It may thus become the responsibility of the government to manage the monetary system so that higher money costs of production can be met, both on the demand and on the supply side. Under these circumstances wage in-

----

[22] Fortunately the first and second causes of the inflationary pressures for wage increases are not always cumulative. For example, a 7 per cent increase in wages, of which 4 per cent is compensation for increased cost of living, is more impressive and probably more acceptable to the managements of labor unions than a 3 per cent wage increase when the cost of living is stationary.

creases may induce monetary inflation. Since compensating upward pressures on agricultural costs and prices do not usually develop of themselves, the government will inevitably be under pressure from farmers to raise farm prices by all possible devices to offset the increased prices of manufactured goods.[23] Consequently, a sort of inflationary "ratchet effect" is likely to characterize an economy of large-scale corporate and labor union organizations accompanied by governmental intervention in the economy. This pattern of encouraging wage increases somewhat larger than increases in industrial productivity and of supporting "parity" farm prices, accompanied by whatever deficit financing is necessary to "underwrite" full employment at the resultant price level, gradually became the basic economic policy of the Truman administration.

While this pattern of wage-price relations evolved under the "laboristic" Truman administration, only recourse to a more restrictive credit policy was to alter this relation substantially under the supposedly more conservative Eisenhower administration which followed. Even the balancing of the budget and the restrictive credit policy of the Eisenhower administration failed to stop the upward movement of wages and prices until these measures had produced a slowing down of production. Indeed, the postwar experience of the national economies of Western Europe indicates that this process is becoming a world-wide characteristic of modern capitalism.

It has been pointed out that the purpose of controls over agricultural prices and production was shifted during World War II to stimulate rather than to limit production. How-

[23] Improved industrial technology, which would have resulted in lowered costs of production and lower prices to consumers (including farmers) for manufactured goods under the assumptions of pure and perfect competition, is reflected under the present corporate organization of industry and labor in higher wages and the maintenance of a rate of profits high enough to induce new investment in industry. By contrast, some millions of individual farmers find it difficult to maintain the rate of return on investment by shifting to other profitable agricultural alternatives. Farmers are likely to find their returns unfavorable compared with those of labor and capital in industry until such time as labor and capital can move out of

ever, the "machinery" for the control of both prices and production remained substantially intact at all times. Since agricultural surpluses had largely disappeared as a result of the emergency demands of the war and immediate postwar period, there had been some hope that it would be possible to eliminate governmental control of farm prices and production at the end of the war. The re-election of President Truman in 1948 disappointed the hopes of those who had counted upon a return to a laissez-faire policy in agriculture. Subsequent experience has demonstrated that even a Republican victory in that year would not have ended agricultural price supports and production controls. Nevertheless, so accustomed have American economists been to considering agriculture, with its millions of independent producers, as the outstanding sector of our economy in which something approaching "pure and perfect competition" still exists that the extent to which governmental intervention has modified the economic system in this sector also is by no means universally recognized. This failure to recognize the significance of the change in the character of the pricing and resource allocation mechanism in agriculture flows in part out of the substantial disagreement about the effects of governmental intervention in this area.

In attempting to estimate the likelihood of governmental controls of farm prices and production continuing as an integral element in our economic system, we now have the experience of well over two decades upon which to base an appraisal of their results. Yet it is extraordinary how much disagreement exists with respect to the conclusions to be drawn from this experience. There is a sort of perverse parallelism in some of the conclusions of the critics and defenders of agricultural price and production control programs.

The hostile critics of these programs have in effect said:

1. The price and production control programs have not been effective in limiting agricultural production and raising farm prices. Instead they have caused large surpluses of farm products to pile up.

2. The control programs have been antisocial in their effects

---

agriculture into other employment. This is a slow process and farmers are not willing to wait for it to happen. More immediate results can be got by political pressure.

by raising the cost of food and restricting supplies available to consumers.

3. The control programs have greatly distorted agricultural production and have caused serious mal-allocation of resources.

The defenders of the governmental agricultural programs have countered by saying, in effect:

1. The price programs have been effective in raising prices through limiting production of farm products.

2. The price programs have not been antisocial in their effects. The production of farm products over the whole period has increased greatly while the real incomes of consumers have also increased greatly.

3. There has been no substantial distortion of agricultural production. Resources devoted to the production of the major crops are just about what they would have been under the guidance of a free price system. In fact, it is argued, governmental controls were necessary to bring about this approximation of the allocation of resources which would have taken place under a competitive, free market system, since it was the disappearance of this system which brought governmental controls into existence.

The defenders generally do not, however, explain how the programs could have raised prices to farmers without limiting supplies and raising prices to consumers beyond what they would have been in the absence of governmental intervention.[24]

With regard to the effects of the programs on resource allocation there has been a wide spectrum of disagreement as to whether they have been the cause of serious mal-allocation

[24] Neither critics nor defenders of governmental price programs in agriculture have, of course, stated their cases as simply and crudely as is done here. For a statement of the position of the defenders and for a criticism of the logic of the hostile critics, see J. K. Galbraith, "Economic Preconceptions and Farm Policy," *American Economic Review,* March 1953, pp. 40–52. Galbraith apparently believes that incomes of farmers were increased by governmental price supports, but does not believe that substantial mal-allocation of resources occurred. He further believes that resources were employed which in the absence of the farm programs would have remained unemployed or might not even have come into existence.

of resources between agriculture and the other sectors of the economy and/or of mal-allocation of resources within agriculture itself.[25] The stark fact of the existing surpluses of wheat, cotton, dairy products and the like does prove some mal-allocation of resources. But this does not tell us whether it is within agriculture or between agriculture and the other sectors of the economy. Neither can we tell from the mere fact of the surpluses whether the manpower and other resources used to produce them would certainly have found alternative employment in other sectors of the economy, although this seems probable in view of the degree of full employment which characterized the United States economy during most of the post-war period. Conversely, the failure of so-called "burdensome" surpluses to accumulate in some cases, as was true for a time of tobacco, does not prove that mal-allocation of resources did not occur or that prices were maintained only at about the level which would have existed in the absence of price supports. It seems probable indeed that the tobacco programs did result in the transfer of income to farmers having a production

[25] See, for example, Gale Johnson, "Agricultural Price Policy and International Trade," *Essays in International Finance*, Princeton University Press, Princeton, June 1954, and his "Competition in Agriculture: Fact or Fiction," *Papers and Proceedings of the American Economic Association*, May 1954, pp. 107–115. Johnson believes that, viewing the period of governmental farm programs as a whole, substantial mal-allocation did not take place because support prices for most of the period were not greatly above theoretically "proper" prices for the inducement of "proper" allocation of resources. He does not believe that income diversion to farmers occurred: ". . . it would appear that at least until mid-1952 the American consumer and tax payer fared reasonably well, the United States farmer may have gained reasonably little, and foreign producers have on the whole been aided by the programs." (It is not easy, however, to see how both American consumers and foreign producers could have been aided by the programs, looked at within the framework of Johnson's analysis.) Indeed, Johnson argues that consumers received farm products at lower prices than they would have had to pay had the quantities actually consumed been produced in the absence of price supports, presumably because of the stabilization of producers' expectations due to price supports. The logical deduction from Johnson's argument would agree with Galbraith's contention that farmers may produce a given quantity of farm products for some lower guaranteed price than for some higher but uncertain average of prices set by the free market through time.

base, and that there was a tendency to freeze resources in less efficient employment, in spite of the fact that large surpluses admitted to be "unmanageable" did not accumulate.

There is disagreement about the results of governmental price and production controls partly because the programs were intended at some times to decrease production and to raise prices while at other times they were intended to increase production. At still other times the programs were simply in abeyance. Consequently, it is not feasible to judge the results of the whole period by the criterion which the government had in mind during any one phase. Furthermore, it is quite unreasonable to attribute the good or bad times for the farmer since the onset of governmental controls primarily to what the government did or did not do in its agricultural programs. It seems likely that farm income during the period was much more affected by governmental policy in deficit financing, by wars and by foreign aid programs, not to mention the factor of weather as illustrated by the droughts of 1934 and 1936, than by the governmental price programs themselves.[26]

Largely in spite of what critics and defenders of governmental price supports and production controls in agriculture have said and written, these programs remain in existence. It has been pointed out that governmental price and production control programs were initiated at the beginning of the New Deal in the belief that it was necessary to accord farmers the same power to maintain prices for their products through withholding production as industry and labor were believed to exercise through their organizations. When the control programs were initiated, the limitation of production by industry was a fact and indeed full employment in industry was not attained until after the outbreak of World War II. During this long period of underemployment in the national economy, governmental controls in agriculture could continue to be represented as a sort of withholding of production by agriculture to match that of industry.

Experience during the postwar period has shown, however,

[26] See Murray R. Benedict's *Farm Policies of the United States, 1790–1950*, Twentieth Century Fund, 1953, for an excellent analytical account of the events of this period.

that even during periods of full employment, when industry as a whole was not limiting production to less than capacity, farm prices could decline to levels unacceptable to farmers. The advocates of governmental price and production controls in agriculture consequently argue that these controls are still necessary even during periods of full employment in industry. They maintain that price supports and production controls are necessary in order to stabilize agricultural prices and thereby eliminate speculative losses to farmers and facilitate well-planned investment, permitting lower costs of production. It is also argued that only by the use of governmental price supports and production controls can farmers receive returns for their labor and capital resources which will give them parity with returns to labor and capital in industry.

It can be shown, of course, that there are likely to be serious contradictions in any agricultural price and production control program aimed both at stabilization of prices and at the maintenance of "parity prices" if such prices are substantially higher than those which a freely competitive market would set. Indeed, the accumulation of agricultural surpluses during the postwar period serves to demonstrate the contradiction. Price supports which are designed to raise farm prices to "parity" will induce the production of larger crops than can be marketed on the domestic and foreign market, in the absence of both comprehensive and complicated crop controls and a two-price system. From the standpoint of social justice it must be pointed out also that government price-support programs which did succeed in increasing the average income of farmers through transferring increased shares in the national income to the agricultural sector would do so largely by increasing the income of farmers in the higher-income brackets. The incomes of almost two million of our somewhat less than five million farms could not be increased materially by price supports for crops which they produced for the market. Their production is too small and any benefit these farmers would receive from price supports would be offset by increases in prices of other farm products which they purchased.

Nevertheless, there is every expectation that some sort of governmental program of price supports and production controls, such as characterized the period of the Truman administration, will continue indefinitely to be a feature of the American economic system. Although the effort simultaneously to stabilize farm prices and to maintain "parity prices" is contradictory, this is because the parity prices have been set so high as to induce a volume of production beyond what the market could absorb. It would be possible to set support prices at levels which would have a stabilizing effect upon prices and which would probably enable production to take place at lower average costs over a period of time than would exist in the absence of government control. In effect, such a price-support program would be designed to accomplish what the old-style, competitive free market had been assumed to do but had failed to do. Such a program of price supports would have the additional advantage of providing some insurance against the possibility of a general economic depression being initiated by a collapse of farm prices.

The fact that a case can be made for the kind of price stabilization program which would be of some benefit to farmers, while neither raising the cost of farm products to the consumer over time nor burdening the taxpayer, is probably not the determining factor in assuring the continuance of governmental controls in agriculture. The evidence of repeated referenda held among growers of cotton, wheat, tobacco and other crops demonstrates that they wish the price and production controls to continue. Growers are in effect asked to vote on whether they favor governmental action to raise the prices of their products by limiting production. This is very much as if the manufacturers of cement or steel or coal, for example, had been asked, during a period when the prices of their products had been falling and threatened to fall further, whether they would agree to limit production, enforced by governmental sanction, in order to raise their prices. The willingness of producers of a particular commodity to raise prices through governmentally sanctioned collective action is not surprising.

Farmers are not impressed by the argument that their total returns will not be increased simply by governmental price supports and production controls designed to give them "parity prices." "High and rigid price controls" do cause surpluses to accumulate. Production controls often do not effectively limit production. The farmer does not worry much about this. He knows by experience that the United States Treasury will eventually take care of the costs of storage and disposal of the surpluses. In the meantime, he has received payment for them just as though they had been sold on the domestic market at the going price. It is no wonder that the vote in agricultural communities in national elections usually confirms the favorable results of the referenda on the price-support and control programs for individual commodities. Even the millions of small farmers who have little to gain from the programs are likely to feel a sense of solidarity with other farmers and in any event to favor whatever governmental program is intended to raise the price per unit of whatever they produce, though the effect upon their total economic well-being may be negligible or even negative. Any argument that such a program will add to federal taxes leaves them understandably cold for they are not likely to be substantial payers of such taxes. Beyond this, a considerable number of marginal farmers have benefited from other governmental aid, such as social security benefits. These people are not inclined to disentangle one form of governmental intervention and aid from another.

Finally, the farmer still vaguely feels that industrial corporations do limit production in order to maintain prices at levels which provide constantly advancing real wages and returns on capital sufficient to induce a continuous flow of investment. True, industrial production in recent years has not usually been limited as it was during the great depression of the thirties by widespread shutting down of factories or by operation of many plants at half capacity. Moreover, large-scale corporate industry does not now generally carry on so-called "cutthroat competition," either by cutting wages or by building excess plants. So long as the general level of demand is maintained by governmental fiscal and monetary policy, it has become generally feasible for large corporations to plan investment and sales policies so as to avoid either greatly excessive inventories or excess capacity in a way which was not feasible when production was carried on by numerous small manufacturers. The prevention of "cutthroat pricing" is facilitated by the floor which industry-wide wage setting places under prices.

Under these circumstances, governmental price supports and production controls in agriculture appear to have become a permanent part of our economic system. The strategic importance of the farm vote is so great that it will be very difficult for some time to come to keep support prices low enough so that a smoothly functioning price and production mechanism in agriculture can be attained.

The Employment Act of 1946 embodied in legislation for the first time the "responsibility of the Federal Government to use all practicable means consistent with the needs and obligations and other essential considerations of national policy . . . to coordinate and utilize all its plans, functions, and resources" for the stated purpose of the act—maximum production, employment and purchasing power.[27] The act did not state the particular means by which the government was to carry out the goal of maximizing production and employment. Although the Council of Economic Advisers was set up, this body had no executive or administrative power over the economy, only analytical and advisory powers. All the means by which the purposes of the act were likely to be carried out had been utilized by the government at one time or another to attain these same ends. However, the purposes for which those means had been used in particular instances had not always been admitted, nor had there ever previously been a legislative mandate for combining various specific measures to carry out the declared purposes of the act.

Though the specific powers of the federal government over the economy were not extended by the Employment Act, its powers and influence could now be exerted more freely, in a more coordinated fashion and for purposes which had not previously been explicitly stated. For example, the level of governmental expenditures required to maintain full employment, the taxation or borrowing required to meet these expenditures, and the extent to which a budgetary surplus or deficit could be expected to have inflationary or deflationary effects could now appropriately be considered by the executive and legislative branches of the government in exercising their

[27] Edwin G. Nourse, *Economics in the Public Service*, Harcourt, Brace, New York, 1953, p. 125.

fiscal functions and responsibilities. The goal of maximizing production and employment may not be the main determinant of whether the federal budget is or is not going to be balanced at a particular time. Yet the recognition of the legitimacy of this purpose was of the greatest importance in the development of the powers of the government over the economy. The level of governmental support for agricultural prices, the attitude of government officials toward raising wage rates either through collective bargaining or through minimum-wage legislation, the question of whether corporate taxes or the personal income tax exemption is to be raised or lowered, may now be considered in relation to maximizing production and employment.

The passage of the Employment Act of 1946 did not specifically increase the powers of the federal government over the Federal Reserve System, and many of the devices for implementing monetary policy depend upon action by that organization rather than by the federal government itself. Yet actions of the Federal Reserve System with respect to the rediscount rate, reserve ratios, open market policy and the like are, to an important degree, determined by the wishes of the administration in power. The legislative mandate which assigned an increased degree of responsibility for the maintenance of optimum levels of production and employment to the federal government unquestionably implied that government officials would furnish more guidance to the Federal Reserve System in exercising monetary powers to the extent that they affect production and employment.

Furthermore, when proposed new legislation in the economic field comes before a congressional committee for consideration, government officials appearing as witnesses are likely to be much freer in arguing, for example, that raising or lowering particular tax rates would expand production and employment.[28] If a member of a congressional committee re-

---

[28] A government official was once sharply rebuked by a member of Congress for arguing that the reduction of trade barriers would shift resources into more productive uses. He was advised that there was no legislative authority whatever for his trying to decide what domestic industries should be curtailed or expanded for the purpose of increasing national income.

bukes such a witness by saying that taxes are levied to meet the expenses of government and not to interfere with or affect the level of production and employment, the witness is now on much safer ground, for he can cite the language of the Employment Act of 1946.

One of the most remarkable of the economic changes which took place during the period of Democratic rule from 1933 to 1953 was the marked decline in inequality in income distribution to which reference has been made. It is true that the most pronounced diminution in inequality is concentrated in the period 1939–44, when war and not New Deal-Fair Deal economic policies were primarily determinative. During that period, however, the change was striking. The share of the upper 5 per cent of the population in disposable income declined by over two-fifths. There is evidence that this decline in inequality maintained itself at least through 1950,[29] and there is no substantial evidence that a reversal of the decline took place under the succeeding Republican administration.

As has been pointed out above, the Democratic administrations of Roosevelt and Truman had evolved an economic and political doctrine which represented the federal government under the New Deal and Fair Deal as acting to provide "countervailing power"[30] to labor, to the farmer, and to lower-income receivers in general to offset the economic power of the great corporations that were no longer effectively regulated

[29] Kuznets, *Shares of Upper Income Groups in Income and Savings,* pp. 37–39. See also Allan M. Cartter, "Income Shares of Upper Income Groups in Great Britain and the United States," *American Economic Review,* December 1954, pp. 877–883, who questions some of Kuznets' contentions with respect to the reduction in inequality in the United States. See also Goldsmith, "Changes in the Size Distribution of Income." A widening dispersion of stockholdings has also sometimes been claimed as evidence of the increased egalitarianism of American capitalism. The evidence for such dispersion is inconclusive, however. For an analytical attack on this claim of widening dispersion of stockholdings, see Victor Perlo, "'People's Capitalism' and Stock-Ownership," *American Economic Review,* June 1958, pp. 333–347.

[30] The phrase is J. K. Galbraith's as used in his *American Capitalism: The Concept of Countervailing Power,* Houghton Mifflin, Boston, 1952.

by competition in the free market. It would be tempting, consequently, simply to conclude that by putting the power of the state on the side of labor, the farmer and the lower-income receiver, the Democratic administrations which held power from 1933 to 1953 were responsible for a planned reduction in inequality in income distribution. Indeed, there is some evidence to justify such a conclusion, in part, as will be pointed out later.

However, some parts of the evidence do not fit neatly into this explanation. In the first place, it seems that diminution of inequality in income distribution occurs in a particular stage in the industrial development of advanced countries.[81] In the second place, the period when the most pronounced diminution in inequality took place was not immediately following the enactment of New Deal legislation but from 1939 to 1944. One might easily conclude that it was World War II and not the New Deal or the Fair Deal which brought this about. In a certain sense, this is true. Probably the greatest single factor responsible for the change was the disappearance of unemployment during the war and postwar period. Millions of people who were formerly without income of their own or had been on relief were added to the total of wage receivers.[82] Some part of the diminution in inequality was the result of heavy wartime taxation. These high rates were no doubt caused as much by the war as by New Deal economic policy. Still another cause was the much higher incomes of farmers during the 1939–44 period, which also continued into the early postwar years. These higher farm incomes were also due to abnormal war and postwar demand and to governmentally supplied funds for purchases for foreign account than to New Deal agricultural policies. It might appear then that, after allowing for the effects of the war, little would remain

[81] Kuznets conjectures that the early effects of capitalistic industrialization may be to increase inequality in income distribution while the later effects tend to narrow inequality. He conjectures that the narrowing process may have begun in England in the last quarter of the nineteenth century and with the first world war in the United States. Simon Kuznets, "Economic Growth and Income Inequality," *American Economic Review*, March 1955, pp. 1–28.

[82] There was apparently also a slight decline in inequality during World War I.

of the economic policies of the New Deal and Fair Deal to account for the change in income distribution which happened to take place during the twenty years of Democratic administrations.

The matter is not even as simple as this, however. Apart from the effects of World War II, it is possible to attribute the recovery from the depression of the 1930s and the maintenance of substantially full employment after the war in considerable degree to New Deal policies intended to maintain mass purchasing power. The principal factor in these policies was deficit financing. During the Truman administration, resort to a budgetary deficit whenever substantial unemployment occurred had become permanent governmental policy. To the extent that this policy was responsible for the maintenance of full employment and to the extent that the employment of persons who would otherwise have been unemployed reduced inequality in income distribution, the New Deal can be credited in some degree with the reduction in inequality. In so far as New Deal policies were responsible for raising real wages, for increasing incomes to farmers through subsidies of many diverse kinds, and for increasing the shares of low-income receivers through relief payments financed either out of income taxes at much more progressive rates or by budgetary deficits, these policies may be credited with some direct effect upon income distribution. To the extent that these measures were favorable to the maintenance of purchasing power in the economy, they helped to keep up the volume of employment as well and thus indirectly increased the income of many persons who would have had much lower incomes or no incomes at all.[33]

In summary, under the Truman administration the New Deal economic legislation which had been initiated by President Roosevelt and which was partially in abeyance during World War II gave evidence of having become an integral part of the American economic system. The process of price and wage determination in industry had become one involving large corporations and large labor unions. It could no longer be

[33] All these factors which add to purchasing power are, of course, simultaneously factors which can produce inflation.

considered substantially an approximation of the purely and perfectly competitive process assumed as characteristic of laissez-faire capitalism. In agriculture, government had come to intervene in the pricing and resource allocation process with the somewhat confused goal of restoring prices and resource allocation to a normality which it was assumed they would have had under old-style competitive pricing. By the Employment Act of 1946 government took over responsibility for the maintenance of full employment in the economy. It had been assumed that full employment would automatically exist in a purely and perfectly competitive laissez-faire economy, but under the changed character of the economy this no longer could be taken for granted. The marked decline in the inequality in distribution of the national income which had manifested itself by the time of the Truman administration could not be attributed directly to the legislative measures enacted with this intent by the Democratic administrations. Nevertheless, the decline in income inequality was attributable in part directly and in considerable degree indirectly to changes in the economic system inaugurated by the New Deal. In any event, this decline in inequality was likely to prove one of the factors which would insure popular support for the continuance of these modifications of the American economic system in the future.

Thus it was during the two terms of President Truman that the new economic system of the United States began to take on an air of permanency. It has been pointed out that the corporate organizational form in industry had transformed old-style, individual-enterprise capitalism long before the New Deal. What the New Deal did was simultaneously to prop up collapsing corporate capitalism, make deficit financing respectable, tremendously strengthen the economic and political power of labor and farm organizations, throw down the shield of inviolability which the courts in the United States had placed over private property, establish the precedent for widespread governmental intervention in the economy, set up a program of social security, and modify the distribution of income in the direction of greater equality.

Yet these great economic changes of the New Deal had not been based upon a previously developed ideology or upon a comprehensive plan. Some of the changes had been represented as only temporary. Consequently, conservatives had hoped that, after the unemployment of the Great Depression was over and after the end of World War II, most of the New Deal measures could be repealed and the old economic system could be restored. But the consolidation of the economic measures of the New Deal under President Truman and his re-election meant that, even in peacetime and even when there was little or no unemployment, politicians could win popular majorities by supporting this new economic system. Politicians now came to feel little hope that popular majorities could be obtained by a conservative party unless the mass of the voters were offered economic inducements as appealing as those of the New Deal and its Fair Deal successor.[34] But if these inducements were offered, could there be any restoration of the economic system to what it had been before the New Deal? The Eisenhower administration had to face this question, just as the Conservative Party in England had to face the same issue in competing for votes with the Labor Party.

[34] This age-old dilemma of the conservatives was well illustrated when Cato in 62 B.C., against all his principles, widened the privilege of obtaining cheap bread-grains at state-subsidized prices in order to win the votes of the masses. Caesar, as the leader of the radical *Populares,* completely outbid the conservative *Optimates* four years later when corn was given out free.

CHAPTER 9

THE CONSERVATIVE
ACQUIESCENCE IN THE CHANGED
AMERICAN ECONOMIC SYSTEM

Conservative businessmen who initially had viewed the complex of New Deal economic measures as a fundamental impairment of "free enterprise capitalism" doubtless believed that the repeal of these measures would be the first order of business after the Republican victory at the polls, if this happy event should ever take place. Long before the Democratic Party gave way to the Republican Party in the election of 1952, however, conservative businessmen had begun to abandon their position that the New Deal had fatally impaired the capitalistic system. Of course, they had never believed that by the early 1930s competition was already so altered by quasi-monopolistic forms of giantism in industry as to reflect a fundamental change in the economic system. During the war and postwar period American industrialists began to push into the back of their minds the changes wrought by the New Deal and to point again with pride to the tremendous productivity of what they were once more coming to think of as *their* American capitalism. They had, for example, seized the opportunity afforded by the Marshall Plan to package advice with aid and to urge European countries both to eschew the evils of industrial monopoly and to refrain from further socialization of their national economies that they might also enjoy the high productivity of "free enterprise capitalism."[1]

It would be incorrect to say that American businessmen had gradually become convinced of the virtues of the economic changes brought about under the New Deal, although even this was partly true for some. American businessmen had, however, learned that they could live with what was once considered the "New Order" and had largely come to take it for granted. The conditioning effect upon some industrialists of their own experience in administering economic controls as wartime governmental officials, on the one hand, and their relief at the elimination of some of the most severe and cumbersome controls after the war, on the other, have been pointed out in the previous chapter. Those New Deal measures which were nevertheless still distasteful were tolerated in recognition that substantial corporate profits could still be earned even though this legislation remained in force. Unquestionably, however, some conservative businessmen had adjusted themselves to this legislation only because the popular support enjoyed by the Democratic administrations of Roosevelt and Truman left them no choice. After the Republican victory in 1952 these conservatives found that they were still not free to dismantle this structure; hostages had been given to fortune in the course of the political campaign by accepting a substantial part of the New Deal legislation.

Thus the newly inaugurated administration found little of the complex of New Deal economic measures which it seemed politically feasible to have repealed. Social security legislation could certainly not be repealed; instead, it was to be broadened. No one any longer advocated substantial modification of legislation regulating the issuance of securities and the security exchanges. The enactment of legislation providing for "flexible" price supports in agriculture, in claimed contrast with "rigid" price supports at some fixed percentage of parity,

---

[1] In 1947, some members of the President's Committee on Foreign Aid, commonly referred to as the Harriman Committee, urged that Marshall Plan aid should not be advanced to those countries which proposed further nationalization of their industries. This recommendation was opposed by the majority of the Committee, of which the writer was a member, and it was not adopted.

represented only a minor divergence from the legislation passed under the Truman administration, which had also provided some degree of flexibility. The Eisenhower administration even proposed to amend the Taft-Hartley Act in an effort to render it more acceptable to labor. Since the proposed amendments did not go far enough to satisfy labor leaders, the act—which had originally been passed over the veto of President Truman—remained in force. It is true that labor leaders could not, as under the Truman administration, count upon the intervention of government in collective bargaining to increase wages. Real wages nevertheless rose, nor did the share of labor in national income decline. Managements of industrial corporations did not stubbornly resist wage increases, since they were eager to attract political support for the Eisenhower administration from among industrial workers by demonstrating that their standard of living would be at least as high under a Republican as under a Democratic administration. This rise in real wages was for a time facilitated by the temporary stabilization of consumer prices, the result of a slight rise in the prices of manufactured goods and a fall in farm prices. While the agricultural price decline was politically most unfortunate, it did serve to mitigate the effect on the cost of living of rising wages and rising profits in industry.

An effort by the more conservative wing of the Republican Party to eliminate the Council of Economic Advisers through failing to appropriate funds for its maintenance, and thus to allow the Employment Act of 1946 to fall into disuse, was frustrated by the President. A vigorous effort to reduce expenditures and to balance the budget was indeed made by the new administration. In some degree this represented a change in policy from that of the previous Democratic administrations. But it inevitably became the operative policy of the Eisenhower administration that the budget should be balanced only during a period of high employment. It gradually became apparent that, if economic recession threatened, the federal budget would be left in deficit or again allowed to become unbalanced. With the onset of the short-lived recession in the fall of 1953, the President announced that he would use all of his constitutional powers to prevent a depression. The restrictive credit policy of raising interest rates to discourage business expansion and other associated anti-inflationary measures which had been inaugurated during the early days of the administration were hastily and temporarily reversed as soon as unemployment began to increase and gross national product began to decline. There is little doubt that taxes would have been lowered with the hope of stimulating both investment and consumer expenditures, in accordance with the New Deal-Fair Deal tradition of budgeting for a deficit to prevent unemployment, if this had proved necessary to halt the recession. In fact, a balanced budget could not even be proposed until the opening of Congress in January 1956.

There was one important difference between the operation of the intertwined wage-price-fiscal-monetary policy of the Eisenhower administration and that of the New Deal and Fair Deal Democratic administrations. It has been pointed out that, except for the war period, the preceding Democratic administrations had not followed a policy of restraint on wages or on farm prices but instead had encouraged increases in both. These increases might have caused either a decline in employment or a fall in consumer purchases or both if there had not been an adequate supply of investment funds available to industry or ample consumer income to purchase the products of industry and farm. The Democratic administration had always seen to it that the monetary supply was large enough and the interest rate low enough to provide investment funds and to support consumer purchasing power. The Eisenhower administration, however, with its more conservative and orthodox attitude towards balancing the budget and controlling inflation, did not accept a definite responsibility for the supply of investment funds at low interest rates or add to funds for consumer purchasing power through budgetary deficits unless substantial unemployment was an immediate threat. When faced with the alternative threats of unemployment or inflation, the Eisenhower administration always was to give greater weight to the inflationary danger than its predecessors had done.

Experience under the previous administrations had taught corporate managements that it was almost impossible successfully to resist increases in wage rates, even though these were larger than increases in labor productivity, in the face of public opinion and of potential or actual governmental intervention. Experience had also shown that such wage increases could be covered out of price increases. Further, corporate managements, generally favorable to an administration which claimed to be more conservative than its predecessor, felt that advances in wages must be at least as large as those under previous administrations if the politically vital votes of labor were to be won.

The result of the increases in wage rates accompanied by a restrictive monetary and fiscal policy was a slowing down of the rate of increase in industrial production, even though restrictive monetary measures did not succeed in preventing a rise in prices. The Eisenhower administration now found itself in the dilemma which was currently confronting almost all modern capitalistic economies: how to provide the requisite supply of investment funds and consumer purchasing power which would permit productivity of the economy to advance at the rate at which it was physically capable, while still preventing inflation. Looked at from the angle of costs, the problem was how to prevent wages and profits from advancing at a rate greater than that sanctioned by increases in physical production when the money supply made available for investment and purchasing power was at such a level as not to prevent inflationary wage and price increases. Upon the solution of this problem was to depend in important degree the question of whether statization of modern capitalistic economic systems could be halted short of the point at which individual liberties would be threatened with substantial curtailment.

Many businessmen were, of course, greatly disappointed that the New Deal and Fair Deal programs were so little changed by the Eisenhower administration. Still, however much American businessmen disliked "government in business," they nevertheless felt much more relaxed and confident now that interferences with and intervention in business were in the hands of a Republican administration. Their acceptance in large part of the "New Order" as "capitalism" naturally helped to obscure recognition both in the United States and abroad of the substantial transformation of American capitalism which had in fact occurred. Communist and socialist opponents of capitalism, both in the United States and in foreign countries, of course denied that any fundamental changes had occurred. They insisted that the contemporary American economic system was undoubtedly capitalism, although a late stage characterized by monopoly instead of by competition.

Curiously enough, there had been developing during the postwar period among some of the leading American economists a contrary doctrine which was also to offer great support to the position that the American economic system had undergone no fundamental change. These economists denied that the American economic system ever had been characteristically oligopolistic or even imperfectly competitive, and that there had been any trend towards an increase in monopoly during recent decades or even any increase in industrial concentration. While this conclusion did not by any means reflect a consensus among economists, its importance was great.

These economists thus challenged the whole economic philosophy upon which the New Deal and the Fair Deal had come to be based. They denied that collective bargaining by labor or control of farm prices and production by government had been necessary in order to offset the "monopoly power" of "Big Business," since this "monopoly power" was largely a fiction. Most of these economists further denied that collective bargaining by labor had increased wages or that the returns to farmers had been increased by governmental price and production controls in agriculture.[2] This recrudescence among an influential group of economists of belief in the competitiveness of the American economy was unquestionably strongly accentuated by the Republican success in the elections of 1952. Nor was it noticeably inhibited by the failure of the Eisenhower administration to repeal any substantial portion of New Deal legislation or to depart very fundamentally from the economic policies of preceding Democratic administrations. These economists maintained that while the unnecessary governmental intervention inaugurated by the New Deal, mistakenly justified by the alleged failure of competition to carry out its regulatory functions, had been costly to taxpayers and had substantially hampered the efficient operation of the economy,

[2] See pp. 204–208, 220–221.

it fortunately had not caused any fundamental change in the nature of the economic system.

This was in sharp contrast to the doctrine which had been in the ascendancy from the late twenties to the end of World War II—that pure and perfect competition, to the extent that it had ever existed, had been superseded by oligopoly, imperfect and monopolistic competition, "administered prices," price leadership and the like. During this period, which corresponded roughly with Democratic control of the federal government, economists had largely supported two opposing viewpoints. One group argued that the decline of competition made a larger degree of regulation by the state inevitable, if it did not indeed necessitate replacement of capitalism by some form of socialism; the other, on the contrary, maintained that competition must be restored by vigorous governmental measures against monopoly and all other imperfections in competition, whether due to the activities of industrial corporations or labor unions. During this period the fact of the decline of competition had not been generally challenged by the active proponents of competition and laissez faire as opposed to monopoly in all its manifestations and to all forms of statism. Indeed, the serious consequences of this decline were vigorously portrayed by the supporters of competition.

It was natural enough that this controversy should have abated during World War II. There was no longer any question of unemployment due to rigidities introduced by the development of monopolistic elements in the economy, since unemployment was nonexistent. Furthermore, wages, farm prices and industrial prices were controlled and regulated by government to such an extent that the question of private corporate monopoly power in their determination became irrelevant. It was also obviously futile to talk about a vigorous program of enforcing antitrust legislation at a time when the energies of both governmental officialdom and corporate management were absorbed in the effort to maximize the production of goods to sustain the war effort.

After the war, the controversy was revived, but it took a curiously new turn. Some of the most articulate of the proponents of competition and laissez faire were among those who now maintained that the economy was still vigorously competitive rather than monopolistic, oligopolistic or even imperfectly competitive.[3] Implied in their belief was the apparent conviction that monopoly, in the absence of positive governmental measures in its support, was both self-limiting and inherently degenerative. As Stigler has put it, ". . . the history of the American economy in the Twentieth Century testifies that a modest program of combatting monopoly is enough to prevent any considerable decline in competition."[4] It was argued furthermore that, in addition to the older forms of competition between firms producing the same products, there was now interindustry product competition, for example, between copper and aluminum, synthetic fibres and natural fibres, plastics and metals. In addition, the development of new processes of production frequently brought in new firms producing old products or producing products which were substitutes for or which displaced older products.[5]

Those who maintained that the economy was still characterized by competition and laissez faire continued to support governmental antitrust policy in general. They insisted moreover that, far from the battle against monopoly having been lost, governmental action against monopoly and in support of

[3] George J. Stigler, Milton Friedman and Sumner H. Slichter, among others, have been exponents of this point of view. See Stigler, *Five Lectures on Economic Problems*, London School of Economics, Longmans, Green, London, 1949; Slichter, "The Growth of Competition," *Atlantic Monthly*, November 1953, pp. 56–70; and Friedman, "Significance of Labor Unions for Economic Policy," in *Impact of the Union*, edited by David McCord Wright, Harcourt, Brace, New York, 1951, pp. 204–234.

[4] George J. Stigler, "Mergers and Preventive Antitrust Policy," *University of Pennsylvania Law Review*, November 1955, pp. 176–184. Nevertheless, there continued to be among American economists vigorous proponents of the position that concentration in industry had reached a point where the maintenance of competition was threatened and that the growth in size of industrial units presented new, complex and difficult problems in the prevention and control of monopoly. For a most useful survey and analysis of the evidence, see George W. Stocking and Myron W. Watkins, *Monopoly and Free Enterprise*, Twentieth Century Fund, 1951.

[5] A highly specialized example of this is the production of itaconic acid by fermentation instead of by chemical synthesis, resulting in the radical reduction in cost of production of this highly versatile compound used in the production of detergents, synthetic textiles and synthetic rubber. *Wall Street Journal*, March 16, 1955, p. 1.

competition had been by no means ineffective and could be made even more effective in the future.

Support for this belief in the continuing competitiveness of the American economy was drawn from various statistical studies, some of which tended to disprove the growth of monopoly and concentration during recent years or at least to raise serious doubts as to the existence of such a trend.[6]

It is possible that the proponents of laissez faire and competition had come to realize the political weakness of representing themselves as the champions of a lost cause, however righteous. It may be that they had decided that, before more effective governmental action to strengthen free enterprise and competition could be hoped for, the system must be depicted at least as "the wave of the present" instead of as "the wave of the past."

There developed simultaneously a curious shift in the other side of the controversy as well. Some of those who continued to maintain that old-style competition, laissez faire and free enterprise were no longer characteristic of the American economy did not now emphasize the evils of monopoly, crying aloud for governmental measures for its eradication or declaring the replacement of monopoly capitalism by socialism inevitable. J. K. Galbraith developed the doctrine of "countervailing power" which held that competition of sellers against sellers and of buyers against buyers had indeed ceased to be the main regulatory process by which prices were set and resources allocated in the economy. Instead, huge producer aggregates of economic power, such as the United States Steel Corporation, were confronted by other consumer aggregates of economic power, such as the General Motors Corporation, in the pricing process for steel. Large-scale corporate producers of foodstuffs, such as flour millers and meat packers, were confronted by the great corporate chain stores when they sold their products. As purchasers of labor, the large corporations had to face other aggregates of power, for example, labor unions in the steel industry and in the automobile industry, in

[6] One such study was that of Warren Nutter, *The Extent of Enterprise Monopoly in the United States, 1899–1939*, University of Chicago Press, Chicago, 1951.

the process of wage determination. Great economic power thus called forth great "countervailing" economic power. If this did not come about, then the power of the state was invoked, as in the case of the agricultural price-support programs of the New Deal, in order that millions of individual farmers might have power to countervail that of the corporate millers of grain or the packers of meat. A series of related concepts were developed by Adolf A. Berle, Jr., and David Lilienthal, the latter maintaining that modern big business has developed a new form of socially effective competition.[7]

In consequence of this resurrection and transfiguration of the controversy concerning the degree of competitiveness and laissez faire which characterizes the American economy, substantially the whole of the annual meetings of the American Economic Association in December 1953 was devoted to an analysis of a series of questions related to this subject.[8] The first session of the 1953 meetings in which Galbraith restated his doctrine, and in which it was criticized, produced marked differences of opinion. The sessions seemed to reflect a decided unwillingness of American academic economists to accept the new form of the thesis that the economy was no longer characterized by competition and laissez faire. The Galbraithian doctrine that oligopoly automatically begets countervailing power which produces net results beneficial to the public was widely questioned on both statistical and theoretical grounds. Reluctance to accept the doctrine of the transformation of our economic system was reflected as well in the sessions which dealt with the effects of labor unions on the determination of wage rates and factor compensation and the sessions which dealt with the effects of governmental intervention in agriculture on farm prices and the allocation of resources in agriculture. Similarly, a vigorous case was made for the usefulness of orthodox economic theory, with its assumptions regarding

[7] See J. K. Galbraith, *American Capitalism: The Concept of Countervailing Power,* Houghton Mifflin, Boston, 1952; David E. Lilienthal, *Big Business: A New Era,* Harper, New York, 1953; and Adolf A. Berle, Jr., *The Twentieth Century Capitalist Revolution,* Harcourt, Brace, New York, 1954.

[8] *Papers and Proceedings of the American Economic Association,* May 1954. A further analysis of the controversy was continued at the annual meetings in December 1954.

competition and laissez faire, in the analysis of the current forces and mechanisms of international trade. Yet the picture which emerges, both from a study of the *Proceedings* of the 1953 and 1954 meetings and from an analysis of the mass of current writing on the subject, even as painted by those believing in the essential competitiveness of the American economy, is fundamentally different from one in which the model of competition and laissez faire would be directly applicable.[9]

A good deal of confusion in the current controversy arises out of the different meanings which are often attributed to the word "competition." Competition among a limited number of large corporations is essentially a different process from competition among a large number of independent firms, but this is sometimes overlooked.[10] Thus in the American Economic Association meetings of 1953, John Van Sickle cited Lilienthal to support the contention that the economic system is still essentially competitive.[11] Lilienthal had insisted, however, that we now have a "New Competition" which differs fundamentally from the old, and that while small-scale business is still an essential part of our economic system it is no longer the norm. "The driving force of our economic life is now large business; no amount of nostalgia for the good old days can change that fact."[12] He further explains that under the "New Competition" *price* is no longer the major issue in the contest for business, and he points out numerous ways in which the "New Competition" differs from the old. With respect to the new role of government, Lilienthal observes: "Of these changes since the twenties none is more pervasive and

[9] Galbraith, in a felicitous phrase reminiscent of Mandeville's *Fable of the Bees,* refers to the contemporary organizational, mixed economy characterized by large-scale producing and bargaining units as the "Bumble Bee Economy."

See the author's "Institutional and Theoretical Implications of Economic Change," *American Economic Review,* March 1954, pp. 1–14, and "The American Organizational Economy," *Perspectives U.S.A.,* Winter 1955, pp. 105–118.

[10] See William Fellner, *Competition among the Few,* Knopf, New York, 1949.

[11] *Papers and Proceedings,* May 1954, p. 387. Lilienthal states: "Indeed, we are living in what is the most highly competitive society men have ever known." *Big Business: A New Era,* p. 47.

[12] *Big Business: A New Era,* p. 6.

none more relevant to the issue of Big Business than the changes in the function and role of government."[13] In their totality the evidence and the analysis set forth by Lilienthal to describe the "New Competition" are curiously similar to the development by Galbraith of his doctrine that competition as a regulatory force has been largely superseded by countervailing power.

Similarly, Sumner Slichter, who maintains that "The economy is undoubtedly more competitive today than it has ever been, and it is becoming even more so,"[14] goes on to explain that two of the reasons for this are, first, the importance of chain stores and mail order houses and, second, the development of modern technological research. Thus two elements reflecting or associated with bigness are advanced as evidence that the economy is highly competitive.

It is not easy to measure the shift in industry from "littleness" to "bigness," but it is plain that a large part of the argument over whether competition has maintained itself or has declined as the regulating force in the economy turns upon whether or not increasing bigness is functionally connected with a decline in competition or with a significant change in its form. It was inevitable that this controversy should be carried on in the courts as well as in the professional and popular journals.[15] A more crucial issue to the economist is whether or not, in an economy of large-scale producing and bargaining units such as ours, with all its current institutional characteristics of the "New Competition," the same assumptions are applicable as in the traditional model of the competitive, laissez-faire economy.[16]

---

[13] *Ibid.*, p. 14.

[14] "How Stable Is the American Economy," *Yale Review,* June 1950, p. 582.

[15] The U.S. Supreme Court on June 4, 1957 ruled that the ownership by the du Pont Company of 23 per cent of the stock of General Motors Corporation was in violation of the anti-monopoly provision of the Clayton Act. This declaration of illegality of an action taken almost forty years earlier apparently reflects an intensified anti-monopoly attitude on the part of the Court.

[16] Recognition of the development of new institutional forms, neither typically competitive in the old style nor yet monopolistic in the traditional sense, is shown in the titles of some books published

Jacob Viner has raised this question with respect to the applicability of traditional international trade theory in the current world.[17] After restating the assumptions of classical international trade theory he shows how imperfectly current national economic institutions, policies and practices fulfill these assumptions. It is impressive how much of Viner's skepticism with regard to the current applicability of the assumptions upon which international trade theory has been based is relevant to traditional economic theory as applied to national economics.[18]

It seems clear that our traditional models for dealing with theoretical pricing problems involved in the operation of the current mixed type of American economy are quite inadequate for their purpose, even if the actual pricing process could be legitimately described by the term "New Competition." In fact, the operation of our current economic system when it is accomplishing socially desirable goals most effectively is likely to be characterized by what has been appropriately called "workable competition," which is substantially different from pure and perfect competition as that term has been de-

---

in recent years by American economists, such as *Competition among the Few* by Fellner, *Big Enterprise in a Competitive System* by Kaplan, and *The Organizational Revolution* by Boulding, although these authors do not in general have a point of view very close to those of Galbraith, Berle and Lilienthal. Boulding, while emphasizing the change from an individual-enterprise and individual-bargaining economy to an organizational economy, minimizes the ability of these organizations to affect the size of shares in income accruing to the factors of production.

[17] "International Trade Theory and Its Present-Day Relevance," *Economic and Public Policy*, Brookings Institution, Washington, 1954, pp. 100–130. Viner quotes Edgeworth's dictum with respect to the catastrophic consequences for economic analysis of the assumption of the existence of universal monopoly without completely accepting it and of course without assuming any close approximation of Edgeworth's hypothetical assumption to current circumstances. This recalls J. M. Clark's comment about bilateral monopoly "in which it seems almost anything might happen."

[18] Berle has also pointed out how differently the present American economy actually operates than it would under the relevant assumptions of traditional economic theory. He argues that corporate planning has in substantial degree displaced the market place as the governor of investment and production.

fined.[19] It has been cogently argued that the economic system may be considered workably competitive even if it does not conform to the economists' model of pure and perfect competition—that this would be so if it is conducive to progress in economical methods of production, if customers have access to an ample range of qualities and types of product, if new products are constantly developed, if the benefits of progress are diffused to customers in lower prices or to workers in higher wages and, finally, if the system permits freedom and opportunity to flourish.[20]

This argument is also developed in the *Report of the Attorney General's National Committee to Study the Anti-Trust Laws* (published in March 1955), which points out that

> Both kinds of difficulties are exemplified by the economists' terms "pure" and "perfect" competition. These are technical terms identifying theoretical models which have defined conditions of equilibrium with logical precision and completeness. They do not purport to indicate ideal conditions. Whatever their views on public policy, economists are in agreement that departures from the model of pure and perfect competition do not necessarily involve monopoly power or substantial lessening of competition in the sense of being a problem for public policy. We do not regard these models as offering any basis for antitrust policy. Indeed, departures from conditions of

[19] The concept of "workable competition" was set forth by J. M. Clark in the *American Economic Review*, June 1940, pp. 241–256. Edward S. Mason, Joe S. Bain, M. A. Adelman and Jesse Markham later developed the concept further. See Stocking and Watkins, *Monopoly and Free Enterprise*, p. 98, notes 36 and 37. J. M. Clark expanded the concept and related it to factor compensation in his "Criteria of Sound Wage Adjustment with Emphasis on the Question of Inflationary Effects," in *Impact of the Union*, pp. 1–33. It is not only the theory of price which has been affected by the development of the "organizational economy" but the theory of distribution as well. It is not sufficient to work out the process of pricing as it is carried out by a particular corporation, even after allowing for departures from the competitive model, in the final pricing of a particular product. The pricing and allocation of the factors of production entering into the price of the end product may well not have corresponded with that assumed by the competitive model.

[20] J. M. Clark, *Papers and Proceedings*, May 1955, pp. 453–456.

pure and perfect competition are inevitable, pervasive and many of them useful to competition as a dynamic process.

These useful departures from conditions of pure and perfect competition may indeed in some instances be those responsible for the socially desirable results in terms of low costs which are often pointed to when the claim is made that our economic system is more competitive than it ever was. The pervasiveness of these departures renders largely abortive any attempt to measure the degree of monopoly in our economy by arraying all industries and assuming that the greater the profit in the industry the greater the degree of monopoly.[21] All industries are in fact certain to be characterized by departures from the economists' model of pure and perfect competition, and the rate of profit, even where there is some correlation with these departures, would not indicate that these profits had been inconsistent with the "competition as a dynamic process" referred to in the Report of the Attorney General's Committee. Indeed, the higher profit rates in some industries may be associated with higher rates of technological progress and lowered costs of production over time.[22] These higher profit rates may also be associated with Slichter's meaning of competition when he says that our economy is more competitive today than it ever has been and is becoming more competitive all the time. Competition of industrial giants in lowering costs of production may result in lower consumer prices and higher corporate profits than existed when producing units were smaller and more numerous.

On the one hand, there has never been a time when the economists' model of pure and perfect competition was actually operative. This is true not only in the sense that absolute

[21] See, for example, Arnold C. Harberger, "Monopoly and Resource Allocation," *Papers and Proceedings*, May 1954, pp. 77–87, and Ruth P. Mack's discussion of Harberger's paper, pp. 88–92. Also Sidney Weintraub's comment on the papers by Harberger, Heflebower and Nutter at the 1953 A.E.A. meetings in "Revised Doctrines of Competition," *Papers and Proceedings*, May 1955, pp. 463–479.

[22] On this point, see the *Report of the Attorney General's Committee to Study the Anti-Trust Laws*, March 31, 1955, p. 324.

purity and perfection are unattainable but for other reasons also. J. M. Clark has pointed out that "The perfect competitive market of theory is one in which prices are identical and each producer knows the others' prices and profits, which implies knowing their costs. In practice, too perfect identity of prices is legally suspect, and so is interchange of information on prices, as in open price associations, or information on costs, or even the use of uniform accounting systems."[23] In other words, if there were no other reason, antitrust law would have prevented the existence of perfect competition.

On the other hand, as both Schumpeter and J. M. Clark have pointed out, it is by no means clear that the most competitive economic system would be the most efficient. Clark argues that competition which operated so drastically as to produce "an excessive rate of elimination of firms may be unhealthy for an industry." Similarly, in a dynamic economy, profits are constantly created by the momentary "monopoly" which an innovating firm enjoys. These profits are eroded as competitors imitate the innovation. Profits can be re-created by renewed innovation accompanied by a renewal of a temporary monopoly position. "This role (of temporary 'monopoly profits' as an incentive to innovation) would be vitiated if the diffusion were instantaneous and complete, since the innovation would bring no rewards to the innovator."[24] As Richard Heflebower puts the matter: "My own view—and it is only a judgment—is that there is a significant degree of truth in the idea that product quality and the structure of costs will be socially more favorable in many industries if there is some insulation from overt price competition. But I do not think that this degree of insulation requires the current size distribution of sellers in some industries."[25] Again, as Clark has also pointed out, unrestricted competition may not bring about optimum production, as in agriculture, where the supply schedule may be such as to bring about, at least in the short run, a perverse response to price changes.

The argument frequently advanced during the meetings of the American Economic Association in 1953, that statistics of

[23] *Papers and Proceedings,* May 1955, p. 453.
[24] *Ibid.,* p. 454.
[25] *Papers and Proceedings,* May 1954, p. 128.

product prices, factor prices and resource allocation in the American economy did not evidence great distortion from the pattern which might be expected under competitive laissez faire, fell far short of proving that the system is in fact competitive and laissez faire in the traditional sense. Still less is such proof furnished by evidence that the current system works as well or even better now than did the economic system at an earlier time, when its competitiveness and the absence of governmental intervention was not in question.[26] Governmental intervention in the control of production and pricing in agriculture had in fact originally been intended to produce essentially the factor prices of the assumed "Golden Age" of 1909 to 1914. Labor union leaders also argue vehemently that they are now only attempting through the countervailing power of collective bargaining to restore the "fair wage" which would exist under a regime of competition and equality of bargaining power, but which the unorganized individual worker can no longer attain in the face of corporate monopsony and monopoly. Consequently, resemblances between the results achieved by the current American economy and those which could be expected under competition might be interpreted as due to governmental intervention and the more purely economic aspects of countervailing power rather than as evidence of the continued existence of old-style competition.

One of the consequences of the failure of the pricing process to approximate the economists' static model of pure and perfect competition is that one cannot assume that in the absence of governmental intervention or of collective bargaining

---

[26] The courts have nevertheless in some cases accepted the argument that monopoly does not exist if a corporation does not act like a monopolist, even though it has potential monopoly power. Thus, in the du Pont cellophane case the court held that even though the corporation was responsible for the major proportion of production and sales of cellophane, the evidence of expansion of production, the research carried on to improve quality, plus price reductions, proved that the corporation had followed a policy in the public interest and hence did not constitute a monopoly. *U. S. v. E. I. du Pont de Nemours & Co.*, 118 Fed. Supp. 41 (D. Del. 1953). See George W. Stocking and Willard P. Mueller, "The Cellophane Case and the New Competition," *American Economic Review*, March 1955, pp. 29–63.

by labor unions there would exist for commodities and for services a series of unique equilibrium prices and wage rates set by the traditional free market.[27] This does not mean at all, however, that actual prices and wage rates are set by individual large corporations in the role of monopolists or monopsonists, or that there are not substantial limitations on prices set by the potential entry of other producers and by the potential or actual introduction of substitute commodities and processes. It does not mean that prices are higher or wages lower than they would be if the actual pricing process were a closer approximation of the economists' model of pure and perfect competition. It does mean that, within a substantial range, prices and wage rates may be varied by the exercise of economic or political power. It can mean that industry-wide labor organizations may compel the corporate owners of the industry to distribute a portion of earnings which otherwise might have been retained in the business or distributed to stockholders. It often means that some part of the increase in wages will be added to the price charged for the product by the corporation or in some instances that the price paid the suppliers of raw materials will be diminished in some degree. None of these possibilities is limitless. The extent to which a wage increase may be passed forward or backward will depend in part upon the elasticity of demand for the product, the extent to which the producing corporations may act as oligopolists, and the extent to which the labor union will be willing to accept a possible limiting effect upon the employment of labor. The extent to which wage increases may cause a decrease in profits will be affected by the above factors plus the long-term effect of a decline in profits upon investment in

[27] Under the contemporary institutional process of price determination, an area of substantial dimensions exists in which the price of a particular commodity or service may be set higher or lower and the quantity offered and the quantity taken may be greater or less than at the dimensionless point at which price equated the quantity offered and the quantity taken in the old-fashioned model of market price determination. Similarly, a range of possible prices and quantities within a substantial area supplants the point determined by the intersection of marginal cost and marginal revenue curves in the abstract and simplified model of price and production of the firm.

the industry. With wages and prices indeterminate over a significant, even though limited, range, pressure for governmental intervention in the modern corporate-capitalistic economy is frequently present. Except for public utilities, agriculture is the only area in which governmental intervention in the pricing process has so far become routine in peacetime.[28] In the field of wages, however, with both wages and prices susceptible of being affected by economic power, the ultimate sanction which determines where wage rates will be set within an appreciable range has come to be the exertion of governmental power, potential or actual.

Thus, as a result of the development of our current organizational economy of large corporations and large labor unions, industrialists and labor leaders as well as government officials are bound to find themselves making decisions on matters which used to be governed primarily by the relatively impersonal operation of the free market or which would have to be dealt with by a directing authority in a centrally planned economy. We cannot any longer be sure that in our current organizational economy these decisions will, in their composite effect, produce equilibrium at full employment. Neither can we be sure that they will produce the optimum allocation of resources or the pattern of income distribution which a fully competitive model or a centrally planned and administered economy would in theory produce.

As an illustration of this: An executive of one of the great pulp and paper companies, when complimented on the good labor relations in his industry, replied, with a sincere sense of pride: "Nowadays the managements of the corporations in our industry consider their basic job to be marketing the labor embodied in our products. We try to sell this labor, embodied in pulp and paper, at the best price we can get for it, in the largest quantities practicable, without resorting to the kind of cutthroat competition which would make it impossible for the stockholders to get a fair return on the investment and, above all, for our labor to earn a decent living. Some folks might indeed charge that the managements of the companies in the industry act simply as selling agents for our labor union." He felt that this represented an immense public gain over the "bad

28 See pp. 219–227.

old times" when the managements of the various corporations in the industry cut prices and wages whenever necessary in order to get business away from the other fellow in the "reprehensible effort" of each corporation to maximize its profits.

Suppose this "laboristic" point of view were to spread to the managements of all large industries where market-wide collective bargaining existed and where the elasticity of demand for the product was such that a price increase could be passed on without an unacceptable decline in sales. Under the circumstances outlined, the industrialists and labor leaders of such industries would be making decisions which determined to a significant degree the shares in the national income of pulp mill workers or steel workers, and indeed of almost everyone else, at least until such time as the labor leaders and industrialists in other industries or perhaps the leaders of farm organizations could counter the move by means of similar action. In the case of such industries it would not be surprising if the government were to intervene, as it has in the past, in the setting of prices and wages. Indeed, if government intervention has seemed necessary in the past because management and labor leaders have *not* been able to agree, it may well be that government will have to intervene in the future because they *do* agree.

It is obvious that in a fully collectivized economy, a democratic government representing the whole population could not tolerate the determination of wage rates by the exercise of the organizational power of particular labor groups. Wage determination under a democratically controlled, collective economy would have to be a planning process, not a collective bargaining process. In actual practice, owing to the failure of the democratic process, a particularly strong economic interest would be likely to use the power of government in a "socialized" economy to increase its share of the national income. Under our own corporate-capitalistic, labor-union economy, the state is also likely to be forced increasingly to assume the onerous task of arbitrating in some fashion the demands of organized group interests for larger shares in the national income. Such a task becomes not primarily a problem of deciding how much shall go to wages and how much to profits but of deciding concurrently how much both wage receivers and profit receivers in a particular industry may be allowed to charge the consumers of the industry's products.

Up to the present time, corporate managements have been functioning in an anomalous role involving a conflict of interests. In opposing wage increases, they are acting as the protectors both of the profits of their stockholders and of the lower prices of their products to consumers which might prevail in the absence of wage increases. There is probably a growing temptation to protect profits rather than prices, however, since corporate managements have no *legal* responsibility to keep prices down and the pressures of competition to do so no longer function in the same way as in the past. The managements of corporations have no clear *moral* responsibility either, since competition was supposed to take care of keeping prices down without involving the exercise of any motive other than self-interest. With the existing divergence between the interests of the managements of corporations and those of stockholders it may be doubted whether the protection of profits as well as relatively low prices by corporate management will always remain in its present state. The increasing tendency of corporate management to acquire an added stake in corporate profits through bonuses, stock purchase options and the like is an offsetting factor, however.

The virtual independence of corporate management of stockholder control has perhaps altered the character of the capitalistic economic system as much as have changes in the nature of competition. Under these circumstances the assumption that profit maximization for stockholders is the almost exclusive goal of management becomes quite unreal. It may often be outweighed by the desire for public approbation, the avoidance of unpleasant clashes with labor union management and the building up of personal prestige. Motives other than the maximization of stockholder profits will usually appear to be much more in accord with social welfare than were the profit-seeking motivations of traditional capitalism. It was, however, precisely profit maximization upon which the capitalistic system depended for resource allocation to the most productive uses, the formation of prices in relation to scarcities and the remuneration of factors in accordance with their productivity. It was this process upon which the argument for the superior efficiency of capitalism over alternative economic systems largely depended. To the extent that corporate managerial capitalism has replaced management by capitalists per se, the system is fundamentally altered. Be it noted that this alteration does not depend directly upon any increase in the degree of concentration in industry or upon any decline in competition in the usual meaning of the term.[29]

However incontestable the evidence might be that at least some forms of competition are being carried on in the most active way possible, and that new forms of competition are developing, this could not logically serve to prove that the character of the economic system has not undergone significant change. Indeed, aggressive "competitive" practices by large corporations are often taken as evidence of monopolistic policies which threaten the existence of small businessmen. Thus, the mergers of the former independents in the automobile industry were indeed caused by the energetic competition carried on by General Motors and Ford. It could hardly be maintained, however, that this type of competition conforms very closely to the traditional competitive model. It is true that the mergers among the independents have improved somewhat their ability to compete with General Motors and Ford and have afforded them some hope of survival. But one could hardly argue that, if the final result were to be the survival of only two or three large automobile producers, this would constitute anything closely resembling the model of pure and perfect competition. Even if as many as five companies survived, the resemblance to the traditional competitive model would not be very close.[30]

[29] For a further development of this point, see Edward S. Mason, "The Apologetics of 'Managerialism,'" *Journal of Business of the University of Chicago*, January 1958, pp. 1–11.

[30] Thus it is reasonable to suppose that General Motors executives have to take public opinion and the possibility of governmental regulation into account in the pricing of their cars. If their cars had been priced lower, General Motors might at times have sold enough additional cars to put one or more of the remaining small producers out of business, with the result that its share of total sales might have increased embarrassingly above the roughly 50 per cent it averaged in 1954. Consequently, the fiercely competitive struggle normally waged between General Motors and Ford was tempered at one period by the really "nightmarish" fear of both concerns that

The actual pricing process often presents a whole galaxy of anomalies which contrast with the model of pure and perfect competition. To continue to use the automobile industry as an illustration, Ford competes vigorously with General Motors in the effort to sell more Fords than General Motors can sell Chevrolets. This has resulted at times in such fierce competition at the retail level that the rate of return on the dealer's investment has been substantially curtailed. This does not, however, result in competitive price cutting at the manufacturer's level such as to limit the profits of Ford and General Motors. The manufacturer's price is not cut in the effort to increase sales because the managements of both corporations take into account factors which would not be relevant if automobiles were commodities produced by large numbers of independent manufacturers. Nor are they influenced solely by the considerations of oligopolists attempting to maximize profits. In addition, there is doubtless the fear that a substantial reduction of price at the manufacturer's level might force all other automobile manufacturers except Ford and General Motors out of business.

Even outside the fields of heavy industry and durable consumer goods, these anomalies exist in profusion where production is confined to a relatively few corporations. Thus, in contrast to the price of cotton yarns, which are produced by a large number of firms, many of which are small, the price of rayon staple fiber did not change between January 1954 and January 1956. The price of rayon filament yarn remained unchanged during the four-year period 1952–56.[31] This price stability was achieved primarily by the adjustment of production to consumption. Under the assumption of the economists' model of competition this adjustment would have come about through the interaction of price changes and production changes, not by production changes reflecting industry-wide policy.

---

they may some day find themselves constituting a duopoly. See *New York Times*, March 19, 1955, for an account of questions along this line asked by Senator Fulbright of General Motors President Harlow Curtice. It was the success of the Chrysler Corporation with its new models which dispelled this "nightmare" for a time.

[31] *New York Times*, February 19, 1956, p. F.9.

The effort to find both meaningful definitions and measures of changes in industrial concentration and competition and monopoly inevitably encounters serious difficulties. It has been pointed out, for example, that the development of industrial giants has fundamentally changed the economic position of very many people who are still classified in the statistics as independent businessmen. Thus the operators of gasoline filling stations, instead of being fully independent businessmen, have a dependent status in relation to the great oil companies, just as retail auto dealers have a similar status in relation to the auto manufacturers.[32]

A report of the Federal Trade Commission on changes in concentration in manufacturing notes the difficulties in measurement and particularly the difference between concentration in industry as a whole, where the emphasis is on over-all economic power, and concentration which effectuates control over particular markets. It is the latter, according to the Report, which, if sufficiently effective, constitutes monopoly.[33]

---

[32] Berle, *The Twentieth Century Capitalist Revolution*, p. 44.

[33] Federal Trade Commission, *Report on Changes in Concentration in Manufacturing, 1935 to 1947 and 1950*, 1954, p. 3. The Report lists the following works which discuss the methodological problems of measuring concentration: Edwin B. George, *Dun's Review*, March, May and September, 1939; Federal Trade Commission, *The Concentration of Productive Facilities*, 1947, pp. 1–14; Clair Wilcox, "On the Alleged Ubiquity of Oligopoly," *Papers and Proceedings of the American Economic Association*, May 1950, pp. 67–73; John M. Blair, "Statistical Measures of Concentration in Business, Problems of Compiling and Interpretation," American Statistical Association, December 29, 1950 (mimeo); G. Warren Nutter, *The Extent of Enterprise Monopoly in the United States, 1899–1939*, University of Chicago Press, Chicago, 1951; M. A. Adelman, "The Measurement of Industrial Concentration," *Review of Economics and Statistics*, November 1951; Corwin D. Edwards, George W. Stocking, Edwin B. George and A. A. Berle, Jr., "Four Comments on 'The Measurement of Industrial Concentration' with a Rejoinder by Professor Adelman," *Review of Economics and Statistics*, May 1952; John M. Blair, "The Measurement of Industrial Concentration: A Reply," and M. A. Adelman, "Rejoinder," *Review of Economics and Statistics*, November 1952. These works afford a review of most of the statistical evidence. See also George J. Stigler's review article, "Monopoly and Concentration," *Journal of Political Economy*, February 1956, and Jesse W. Markham, "Merger Policy under

The Report shows a small increase in concentration in manufacturing as measured by the percentage of total value of product of all manufacturers accounted for by the 200 largest manufacturing companies between 1935 and 1950, from 37.7 per cent to 40.5 per cent. The smallness of the increase was doubtless due in part to the already high concentration of industrial production in large corporations in earlier years.

Other data are somewhat contradictory. The total number of business concerns increased by 124 per cent from 1900 to 1952, or substantially more than the increase in population for the period.[34] This would seem to reflect no tendency for giant corporations to squeeze smaller businesses out of existence. During the same period, however, the number of farms, always the outstanding field for the independent operator, after reaching a peak of almost 7 million in 1935 decreased to less than 5 million, which was somewhat less than the number at the turn of the century.

Paradoxically enough, while the concept of the continuing competitiveness of the American economy was attracting renewed support among American economists, a new wave of mergers began to cause concern in Congress. These affected banking, automobiles, textiles, steel, newspapers and hotels, among others. This movement had two characteristics which differentiated it somewhat from other merger movements in the past. Mergers of the current movement have not usually been between the largest corporations in the industries, although a large corporation often acquired a smaller one. In any event, the proposed or actual mergers did not usually result in corporations which were the largest in the industry. In almost none of the cases did the mergers produce firms which came close to controlling the bulk of production in an industry. Such mergers would almost certainly have been held illegal by the courts.[35] Secondly, the mergers were often between corpora-

---

the New Section 7: A Six-Year Appraisal," *Virginia Law Review*, May 1957.

[34] Dun & Bradstreet, *Commercial Failures in an Era of Business Progress, 1900–1952*.

[35] See Federal Trade Commission, *Report on Corporate Mergers and Acquisitions*, May 1955, for an analysis of the characteristics of the mergers which occurred in the period 1948–54.

tions in quite different industries, so that no direct charge could be made that competition would be reduced. Indeed, even in the case of mergers in the same industry, it could well be argued that the results would be to strengthen competition when two smaller corporations after the merger more nearly approached the size of the corporation previously dominant in the industry. Yet there was an uneasy feeling in Congress that even this type of merger movement, if left unrestricted, would hasten the trend away from a competitive, free-enterprise economic system.

Naturally, the managements of corporations involved in the current wave of mergers have been anxious to prove that the motive is not to control a larger proportion of the market. It is usually claimed that, on the contrary, the purpose is diversification or integration or the reduction of overhead costs. A steel company, for example, which formerly was not fully integrated or did not produce a full line of products would be able, by merging with a corporation whose productive facilities were complementary, to improve its productive efficiency. Similarly, an oil company with excess refining capacity will merge with one which possesses properties producing crude oil, or a New York bank with large financial resources but without many branch offices merges with one which is well supplied in this latter respect. In some cases the motivation has been to stabilize earnings through merging firms with compensating seasonal or cyclical fluctuations. In other cases the motive has been to diversify the product mix to cope with technological change which might threaten the firm's previous product lines.[36]

The process of corporate diversification, sometimes carried out by merger of equals, sometimes by the acquisition of smaller companies by larger ones, sometimes simply by corporations undertaking new lines of production, went to almost fantastic lengths. A bus and truck manufacturer bought a chain of grocery supermarkets. A corporation already in coal, oil and shipping added a machine tool company to its agglomerate of enterprises. A mining and manufacturing company broadened its line to include insulating materials, adhesive

[36] A. D. H. Kaplan, "The Current Merger Movement Analyzed," *Harvard Business Review,* May–June 1955, p. 95.

tape, office equipment and chemicals. An international shipping company moved successively into banking, textiles, outdoor advertising and agriculture.[37] An aircraft company purchased a wholesale company dealing in plumbing, heating, refrigeration and industrial supplies. A big mail order company went into insurance on a wide scale by setting up a subsidiary. A coal and iron company went into the underwear business. A tire and rubber company went into radio and then continued to expand into one widely separated line after another. The bizarre list could be extended indefinitely. However, a number of these mergers in which there was little functional relation between the merged companies of either a complementary or supplementary nature proved financially unsuccessful and were dissolved.

Granted that integration and diversification are often false arguments to disguise an effort to extend control of the market, there can be no doubt that they both constitute bona fide motives for mergers. There are purposes which are not directly connected with immediately increased profits for the enlarged corporation. Sometimes mergers afford a means of "spreading" scarce top managerial ability over a larger area of production. Reciprocally, the sense of economic security of the managerial personnel, particularly with respect to pension rights and the like, is increased through becoming a part of a larger bureaucracy with greater diversification of product. The possibility of becoming "stranded" either temporarily or permanently, as demand for a particular product happens to contract or even disappear, lessens considerably with the larger and more diversified corporate organization.

A series of functionally intertwined causes and results have accompanied the current integration and diversification in American industry through merger, through internal expansion and increasingly through joint investment in new productive facilities by two corporations hitherto in different lines of production.[38]

[37] *New York Times*, August 1955.

[38] For example, the joint venture of the American Viscose Company and the Monsanto Chemical Corporation in setting up the Chemstrand Corporation to produce Acrilan and nylon. In addition to the supplying of financial resources, the combination of technical know-how of the two companies was an important factor in motivat-

For one thing, the opportunity for carrying out what is in some respects a more sophisticated investment policy for funds earned by a corporation expands with integration and diversification. Corporate management has been generally reluctant to disburse unusually large dividends, even apart from their effect in increasing the tax liabilities of large stockholders. Among other reasons, corporate managements are reluctant to raise the expectation of a permanently high dividend rate without expanding the investment base upon which earnings can continue to be made. Furthermore, dividends paid out no longer contribute to the growth of the corporate entity, which has often become the embodiment of management's ego. However, there may not be investment opportunities in a single type of production that do not involve an unacceptable degree of price competition, perhaps the shattering of an existing *modus vivendi* with competitors and a decline in the rate of earnings on investment that could be expected in the existing type of production. The alternative of giving higher dividends to stockholders is excluded for the reasons noted above. The management of such a corporation may find it advantageous to integrate forward or backward in order to obtain captive sources of supply of its raw materials or to obtain captive outlets for its product and in so doing find an investment for its funds at a higher rate of return than that attainable through horizontal expansion. The management may alternatively or concurrently invest in the production of an entirely different type of commodity or service, where the rate of return seems more promising. By this process of simple or compound integration and diversification the field for potential expansion of

---

ing the joint venture. The American Viscose Company also joined with the Puget Sound Pulp and Timber Company in forming the Ketchikan Pulp Company to construct a giant pulp mill on the West Coast, using the latest and most efficient techniques. The Freeport Sulphur Company joined with the Pittsburgh Consolidation Coal Corporation to exploit potash deposits in Arizona. A venture which represented perhaps the widest corporate participation of all was the Iron Ore Company of Canada, set up to exploit the huge iron ore deposits on the Quebec-Labrador border. Republic Steel, Armco Steel, National Steel, Youngstown Sheet and Tube Company, Wheeling Steel, Hollinger Consolidated Gold Mines and M. A. Hanna Company participated.

investment within the growing corporate empire widens. Thereafter, the management of the corporation can choose among a greater number of investment opportunities of which it has intimate knowledge. It can avoid pushing down the rate of return on investment which might result if horizontal expansion were the only alternative to paying out additional dividends to stockholders. Essentially the same process may take place through merger as through the investment of excess funds, or diversification may take place through a combination of the two processes.

As the corporate empire expands, the potentialities for supporting large-scale research, engineering and financial staffs and facilities increase. With diversification a wider range of employment opportunities together with alternate routes to promotion can be made available to executive and technical personnel with diverse talents and training without jeopardizing the pension rights of such personnel as well as other attributes of status and security in the corporate hierarchy.

The way in which these mergers, even though not intended as a step toward monopoly, represent a departure from the economists' model of the free market is illustrated by the relation between corporations, say, in the chemical industry and those in the oil industry. A chemical firm producing or using petrochemicals may merge with an oil company which furnishes raw or semiprocessed materials for petrochemicals. The same oil company may furnish an important market outlet for chemicals used in refining petroleum. The oil company may have other commercial activities which do not serve either as a source of supply or as a market for the chemical company, but these activities can be accounted part of the diversification process. In conventional terms this type of merger does not restrict competition. There may still be twenty or more large, independent firms in each of the two industries. However, as more and more of them "choose partners" through merger, through investment in new facilities or through long-term contracts, the firms without "partners" are likely to be at a disadvantage in control over supply and in dependability of sales outlets,[39] although the liabilities incurred may also be substantial.

[39] The merger of the Monsanto Chemical Company and the Lion Oil Company in 1955 is an example of this type of merger.

Sometimes the very purpose of merger itself illustrates a departure from the economists' model of the free market. Thus, in early 1956 the Olin Mathieson Chemical Corporation, itself a result of merger and an outstanding example of diversification, purchased 40 per cent of the stock of F. H. McGraw & Co., heavy construction engineers. A consideration of the sale was that McGraw receive from Olin Mathieson the engineering and construction contract for a proposed ninety-million-dollar aluminum plant.[40]

These are random illustrations drawn from an indefinitely large number of such departures from the economists' model of the market. As they multiply in number, more and more transactions become part of the process of internal administration within the corporate structure and are withdrawn from the traditional market process of price determination. Yet the effect is not necessarily or even usually exploitative with respect to either the consumers of the products of such industries or the workers employed in them. Such developments almost defy any effort at statistical measurement of change in the degree to which monopoly or competition characterizes the economic system. In the case of the oil and chemical companies, for example, any attempt to measure the degree of monopoly, industry by industry, would be frustrated since it would be almost impossible to tell to which industry a monopolistic profit, if attained, had accrued. Further, the "monopolistic" advantage of one concern in an industry might be accompanied by a competitive disadvantage to others, so that the data on average profits, industry by industry, would be largely meaningless even if obtainable.

These myriad, complex and variegated departures in the current merger movement from the traditional model of pure and perfect competition naturally present extremely difficult problems in public control of "monopoly" since they do not fit the historic pattern of monopoly. It would hardly be practicable to forbid all mergers, and still less feasible to forbid expansion through corporate investment in the construction of new facilities in diverse lines. There seems no escape for Congress and the courts from the tedious task of attempting to define what corporate mergers tend to restrict the competitive

[40] *New York Times*, February 8, 1956.

character of the economic system to the detriment of the public. Yet there is little prospect that the trend towards this type of merger can be reversed, and it will be difficult to deny to unmerged corporations the advantages attained by those already merged or by those which acquired a similar status through the investment of internal financial resources.

The progress of diversification has strengthened the approach of large corporations to the status of immortality. Adaptation to a fall in the demand for an important product of a large, diversified firm can more easily be made by internal adjustment. Large corporations are able to afford statistical studies of the probable future demand for their product and to carry out a planned investment program which effectuates such internal adjustment. It is true that the investment program of each corporation is contingent upon that of its competitors but, if these are few enough in number, the different investment programs are by no means planned in ignorance of competitors' intentions. Where the estimated future demand is insufficient to absorb current earnings in excess of desired dividend payments, specific motivation towards diversification comes into force.[41] This trend towards immortality of large corporations is reflected in the statistics of business failures in the United States. Since the end of the depression of the thirties, the total number of business failures yearly has shown a pronounced downward trend. Indeed, the failure rate declined from 92 firms per 10,000 in 1900 to 34 in 1950. Of the total of 8,862 commercial failures in the United States in 1953, 58.5 per cent had been in business less than five years. The total liabilities of all commercial failures amounted to only $394,-153,000, not much more than one-tenth of one per cent of gross national product. These data reflect the fact that no large corporations whatever failed during that year. In fact, there has been no failure of a corporation with liabilities of as much as $100,000,000 in recent years.[42]

It is true that even large corporations would fail in the event of another depression as severe as that of the thirties and in

---

[41] As in the case of Kennecott Copper Company's investment in the stock of Kaiser Aluminum Company.

[42] Dun & Bradstreet, *Commercial Failures in an Era of Business Progress, 1900–1952*, and *The First Five Years Are the Hardest.*

the absence of massive credit extension by the government. But the experience of that depression proves that such a situation is hardly conceivable. The government did intervene at that time on a massive scale through the Reconstruction Finance Corporation, the Farm Credit Administration, the Homeowners' Loan Corporation, and through a general program of relief payments. The whole was financed through the expansion of bank deposits induced by deficit financing, which prevented wholesale business failures. In the light of that experience and of accepted economic policy by both political parties, it is certain that governmental action would take place much sooner and on an even larger scale if necessary to forestall the failure of any appreciable number of large corporations.

It has been pointed out that as the size, diversity of product and interrelatedness of corporations increase, the determination of prices and the allocation of resources are to the same extent withdrawn in a substantial degree from the "free market" and administered instead within the corporation. This does not mean that prices can be set and resources allocated by the exercise of the arbitrary will of a corporate official. Yet the pricing and costing process as iron ore is turned into structural steel by the United States Steel Corporation is significantly different from what it would be if iron ore, raw steel and structural steel were produced by large numbers of competing firms at all stages of the production process. Similarly, the process by which the compensation of corporate officials is set is quite different from the way in which such compensation would be determined if property owners were to hire management "on the free market."

The corporate structure in the United States thus represents a fundamental departure from purely individual free enterprise. The large corporation begins to approach in some respects the status of a governmental bureaucracy. Indeed, the position of the management would not necessarily be much changed if the corporation were nationalized. The management, like the bureaucracy of a labor union, a farm organization, a cooperative or any other large organization in our economic system, tends to be self-perpetuating. The process by which this self-perpetuation takes place follows no set pattern.

The extent to which the president who is retiring to become chairman of the board is able to dictate his successor depends upon factors varying from one corporation to another. There is, of course, no invariable pattern by which the retiring president becomes chairman of the board. The influence of holders of important blocks of stock may weigh heavily in the decision. Yet it is still true to say that it is not the owners of the majority of the voting stock who really elect the management of corporations. As a matter of fact, it is highly doubtful whether the selection of the managements of corporations would be more in the interests of either the stockholders or the public if it were actually made by the owners of a majority of the voting stock. In the rare cases in which the existing management has been displaced by a contesting group of stockholders, the evidence is quite unclear as to whether their interests have really been better served by the new management. Such a contest is likely to be extremely costly if the contesting group is to have any hope of success. Naturally the contesting group will cover its costs at the expense of the corporate treasury if it is successful. The contest is thus a gamble in which the stakes are high and the cost of running the contest is borne by the stockholders who may be in reality only helpless bystanders.

The exposure of reprehensible corporate actions which led to the establishment of the Securities and Exchange Commission in the early 1930s did much to discredit modern capitalism in the eyes of the intelligentsia and even small investors. It seems probable that some of the current practices may cause mushrooming hostility toward corporate management reminiscent of earlier years.

The bestowal of stock options by corporate management on itself, permitting the dilution of stockholder equities in the name of executive incentives, is a widely accepted practice. When their value depends largely on the demand for the products of the industry rather than for those of a particular corporation and on the level of the stock market at the time the options are bestowed—as compared with the level when they are exercised—it is difficult to present these stock options as simple incentives. The supplementing of pensions at retirement with lifetime consultantships, at even more generous rates, is also becoming a common corporate practice. To present corporate management to intellectuals in the role of the champion of the consuming public against inflationary wage demands by labor union management is not easy in the light of current corporate practices of the kind described.

The logic and propriety of corporate management personnel dominating, through their own membership and control of the proxy committees, the boards of directors which set their own compensation is coming to be increasingly questioned. In the course of the U.S. Senate's steel pricing inquiry it was brought out that the Bethlehem Steel Corporation had eleven of the eighteen highest-paid corporation executives in the United States. In 1956 the Chairman of the Board received compensation amounting to slightly more than 800,000. Senator Kefauver of the Committee pointed out that "with officers receiving such compensation, that becomes a challenge, a goad, a red flag to labor unions and individual workers to seek and receive all they can."[43] The tightened rules of the S.E.C. governing the conduct of proxy solicitation in such contests may well presage the formulation of a procedure laid down by law for the selection of the management of corporations.[44] It is not certain that such legislation would actually improve the selection process.[45] It may be that the present method, by the degree of corporate autonomy and diversity it allows, is superior to a much more logically codified system.

Internally, the organization and functioning of the modern American corporation has similarities to that of a "trust" or other corporate entity in a country where industry has been nationalized. The management of an American corporation has, of course, far greater autonomy than the management of

[43] *New York Times,* October 22, 1957.

[44] Professor Adolf Berle has considerable confidence in the development of a kind of "public consensus" which checks or guides the managements of corporations in their exercise of economic power. For a brilliant analysis of the subject, see his *Power Without Property,* Harcourt, Brace, New York, 1959.

[45] By analogy, the introduction of Civil Service did correct corruption and political favoritism in the administration of political government, but there have also been losses in terms of rigidities introduced, e.g., the lag in promotion for merit or discharge for inefficiency.

a Soviet trust, and this autonomy is an important factor in the maintenance of a free society. The management of a Soviet trust is appointed by a government which is not responsible to the population. The authority of the management of a Soviet trust is not restricted, as in American industry, by the power of labor unions. The differences thus outweigh the similarities, but it is evident that the most fundamental differences are those which stem from the fact that the American corporation functions in a free society while the Soviet trust does not. In terms of internal organizational form the similarities, even if far from complete, cannot be overlooked. In fact, the organization and functioning of a modern large corporation is such that the take-over of industry by government would be facilitated. This was illustrated in Germany by the way in which the Nazis were able to substitute control through board of directors for outright seizure by the government. It is illustrated as well by the experience of the British steel industry when it was nationalized by the Labor government and in turn denationalized by the succeeding Conservative government. It was astonishing how little difference was noted by management or the workers as a result of the change in the legal ownership of the industry.

The transfer of governmental control from Democratic to Republican hands did not result in a return to an individualistic, free-enterprise economic system. Governmental spending was somewhat curtailed, the expansion of the governmental bureaucracy was slowed down, the extension of governmental activity into new areas was at least temporarily halted, and the powers of government could no longer be counted upon to settle wage disputes in favor of labor unions. There was, however, no significant withdrawal of governmental power in the monetary and fiscal field nor even a basic change in policy in this field. Governmental controls over production and prices in agriculture continued in effect with only slight modifications.

Above all, the shift of the economy itself away from an individualistic to an organizational type of system continued. This was in spite of a rather more energetic antitrust policy on the part of the Republican administration than had characterized the preceding Democratic administrations. (The most striking example was the Supreme Court decision in June 1957 declaring the du Pont Company's ownership of stock in the General Motors Corporation illegal.) In the field of labor the A.F.L. and C.I.O. merged. In industry, there was the new merger movement, characterized by diversification and integration rather than by efforts to attain monopoly. Even if this evolution of the American economy could not adequately be described by terms such as the "New Competition," "workable competition" or "countervailing power," the basic and organic character of the transformation was evidenced by the failure of the trend to reverse itself in the changed political climate.

The evidence is inconclusive as to whether the changes in the economic system which began with the New Deal and were continued under the Fair Deal and modified only very slightly under the succeeding Republican administration substantially affected the trend in the rate of economic growth. The annual rate of increase in national income during the past eighty years has been estimated to average between 3 and 3.5 per cent.[46] There are some indications that the somewhat greater concern of the Republican administration for balancing the budget and for the danger of inflation may have led to

[46] Moses Abramovitz estimates the net national product to have increased during this period at an average annual growth rate of 3.5 per cent or at a per capita growth rate of 1.9 per cent. "Resources and Output Trends in the United States since 1870," Occasional Paper 52, National Bureau of Economic Research, New York, 1956, p. 7. The staff of the Joint Economic Committee estimates the rate of growth in the gross national product during the past fifty years at 3 per cent. *Productivity, Prices and Incomes*, Materials Prepared for the Joint Economic Committee, 1957, p. 15. Fluctuations in the rate of increase or decrease during a particular year have been at times as high as 15 per cent, however, so that it is difficult to judge when a change in trend is occurring. During the early months of 1958 industrial production in the United States fell below what it had been two years earlier. For a comprehensive description and analysis of economic growth in the United States see J. Frederic Dewhurst and associates. *America's Needs and Resources: A New Survey*, Twentieth Century Fund, 1955. Projecting a trend line to 1960, the estimated annual increase in real private income per private man-hour is estimated to be 2.3 per cent a year (pp. 42–43).

restrictive fiscal and monetary policies which have resulted in a diminution in the rate of economic growth.[47]

Thus the Eisenhower administration, having inherited the evolutionary transformation of the organization and control of industry which gave rise to the New Deal and Fair Deal and having accepted most of the economic measures of the New Deal and Fair Deal, in its actual economic policies signalized the permanence of the changed economic system. This new system might be variously called the Mixed Economy, Welfare Capitalism, Progressive Capitalism or simply the Organizational Economy, to distinguish it from the individual-enterprise, laissez-faire, private-property economy of old-style capitalism.

The changed system in the United States, characterized by a great relative improvement in the standard of living of the former lower-income classes, a sharp increase in the power of labor organizations, a diminution in the degree of absolute authority of management over workers in industry, a far greater role of the state in the economy, a substantial shrinkage in the rights of private property, the acceptance by the state of responsibility for full employment plus a wide system of social security, was not easily distinguishable from the economic system existing in the United Kingdom under the Conservative government which succeeded the postwar Labor government. But this is nearly the equivalent of saying that the changed economic system in the United States as it had consolidated itself under the Eisenhower administration was not very different from the economic system in the United Kingdom under the Labor government. For in Britain also, the changes in the economic system under the Conservative regime were not great. The new system in Britain might have been called State Capitalism, the Welfare State, the First Stage of Socialism or the like, yet the similarities between the two national economic systems were far greater than their differences.[48] The economic systems of the two countries remained alike in that

[47] See Chapter 5 for an analysis of the rate of Soviet economic growth.

[48] Much the same point is made by C. A. R. Crosland in his "The Transition from Capitalism" in *New Fabian Essays*, Turnstile Press, London, 1952, p. 43.

individual freedom had not been dangerously impaired in either and that in neither had the whole economy been forced into an organizational strait jacket. In both systems the changes had stopped far short of full statization of the economy.

The continued existence under modern capitalism of countless individually owned businesses, together with thousands of small corporations producing or selling independently, or at least quasi-independently, alongside the great corporations, contributes immeasurably to flexibility and efficiency in the growth and operation of the economy. This remaining area, within which the individual personality may develop and be expressed more freely than as an employee of a large corporation or of government or as a member of a large labor organization, and which can exist when dogma and authority do not rigidly determine economic organizational forms, is of even greater importance to liberty than to efficiency.

Whether the movement towards statization in either of these modern capitalistic economies of the West can be permanently halted short of the danger zone where liberty begins to be seriously curtailed remains uncertain, since unfortunately the limits are nowhere sharply defined.

CHAPTER 10

MIXED ECONOMIC SYSTEMS:
(1) THE BRITISH
ECONOMIC SYSTEM

It is a remarkable anomaly that the experience of the United Kingdom and the Labor Party's reaction to it afford the clearest case to be found in any country for the analysis of the relation of a socialist party to the peaceful nationalization of industry. The experience of Soviet Russia could not, of course, serve as an example since the political and economic system and the whole cultural background were so different there. Nationalization in Russia took place through violent revolution, moreover, and the economy never came to be operated under democratic control. Nor does any other continental country serve well as an example. It might have been expected that nationalization as a means of attaining socialism would have taken place earlier and proceeded further in the other countries of Western Europe than it did in Britain. The socialist movement had developed earlier in those countries and had been dominated by doctrinaire Marxism; class consciousness had been stronger; and socialist parties had always advocated outright, even if gradual, nationalization of substantially the whole economy as a matter of principle. Yet, even though Social Democratic parties have controlled the governments of countries such as Sweden and Norway for a number of years, and strong socialist parties have existed in all countries of Western Europe, nationalization on any wide scale has failed to take place.

The Marxist orientation of the continental socialist parties was in fact to inhibit experimentation with the gradual nationalization of industry by peaceful means. Furthermore, the profound disillusionment of the non-Communist, Social Democratic parties on the Continent with Marxism on account of the record of the Soviet economic and political system eventually robbed these parties of both their sense of direction and their sense of mission. At the same time the improving economic status of the workers under the modern forms of capitalism made ridiculous the Marxist doctrine of the increasing misery of the working class under capitalism and so took the steam out of demands for its replacement by a totally different system. Instead, socialist parties everywhere had to strive to find issues with a less doctrinaire appeal, such as demands for higher wages, increased social security payments, rent control laws, and the like.

The split of the Social Democratic parties in all countries of Western Europe into Communist and non-Communist parties was an additional major factor in preventing the pushing forward of any program for the nationalization of industry. A momentary exception was France, where a wave of nationalization of a limited number of industries took place immediately after World War II, although the split between Communists and non-Communists, temporarily and partially bridged over, was later to widen again here too. This program of nationalization quickly came to an end, and there have been few signs of its renewal. Moreover, in contrast to the United Kingdom, there has been relatively little analysis of the results of nationalization in France and consequently little discussion of the limitations on the attainment of socialism through the nationalization of industry. This has been true in part because of the preoccupation of public opinion with so many other more pressing issues and in part because the multiplicity of parties and group interests in France has prevented the consideration of broad economic issues.

Concurrently, in Sweden and Norway where very limited nationalization took place, there began to develop among the leaders of the Social Democratic parties a realization of the limitations on achieving socialist goals through the nationalization of industry. But it was only in the British Labor Party that the relevant issues were to find wide and full discussion. The British Labor Party had suffered neither from disillusionment with Marxist doctrine, since the labor movement had not been based primarily on Marxism, nor from the feeble competition of the Communist Party for leadership of the movement. Nor did it suffer from the splintering of political parties which existed on the Continent and which might have paralyzed the inauguration of any attempt at the comprehensive nationalization of industry. The Labor Party when it came to power in 1945 was consequently able to embark upon a program for the nationalization of a limited number of key industries with the implicit understanding among its leaders that, after experience with these industries, nationalization would be extended step by step to others.

Thus it is possible to study in at least one country the principles and problems involved in the nationalization of industries under peaceful circumstances, where parliamentary institutions existed and where democratic controls remained unimpaired while the experiment went forward. Furthermore, it is possible in Britain to study the principles and problems of the nationalization of particular industries. If the whole of industry or even the majority of industries had been statized at one time, this process of itself might have so impaired the system of parliamentary democracy that the relations between a statized industry and democratic institutions could not be examined.

Competition has never been enforced in Britain by statutory provisions such as those of the Sherman Antitrust Act and the Clayton Act in the United States. Nevertheless, in spite of the existence of many agreements and arrangements among British firms which would have been considered in restraint of trade by United States courts, the British economic system was still largely characterized by competition until the beginning of the Great Depression of the 1930s. During the decade immediately preceding World War II, however, as G. C. Allen has shown, the transformation which had gradually been taking place from a system of competitive individual enterprise towards a highly organizational type of economy was actively pushed forward by governmental policy and actions.[1] It was brought about in part through combination and financial consolidations, but primarily through restrictive agreements among individual firms. The government and the banking authorities were active agents in facilitating this process. In industries suffering from overcapacity, rationalization, which often meant consolidation, was encouraged by fiscal relief and financial aid. In coal mining, compulsory cartels were set up. In cotton spinning, the decisions of private cartels received official sanction. In agriculture, marketing boards run by the producers themselves were set up, much as they were in the United States under New Deal legislation. Substantially all these governmentally supported cartel-like arrangements were anti-depression measures, intended to serve much the same purposes as those of the National Recovery Administration set up by the Roosevelt administration in 1933. Apart from legislation implementing agreements of the cartel type in particular industries, the law also had come to take an increasingly favorable position towards contracts in restraint of trade. Indeed, the courts began to show a readiness to enforce such contracts.

Sources cited by Allen indicate the increased degree of concentration in British industry by the beginning of World War II, although, as in all countries, statistical measurement of the degree of concentration or of the extent of the decline in competition or of the growth of the variant forms of "monopoly" presents almost insuperable complexities.

With respect to labor, the evidence is quite clear that collective bargaining carried on by giant unions had long superseded individual bargaining. This had largely taken place by 1929. By 1939 the network of collective bargaining covered substantially the whole economy. The fixing of minimum wages by government and the legal sanction of collective wage agreements had become well established. The net result was

---

[1] See G. C. Allen, "The British Economy" in *Economic Systems of the West*, Vol. I, List Gesellschaft, Kyklos-Verlag, Basel, 1957, pp. 65–99. Allen's study has been heavily drawn upon as a source for this chapter. See also Ben W. Lewis, *British Planning and Nationalization*, Twentieth Century Fund, 1952.

the development of what J. R. Hicks has called the "labour standard" as a major determinant of the price level.[2] Wage reduction could no longer be used as a means of restoring equilibrium in the economy. A formerly flexible element had thus become inflexible or rather had become flexible only upward.

The transformation of the British economic system was obscured by the outbreak of World War II. The whole economy ceased to be a market economy. The managing personnel of industrial firms in effect became government functionaries. A similar transformation, differing only in degree, took place in such of the other belligerent countries as had not already installed governmentally directed economies. Yet in none of these countries did this necessarily mean that the trend away from competitive, free-enterprise capitalism had been permanently accelerated. Eventually, almost all of this governmental wartime apparatus by which the economy was controlled was dismantled. For a time the economic system reverted largely to the system of competition, limited by the development of dominant firms and the widespread cartel-type agreements of the immediate prewar period.

With the abandonment of the elaborate wartime system of rationing, price and wage controls, and subsidies designed to keep down prices of consumption goods, the enhanced power of labor unions in collective bargaining could be more freely exerted. Increasingly, the wage settlements in major industries came about through compulsory arbitration on the national level, so that factors affecting the entire economy, as well as those affecting the parties directly involved, needed to be taken into account. One such factor invariably was the extent to which a proposed wage increase would have an inflationary effect. Under full employment, however, the consideration of this potentially inflationary effect has been quite unsuccessful in preventing a generally inflationary movement of prices. The managements of labor unions evidently feel a greater necessity to obtain advances in money wages for their constituents

---

[2] "Economic Foundations of Wage Policy," *Economic Journal,* September 1955, pp. 389–404. At the present time this development of the "labour standard" has become universal, except in countries having the Soviet economic system.

than do the managements of industrial corporations to secure profits for their stockholders. Nevertheless, since wage increases are so often made on a nationwide basis, general price increases to meet such wage increases are greatly facilitated. In a full-employment economy there is almost no motive for a firm to fail "to go along with" such price increases.

With the passage of the Monopolies and Restrictive Practices Act in 1948, followed by the Restrictive Practices Act of 1956, a governmental policy definitely intended to restrict agreements in restraint of trade was inaugurated. Even though this did not bring British antitrust policy up to the level of stringency reflected in United States legislation and court decisions, it did indicate a substantial change in policy. Concurrently, the reduction of protective measures accorded to industry by government and the movement towards participation in the European Free Trade Area offered promise of limiting the effectiveness of monopoloid arrangements in British industry.

The Conservative Party has always been instinctively more adverse than the Labor Party to regulatory measures and controls of the national economy and to economic planning in general. The disappearance of wartime shortages facilitated the carrying out of the Conservative policy of withdrawal of controls within practicable limits. Since British labor unions do not feel the same proprietary concern for the Conservative government that they did for the Labor government, there has in recent years been less coordination between government and industrial and labor managements on national wage and price policies.

Apart from fluctuations in the extent of controls over the economy is the trend of governmental participation in the economy. In 1938 governmental expenditures were some 20 per cent of the gross national product; in the middle 1950s this figure had increased to about 30 per cent, exclusive of the product of the nationalized industries. About one-twelfth of the gainfully occupied population was still employed in nationalized industries even after iron and steel, long-distance transport and raw cotton marketing were returned to private hands. The industries remaining nationalized included railways, electricity, gas, coal mining, cables and wireless, and the Bank of England. The denationalization of the iron and steel industry by the Conservative government did not mean that steel prices were thereafter to be set by competition, for the structure of prices remained under the supervision of a governmentally authorized agency, the Iron and Steel Board. Moreover, a complete rollback of nationalization in industry was advocated by almost no one. Thus it was not proposed that either the coal industry, the railroads or the airlines should be denationalized any more than it was proposed that the comprehensive "cradle to the grave" social insurance system be dismantled.

While the transformation of the British economy away from old-style capitalism was occurring, a substantial diminution in income inequality was also taking place. Though this trend had been in operation since the last quarter of the nineteenth century, it had accelerated during the late 1930s. This diminution in inequality was by no means due solely to the tax policies of the Labor Party, since the more progressive rates of taxation had been essential to carrying out governmental expenditures on which substantially all parties were, however reluctantly, in agreement. Indeed, the decline in inequality was by no means due to changes in the progressiveness of taxes alone. Between 1928 and 1948–49 the percentage of personal income which would have had to be redistributed to attain complete equality declined from 30 per cent to 24 per cent *before taxes*. During the same period the decline in the amount of disposable (post-tax) income which would have had to be redistributed fell from 30 per cent to 16 per cent. Thus, increasingly progressive tax rates strongly intensified a trend which was taking place for other reasons as well.[3]

[3] See Allan M. Cartter, *The Redistribution of Income in Postwar Britain,* Yale University Press, New Haven, 1955. Cartter includes a comparison of inequality in income distribution between Britain and the United States. The analytical method he uses appears to minimize the reduction in income inequality in both countries, and shows a greater reduction in inequality in Britain than in the United States. However, as Cartter points out (footnote 6, p. 85), if the data are computed for the top 5 per cent of income receivers as Simon Kuznets has done for the United States, the reduction in inequality in both personal and disposable income was greater in the United

The trend towards a narrowing of the gap between skilled and unskilled wages diminished inequality somewhat in the lower brackets of income. The movement of labor out of low-paying employment into industries of higher value productivity was probably also a factor. The reduction and eventually the virtual elimination of unemployment was another. The decline of investment income as a percentage of personal income from 24 per cent in 1938 to 13 per cent in 1948 reflects the reduction in income from rent, interest and profits, even before the payment of personal income taxes. In other words, income from property was declining in proportion to income from wages and salaries.

It is impossible to make a precise comparison of the degree of inequality in income distribution between Britain and the Soviet Union. Even if statistics were available for the Soviet Union, they would not be directly comparable with those for Britain in view of the fundamental differences in the two economic and political systems. However, very limited and fragmentary data indicate that the gap between the highest and lowest incomes in Britain is about the same as in the Soviet Union.[4] If the nonfinancial perquisites of higher-income recipients in the Soviet Union are taken into account, inequality

---

States than in Britain between the pre-World War II and postwar periods. The share of the top 5 per cent was also smaller in the United States than in Great Britain at the end of the period. Kuznets ("Economic Growth and Income Inequality," *American Economic Review,* March 1955, pp. 1–28) points out that the share of the top quintile was 44 per cent in the United States and 45 per cent in Britain, while the shares of the lower 3 quintiles were 34 per cent in the United States and 36 per cent in Britain, *before direct taxes and excluding free government benefits* (which would, of course, substantially reduce inequality). In other words, the distribution of income between these larger brackets of national income was about the same in Britain and in the United States, before the redistributional effects of personal taxation. Although there are many alternative methods of measuring comparative inequality which yield different results, one may conclude that, roughly speaking, changes in income inequality in Britain and the United States have followed a similar trend and reached a comparable level.

4 See Abram Bergson, "On Inequality of Incomes in the U.S.S.R.," *American Slavic and East European Review,* April 1951, pp. 95–99.

of income is perhaps greater there than in Britain. That this has come to be realized by at least some of the members of the Labor Party is shown by the statement of Roy Jenkins, M.P. for Birmingham, that Soviet Russia has less equality than any of the welfare states of the West, and even less than some of the more purely capitalistic countries.[5]

Although wartime controls were abandoned in Britain, as Allen points out, the managements of large corporations were now "more sensitive than in the past to public criticism, more amenable to governmental restraints and influences, and readier to accommodate their activities to official policy." This meant that even if not legally required to do so, as in wartime, the administrative personnel of large corporations had more and more come to regard themselves and were regarded by governmental officials as instruments of public policy. Informal understandings between governmental departments and representative industrial organizations with respect to the proportion of output to be exported had, for example, long existed.

This gradual and partial movement toward the role of public administrator did not primarily represent the abdication of self-interest by the top industrial administrative personnel. On the contrary, with property ownership declining in importance in the control of corporations and with earnings ceasing to be so much the major concern of corporate managements, the relative importance of good public relations and of the approbation of segments of society other than stockholders has increased. The perquisites of management—which have come to be perhaps more important than nominal salaries, since they escape income tax—are not diminished at all by this increased managerial susceptibility to governmental pressures or to pressures from "the public" as represented by the press, radio or other mass media of communication.

The British Labor Party has shown itself keenly aware of the extent to which corporate managements have become divorced from property ownership and have in effect come to be administrators who serve the public interest. At the same time the Party has expressed concern lest a managerial class should

[5] "Equality," in *New Fabian Essays*, Turnstile Press, London, 1952, p. 69.

be developing with special perquisites in lieu of those which used to accrue to the ownership of property. It has also been concerned about the self-perpetuating character of corporate managements. This recognition of the greatly diminished role of property in the British economy and the changing attitude of the Party towards the managements of industrial corporations have been expressed in the pamphlet *Industry and Society*.[6]

> In the large companies, it is the managers who now undertake the functions once performed by the capitalist owners. . . . For the world of the managers is not the world of the shareholders. Their concern is with production as much as with profits and with expansion far more than dividends. Salaries, pensions, status, power and promotion—these rather than wealth are their operating incentives. . . . In the first place, the large companies are increasingly controlled by men who have little or no stake in the companies they run. . . . Company aggrandisement, conceptions of the national interest, prestige and power, pensions and pay for chief executives—these are now the main incentives . . .

The pamphlet goes on to cite the case of the Volkswagen plant in Germany, which has been operated so successfully without any stockholders at all, and the case of the Steel Company of Wales, which in the status of "suspended ownership" for four years up to 1957 grew and prospered without having stockholders.

> The Labour Party recognizes that, under increasingly professional managements, large firms are as a whole serving the nation well. Moreover we recognize that no organization, public or private, can operate effectively if it is subjected to persistent, and detailed interventions from above. We have, therefore, no intention of interfering in the management of any firm which is doing a good job.
>
> Nevertheless, the virtual absence of shareholder con-

[6] Labour Party, *Industry and Society: Labour's Policy on Future Public Ownership*, Transport House, London, 1957.

trol does mean that the Boards of large firms are almost wholly autonomous. They exercise enormous power without being accountable to anybody. . . . The essential point is that the Boards of these companies should conduct their affairs in a manner which coincides with the interests of the community. This involves not only good relations with their employees and full consideration of the consumer interest but also a sense of responsibility to the nation as a whole through Parliament and the Government.

Finally, the pamphlet warns,

Indeed, from existing Board Room policies it is not difficult to envisage a managerial caste taking on the former role of the owners of wealth and using its economic power to buttress class privileges and institutions. . . . As vast disparities in individual wealth begin to disappear, we do not wish to see a new order of privilege based upon control, as distinct from the ownership of corporate wealth, taking its place. Nor do we wish to see the sharp distinctions of opportunity and status which in the past have largely been based upon personal wealth, replaced by new and equally sharp distinctions determined by the social policies of corporate managers.

It is no longer probable that a Conservative defeat by Labor would result in a substantial increase in the number of nationalized industries. True, if Labor were to win the next election it is almost certain that the steel industry and long-distance transport would again be nationalized. But this would be primarily for reasons of Party prestige and morale. It was not only defeat at the polls in 1955 which brought an end to the Party's program for further nationalization of entire industries. The defeat did make it quite evident that the nationalization of industry was a poor issue to take to the polls; issues such as the increased cost of living, the restoration of rent controls, larger old-age pensions and the relaxation of "tight money" anti-inflationary measures were the ones on which the Party was going to have to depend for votes.[7] In the

[7] See Herbert Morrison, "Election Afterthoughts: Some Lessons of 1955," *Socialist Commentary*, July 1955, pp. 201–204.

main, however, it was the experience with nationalization itself which raised in the minds of Party leaders a question which would have seemed absurd a generation earlier, namely, "What does the nationalization of industry contribute towards the fundamental goals of socialism?"[8] Not that the experience of the nationalized industries was a record of disastrous failure or even of notorious inefficiency.[9] But there was almost no evidence that laborers in those industries worked with more zeal as employees of the state than they had as employees of private corporations. Furthermore, it had not proved politically feasible to charge high enough prices for the goods and services of the nationalized industries to cover all costs and to provide capital for replacement of depreciated equipment and construction of up-to-date equipment. Consequently, it had been necessary to resort to the capital market to obtain investment funds. Indeed, some two-thirds of the capital requirements of the nationalized industries have been supplied by loans under government guarantee. In a certain sense, therefore, the "net public equity" in the nationalized industries was contracting instead of expanding.[10]

Even more important was the recognition by the Labor Party that nationalization had proved almost totally ineffectual as a means of diminishing inequality in income. So long as compensation had to be paid to the former owners of the industries, payments on government bond issues largely duplicated former dividend payments. Compensation to private owners could not be denied, since it would have been intolerably inequitable to have confiscated the property of, say, railway shareholders while leaving intact the property of share-

[8] For a brief but brilliant analysis of the relationship between nationalization of industry and socialism, see Arthur Lewis, "A Socialist Economic Policy," *Socialist Commentary*, June 1955, pp. 171–174. Lewis maintains that a government which owned all property and in which all opportunities for employment were concentrated would be a totalitarian state rather than a socialist society. He thus states in different language the doctrine of Milovan Djilas in *The New Class*...

[9] Indeed, in a Labor Party pamphlet, *Public Enterprise: Labour's Review of the Nationalized Industries*, Transport House, London, July 1957, the record of the nationalized industries is presented as one in which the Party takes pride.

[10] *Ibid.*, p. 52.

holders in non-nationalized industries.[11] Further, it had become obvious to the leaders of the Labor Party that the managing personnel of the nationalized industries would have to be compensated at about the same rates as those in non-nationalized industries, if competent management were to be secured and kept.[12] Consequently, there could be no decrease in income inequality to the advantage of the workers in nationalized industries or to the general public from this source. While very substantial decreases in income inequality had taken place, they were thus not traceable to the nationalization program.

Finally, the leaders of the Labor Party had come to realize that a most serious problem of management existed. Were the nationalized industries to be run simply like any governmental department and to be directly answerable to Parliament? This alternative had to be rejected at once, since the impossibility of effectively managing and operating entire industries under such a system was clear. The setting up of autonomous "boards" or "authorities" was far more practicable from the standpoint of efficient operation. But if this alternative were chosen, how was effective representation of the public interest to be insured? Why could the management of such a public corporation be relied upon not to develop much the same characteristics as the managing boards of private industrial corporations? The concern expressed by Labor Party leaders about the boards of large firms which "exercise enormous power without being accountable to anybody" would inevitably apply even more to the board of management of a nationalized industry organized as an autonomous authority over an industrial monopoly. Similarly, the distaste for seeing "the sharp distinctions of opportunity and status which in the past have been based upon personal wealth, replaced by new and equally sharp distinctions determined by the social policies of corporate managers" would pertain even more to the case of managers of nationalized industries.[13]

[11] See Hugh Gaitskell, "Public Ownership and Equality," *Socialist Commentary*, July 1955, pp. 165–167.

[12] See the passage on "Recruitment and Training" in the pamphlet *Public Enterprise*, p. 27.

[13] For an excellent survey of the writings of the leaders of the

Finally, the record of Soviet Russia had sharpened the apprehensions of socialists in Britain concerning the threat of exploitation by a ruling bureaucracy. The elimination of property owners and the complete statization of the economy in Soviet Russia had substituted the exploitation of the workers by the ruling bureaucracy of the state for their exploitation by the owners of property. On that record it was abundantly clear that the new exploitation was at least as bad as the old. This realization that the Soviet system was not a workers' state had developed slowly, but it had come to limit substantially the desire for any comprehensive program of nationalization.[14] The possible effect upon personal liberty of the management of an entire statized economy by a huge bureaucracy, while obviously not a near danger, had come to be a factor in setting the policies of the Labor Party.

Recognizing the limitations on further extensive nationalization of industry as a means of achieving socialism, leaders of the Labor Party have proposed that, instead of whole industries, particular firms might be nationalized.[15] It was apparently the hope that somehow the difficulties and limitations involved in the nationalization of an entire industry could thus be avoided. But this raises the question of what the original purposes of nationalization were supposed to be and whether the advantages to be gained thereby could be expected to accrue to the nation if only single firms (presumably large ones) instead of entire industries were nationalized.

It had now become obvious that the elimination or even the reduction of inequality in income distribution was not a function of the nationalization of industry. Consequently, there would be no reason to suppose that the nationalization of even a number of single firms instead of entire industries

---

Labor Party with respect to the seriousness of the management problem in nationalized industries, see Paul T. Homan's "Socialist Thought in Great Britain," *American Economic Review,* June 1957, pp. 350–362.

[14] See, for example, the statement of R. H. S. Crossman which sharply points out the fallacy of supposing the Soviet Union to be a workers' state" and the negative effect of this realization upon the movement for the nationalization of industry. "Towards the Philosophy of Socialism" in *New Fabian Essays,* p. 13.

[15] See *Industry and Society,* p. 47.

would further the equalization of income. This originally expected advantage could not be resurrected by any shift from whole to piecemeal nationalization.

Another advantage of nationalization of industry was supposed to be the operation of an industry "in the public interest" rather than for private profit. But what did this mean? It might have meant at one time that nationalized industries could avoid unemployment by not restricting production so as to maintain selling prices. Since in recent years there had been almost no unemployment in private industry, there would, of course, be no advantage in this connection in the nationalization of a single firm. There could, however, be a conceivable advantage to the public in lower prices due to the disruptive effect the existence of a nationalized firm might have on any price maintenance agreements of private firms in the industry.

The nationalization of an entire industry might have avoided duplicative investments and the construction of duplicate productive and marketing facilities, though under full employment conditions there was scarcely any evidence of idle capacity due to duplicative investments. But even this potential advantage would not accrue from the nationalization of a single firm.

It might further be argued that if only one firm were nationalized the stimulant of competition with non-nationalized firms would be retained, as it could not in a state monopoly created through nationalization of an entire industry. Yet there was no very robust belief that a single government-owned firm was likely to come off advantageously in competition with non-nationalized firms. Thus scarcely any of the "planning" advantages of nationalized industries over the alleged "unplanned chaos" of private industry could be expected to result from the nationalization of single firms.

Finally, many of the difficulties of administrative relationship to the state would remain unsolved by the nationalization of single firms instead of whole industries. However, the grant of power to the administrators of a nationalized firm would be less than that to a nationalized and hence monopolized industry. Both the negative and positive aspects of this difference cannot be gainsaid. The management of a single nationalized firm could not be responsible, for example, for technical stagnation of an entire industry nor would the management be likely to become part of a national one-party bureaucracy with authoritarian power over its employees.

Apart from the nationalization of entire industries or of single firms in an industry, the leadership of the Labor Party has proposed as another alternative that shares of individual firms should be purchased for governmental account. The primary argument advanced in support of this policy is that the public could thereby capture the appreciation in value of shares of industrial corporations which has largely escaped taxation. By "plowing back" profits instead of paying dividends, particularly in the presence of inflation and in the absence of capital gains taxes, firms have been able to build up large equities for individuals which were exempt from the socialist purpose of greater equalization of income and wealth. The Labor Party has argued that the walls of this "city of refuge" for capitalists might be effectively breached through government purchase of shares in industrial firms. It has been proposed that old-age pension funds and the like might be thus invested for public account and that death dues might be paid directly in securities of industrial firms. It is clear, however, that this could not be done unless there were a governmental budgetary surplus or unless (a not very logical or likely prospect) the government should borrow funds on the capital market for such investment. In order to attain a budgetary surplus it has been proposed that a capital levy might be made which would cover not only corporate securities but substantially all privately held wealth.[16]

The difficulties inherent in carrying out such a proposal are many and obvious. Basic would be the question of whether or not the government would have membership on the boards of management of the companies in which it had large investments. If so, many problems of administration would arise, most important of all that of whether governmentally appointed directors would have to take an assigned position on particular issues or whether they would be free to use their discretion on all matters of policy and detail. It may well be that the proposal has not been made by the Labor Party lead-

[16] *Ibid.*, pp. 31–41.

ers very seriously but only represents a purely theoretical alternative to outright admission that nationalization has been abandoned as a policy. On the other hand, the Party leadership, for the very reason that it has had to abandon nationalization as a way of reducing inequality in income and wealth, has turned to the problem of how further equalization can be accomplished by other methods. Recognizing that progressiveness in the current income tax structure has reached the limit, the Party has been studying various means such as a capital levy and the capture of a portion of the retained earnings of firms. It may well be that governmental acquisition of shares in industrial firms is being considered seriously as part of this renewed interest in relatively direct methods of equalizing income and wealth alternative to nationalization. Indeed, most leaders of the Labor Party, instead of thinking of socialism in terms of a statized economy, are now beginning to visualize socialism as consisting primarily of a wide distribution of property holding among individuals, a moderate further degree of equalization of wealth and income, and the reform of the boards of management of firms still further in the direction of responsibility towards the public. This would be as much of a departure from old-style socialism as from old-style capitalism.

There can be little doubt that if the Labor Party is returned to power there will be a further development of the role of the management of industrial firms as public administrators. The process by which this will take place is likely to be a very complex one, involving as it necessarily does the difficult problems of how the public interest is to be interpreted and reconciled with the interests of management and shareholders. Even with the renunciation of nationalization as a major campaign issue, the emphasis on increases in old-age pensions, the reintroduction of food subsidies, the relaxation of monetary and credit restraints, and the increases in expenditures for education, housing and the like make it almost certain that an expansion of governmental controls will take place in the event of a Labor victory. This would occur because the net effect of these proposals would be to increase inflationary pressures. It appears probable that this increase of controls would not only take the form of "outside controls" exerted by government officials upon the managements of industrial firms and labor unions, but would include a return and even an intensification of the efforts to induce these managements themselves to restrain price and wage increases, operating as quasi-public administrators. Indeed, the inflationary pressures in the British economy are already so strong that, even if the Labor Party is not returned to power, the Conservative government may be forced to move to reinstitute a number of governmental controls. An escape from inflationary pressures so successful that it resulted in an economic depression might paradoxically have somewhat similar results. Moves in this direction by a Conservative government would naturally be minimal compared with those of a Labor government.

The increase in gross national product of the British economy during the five-year period 1955–60 has been estimated to be 15.3 per cent, or slightly less than a 3 per cent compound rate annually. This is substantially below the average rate of 26.5 per cent projected for the O.E.E.C. countries of Western Europe, including Britain, for the same period.[17] The British rate of increase has been held down by the necessity for restrictive money and credit and public expenditure policies in an effort to restrain inflation. During the past ten years consumer prices have increased almost 50 per cent—one of the highest rates in the countries of Western Europe. Thus, although inflation is a serious problem in all European countries with the exception of Western Germany, the British economic system has performed less efficiently than most of the other Western European economies both in terms of increases in productivity and in terms of failure to prevent price increases. The evidence suggests that some more direct national effort to carry out policies of agreed restraint on wage and price increases is likely eventually to become essential in Britain.

If inflation could be kept within tolerable bounds without producing depression or preventing economic growth, an economic system in which both the managements of large firms and the managements of labor unions had gradually taken on

[17] Organization for European Economic Co-operation, *Europe Today and in 1960*, 8th Report, Paris, Vol. II, "Europe in 1960," p. 21.

the role of quasi-public officials would still leave a large degree of autonomy to industrial firms. This would be true even if an economic *condominium* of representatives of government, industrial and labor managements were also set up to work out agreements with respect to national price and wage levels. The independence of thousands of small firms would not necessarily be substantially reduced thereby. Nor would the entrance of new firms into production necessarily be made more difficult. New inventions and techniques of production would not need to be restricted, although there might be some decline in incentives inherent in such a system. The difficulties of working out the structure and functioning of a system in which profit maximization would not be the single-minded purpose of the managements of firms, and the highest possible wages the exclusive goal of the managements of labor unions, would be very great, conceivably insuperable. Yet this single-mindedness of the managements of firms and of labor unions no longer exists anyhow. Further complexities in the motivations of the two types of managements might impair the functioning of the economic system, but the development seems almost inevitable, not only in Britain but in all the economic systems of the West.

Even such a system, stopping far short of nationalization, would be more vulnerable to a take-over by a Soviet or Fascist regime than would an old-style capitalistic economy of small firms and individual free enterprise. But old-style capitalism is gone and not retrievable. So long as the system of modified capitalism of the type sketched herewith avoided crises of inflation or deflation and prevented stagnation, there would be no necessity for a one-party political system. Numerous autonomous groupings of economic power could still exist. There need be no doctrinaire forcing of producing and marketing entities into rigid forms. So long as such a system could be made to function, there would not appear to be a net diminution in personal liberty.

CHAPTER 11

MIXED ECONOMIC SYSTEMS:
(2) THE ECONOMIC SYSTEMS OF
WESTERN EUROPE

With their varying historical and cultural backgrounds, their different natural and capital resources, the diverse impacts of revolutionary ideologies, and their somewhat differing political institutions, it is inevitable that the countries of Western Europe show substantial divergencies in their economic systems.[1] This is in contrast to the imposed uniformity that existed in the sovietized economic systems of Eastern Europe until the time when somewhat deviant forms began to develop in Yugoslavia and Poland. It is not easy to visualize general trends or changes in trends which have taken place in these diverse national economies of Western Europe in recent times, even if a

[1] That only two chapters are devoted in the present study to the national economic systems of Western Europe compared with the much larger space devoted to the United States and Soviet Russia does not, of course, reflect their order of importance. As explained in the Prologue, studies have been made by economists of each of the countries of Western Europe and have appeared in *Economic Systems of the West*, Rudolf Frei (ed.), published by List Gesellschaft, Kyklos-Verlag, Basel, in two volumes, in 1957 and 1958. The writer has used these volumes as an important part of the source material for the present as well as the preceding chapter, although only a portion of the second volume was available in galley proof.

country such as Spain, where a type of authoritarian politico-economic system exists, is omitted from consideration.[2]

In none of the Western European countries did capitalism ever attain the levels of development which were reached in the United States before the Great Depression of the 1930s. Only in Germany, and to a lesser extent in the United Kingdom, did assembly-line techniques in large-scale industry even approach those of the United States. Thus, paradoxically, capitalistic production was carried on in Western Europe in industrial plants of smaller scale than the huge industrial units in the United States, where there had developed a politico-economic doctrine far more devoted to the maintenance of competition among numerous independent units than was true in Europe.

Since there have not existed generally in Europe the legal prohibitions against cartels and other forms of agreements restricting competition, it would not be logical to use evidence of departures from competition as proof of a developmental change in capitalism there.[3] On the contrary, monopolistic or quasi-monopolistic industrial and commercial practices and institutions in Western Europe tend to be customary survivals rather than developmental innovations.

An examination, country by country, of the extent of the nationalization of particular industries also would not yield an index of much precision in measuring the degree of socialization of a particular national economy. Thus, some of the state-owned mines of Germany were a heritage from the Prussian monarchy. State-owned industrial plants such as the Volkswagen plant are left-overs from the Nazi regime. Similarly, state-owned industry in Italy is largely a legacy from fascism, while in Austria some plants and banks had been seized by the Russians as German assets and then transferred to the Austrian government.[4] In France, a wave of nationalization of

[2] For an analysis of the Spanish economic system, see Higinio Paris Eguilaz, "Staatsintervention und Wettbewerb in der Spanischen Wirtschaft," *Economic Systems of the West,* Vol. I, pp. 197–211.

[3] Indeed, in the case of Western Germany, we even find some shift since World War II towards the doctrine of legally enforced competition instead of legally enforceable cartels.

[4] For an analysis of the Austrian economic system, see Wilhelm

industries immediately following the war carried so far as to include banks, insurance companies, coal mines and aviation plants. This surge of nationalization could properly have been considered as a step towards the statization of the economy, even though the nationalization of a major automobile plant represented the confiscation of the property of an alleged Nazi collaborator. As mentioned in the preceding chapter, the wave subsided, however; not primarily for reasons of principle or because of dissatisfaction with results, but because political confusion had produced general stalemate. In general, there has been only limited nationalization of industry in Western Europe since the immediate postwar period, nor is there strong prospect of further nationalization. Indeed, in some cases governments have recently divested themselves of ownership.[5]

One other difficulty exists in trying to assess trends towards or away from greater statization of the various European national economies. The depression had been responsible for the installation of a whole series of interventions and controls by the state intended to combat unemployment. The outbreak of World War II had brought an even more drastic and intimate series of state controls. With the end of the war these controls began to be lifted, and this process of relaxation was to continue almost to the present time. Similarly, under conditions of full employment such as have now existed for a decade in Europe, some of the obstacles to trade between the national economies have been gradually removed. It might be tempting but it would almost certainly be deceptive to offer these changes simply as evidence of a return to traditional capitalism.

In spite of these difficulties in the interpretation of evidence

---

Weber, *"Die Österreichische Volkswirtschaft—Ein 'Gemischter Typus' Mit Ausgeprägter Verbandwirtschaft,"* in *Economic Systems of the West,* Vol. I, pp. 169–195, and his *"Österreichs Wirtschaftsverfassung und Wirtschaftsordnung im Lichte moderner Wirtschaftstheorie und Wirtschaftspolitik,"* in *Zeitschrift für Nationalökonomie,* Band XVII, Heft 1, 1957, pp. 55–101.

[5] In 1957 the Austrian government disposed of two banks and the Netherlands government disposed of its holdings of K.L.M. Airlines stock.

and in spite of national divergencies, some tentative generalizations may be made with respect to the Western European economic systems and developmental trends in these systems. First, there is substantial evidence of the declining political and economic role of the capitalist, just as has been true in the United States. This has been accompanied by the shrunken role of property, as such, in the control of corporations and in the increasing power and perquisites of the corporate bureaucracies, just as in the United States. It appears that income from property after taxes, and particularly from property in land, has diminished in relative importance in Western Europe as it has in the United States. This decline in the role of the capitalist is reflected in a number of ways. It shows itself intangibly in the lessened social prestige of upper-income groups, and manifests itself in the disappearance of political parties which openly espouse the interests of capitalists in the various national parliaments. It can be seen in the spread of social security benefits for the whole population, and in the reduced ability of industrial managements to resist demands for wage advances.

A second generalization with respect to the changed character of the Western European economic systems is the acceptance of responsibility by all national governments for the maintenance of full employment. This has been partially responsible for a change in the economic systems not recognized so widely—the development of what might be called an economic *condominium* or joint rule by the bureaucracies of government, industrial organizations and labor organizations for the working out of national economic policy with respect to wage and price levels and the volume of employment. The economic *condominium* takes varying institutional forms in different countries. It works relatively smoothly in some countries and hardly works at all in others. By means of this *condominium* an effort is made to coordinate wage and price levels, the volume of saving and investment, and the volume and prices of imports and exports with credit, fiscal and monetary policy. No longer are these elements left simply to the free play of the market and the composite effects of the decisions of individual industrialists.

The economic system which has developed in the Netherlands since the end of World War II serves well as an example of the joint control of the economy by the governmental bureaucracy, the managements of industry and the managements of labor organizations. This joint control is exercised over an economy characterized by increasing concentration in industry, trade and banking. On the one hand, very little nationalization of industry has occurred. Nevertheless, the national economy is in effect now managed largely upon the advice of the Social and Economic Council, the recommendations of which are implemented by the decisions of a complex hierarchy of organizations of varying kinds of "jointness" and degrees of "governmentalness." The development of this organizational, quasi-managed economy has not been accompanied by any diminution in the democratic character of the government of the Netherlands.

Employer organizations and labor unions are expected to work out through their representatives on joint bodies agreements on wage increases. These agreements have governmental sanction. Employer organizations are expected to refrain from raising prices to cover wage increases except when increased costs necessitate this. The working out of wage agreements in the Netherlands is carried on through an agency set up jointly by the employer organizations and labor unions, Stichting van den Arbeid, upon advice from which a higher Kollegium with governmental powers gives legal authorization to wage rates.

The government is depended upon to take appropriate measures, through the central bank and other public institutions, to restrict investment or to permit it to expand, to tighten or to relax import controls, and in general to increase or decrease consumer investment expenditures in the economy, so that full employment can be maintained and inflation avoided.[6] To facilitate this kind of control the powers of the

[6] For example, in February 1957, the government of the Netherlands on the basis of a report from the Social Economic Council (S.E.R.) drew up a program for the limitation of *expenditures* in the economy in view of the then existing unfavorable economic tendencies in the country. The burden of limiting disbursements was to be borne by consumers, by the private sector of the economy and by the public authorities. In the latter connection the government had asked the municipalities not to finance any fresh construction

Nederlandsche Bank over the private banking system and over the whole monetary and banking system were progressively strengthened and extended. This control was accentuated when the Bank was nationalized in 1948. Beyond this the government furnishes a substantial amount of capital to the economy through a number of different devices and institutions, including the purchase of stocks in undertakings and the guarantee of certain investments in industry.

A comprehensive network of governmentally sanctioned economic bodies representing the employers' organizations and labor organizations has been set up on both a horizontal and vertical basis to integrate and give direction to the economy. These bodies can issue regulations dealing with a wide variety of matters including production, markets and distribution of products. They carry on research concerning the competitive situation, mechanization and rationalization, educational training programs, unemployment compensation, the creation of employment opportunities and many other matters. They may not, however, issue regulations concerning the formation of new enterprises or the expansion of old ones, nor for the closing of existing enterprises. The actual negotiation and setting of wages is outside their powers, although it has been proposed that this also might be included. Most of the regulations of the public economic organization thus formed (known, by its initials, as P.B.O.) require the concurrence of one or more cabinet ministers to be valid. One-third of its members are named by the government, one-third by employer organizations and one-third by labor organizations. Codetermination is provided on a plant basis through joint representation of management and labor. At the top of the structure of quasi-

of dwelling houses with short-term money. *Quarterly Review Amsterdamsche Bank*, No. 117, Second Quarter, 1957, p. 39. See the note by Jan Tinbergen, "The Netherlands Social and Economic Council," in which he gives a brief account of the Council's functions as well as a résumé of one of its reports, "Advice Concerning National Expenditures." The report, recommending limited wage increases, price controls limiting profit margins, reduction of public expenditures, a rise in taxation, the abolition of certain consumer subsidies and a rise in some public utility rates, was adopted unanimously by the Council on November 28, 1956. *National Planning Association Bulletin*, October 1957.

governmental bodies is the Social Economic Council (S.E.R.), carrying out central planning functions with advisory powers. This whole complex of governmentally sanctioned economic bodies is far too comprehensive to describe here. While most of the decisions with respect to production and sale of goods are still made by the autonomous corporate managements in industry rather than by these quasi-governmental organizations, the net result of the reorganization is that the Dutch economy has become substantially a more directed or managed economy than before the war.[7]

In Belgium, as an additional example of the joint control of the economy by the bureaucracies of the state, industrial managements and managements of labor unions, the government has actively stimulated industrial mergers with the purpose of improving productivity and insuring full employment. It has even extended certain tax exemptions and made substantial loans to encourage mergers. It has made financial support of research institutes compulsory under some circumstances for all the firms in an industry. The already existing web of interfirm and interindustry relations, strengthened by the relations of the investment banks to industry, has been further developed by governmental policy and the setting up of quasi-governmental economic organizations. However, the economy of Belgium is, on balance, substantially a less controlled and directed economy than that of the Netherlands.

A law of September 20, 1948 substantially affected the social structure as well as industrial relations by setting up a network of institutions which brought government, industry and labor unions into a complex of consultative relationships. A Conseil Central de l'Économie was established with equal numbers drawn from organizations representing industry, agriculture, commerce and the handicrafts on the one side and from the organizations representing labor on the other. The Council was charged with the responsibility for giving advice

---

[7] See C. Geodhart, J. F. Haccoû, P. Hennipman and J. H. van Stuyvenberg, of the Institute of Economic Research of the University of Amsterdam, "Das Wirtschaftssystem Der Niederlande Nach 1945," in *Economic Systems of the West*, Vol. I, pp. 131–167, from which this section on the economic system of the Netherlands is largely drawn.

and making proposals concerning problems relative to the national economy. A number of *conseils professionnels* charged with the same sort of responsibility for a particular branch of industry were also set up. They have so far been set up for textiles, metals, the construction industry, fisheries, chemicals and food. The *conseils d'entreprise* perform a different function, and were intended to provide for a limited sort of codetermination by representatives of plant management and plant workers on matters connected with employment in individual plants. They have consultative functions in respect to other matters. These institutions are in addition to the employer organizations and the labor unions which negotiate wage agreements.

Thus, in spite of the fact that there has been no postwar nationalization of industry in Belgium, a comprehensive and intricate set of institutional relations has developed among government, industrial and labor organizations. Nevertheless, the Belgian economic system still permits a high degree of autonomy and liberty among firms in the various industries. Decisions relating to investment, the volume of production, and prices are still largely made by individual corporate managements but within the constraints of institutional understandings, agreements, and pressures and controls. It does not appear that the net result has been to saddle the economy with the high costs and the mal-allocation of resources that might result from a highly cartelized, private, monopolistic economic system. The liberal international trade policy of Belgium insures effective competition from foreign producers and thus reduces the tendency towards monopoly.[8] In any event it would be as incorrect to designate the Belgian economic system simply as a cartelized economic system as to maintain that it is still an example of old-style, individual-enterprise capitalism. Instead it has become a complex organizational economy with working rules designed to maintain some sort of balance of power among economic groups and to minimize overt combat among them.

[8] See Valéry Janssens, "La Belgique: Régime Économique Essentiellement Libre," *Economic Systems of the West*, Vol. I, pp. 19–48, from which the section on the Belgian economy is largely drawn.

The development of the economic system in Sweden away from old-style capitalism has taken place during recent decades under a government in which an avowedly socialistic party has played the dominant role. As Hugo Hegeland points out, it was originally the belief of the Social Democratic Party that the goals of income equalization, full employment, social reforms and a rising standard of living could be attained only by the transformation of the private, capitalistic society into a socialistic one in which collaboration would be substituted for competition.[9] In fact, the transformation of the Swedish economic system has taken place with relatively little nationalization of industry. Nationalization has not, however, been formally abandoned as party doctrine, and there have been some instances of it since World War II, as in the case of the Lapland iron ore corporation in 1956. There seems little prospect, however, that the Social Democratic Party will press actively for extensive further nationalization of industry. It has come to realize, first, that further nationalization has little appeal to the electorate as a political issue, second, that there are decided limitations upon the extent to which further nationalization would aid in attaining the goals desired, and, third, that the desired goals have been and are being achieved in large degree by other means.

The evidence indicates that in spite of increasing industrialization the share of large industrial enterprises in the total employment of labor has not been increasing during the last couple of decades. The importance of cartels in the economy has also apparently been declining. Recent legislation limiting the powers of cartels has been only a minor factor in this development. In larger part, it is due to full employment and a strong market demand for the products of industry, which have diminished the motivation for the formation and maintenance of cartels. Cooperative associations employ less than 1 per cent of the total labor force and control only about 14 per cent of retail trade.

Yet group interests are probably more thoroughly organized

[9] See Hugo Hegeland, "The Structure and Functioning of Sweden's Political Economy," *Economic Systems of the West*, Vol. I, pp. 213–242, from which the source material for this section on the Swedish economy is largely drawn.

in Sweden than in almost any other democratic country. Over 90 per cent of the workers in industry are organized in trade unions. These unions in turn are linked together in the Swedish Federation of Trade Unions (L.O.). Salaried workers are also organized in unions on a national basis. Employers forming 43 federations are linked in the Swedish Employers' Confederation (S.A.F.). The Swedish Federation of Trade Unions has followed a policy tending towards wage equalization through negotiating wage agreements giving greater percentage increases to unskilled than to skilled labor. Agreements with respect to the general level of wages and hours of labor in relation to the cost of living are worked out between the two organizations. For example, a comprehensive agreement covering the two years 1957 and 1958 was signed in February 1957.[10] As Hegeland points out, the government has intervened in wage disputes only in tense situations in the early stages of wage negotiations and has then left it to the labor unions and employer associations to act "with a sense of social responsibility." This sense of social responsibility has been interpreted to mean limiting wage increases to those consistent with a stable price level. While this particular aspect of the *condominium* of government, labor unions and employer associations in the management of the economy has served well in maintaining industrial peace, it has not been so successful in maintaining a stable price level. Nor has it been wholly successful in protecting the interests of the less well organized elements of the population. However, the elaborate system of social insurance provides a welfare "floor" below which almost no one may fall. Since wage agreements provide only the minimum which may be paid for the various jobs, in a period of over-full employment wages have risen above these minima. It has been estimated that during the past decade from one-half to two-thirds of the increase in wages has been a direct result of collective bargaining.

Even though agriculture is overwhelmingly characterized by small-scale individual proprietors, agricultural prices are so regulated by the government that farmers receive the same income as "other comparable groups" in society, and farm

[10] International Monetary Fund, *International Financial News Survey*, March 8, 1957, p. 270.

laborers receive substantially the same wages as comparably employed industrial workers.

In spite of the abandonment of any dynamic policy for the nationalization of industry, the role of the state has continued to expand. Total taxes as a percentage of national income increased from 18 per cent in 1939 to 36 per cent in 1956. The current budget, as distinguished from the capital budget, of the national government now constitutes about one-fourth of the national income compared with one-tenth in 1938–39. Social expenditures such as old-age pensions, child contributions and rent contributions have grown from 23 per cent to 33 per cent of the governmental budget during the same period.

During a period when the proportion devoted to investment in total production increased from 25 per cent of gross national product in 1938–39 to 30 per cent in 1955, while the percentage of total production devoted to consumption shrank in proportion, public domestic capital formation doubled from 6.5 to 13 per cent of gross national product. Public investment amounted to 42 per cent of total gross investment in 1956. The total percentage of the gross national product attributable to the public sector increased from 14 per cent in 1938–39 to 25 per cent in 1956.

Perhaps the greatest instrument of governmental control over the economy has been the monetary and credit system. Comprehensive control over investment has developed primarily in an effort to prevent inflation. Governmental agencies have the power to set interest rates. New loans on the capital market have to be authorized by the central bank. As a consequence the traditional market mechanism no longer functions in the capital market. As a result of the difficulty of obtaining new funds for investment from outside sources, industrial corporations now depend very largely upon internally generated funds "plowed back" into the business. It is extremely difficult to obtain capital funds for new enterprises.

As Hegeland states:

> In its attempt to stabilize the economy, the Government has not only controlled the money supply but also the use of the country's "real resources." On the basis of the annual forecast by the national budget delegation con-

cerning the expected changes in total current resources for the following year, the Government decides upon the distribution between an increase in total investment and in consumption. And it does not only determine the amount of total investment for the following year; it also determines its distribution between private and public investment, as well as its detailed allocation within each section of the economy and between factories, housing, highways, railroads, power dams, etc. Investment activity has been almost completely regulated during the whole period. In this way the Government has steadily increased the public sector of investment, as it considers public investments more profitable and necessary to society than private ones.[11]

In spite of the extended role of the government in the control of the Swedish economy and in spite of the transformation from an individual-enterprise system to an organizational economy, a large role is left for the individual entrepreneur in small-scale industry, in trade and in agriculture, and for the managements of corporations in larger-scale industry, banking and commerce. The majority of operational decisions are still made by private and corporate managements.

During the period under review a substantial diminution in income inequality occurred. The percentage of total national income which would have to be transferred in order to attain complete equalization of income decreased from 41 per cent in 1935 to 34 per cent in 1948. The share of disposable income of the four lowest decile groups increased from 10 per cent to 14 per cent while the share of the tenth decile group, the highest, decreased from 37 per cent to 27 per cent. The share of employees in the national income increased from 70 per cent in 1930 to 77 per cent in 1954, while the share of employers declined from 21 per cent to 16.5 per cent. This change is largely accounted for by an increase in the number of employees in proportion to the number of employers. There has been a substantial diminution in the proportion of dividends in national income during the period. Individuals' income from

[11] Hegeland, "The Structure and Functioning of Sweden's Political Economy," p. 237.

capital fell from 7 per cent to less than 3 per cent. There has been a similar tendency towards the equalization of wealth. Tax policy has apparently played a relatively minor role in this tendency towards the equalization of income and wealth. The elimination of unemployment, the increase in productivity, the movement of labor from industries of low productivity to industries of higher productivity, the inflationary movement of prices acting upon a very progressive tax structure, compensation for increases in the cost of living extended to the lower-paid workers, and trade union policies favoring wage equalization, have all tended towards equalization.

During the period 1946–51, economic growth as reflected in the gross national product increased at an average rate of 4.5 per cent a year. With full employment and the necessity for restricting both consumption and investment through tightening money and credit, the rate of increase had fallen to 2 per cent by 1957.

Regardless of whether or not the economic and social policies of the Social Democratic Party have been the cause of full employment, a rising standard of living and a greater equalization of wealth and income in Sweden, it is easy to understand why that party no longer presses strongly for further nationalization of industry. Experience with a managed economy without extensive nationalization has demonstrated rather clearly that little if anything would be gained by nationalization and much might be lost. It has been demonstrated, for example, that restraining inflation while maintaining full employment is the major and extremely difficult problem of a managed economy. It has become clear that the attainment of a higher rate of capital investment and the further expansion of production are limited by the necessity for credit controls to prevent inflation. None of these problems would be ameliorated by the nationalization of the economy, but would instead be intensified. Similarly, it has been demonstrated, in Sweden as elsewhere, that a considerable degree of equalization of income and wealth can take place without nationalization. It has also become quite clear that a substantial degree of inequality would have to be retained even under nationalization.

The trend in the development of the Danish economic system is not very clear.[12] Contrary to the experience of some of the neighboring economies, the number and importance of cartels has increased somewhat. On the other hand, while there has been some increase in the size of industries, any increase in concentration in Danish industry seems to have been of minor importance.

Rents are still controlled as in most European countries, but the comprehensive governmental price controls of the war and postwar periods have shrunk to those involving price-fixing by cartels. Governmental controls in agriculture have largely been abandoned. Agricultural cooperatives function as cartels of a sort. However, the general liberalization of import policy in recent years has limited any monopolistic tendencies which might have existed.

The principle of adjustment of wages to the cost of living, which formerly applied only to civil servants, has now been accepted as a major factor in the setting of wages by labor unions and employers' associations. Ordinarily the government does not intervene in wage negotiations, but on occasion it has done so. An effort has been made to set up collaboration committees in all large firms so as to provide for a kind of co-determination by employee representatives with managements. These committees have only consultative powers.

The government and the central bank have manipulated money and credit in an effort to prevent inflation and to maintain a viable balance of payments in foreign trade, even at the cost of interference with full employment, the proclaimed policy of the government. As in many other countries of Western Europe there has been some diminution in inequality in income distribution. There has been a substantial increase in the share of social expenditures in national income, with old-age pensions increasing and sickness and unemployment payments diminishing in relative importance. The share of the governmental budget as a percentage of gross national product increased from about 4 per cent in 1938–39 to 15.5 per cent in 1954–55. During the same period the share of public investment in gross

[12] See Bjarke Fog, "The Relevance of the Competitive Laissez-Faire Model to the Danish Economy," *Economic Systems of the West*, Vol. I, pp. 49–64.

national investment increased also, and the government has come to have a leading role in the capital market.

In practice, in these tripartite institutional arrangements among governments, corporate managements and the managements of labor unions it has proved difficult to induce the managements of labor unions to follow a policy of sufficient wage restraint, to induce bankers to restrict investments, to induce industrialists "to hold the line on prices," to induce economic pressure groups to accept limitations on governmental subsidies, and to induce taxpayers to pay higher rates of taxes. Consequently, during the past decade a general inflationary movement in these countries has occurred. Yet these very inflationary difficulties increase the feeling that joint action with organized economic groups by the governments of the different countries is an absolute necessity. The economic *condominium* has been a potent factor in reducing conflict both among the managements of business enterprises and between these managements and the managements of labor organizations. In general, the *condominium* has greatly facilitated the carrying out of an integrated national economic policy, although at some cost to the unorganized elements of the population. Since the *condominium* has not been part of a totalitarian society, and since it has not been dependent upon the monopoly of power by one political party, up to the present time it does not appear to have brought about a diminution of personal freedom. If a still more comprehensive and intensive control of the economy were to prove necessary to combat inflation or to prevent depression, there can be no certainty that this would continue to be true.

Gross national product of the fifteen O.E.E.C. countries of Western Europe increased by an average of 26.5 per cent during the five-year period 1950–55. Taking into account changes in the total labor supply, this increase represented an average annual compound increase in G.N.P. per man-hour of 3.1 per cent.[13] The annual rates of per capita increase for individual

[13] By comparison, the rate of increase for the United States was 2.4 per cent. The rate of increase fell during the two years following 1955, as was also true in the United States. "Europe in 1960," Organization for European Economic Co-operation, *Europe Today and*

countries during the period showed a substantial range, from a high of 6 per cent for West Germany to a low of 1.2 per cent for Denmark. The rate for Britain was almost as low, at 1.7 per cent.

One of the main limiting factors in the rate of productivity increase seems to have been the degree of necessity for following a restrictive money and credit and budgetary policy in order to limit inflation. This did not mean, however, that those countries which followed the most restrictive policies had the smallest price rises. Instead, as might be expected, really restrictive policies seem to have followed large price increases. There seems to have been a tendency for those countries which had the largest price increases to have been those with the smallest increases in productivity. In countries where price increases reached serious proportions, restrictive monetary and credit measures eventually had to be invoked. These measures were sometimes more effective in limiting production than in holding down prices. This suggests that one of the major tests of the efficiency of a country's economic system is the extent to which a national policy restraining increases in costs of production, particularly in wage rates, can be made effective without having to restrict the money supply so sharply as to limit production short of its physical potential. In those national economies in which old-style competition among entrepreneurs can no longer be relied upon to restrain the upward movement of prices nor the resistance of industrial managements to collective bargaining by labor managements relied upon to limit wages, this presents an organizational problem of the first magnitude.

Unfortunately an examination of the record does not suggest an easy answer to the question of the organizational form most likely to be effective. The country which has had greatest success in increasing productivity and preventing inflation, West Germany, does not have a formal comprehensive system for working out agreements regarding wage and price levels on a national basis, although the government has the power to intervene to protect the public interest if necessary. Indeed, the West German government has followed a positive policy of attempting to create a freer and more competitive market economy than has ever before existed in Germany. This policy has been under the leadership of Economics Minister Ludwig Erhard. It has had the support of an influential group of neoliberal German economists who have idealized and publicized what they call the *Marktwirtschaft* or free market economy.[14]

But competition is not enough. The West German government's current denationalization of industry program shows that Dr. Erhard recognizes what has always been a most vulnerable spot in the capitalistic free market economy. Even when the prices of products and the compensation of factors of production have been set competitively, the distribution of income under capitalism has always departed from the vaunted principle of "from each according to his ability, to each according to his productivity." Instead, the real distribution has been "from each according to his ability, to each according to his productivity *and the productivity of his property.*" So long as this remained true, a conflict between the interests of those who had only labor to sell and those who could sell the services of property was inherent in the capitalistic free market system.

In a move that has aroused great interest in other Western European countries, the West German government this year began to sell off industries which it had inherited after World War II. In April 1959, the government sold a large part of its holdings in Preussag, an industrial combine engaged in oil refining and coal mining with a yearly turnover of some $180 million. The Bonn regime also plans to sell its interest in Viag, a heavy industry combine, in Volkswagen, producer of automobiles, and in other enterprises in the near future.

The West German government has thus sought to use its sale of government property as a means of broadening stock ownership and democratizing capitalism in general. In selling Preussag, for example, the government deliberately provided its lower-income citizens with a bargain investment. Only persons with incomes of less than $3810 a year could subscribe and no individual could buy more than five shares (reduced to four shares when additional issues were offered later in the

[14] See Henry M. Oliver, Jr., "German Neoliberalism," *Quarterly Journal of Economics*, February 1960.

year). Employees of Preussag were given first bids. Shares could not be resold until six months after purchase. Most important, the stocks were priced so low that buyers enjoyed an immediate capital gain of some 25 per cent. The public's response was enthusiastic. In fact, the sale of the first 300,000 shares was so successful that an additional 530,000 shares were offered for public sale.

Policies of restraint in regard to wage increases and the prices of the most important commodities have been in successful operation in West Germany. In turn, price and wage restraint in Germany has been facilitated by productivity increases large enough so that reasonably satisfactory profits and wages could be paid to stockholders and wage earners. A policy of restraint consequently did not preclude rising compensation to both. In Britain, where likewise no formal and comprehensive machinery has been developed to deal with price and wage levels, both price and wage restraints have been generally unsuccessful, in part because productivity increases have been relatively so small. It would be easy to conclude that where large productivity increases take place the line can be held against wage and price increases and where productivity increases are low the line cannot be held. There can be no doubt that inflation can be held in check more easily when productivity increases are large than when they are small, all else being equal. But an inflationary situation often exists which combines high capital investment, large increases in productivity, large demands for wage increases and the upward movement of prices. To prevent an inflationary situation of this type from arising is likely to require a combination of the correct money, credit and fiscal policies by governmental agencies together with organizational forms in the economy which will make possible the implementation of price and wage restraints. Even then, the attitudes of the managements of industry and of labor unions are likely to be as important as the organizational forms. The willingness of German labor to postpone demands for wage increases until a revived economy could pay real increases out of increased product has been a major factor in Germany's stable prices. This self-restraint was the product of the disillusionment of German labor with violent and revolutionary economic and political means and goals. It was reinforced by the influx of Soviet zone labor. The Nazi regime, the war and the Soviet occupation of East Germany had taught German labor some unforgettable lessons.

The rather complex conclusion must be that different organizational forms may be required in different countries to maintain a tolerable degree of price stability while facilitating productivity increases, depending upon existing attitudes. Since it is clear that neither competition between individual entrepreneurs nor unrestrained collective bargaining can be relied upon to facilitate economic growth and price stability, a continual groping towards the organizational forms appropriate to particular national economies is presently taking place. The variants of the *condominium* or joint controls by government, the managements of industry and the managements of labor unions, which exist in only embryonic form in some of the countries of Western **Eur**ope and in more advanced forms in others, seem certain to continue and to undergo further development.

CHAPTER 12

ECONOMIC SYSTEMS
AND LIBERTY: ANALYSIS
OF THE RECORD

That the extension of the power of the state over the individual—whether or not it be in the best interests of society—represents a curtailment of personal liberty has generally been considered a truism. The national economy has always been viewed as one of the most crucial areas in which this curtailment of personal liberty might occur. The protagonists of laissez-faire capitalism have, of course, always maintained that this is so. It was the bourgeois class that took the lead in developing constitutional protection for the liberties of the individual against the state, insisting at the same time upon the minimization of interference in or control of the economy by the state.

Viewed abstractly, laissez-faire capitalism differed from anarchism as a politico-economic system primarily in its recognition of the necessity for the existence of the state to perform the absolutely essential, minimum functions, even though these limited the liberties of individuals, and to establish and protect the institution of private property. Like the anarchists, Communists viewed the state as an evil. One of the major advantages that Marxian Communists expected would flow from the destruction of capitalism and the bourgeois state was the opportunity for the complete "withering

away" of the state—even the workers' state which would temporarily succeed the bourgeois state. Only through the elimination of the state in any form could full liberty be attained.
Thus anarchist, capitalist and Communist philosophers have
historically been agreed on the doctrine "The more state, the
less liberty."

It has been primarily the advocates of gradual economic
reform and the less doctrinaire advocates of socialism by
peaceful and parliamentary means who have defended the
position that the extension of the powers of the state over the
economy does not, on balance, limit liberty but instead ex-
tends it. They have argued that the extension of state power
holds no threat to individual liberty because legislators are
followers, not leaders. Politicians desiring to be re-elected
would not pass legislation to restrict the liberties of citizens.
Politicians who would try to do so would never be in the
majority.[1]

This argument disregards the fact that whenever politicians
favor the extension of the powers of the state they never admit that it might endanger personal liberty. Instead, they take
a stand for a particular extension of governmental power
which will ostensibly benefit at least some group of voters.
It may indeed be that the proposed extension of power would
not of itself critically limit personal liberty. The cumulative
effect of such measures might, however, critically endanger
liberty without the electorate ever having deliberately considered, much less voted upon, the desirability of statization
of the economy. At a time of economic crisis when critical
extensions of governmental power are likely to occur, whether
as a part of this cumulative process or not, there is little opportunity for a meaningful vote on whether or not, as a matter
of principle, the powers of the state should be extended. Instead, there is likely to be an insistent demand for emergency
action of some sort and relatively little consideration of what
the permanent effect will be. There was, for example, nothing like a coherent majority *against* the Nazis when they came

[1] So staunch a defender of the current form of the capitalistic
system as Professor Sumner Slichter advances much this type of
argument. "Government Expansion in a Dynamic Society," *Commercial and Financial Chronicle*, April 25, 1957.

to power in Germany. On the contrary, the Nazis had received a substantial plurality of the vote in the election just before Hitler was granted extraordinary powers by the Reichstag. This is not to say that Hitler came to power legally—a totalitarian dictator never does. Under circumstances favorable to a dictatorship, involving, of course, an immense increase in the power of the state over the individual, the wish of politicians to be popular with the voters would be quite unlikely to protect individual liberties effectively.

The position that personal liberty might be extended by increasing the power of the state was embraced by socialists and by many reformers out of what appeared to be necessity. Whatever the defects and injustices of old-style capitalism and its institutional keystone, private property, the anarchists' solution of eliminating the state and with it property in any form had obviously become impossible to apply in an industrialized society. If the evils of private property were to be eliminated or even mitigated, the only alternative appeared to be the substitution of state property for private property in whole or in part, or at least the curtailment of private property rights by the state.

Socialist parties such as those of Western Europe, which defended the extension of the powers of the state as a means of eliminating or ameliorating the claimed inequities of capitalist private property, maintained that the state thereby only exercised powers previously exercised by capitalists, as individuals or as managers of corporations, over the mass of workers and consumers. This extension of state power, non-Marxian socialists reluctantly conceded, would indeed involve the exercise of the power of men over men. But, they argued, this would not be more so than under private-property capitalism, and with the difference that the appointees of the state would be assumed to exercise power in the public interest rather than for private gain. Moreover, it was maintained that, since public administrators would not be operating industry for private gain and since workers would be producing for consumers rather than for the profit of capitalists, the rule of men over men for selfish ends would be much reduced. Thus, for some esoteric reason, public administrators could be counted upon to act in the public interest and not in their own personal interests. There was consequently little concern about the exercise of arbitrary power by administrators of the state monopolies which were proposed as substitutes for production carried on by corporate managements.

Under old-style, laissez-faire capitalism there had been in fact substantial limitations upon the power of the capitalist to act in his own interests. Apart from the minimum limitations enforced by the state, the capitalist enterpriser had no choice but to offer his goods at prices which would move them off the market in competition with other products and to offer wage payments and working conditions which would induce workers to accept employment with him rather than with another. Granted that these limitations upon the power of capitalist enterprisers did not result in a distribution of income satisfactory to a large part of the population from the standpoint of social justice, they were nevertheless real limitations upon the capitalist's power over others. Even when old-style capitalism was superseded by modern corporate capitalism, the restraints of new and old forms of competition plus the countervailing power of labor organizations limited the power of corporate executives over the liberties of workers and consumers, perhaps to an extent greater than before.

The capitalistic system is the only economic and political system in which it has been possible for substantial numbers of individuals to have incomes allowing them to live without functional duties, responsibilities or authority in relation to the system. Under capitalism a person may and usually does enjoy wealth and its perquisites even though he has no governmental power. Men who possess property may live without doing any work at all for periods of time of varying length depending upon the amount of property they possess and the standard at which they live. This situation greatly facilitates the exercise of liberty by the individual who possesses even a little property. On the other hand, it means that this dimension of liberty has, during most of the capitalistic era, existed among persons with little relation to equity. However, under modern modified capitalism, in virtually all countries governmental power is exerted to reduce the inequality in income from property. Consequently, this liberty which depends upon property has become of some value to a major fraction of the population.

In the totalitarian state a much tighter connection exists between receipt of income and performance of what those who wield authority consider service to the state. Thus in Soviet Russia men may receive income for work on a factory assembly line, for work on a state farm, as a member of the security police or as a member of the Presidium of the Communist Party. With few exceptions, however, they cannot receive income, except for paid vacations and limited retirement allowances, apart from some functional relation to the state. At higher levels the inability to receive income apart from one's connection with the state has been associated with the inability of men who wield state power to retire from the exercise of that power. There have been, of course, other more cogent reasons in Soviet Russia than the absence of personal property for this inability to retire from positions of power. Nevertheless, the possibility of having an income from property which is independent of the authority or whim of those who happen to wield the state power is an important factor in making the thought of relinquishing power in some degree tolerable in free societies.

In the lower reaches of capitalistic society, the opportunity of men to choose to work when, where and if they wish is restricted, in addition to other miscellaneous restraints, by the amount of property they hold. Yet the right to quit a job, to loaf for a few days or months, to change from one job to another without having to observe universally applicable rules, and the opportunity for at least temporary self-employment, make up a vastly important part of the liberties of men. These particular capitalistic liberties are among the most precious and widely shared of all. Yet they are so taken for granted that they are not generally thought of as liberties which might be lost under an alternative form of economic and political system.

There can be no question, however, that in all countries the trend has been towards extension of state power, whether as a result of revolution or by conscious choice through parliamentary actions or by gradual and almost imperceptible change. The problem is the extent to which this growth of state power has diminished liberties formerly protected by capitalistic institutions and the extent to which this has been offset by the enlargement of other liberties.

The changes which have taken place in economic and political systems since World War I have been reviewed in previous chapters. They reflect differentiated national patterns. It would be easy to conclude that, however differentiated these patterns have been, the extension of state power has clearly reflected an accelerated trend away from capitalism towards socialism. This trend might appear to have manifested itself in all countries—in Soviet Russia, where capitalism long ago ceased to exist; in Western Europe, where partial nationalization of the economy has taken place in various degrees in different countries; and even in the United States, where capitalism has been substantially modified. We might then simply ask: How has this trend towards "socialism" affected human liberty? It would appear a simple matter to examine the record and to come up with an answer.

Closer analysis of the experience of all countries where these changes have taken place raises serious doubts whether this question is really pertinent and meaningful. The departure of national economic systems from old-style, laissez-faire, individual-enterprise capitalism cannot be disputed, or the fundamental nature of these developments questioned. Yet the movement has by no means been unequivocally towards the type of economic and political system visualized by the nineteenth and early twentieth century protagonists of socialism. This is quite clear in the case of Soviet Russia, but the analysis in the preceding chapters of the political and economic systems of other countries, where there have been varying degrees of change from old-style capitalism, also discloses reasons for skepticism with respect to an unambiguous trend toward what used to be generally understood as "socialism."

The protagonists of socialism have in the past had unquestioning faith that the reduction or limitation of private property would result in a very great increase in the amount of income from production available for distribution to workers, and that none of the former return from private property would have to be used to increase the rates of pay to public administrators or to pay greater numbers of such administrators. Far greater equality of income distribution would therefore result. They believed that workers would work far more willingly and productively when working for the benefit of consumers who were themselves workers than when working for the profit of capitalists, and that consequently far less industrial discipline would be necessary. They believed that the productivity of the economy would be much greater under planning for public purposes than under the wastes of competition or the restrictions of private monopoly. Above all, they believed that the effect of the elimination of private property would be a large net gain in individual liberty.

Significant changes in the institutions of old-style capitalism have indeed taken place in all countries. In the cases where private property has been abolished and the powers of the state have been extended without limit, however, progress towards the goals of socialism, as these goals were understood in the past, has been least. On the other hand, substantial progress towards the commonly accepted goals of socialism has been made in some countries without any deliberate move towards socialism and without even partial nationalization of industry.

Thus, the question of the relation between the type of economic system and the status of individual liberty cannot be answered simply by comparing the degree of socialism attained in different countries. It is possible, nevertheless, to arrive at some conclusions of general validity by analyzing the records of the different economic systems as they have functioned during recent decades, drawing upon the experiences of these countries as set forth in detail in previous chapters.

In the one major country in which capitalism has been completely eliminated, Soviet Russia, the record of events and developments has answered in the most emphatic negative the question of whether or not an economic system which destroys the institution of private property thereby automatically increases the economic and political liberty of the worker, as it was supposed to do according to Marxist doctrine. It has been pointed out that the Soviet regime did not follow the Marxist timetable in coming to power, that the causes of the Revolution were not consistent with Marxist theory, and finally that the political and social system which the Bolsheviki imposed upon Russia has turned out to be in almost total contradiction to that envisioned by substantially all socialist philosophers prior to that time. According to Marxist doctrine, the overthrow of capitalism should have meant the elimination of both the capitalist as economic boss and the police state, which was considered to be the creature of the bourgeoisie. This was eventually to bring about the end of the rule of man over man and the full blooming of individual liberty. Capitalists were eliminated in Russia, the provisional government which had momentarily replaced the tsarist state was destroyed, and the Bolshevik dictatorship took over power. Since the socialist society forecast by Marxist doctrine never came into existence, however, one cannot simply say that the Russian experience proves that personal liberty is bound to be most sharply limited under socialism. What the Russian experience does prove is that a socialism which embodies liberty is not to be attained by the Soviet route.

Soviet experience has not, of course, definitively demonstrated the productive superiority of a collectivist economy, as compared with the production record of the United States and of Western Europe. Before the Soviet experience, however, it had been widely questioned whether a collectivist economic system could function at all. This question has now received a positive answer. We now know that an authoritarian collectivist economic system can function over a huge area with a large population at a level of production high enough to maintain a tolerable standard of living, provide for an enormous armament effort and permit the saving of capital essential for an impressive rate of economic growth.

Socialist critics of capitalism including the Marxists, however, had always maintained not only that a higher standard of living for the masses would be attainable under socialism but that mankind would be far freer as well. The Soviet leaders consequently have always claimed that their one-party-list "elections" with an almost unanimous popular vote, the absence of even one dissenting vote in the Supreme Soviet, the complete unanimity of opinion in the Party Congresses (on the infrequent occasions when these have been held), and the monolithic position of all organs of public opinion on all issues, showed that in a truly "socialistic society" popular solidarity and unanimity of opinion were somehow automatically attained. Thus, it was claimed, all the divisive forces of capitalism had disappeared, and with them political corruption, parliamentary "maneuvering" and all the problems of rendering the state and the economy responsive to the people's will.

Communists outside the Soviet Union unwaveringly insisted this was so, even if many knew it was not. Many liberals outside the Soviet Union, even if they did not accept the explanation in its entirety, still felt that significant progress in the direction of enthusiastic popular solidarity had in some undefinable way been attained by the elimination of capitalistic exploitation. The repeated purges and executions which seemed to give the lie to any such claims of popular solidarity and national unity were represented by the Soviet rulers as the just punishment of individual traitors, who, as enemies of the people, were invariably and unanimously execrated once their evil machinations had been exposed to the populace. Thus it was maintained that the Stalinist regime simply embodied the people's will in carrying out these wholesale purges and executions. The official disclosures by Khrushchev of the appallingly coercive character of the Stalinist state showed conclusively, however, that this "popular solidarity and national unity" was simply the product of unlimited force which had induced total submission to the will of the tyrant.

Upon the basis of the Russian experience we must conclude that where a collectivist economic system is set up by violence under the control of one man or of a junta, unaccompanied by democratic and parliamentary responsibility in a country technologically and culturally retarded, such a system is bound to remain authoritarian and totalitarian over a long period of time. The Russian experience does not, however, definitively prove that a collectivist economic system which came into existence by peaceful, democratic, parliamentary means in a culturally and technologically advanced country would inevitably be characterized by a loss of personal liberty. Some have even argued that there is no functional relation between the establishment of a collectivist economic system as such and the loss of personal liberty. There is, indeed, evidence that the causal relation sometimes runs in the opposite direction, since it was the initial military *coup d'état* of the Bolshevist junta which enabled the Leninist and later the Stalinist bureaucracy to repress personal freedom both politically and economically. Again, in Germany, it was not the increase in the economic role of the state which was primarily responsible for the loss of personal liberty under the Nazis.[2] It was, on the contrary, political-military power which enabled the Nazis to impose on Germany an economic system characterized by greatly increased state participation.

The Soviet experience affords conclusive evidence, if any were needed, that the elimination of private property and the cognate institutions of capitalism does not automatically change the personalities and characters of men by causing human acquisitiveness to disappear. There is no evidence that material incentives or penalties are of less importance in reducing performance of economic and political functions in Soviet society than they are in capitalistic countries. Indeed, material incentives and penalties appear to play a much greater role in Soviet society. There is no evidence whatever that with the passage of time "the Soviet man" is losing any of the selfish characteristics which were supposed to be almost unique to capitalism.

The Soviet experience in this respect parallels that of Western countries in which the nationalization of particular industries has taken place. No measurable gain in productivity attributable to "the worker now working for himself and not for the capitalist boss" has been noticeable in these countries any more than in Soviet Russia. Nor was it reasonable to expect this to happen. After nationalization the individual worker in most cases continues to receive orders from the same boss as before, and he finds almost no evidence of betterment in wages or other working conditions which he can attribute to the new status of the industry. Hence, there can be little expectation that the problems of planning, organizing and directing a collectivist economic system would be made easier

---

[2] The Nazi revolution occurred under circumstances much more like those which, according to Marx, would have resulted in the overthrow of capitalism and the dictatorship of the proletariat than did the October Revolution in Russia in 1917. As related in Chapter 6, it was the economic depression which was crucial in bringing the Nazis to power in Germany in January 1933.

by a greater concern for the public interest as self-interest declines among workers, since there is no evidence that it does decline.

One reason for the harsher discipline encountered by the worker in Soviet industry compared with that in a typical modern capitalistic country is that industrial discipline had to be restored in Russia by the same leaders who had proclaimed the necessity for its destruction and had succeeded in destroying it. The maintenance of worker discipline was rendered somewhat more complicated by the continual reiteration of the doctrinaire myth that the workers owned and controlled industry.

The structure and functioning of Soviet society has departed from the socialist ideal in another basic respect. Elimination of the greater part of the inequality of income which characterized capitalism had always been a major element in socialist doctrine. But in Soviet Russia inequality in income distribution, contrary to socialist doctrine, has been associated with maintenance of the pyramid of authority in industry, and indeed throughout the economy.

A substantial portion of the inequality of income which characterizes the Soviet system in essence simply reflects the setting by those in authority of their own compensation.[3] There is substantial evidence, however, that the amount of reduction in inequality in income distribution which could be expected to result from any form of statization of a formerly capitalistic economy is much smaller than most protagonists of socialism have assumed. The experience of countries where limited nationalization of industry has occurred also indicates the need for much the same pattern of differential compensation of skills and responsibilities that existed before nationalization, and the continuation, therefore, of much of the inequality in income distribution which characterizes modern capitalism.[4] The trend in recent years both in the United

[3] In this respect the process is not wholly unlike the setting of the salaries of the top echelon of executives in the capitalistic corporation, which is not typically market-determined.

[4] Statistical evidence indicates that the effect of redistributing income from private property in an economy like that of the United States, for example, would not be of major importance. Kuznets has

States and in most of the countries of Western Europe towards a diminution of inequality in income distribution accentuates this observation.

Beyond the causes of the authoritarian character of Soviet industry which might be considered largely historical in character there are others which appear to be inherent in the nature of a statized economy. If the state, even by the process of free elections, once assumes the task of determining all distributive shares, there is doubt whether it can remain a parliamentary, libertarian state. This process of share determination has many facets. It involves, for example, not merely the setting of wages, salaries and prices but also the provision of funds for further investment if economic progress is to continue. The record of nationalized industries in countries where democratic institutions continue to exist is poor in this respect, compared with that of private corporate industry. The temptation to give in to demands for higher wages and the fear of consumer resentment if prices are allowed to rise as an offset to wage increases usually means that little in the way of

---

estimated that property incomes constitute about one-sixth of the total income receipts of individuals. If property incomes (rent, interest and dividends) were to be redistributed equally, the effect would be to decrease the share of the upper 5 per cent of income receivers from 24.7 per cent to 19 per cent. (Since undistributed corporate profits as well as some portions of other entrepreneurial income which might be considered property income are not included in this estimate, the share of property in national income may be somewhat understated.) In other words, the income of the top 5 per cent would be reduced by about one-fifth. The share of the lowest 95 per cent of income receivers would be increased from 75.3 per cent of total income to 83.1 per cent. Kuznets further estimates that even if the definition of property income is made as inclusive as possible, at least two-thirds of the inequality in income distribution would remain after property incomes were equally distributed. Simon Kuznets, *Shares of Upper Income Groups in Income and Savings,* National Bureau of Economic Research, New York, 1953, pp. 27–31.

After the nationalization of private industry, the state would have to retain for its own administrative expenses and for general welfare purposes funds now secured from property through taxation, plus whatever funds are now obtained from the income of private property for use in further investment in the economy. This means that the proceeds from the confiscation of "surplus value" in the Marxist sense would probably be disappointing.

plowed-back profits will be available for capital expansion or even renewal.

In a fully nationalized economy the state has no choice but to assume responsibility for the determination of distributive shares. The ruling bureaucracy must then either resist or succumb to the efforts of organized groups by exercising the power to interfere with the process of share determination at the expense of consumers or other workers, or at the cost of adequate capital investment. So long as free parliamentary elections existed, politicians and parties would be certain to try to intervene in the process of share determination, just as would labor union managements.

The temptation for the ruling bureaucracy to shut itself off from intolerable pressure and confusion in the complex process of share determination is inevitably great. The pressures of economic groups and of individuals for preference in income distribution could indeed become unendurable unless the responsible hierarchy were armed with sufficient authority to moderate these pressures. In the face of such pressures, actual or potential, the power grasped by the bureaucratic hierarchy is likely to be far greater than the minimum necessary for efficient operation of the economy. The ruling bureaucracy of a completely nationalized economy is almost inexorably driven to refuse workers permission to strike, for example. Once having accepted responsibility for planning the national economy, the ruling bureaucracy cannot logically allow the weapon of the strike to be used either to push up the general wage bill beyond an amount the economy can endure without inflation or to increase the wage rates of one economic group at the expense of another without restraint. Thus, the government of a statized economy is almost certain to be confronted with the alternative of allowing economic anarchy or assuming dictatorial power.

This principle is well illustrated by the experience of Gomulka after he took over power in Poland following the riots in Poznan in June 1956. In a speech on March 21, 1957, Gomulka warned of "economic ruin" unless "financial discipline" was restored. The speech pointed out the threat to the national economy of strikes for higher wages, at a time when a strike for a 40 per cent wage increase in the car repair works at Poznan had just been settled by granting a 15 per cent increase. Gomulka went on to say, "If our party organization does not know how to oppose a group of squabblers but keeps silent and allows the squabblers to talk, the latter can frequently do much harm. They can instigate a section of the working class; they can provoke a strike. I tell you that in the present circumstances a strike could not achieve anything. It would not improve the economic situation but only worsen it. Under the pressure of a strike we would not yield to unrealistic demands because we would not permit the breakdown of the whole economy."[5]

The power to resist what the ruling bureaucracy feels to be intolerable pressures can be effectively implemented by the institution of the one-party monopoly. Here we have the example of the Nazi, the Fascist and the Soviet economic systems. We also have the example of Red China, the Soviet satellite states and even those satellite states which have achieved some degree of independence of Moscow. In the Nazi and Fascist systems the decision to permit but one party was always a part of doctrine. In statized economies of Marxist origin, the decision for the one-party state has been both disguised and facilitated by Marxist doctrine and terminology. The experiences of Tito in Yugoslavia, of Gomulka in Poland and even of Khrushchev in Russia furnish abundant evidence that once a statized economy comes into being, set up by revolutionary force on the Marxist-Leninist-Stalinist model, the relinquishment of any part of the monopoly of power by one party is attended with the greatest difficulties and obstacles.

It seems probable that some of the same factors that make relinquishment of the one-party monopoly difficult, once it has been established, also operate to bring the one-party monopoly into being in the economy which has been statized, however peaceful the process of statization may have been. Not all the pressures towards a one-party monopoly of political power in a statized economy are dependent upon the Marxist revolutionary origin of the economic and political system. Communists have indeed argued that there is no ideological basis for more than one party once private property has been abolished. This argument implies that the only basis for

5 *New York Times*, March 23, 1957.

differences between political parties is the one issue of nationalization or non-nationalization of the economy. But it is not
because of the absence of issues in a fully nationalized economy that one-party monopolies are maintained; it is because
in such an economy the difficulties of administration under a
democratic and parliamentary system are likely to be almost
insuperable.

At least until complete statization of the economy has been
achieved, there would be the issue of a little more or a little
less statization. Statization is not an easily reversible operation: it is hardly feasible to nationalize or denationalize sectors
of the economy as popular sentiment might shift from one
election to the next. This is one of the reasons why a party
fundamentally committed to nationalization is likely to refuse
to allow an opposition party to exist.[6]

Even if the statization of the economy were substantially
complete and therefore not a subject for political controversy,
there would still be issues which could be arrayed by the politicians of two contending parties in such a way as to provide
election issues and thus provide at least one continuing *raison
d'être* for political parties. Should the state increase or decrease the proportion of national income devoted to investment in comparison with that made available for consumption through wage payments? Should the national planning
authorities be instructed to increase the compensation of
teachers in comparison with the compensation of steel workers
or agricultural workers? Should current wages be higher or
lower in relation to old-age payments? Should more roads, hos-
pitals, sports stadiums and airports be built in this or that
area? Who should have the jobs in the economic hierarchy
which provide greater power and compensation?

Some of these issues now enter into political campaigns but
most of them are resolved by the operation of the pricing system of capitalism, even though under modern capitalism this
pricing system is by no means purely and perfectly competitive. All of these and countless other problems would consti-

[6] It is true that this process of nationalization and denationalization did take place in the case of the steel industry in the United
Kingdom, but the process could probably not be repeated without
most serious difficulties.

tute political issues upon which politicians and political parties might divide. Thus, there would be no lack of issues "which might be poured into the empty vessels which political parties are." It has been pointed out, however, that in a fully statized economy the governing bureaucracy could hardly endure having these decisions made through political campaigns and would be likely to seek protection behind the shield provided by the disciplinary apparatus of the one-party system.

This problem of how to avoid the extension of the coercive powers of the state whenever it assumes increased responsibility for the planning and direction of the economy arises long before the state has formally and permanently assumed such responsibility. It arises as soon as the free market begins to be impaired by the growth of corporations and labor unions to a size which prevents the largely impersonal and competitive determination of prices and costs as under traditional, individual-enterprise capitalism. So long as personal private capital provided the means for directing the allocation of resources through new investment and the expansion of existing investment, the necessity for the use of coercive power in the control of the economy by the state did not normally arise. But the role of the capitalist, as an individual, diminished under modern capitalism; more and more of such investment came to be financed out of the internal resources of corporations and a large part of the remainder was carried out with the private, personal suppliers of capital playing a largely passive role, while the large insurance companies, pension funds and the like placed capital resources at the disposal of large corporations. These corporations, rather than individual capitalists, now carry out the actual planning and effectuating of investment in new or old lines. This is not to deny that the element of flexibility and the degree of economic autonomy which is insured so long as there is no prohibition of private investment for doctrinaire reasons remain of great importance in limiting the extension of the power of the state over individual liberty, even though capitalism has become corporate rather than private and individual.

The large corporations, large labor organizations and even large cooperatives and farm organizations which are typical of the modern capitalistic economy begin themselves to resemble governmental bureaucracies. Do not much the same questions concerning the liberty of the individual arise in the case of corporate bureaucracies as in the case of state bureaucracies? It has been argued that there is no more necessity for the police power of the state to be exercised in the operation of a nationalized industry than in a private corporate industry. The examples of the Tennessee Valley Authority in the United States and the London Transport Authority in the United Kingdom have been offered in support of this argument.

Under the modern type of capitalism, corporations have, indeed, become more and more like public bodies, retaining nevertheless a considerable degree of autonomous power to make decisions. The degree of autonomy which the state still permits corporations to retain does not, however, exclusively or even primarily mean the retention of control of corporations as the private property of the stockholders. The managements of corporations may, consequently, be expected to operate them in their own interests. They can do so, however, only within the limits of the residual powers of the stockholders (perhaps the least effectual limitation), the power of the managements of labor unions in their plants and the power of the bureaucracy of the state. Just as government officials all through history have often partially sublimated their personal interests in those of the national state and labor union managers have often sublimated their interests in those of the union, so in some degree do corporate managers sublimate their personal interests in those of the corporation. The larger the corporation, the greater the tendency for its managers to regard its interests as parallel with those of the public and to begin to sublimate their own personal interests in what they conceive to be the interests of the public rather than those of the corporate stockholders.[7]

Thus corporate managements, having largely escaped from control by private property, are likely by that fact to have a

[7] As, for instance, when corporations make "untied" fellowship grants to support research in educational institutions. Although the stockholders may benefit in the long run by the additions to general knowledge and to the total number of research personnel in the nation, this advantage is spread over the whole economy and does not accrue primarily to the endowing corporation.

more "public-spirited" attitude than if property ownership controlled corporate operational policy. The recognition by the British Labor Party "that, under increasingly professional managements, large firms are as a whole serving the nation well"[8] thus seems of general applicability in countries characterized by large modern capitalistic corporations. But the recognition of a considerable degree of public spirit among corporate managements, and the frequent exhortations that they should be even more public-spirited, raise substantial problems. So long as corporate management could concentrate single-mindedly on profit maximization for the benefit of the stockholders, the goal was unambiguous, even though competition had to be relied upon to see that consumers and employees were not exploited through monopoly profits. Once this simple goal is abandoned, obvious difficulties arise, not only in pricing and wage setting but even in delineating the fields in which the corporation's power and resources are to be employed. For example, should the management of a corporation be expected to exercise its power and resources in carrying out national policy in the foreign field? The question even arises whether corporate management should continue to be allowed to dominate the board of directors and determine its own compensation,[9] or whether instead the active management of a corporation should be restricted to a minority of the membership on the board.

Thus it is no longer true that private property determines the distribution of economic power under modern corporate capitalism,[10] and much of the hatred of private property as the source of privilege which has characterized socialist movements becomes anachronistic. Instead it is perfectly rational that much of this antagonism should be transmuted into concern about the powers and privileges of corporate manage-

[8] *Industry and Society: Labour's Policy on Future Public Ownership,* Transport House, London, 1957, p. 39.

[9] For some relevant observations in this connection, see "The Evolving Role of the Corporate Director" in *Adventures in Thought and Action,* School of Industrial Management, Massachusetts Institute of Technology, April 9, 1957, pp. 46–56.

[10] This is clearly put by C. A. R. Crosland in "The Transition from Capitalism," *New Fabian Essays,* Turnstile Press, London, 1952, p. 36.

ment, whether the corporation be private or public.[11] As stated by the British Labor Party, ". . . it is not difficult to envisage a managerial caste taking on the former role of the owners of wealth and using its economic power to buttress class privileges and institutions."[12] The pamphlet in which this appears refers also to the way in which the purchase of privilege through simple property ownership has become extremely difficult for individuals but extremely easy for corporate executives through their access to generous expense accounts, cars, travel, entertainment, holidays, "top hat" pension schemes and the like.

Nevertheless, the risks of undue power and privilege are not likely to become critical so long as there continue to be in all important industries a number of autonomous corporations, carrying on substantial degrees and kinds of competition, together with independent labor unions and supervision by government. If, however, an entire industry is nationalized so that there is only one corporate management, the risk of inordinate privilege and power for the management is much increased. If, in addition, as in Russia, there are no independent labor unions and the government is not separated from corporate management but is part of it, the risk, as we have seen, becomes fact.

An intermittent struggle of greater or lesser intensity will normally be carried on within the bureaucracy of the capitalistic corporation in competition for the more desirable administrative positions. The competitors in this struggle for power and its perquisites do not, however, succeed or fail wholly according to their relative efficiency in directing the profitable production and sale of the corporation's goods or services. If the management becomes notoriously inefficient in extending or at least maintaining profits, it may have difficulty in maintaining itself in power. Even though stockholders cannot easily get rid of unsuccessful managerial personnel, the top leadership is not likely to remain monolithic in the face

[11] On this point, see R. H. S. Crossman, "Towards the Philosophy of Socialism," in *ibid.*, p. 27. "The main task of socialism today," he notes, "is to prevent the concentration of power in the hands either of industrial management or of the state bureaucracy . . ."

[12] *Industry and Society*, p. 51.

of continually poor financial results. Factions may form within the management and it then may become possible for one faction to force out the unsuccessful managerial personnel, perhaps even through enlisting the support of factions among the stockholders.

The struggle for position within the corporate bureaucracy thus is largely analogous to the struggle which goes on within a governmental or a labor union bureaucracy, or within a university faculty for that matter. The circumstance that the corporation must be able to sell its product on a market characterized by some form of competition without incurring continued substantial loss does serve to keep the link between efficiency and success in the struggle for position in the corporate hierarchy somewhat closer than it is likely to be in other types of bureaucracies. It also gives consumers some indirect control over corporate management through the market. Furthermore, expansion of the corporate bureaucracy is limited by the availability of funds for payment of salaries and other expenses of the bureaucracy. Poorly managed corporations are thus more limited in their ability to expand their bureaucracies than are the more successful ones. Poor management usually means inability to serve the consuming public satisfactorily.

These limitations do not exist within governmental bureaucracies. It is true that governmental bureaucracies are limited by their ability to persuade the executive branch of government to budget and the legislative branch to appropriate funds for their purposes. But the relative efficiency of the various divisions of the governmental bureaucracy is not a major influence in the allocation of funds. Eventually the amount of funds available to support a governmental bureaucracy depends upon the ability of government to raise funds through taxation, borrowing or monetary expansion. But this ultimate limitation is a less effective one than the limitation set upon a corporate bureaucracy by the necessity for selling goods and services on the market to obtain such funds.[13] The greatest difference between the corporate bureaucracy which largely manages the economy of modern capitalism and

[13] The nearer corporations approach to monopoly, with or without the aid of labor unions, the more this limit is impaired.

the state bureaucracy is the absence of police power in the case of the former. The arbitrary right of corporate management to hire and fire is sometimes held to be the equivalent of police power. But in a modern capitalistic economy characterized by powerful labor unions, full employment or the payment of unemployment compensation, this argument has little validity. The growth of the corporate form of industrial organization has consequently not been accompanied by a measurable decline in personal liberty within corporate organizations themselves, while the survival of some forms of competition and the growth of new forms, the development of the countervailing power of labor unions and the growth of governmental controls have substantially limited the power of corporate managements over workers and consumers.

Analysis of the economic systems of the Western European countries has clearly shown that most of them are characterized, to an even greater extent than the United States, by large though varying degrees of state intervention in and control of the economy.[14] The extent to which state participation in the direction and control of the national economy represents a new development rather than a continuation of a past situation differs from country to country. It has been pointed out that in the United States the trend from a "free-enterprise" economy of laissez faire and simple competition to an economic system characterized by large corporate entities and governmental intervention and controls culminated with the New Deal, but has continued without reversal to the present time.

The term laissez faire implied that *any* expansion of the role of the state would mean less freedom for the individual. To what extent, then, has the expansion of the role of the state in the countries of the West resulted in a net diminution of personal liberty? The paradoxical answer is that there seems to be no close correlation either in Western Europe or in the United States between the degree of state intervention and control of the economy and the net limitation upon personal liberty. This seems to be true whether we make a comparison country by country or whether we analyze the change through time as a greater degree of governmental control of the econ-

[14] See Chapters 10 and 11.

omy has superseded laissez faire and simple competition. This finding seems to contradict the theory that extension of the power of the state is incompatible with the maintenance of personal liberty. The apparent lack of correlation between the degree of statization of the economy and the degree of limitation of the liberties of individuals offers a striking contrast to the close correlation which existed under the Nazi and Fascist regimes, and which continues to exist under the Soviet economic and political system. The conflicting evidence is due partly to the fact that the basic differences between the totalitarian regimes and the Western regimes of modified capitalism are less economic in character than they are political and cultural. While the standard of living is much lower in Soviet Russia than in the capitalistic countries of the West, by far the most important difference between life under the Soviet system and life in the United Kingdom, the United States, France or West Germany is the degree of personal freedom. The limitation of personal liberty in a totalitarian state is indeed so complete that the difference cannot appropriately be described as a matter of degree.

The typical worker in the quasi-capitalistic economy of the West does work under industrial discipline. But this is not a police power discipline of the sort exercised in Nazi, Fascist and Soviet industry. He is an employee of a corporation, not an independent producer as he might have been at an earlier stage of economic development. He usually works for a large corporation under a hierarchy of control extending from the foreman through the superintendent up to the higher echelons of management, or he is himself a member of the hierarchy. Viewed from this angle, his position organizationally might appear not very different from that of the Soviet worker. But in the Soviet system hierarchic rank is associated with substantially greater authority over those of lower rank, and therefore the authority of men over men is far greater than under Western capitalism. This was also true of the Fascist and Nazi states. The employee in the modified capitalistic economies of the West usually has the protection of trade union organizations in his relations with the managerial hierarchy. He has some degree of control over the selection of the management of his trade union. Even though in practice this control may be infinitesimal, at least the management of the labor union is not appointed as in the Soviet Union by a party hierarchy which also controls the apparatus of the state. Moreover, the worker under modern capitalism has alternative sources of employment. Finally, he can, as one among the mass of citizens, vote for representatives in government who may be able to restrain either the managements of corporations or the managements of trade unions from arbitrary and anti-social action.

With the relatively low degree of consumer sovereignty in the Soviet system[15] and the absence of parliamentary control over the rate of saving, or over expenditures on capital investment or for public buildings and the like, in these aspects the influence of individuals over the economy, exercised as part of a majority, is reduced to a very low level. In the most basic sense this represents a diminution of personal liberty in comparison with capitalistic countries.

These particular differences between the fully collectivized states and capitalistic countries are, as has been said, as much political as economic. If it could not be shown to have a functional relation to the control or operation of the economy by the state, the denial of personal liberty might be considered as the result of the political philosophies and the personalities of the ruling class of the totalitarian states rather than as the result of the statization of their national economies. The assumption of responsibility by the state for the full control of the economy, however, is likely to induce the development of a political outlook inimical to personal liberty. This relation between the growth of state control and possible restriction of personal liberty is extremely complex and most difficult to measure and analyze.

Since the decline of laissez faire in the West has meant that there are more and more kinds of actions by the individual that are either forbidden or required by government, regardless of the individual's preferences, the modern form of the capitalistic state might appear to stand midway between the

---

[15] It would be conceptually possible to have at least a considerable degree of consumer sovereignty in a statized economy if a democratic and parliamentary political system were to accompany such an economy. A very limited degree of consumer sovereignty has been allowed to exist even in the Soviet economy.

laissez-faire state of the past and the modern totalitarian state in terms of restriction of personal liberty. But there are at least three reasons why this increased role of the state in the capitalistic countries of the West does not appear on balance to have diminished personal liberty as yet.

In the first place, most of the actions of individuals which are now controlled by the modern capitalistic state represent the limitation of what men usually think of as "business liberties" rather than "personal liberties."[16] It is by no means certain that there is in fact a clear distinction between personal liberties and business liberties; historically they seem to have almost always been found in close conjunction. The general run of mankind, however, appear to think of the two as being quite different. If the state forbids an employer to offer employment to workers at less than one dollar an hour, it may be argued, as it has been, that this is a limitation on the liberty of both the employer and the employee. Similarly, if the state forbids a farmer to raise tobacco beyond the quota assigned by law, on pain of payment of a prohibitive tax, unquestionably liberty is curtailed. Yet most men apparently do not consider this a diminution of personal freedom of the sort which is protected by constitutional guarantees, such as freedom of the press, freedom of speech, freedom of religion, protection against self-incrimination, and the like. It may be that, if "business liberties" are curtailed, those liberties which are considered to be peculiarly personal are likely also to be curtailed. It may be

[16] The possible distinction between business and personal liberties first arose in the writer's mind while he was serving as Economic Adviser in the Agricultural Adjustment Administration in 1934 and was mentioned in a discussion with Secretary Wallace. The Secretary in a subsequent press conference vigorously defended the position that any limitations of the liberty of the individual embodied in New Deal legislation were solely restrictions on business liberties and not restrictions on personal liberties. This distinction between business and personal liberties has been further developed by J. M. Clark in his *Economic Institutions and Human Welfare*, Knopf, New York, 1957, Chapter 4. Fred Gottheil has called the writer's attention to Marx's distinction between the liberty of an individual in relation to another individual and "the liberty which capital has to crush the workingman," which Marx identifies with "commercial liberty," in his "Discourse on Free-Trade" delivered in Brussels, January 9, 1848.

that, in the process of the enforcement of laws limiting business liberties, the more strictly personal liberties are inevitably involved. Nevertheless, a persistent feeling that these liberties are in separate categories continues to exist.[17]

The second reason why the decline of laissez faire does not appear to have been associated with a decline in personal liberties is that the extension of state economic intervention and controls usually followed upon a prior increase in the power of some economic organism over individuals. The growth of the power of the managements of large corporations placed them at an advantage in transacting the wage bargain with the individual worker and in selling goods and services to the consumer. Hence, limiting the business liberty of corporate managements appeared to and sometimes did increase the relative liberty of the average individual citizen vis-à-vis the corporation. State intervention often takes the form of giving power to the managements of countervailing organizations. In the United States the Wagner Act is a case in point. Here the power of the state was used to extend the power of labor unions. Similarly, with the growth in the power of labor union managements, limitations upon their liberties by government could mean a relative increase in the liberties of union members, corporate managements and the consuming public. The development of the modern complex, technological society had thus made it inevitable that the role of the state could no

[17] The development of the concept of personal as separate from business liberty in the United States closely parallels the attitude of the Supreme Court with respect to "liberty" and "property." The Court did not originally distinguish between the terms "liberty" and "property" as referred to in the Fifth and Fourteenth Amendments. The general tendency of Court decisions during the half century before the New Deal was to expand the concept of property and to grant it a high degree of invulnerability, along with liberty, against either state or federal regulation. If anything, property was more jealously protected than liberty. "Business liberty" was protected both as part of "personal liberty" and as property. A man's property was considered, in effect, an extension of his personality. See Chapter 1, and John R. Commons, *The Legal Foundations of Capitalism*, Macmillan, New York, 1924. With the reversal of the Supreme Court's position in 1936 in the Washington State Minimum Wage Act case, the Court progressively abandoned its defense of property and business liberty.

longer merely be that of "holding the ring" within which innumerable small producers, limited only by the restraints of each other's competition, could do battle for the consumer's dollar. The development of large aggregates of economic power had made it necessary for the state to step into the ring both to protect the rights of individuals and to prevent all-out battles between economic giants which might otherwise have wrecked the economy. It was inevitable that to the masses of the people this expansion of the role of the state should appear as the protection of personal liberty rather than its suppression.

Third, although there is a notable tendency for the expansion of the role of the state to be compulsive and cumulative, there may be no ostensible loss of personal liberty so long as the process of statization is gradual and does not result in some type of economic crisis. The bureaucracy of the state may quite unwillingly intervene in the economy in order to prevent an interruption of the productive process due to an uncompromising clash of countervailing powers. Through "mediation" or "arbitration" the bureaucracy of the state may then have to set wages, and indirectly prices, but an otherwise insurmountable crisis would appear to have been averted. The assumption of responsibility by a public administrator under such circumstances is not likely to be assessed by the public as an avid grasp of power. The assumption of responsibility for wage and price fixing by the state may come about when, in a political campaign, substantially larger wage increases are promised by a political party than the economy can bear without serious inflation. A party which wins an election after having made such promises can hardly avoid setting up a comprehensive system of economic regulation if it is to continue in power.

The state may not find it necessary to intervene so long as corporate management and labor union management in a particular market can come to an agreement whereby wage increases do not exceed the increase in labor productivity in the industry, even though they may exceed the increase in productivity for the whole economy and therefore have an inflationary effect. Wherever industry-wide wage agreements can be arrived at and the demand for the industry's products is elastic enough to permit price increases without too large a falling off in sales, wage-price increases ordinarily will obviate the immediate necessity for intervention by the state. If such wage-price increases can be absorbed by the average increase in productivity for the whole economy, no serious difficulty may arise. Likewise, when wage-price increases result in only mild inflation, no crisis is likely to arise which necessitates intervention by the state. Consequently, there is no fixed time at which the government of a particular country is required to face the problem of choosing between allowing inflationary pressures to continue and explicitly assuming the responsibility for determination of distributional shares. If some degree of restraint in the wage increases demanded and in the "compensatory" price increases imposed on industrial products is exercised by both managements of labor unions and managements of corporations, the upward movement in the price level may be moderate enough so that the assumption of economic responsibility by the state may be indefinitely postponed.[18]

The problem of assumption of responsibility for wage and price fixing by the state inevitably arises, of course, wherever outright nationalization of one or more industries has taken place. However, so long as only a limited number of industries have been nationalized, price-wage determination may be carried out by the state bureaucracy without such an extension in the coercive power of the state as to cause a serious diminution of personal liberty. The very realization that the state must, if necessary, deny the right to strike, may, at least for a time, keep demands for wage increases within limits which can be met. These demands also may be met in part out of the productivity of the non-nationalized industries. They consequently may not involve the use of the coercive power of the state any more than in the case of a threatened strike in an important non-nationalized but highly organized industry where essentially the same sort of situation may arise under modern corporate capitalism. So long as the nationalized sector embraces only a limited area of the national economy and so long as most wages and prices are determined in part by

[18] This would assume that corporate managements do not attempt to maximize profits and that labor union managements do not attempt to maximize wages, which, of course, is contrary to the assumptions upon which laissez-faire capitalism has been based.

competition (even if competition is less than perfect) and in part by bargaining agreements which do not set up intolerable inflationary spirals or produce severe economic depression in the effort to halt inflation, the degree of governmental intervention in, control of, or even operation of, the economy may not become so great as to curtail personal liberty substantially.

One of the threats to personal liberty from expansion of the role of the state in the economy lies in the strengthening of the executive branch of the government at the expense of the legislative.[19] In modern society a substantial expansion of the role of the state has been inevitable and has usually been sanctioned by the legislators, and, as in the United States, by the courts acting in a quasi-legislative capacity. This has meant the wholesale delegation of legislative powers[20] and the potential emasculation of the principle of self-government as the gap between the will of the citizenry and the operation of laws by the bureaucracy has widened.[21]

The strengthening of the executive arm of government in relation to the legislative inevitably increases the risk of exercise of arbitrary power and conceivably increases the risk of illegal seizure of power. This is so even though executive power as well as legislative power is continually delegated as the expansion of executive power takes place. Here, too, the distance

[19] It is noteworthy that it is the mob, even if a highly organized mob, demanding economic benefits, plus the armed forces, upon which modern dictators depend to put themselves in power. In turn, the mob sees the dictator as wielding executive power on behalf of "the working class," "*das Volk*," "the Italian people," or the "*descamisados*" as in the cases of Lenin, Hitler, Mussolini and Peron. During the closing days of the Roman Republic, it will be recalled, it was the *Populares* who demanded power for Caesar that he might continue to provide them with bread and circuses after the legislative machinery represented by the various forms of the *comitia* had disintegrated.

[20] The process by which this delegation of powers has taken place is well described by Spencer Gervin in his *The Delegation of Legislative Power* (doctoral dissertation), Duke University, Durham, 1957.

[21] The extension of the executive power has also been accompanied in the United States by an extension of the powers of the federal government in relation to those of the state for kindred reasons. The Supreme Court since the shift in 1936 has greatly facilitated this process.

between the will of the citizenry and the operation of laws is widened. The vulnerability of the citizen to possible arbitrary actions by lower levels of the bureaucracy may thus be increased, as the power of the individual at the apex of the pyramid of administration becomes diffused in the process. This may be remedied by a tightening of discipline in the hierarchy of administration, but this in turn involves the risk of strengthening the power of the upper levels of the hierarchy.[22]

Even when the exercise of police powers by the management of nationalized industry is not importantly involved, a real dilemma exists with respect to the means by which any meaningful public control of the nationalized industry can be maintained. It is obviously impracticable to have intimate intervention in the management of such an industry by legislative bodies. Indeed, in the British experience with nationalized industry, a determined effort has been made to insulate management from political influence by setting up organizations such as the London Transport Authority or the National Coal Board. But since nationalized industries are almost always monopolies, and since they are regulated neither by the market nor by a combination of market forces and public regulatory agencies as would typically have been true before nationaliza-

[22] It is probably no accident that during the period when the powers of the federal executive have been so greatly extended in the United States, the Supreme Court has made an effort to extend its protection of personal liberty in the more limited sense. This has shown itself in cases where the Court has ruled that the defense must have the right to examine certain of the files of the F.B.I., where the Court has upheld the right of individuals to invoke the protection of the Fifth Amendment, and the like. It seems almost as though the Supreme Court were saying, "We have felt it necessary greatly to extend the area of governmental control. We must now restrain the powers of government over the *old areas* of control." One might even see in the du Pont–General Motors case a determination of the Supreme Court to restore old-style competition and hence to obviate extension of the areas of governmental controls over the economy. This interpretation of the causal connection between increased concern by the Court for personal liberties and the expansion of the area of governmental control is somewhat limited by the fact that the cases where the Court has pressed its defense of personal liberties have rarely involved those areas where the powers of the government over the economy have been expanded by the legislative, executive or particularly the judicial branches.

tion, the management is likely to be less responsible to the public than before nationalization. As Hugh Gaitskell, the Labor Party leader, puts it, "I doubt if there is any escape from the dilemma that the more independent the boards [of nationalized industries] are allowed to be, the more they will exercise power without responsibility, and the less independent they become, the greater the risk of overcentralization and lack of enterprise."[23]

At what point short of complete statization the devitalizing of individual liberty would become critical is not likely to be easily recognizable. Liberties commonly regarded as personal are likely to suffer wholesale repression by a government coming to power at a time of economic crisis when the previously existing government had not been ostensibly limiting purely personal liberties. It is likely under such circumstances to be the new government which decisively limits personal liberty at the moment of taking complete power and responsibility over the national economy. There can be no doubt that the more advanced the process of statization of the economy, the easier and quicker is the task of a dictator in bringing a country completely under control. Likewise, the more completely statized the economy, the greater the ease of maintaining such control. Few sanctions are so efficacious in inducing submission to the will of a dictator as the knowledge that one's job can be taken away and that no alternative employment is permitted. Men seem to fear the loss of their jobs even more than death itself if alternative jobs are forbidden to them by state authority. In a fully statized economy this powerful sanction is always operative. It all but eliminates the possibility for the development of autonomous centers of resistance to tyranny, moreover, for they can hardly exist without an economic base.

Thus, while a functional relation between the devitalizing of personal liberty and the complete statization of the economy clearly exists, the causal relation between the two and the rate at which one affects the other remain highly complex. Neither the development of the corporate organization of the modern economy, together with the countervailing power of labor unions, nor the great increase in the role of the state in

[23] Quoted by Paul T. Homan in "Socialist Thought in Great Britain," *American Economic Review*, June 1957, pp. 350–362.

controlling the economy, nor even the piecemeal nationalization of industries in some countries of Western Europe has yet resulted in a demonstrably serious net diminution of personal liberty so far as this can be separated from business liberty. It seems inevitable, however, that substantially complete statization of the economy would result in a critical diminution of liberty.

Since the trend has been in the direction of statization of the economy, only by examining the forces retarding this trend compared with those accelerating it can one make some forecast of the future of personal liberty. This will be the task of the next and concluding chapter.

CHAPTER 13

THE PROSPECT FOR
THE SURVIVAL OF LIBERTY

What is the prospect for the revival of liberty in countries with Communist regimes—Russia, the satellite states, Yugoslavia and China? The record demonstrates that so long as the ruling class remains sufficiently ruthless and the hierarchy enforces complete personal and ideological discipline, only defeat in war is likely to overthrow a totalitarian regime.[1] It has been pointed out, however, that after the death of Stalin, and later after the execution of Beria, there was a substantial relaxation of repression in Russia. Thousands were released from prisons and forced labor camps, the powers of the secret police were curtailed, controls on literature were somewhat relaxed, the reign of Lysenko as a kind of dictator in the field of genetics was ended, at least for a time. The privileged position and standard of living of the new ruling class came under mild criticism and some measures were taken to improve the relative position of the lower-income classes. The crushing of the revolt in Hungary by Soviet troops was a severe setback to hopes that the changes were fundamental in character. There was nevertheless discussion and criticism among Russian stu-

[1] The overthrow of Peron offers the one possible exception to this statement, but the Peronist regime cannot be considered to have been a fully developed form of the totalitarian state.

dents of Soviet action in Hungary. Unfortunately, the relaxation of repression did not continue unabated. In this respect events have so far followed the pattern of previous relaxations of repression. Students who had attempted to question the actions of the Soviet government in Hungary were sharply rebuked. Dudintsev, whose novel *Not by Bread Alone* had reflected a critical attitude towards the self-seeking and callous character of the Soviet bureaucracy, was sternly called to account.

Nevertheless, the present Soviet regime has not been able to maintain the complete personal and ideological discipline which characterized the rule of Stalin. Indeed, there is evidence that the successors of Stalin were not opposed to some relaxation of discipline. The limited relaxation which they permitted, has, however, severely shaken the monolithic character of the Soviet ruling class. It is quite probable that the partial dismantling of the terror apparatus and the limited relaxation of tension in Soviet Russia is temporary, since it is unclear whether this limited relaxation will strengthen popular support or at least popular tolerance of the Soviet regime or whether on the contrary it will permit the development of elements hostile to it. The deep-seated hatred of the population for a totalitarian regime is evident only after such uprisings as those in East Germany, Poland and Hungary. Even though nationalist anti-Russian sentiment was a major force in these revolts in the satellites, there is little doubt that a bitter distaste for its rulers by a large proportion of the population normally accompanies popular subservience in any totalitarian state. Consequently, the possibility of a revolutionary outbreak either accompanying a renewal of the struggle for power among the ruling hierarchy in the Soviet Union or occasioned by the intervention of Soviet forces to put down anti-Soviet uprisings in satellite countries cannot be wholly excluded from consideration. The possibility at present seems remote, however.

The end of the so-called collective leadership and the emergence of Khrushchev at the top of the pyramid of power is not reassuring. So long as there is no representative government, state power rests on force alone and human liberty cannot rely upon any sanctions to protect it. Finally, the degree of success achieved by the Soviet economic system appears to have demonstrated disturbingly that men can be compelled and induced to produce without having liberty. The great majority of the Polish and Hungarian people did indeed demonstrate by the risk of their lives their hatred for the Communist governments which ruled them. The near-unanimity of the Polish and Hungarian people in rising against their oppressors was based upon nationalist sentiment and bitter economic dissatisfaction as well as the desire for liberty. If a Communist totalitarian regime can provide a tolerable standard of living for the masses, plus higher rewards and positions of authority and prestige for scientists, engineers and bureaucrats, as has been done in Russia, the wish for liberty may not of itself be the decisive force in determining the kind of economic and political system which will endure.

In the absence of representative government, power can hardly pass from one ruler to another without violence. Yet in the forty years of the Soviet regime, the violence has not been so great as to prevent the functioning of the economic and political machinery. Nor has it served as an opportunity for the people to take advantage of confusion to seize liberty for themselves. It is not easy to visualize the type of economic and political system which might succeed the present system in the unlikely event of its overthrow under whatever circumstances. Assuredly it would not be a replica of the political and economic system of tsarist times. But what kind of economic organization could be put in place of the existing complex structure of state industries? The process by which these industries could be transformed into something like the industrial corporations of modern capitalistic countries cannot easily be visualized.

If violent overthrow is completely excluded from consideration, is there a possibility that in time the Soviet regime might continue to advance along the path of relaxation, so that personal liberty and representative government might eventually be restored, while the economic system would continue virtually unchanged in its organization and functioning? It does not seem likely that Khrushchev and his subordinates, trained under Stalin as they were, would be at all willing to have the relaxation of their power go anything like so far as this.

Still, the possibility of the restoration of some degree of

personal liberty and representative government either by revolution or by evolution cannot be completely excluded from consideration. But if this happened, would it be possible any longer to carry on the type of fully statized economy which now exists? Or to turn the question around, could a political system embodying personal liberty and parliamentary institutions come into existence so long as the fully statized economy continued? For reasons developed in the previous chapter, it seems very doubtful that a fully statized economy could be operated by a bureaucracy in which a high degree of personal liberty and representative government existed. This means that the restoration of personal liberty and representative government would depend upon the development of some form of economic organization of industry which would allow a considerable degree of autonomy in operation, while still somehow solving the problem of wage and price determination, so that the state would not have to assume full responsibility.

In Soviet Russia, in 1957, a great effort got under way to decentralize industry and give more autonomy through setting up over a hundred industrial regions to supplant the direction of industry from Moscow. The reasons for so doing were primarily to increase efficiency through breaking the strangling grip of the tremendous bureaucracy which had grown up. What this will amount to is as yet uncertain. It could possibly be a step in the evolution of more autonomous industrial units of production which after considerable development might prove compatible with a much higher degree of personal liberty and representative government than now exists. So far, however, there is no evidence that this recent movement towards decentralization is connected with any intention to restore liberty or representative government.

What is the prospect that an economic system embodying more liberty might develop in Communist countries outside Russia? It is clear that the Soviet government will not permit non-Communist regimes in the adjoining satellite countries without resorting to armed intervention if necessary. Following Khrushchev's concession to Tito that there are "many roads to socialism," however, one might have supposed that on some of these variant paths personal liberty might be found. It seems likely that this statement by Khrushchev played at least a minor role in touching off the Polish and Hungarian struggles for independence. Even though the Polish movement stopped far short of independence and thus saved Poland from the fate of Hungary, the new Polish Communist regime soon showed that liberty was still to be sharply repressed. The failure to allow free elections, the closing of the student newspaper *Po Prostu*, and the forbidding of strikes all indicated that the government of Gomulka was still essentially totalitarian.

In Yugoslavia under Tito, the partial relaxation of the power of the secret police, the end of the forcible collectivization of agriculture and the setting up of workers' councils to operate industrial undertakings give some hope for the development of an economic and political system which would be less than fully totalitarian. It is too early to say with certainty whether this can take place.

In China the publication of Mao's speech "Let All Flowers Grow" in February 1957 supported the idea of recognizing variant means of attaining socialism. More important, he recognized the danger of the development of a new class of economic and political administrators whose interests would diverge from those of the masses and who might themselves become exploiters. The speech appeared to welcome some criticism of the regime. Hopes that it represented the beginning of greater liberty were, however, promptly shattered. As soon as any criticism began to be offered, Mao savagely attacked all critics both within the Party and without. It almost looked as though the speech had been made in order to tempt critics to unmask themselves so that they could be arrested. The purges which followed the speeches show no signs of ceasing.

The speeches of Gomulka, following his coming to power in Poland after the Poznan riots, contained numerous castigations of the administrative bureaucracy of state and Party which had misruled Poland under Soviet Russia's tutelage. Yet he quickly backed away from allowing really free elections, which would have been the only effective means for preventing the exploitation of the people by the new ruling class.

While Mao's speech was published in Russia, the possibility of the exploitation of the people by the bureaucratic hierarchy which had replaced the capitalists and their government was not admitted. That this danger had indeed become a reality on a massive scale under Stalin was dismissed as only the temporary manifestation of "the cult of personality." The prospect that measures will be taken to prevent the growth of a privileged class over which the masses have no control seems only a little more likely outside Russia than within.

Since the prospect for the revival of liberty in countries which now have the Soviet political and economic system does not appear promising, except to some extent in Yugoslavia and possibly in Poland, the survival of liberty seems to depend upon the ability of the modified forms of capitalism of the Western world to endure. Even in these countries, however, the survival of liberty depends upon the end result of the evolutionary process through which capitalism has been going in recent decades in which the roles of the state and of organizations have grown so tremendously. Already we can speak of capitalism as characteristically an organizational economy rather than an economy of individual enterprise. Consequently, the question of modern capitalism's survival must first be considered and then the question of whether capitalism is likely to develop further in such a way as substantially to inhibit individual liberty. Actually the two questions are overlapping, since at the moment when individual liberty has been definitely and substantially curtailed we might conclude that capitalism had not survived.

What is the likelihood that within the next two or three decades the modern type of capitalistic economic system will be supplanted in any important country of the West by a collectivist economic system? At the present time there is almost no chance that this would happen by the conscious will of the majority. Yet the possibility of the take-over of Western Europe by Communist satellite governments was very real in the years immediately after World War II and the possibility, while very remote, cannot be totally excluded even now. The economic crisis due to wartime destruction and shortages which confronted Western Europe at the end of World War II doubtless would not of itself have threatened the end of capitalism on the Continent. In the presence of the aggressive and expansionist policies of Stalinist Russia, however, the threat to capitalism and to democratic and parliamentary institutions in Europe was indeed critical. It was not a question of an outright victory for the Communist Party at the polls in any country of Western Europe. All that would have been necessary for a Communist take-over would have been a continuing economic and political crisis, in which the Communist Party would eventually have been able to force its way into a coalition government. In such a coalition the Communists would have pushed progressively for the key cabinet posts controlling internal security and the armed forces, as has become the familiar pattern for setting up Fascist, Nazi or Soviet totalitarian states. This process would have been enormously facilitated by the ever-present menace of the intervention of Soviet armed forces. In the event of domestic armed resistance to a Communist seizure, Soviet armed intervention would in all likelihood have become actual as well as threatened.

Why did this sequence of events which would have meant the end of capitalism in Europe fail to take place? The answer is that the threatened economic crisis was averted and with it the political crisis as well. The economic crisis was averted largely through American financial assistance rendered by the Marshall Plan. The temporary American monopoly of atomic weapons made it possible to require the Soviet evacuation of Iran, to stop Soviet pressure on Greece and Turkey through the announcement of the Truman Doctrine, to break the Berlin blockade by the American airlift and finally to repulse the North Korean invasion by American armed intervention in aid of the Republic of Korea. The economic aid afforded by the Marshall Plan was supplemented in Europe by military power eventually organized within the NATO framework, which prevented the use of Russian military forces to impose the Soviet form of totalitarianism beyond those territories occupied by Russian troops at the end of the war.

The threat of a Communist take-over disappeared during the period of unprecedented prosperity and economic growth which has characterized Western Europe since about 1950. If the recent prosperity of Western Europe should be interrupted by a serious economic depression, the possibility of the end of capitalism in Europe through a Communist take-over could not be completely discounted. The probability of a deep and long-continued economic crisis in Western Europe is not great, however. No government would allow such a thing to happen without taking the most extreme anti-depression measures. However imprecise in their operation and however undesirable their "side effects," these measures are now well enough understood that their utilization would be certain. Unlike the situation existing at the end of World War II, when American financial aid for the purchase of food and raw materials to meet serious shortages was the chief need, the principal aid which the United States could render in preventing such a depression would be to avoid a depression itself. One of the chief dangers for Europe is that a depression in the United States would reduce the total demand for European goods.

Relative Soviet military power is, of course, now greater than at any previous time. On the other hand, Khrushchev does not appear to be the paranoiac that Stalin had become in his later years. Khrushchev's participation in the crimes of the Stalinist era as well as his responsibility for the crushing of the Hungarian revolution rule him out as "a man of peace." Yet it appears that he is able to understand the mutually annihilating potentialities of atomic war as Stalin emotionally could not. Since Khrushchev, like Stalin, long ago ceased to be impelled by the crusading aspects of the "World Revolution," even though the Communist movement throughout the world is still utilized primarily as an instrument of Soviet foreign policy, the danger has been reduced that the Soviet Union might undergo great risk of war under favorable circumstances in order to expand its empire. The conclusion must be that Soviet military forces would be likely to intervene in Western Europe in the event of an economic and political crisis only in support of a Communist take-over of a national government which had at least some shadow of legality.

In the event of a serious economic depression in Western Europe, the possibility of a Communist take-over would once more exist. The degree of economic success achieved by the Soviet state in recent years would lessen popular repugnance to such a system, and the enhanced prestige of Soviet science and technique would play a role as well. Such a take-over would not have to wait upon securing a popular majority. For that matter, most European governments are not now and usually have not been based upon a popular majority for one party. Certainly Communist dominance of governments has never depended upon securing such a popular majority. As indicated above, Communist control of the ministries responsible for internal security and the armed forces is enough. The degree of legality, constitutionality and popular support needed for such a Communist take-over is in inverse proportion to the military power of the Soviet regime.[2]

The opportunity for putting the Soviet take-over technique into operation in Europe rapidly faded away after 1948, and there seems little prospect that it will present itself again soon. Once the direct ravages of World War II were repaired, there was an almost uninterrupted increase in industrial and agricultural production in capitalistic countries. The level of consumption has everywhere been raised. In the United States and in many other countries of the West inequality in the distribution of income has declined. Social security programs have become universal. Full employment has come to be largely taken for granted. The combined effect has been that really grinding poverty is in the process of being eliminated. The Marxist doctrine of the increasing misery of the working class under capitalism has never been so manifestly false as it was in 1957 on the occasion of the celebration of the fortieth anniversary of the overthrow of capitalism in Russia.

For the first time in history the great majority of the population can afford a diet so rich in fats and sweets that almost no one is any longer immune to the diseases which used to be almost exclusively the curse of the rich. The problem of what to do with the leisure provided by the decline in hours of work would have caused a major psychic crisis if it had not been partially alleviated by the "do-it-yourself" development. This in turn had been partially caused by the tremendous in-

---

[2] All of this discussion of the possibilities of a Communist take-over in Western Europe avoids any attempt at analysis of the effects of an atomic missiles war. In fact, the possibilities of such a war occurring or being avoided will turn importantly on the very matters here discussed. Needless to say, if an atomic missiles war does occur, the above analysis is largely irrelevant.

crease in the demand for servants, repairmen, odd-jobs men and the like due to the great increase in income of the mass of the population. The supply of these services had been made far more costly for much the same reasons plus the reluctance of persons with opportunities for alternative well-paid jobs to serve in these capacities. Automobiles, television, household appliances, suburban housing for millions of workers, accompanied by the decline of the large mansion-*cum*-servants style of living even among the upper-income classes—particularly in the United States but increasingly also in other capitalistic countries of the West—reflect a growing tendency towards uniformity in the style of living. These changes might well be thought finally to have given the lie to the Marxist doctrine of the weakening of popular support for capitalism due to the pressing down of the former members of the lower middle class into the proletariat.[3] So long as these conditions continue there appears little reason to expect a bitter and determined demand from the masses of the population for the overthrow by either revolutionary or parliamentary means of a system the benefits of which are so obvious and widespread.

The change in status of what is still generally called "the working class" in capitalistic countries is thus of major importance. The number of workers who are engaged in purely physical labor is declining steadily. The physical effort required even in "physical" labor is being reduced, while con-

---

[3] Marxist doctrines have, of course, played an enormously important historical role even in the present century. Marxist theory, as a theory of current applicability, is with few exceptions, however, no longer taken seriously in Western countries outside the Communist Party. The total downgrading of Marxism as a guide to practical policy, as an analysis of current society or even as a conceptual tool is, for example, well expressed by C. A. R. Crosland, member of the British Labor Party and former Member of Parliament, in *The Future of Socialism*, J. Cape, London, 1956, particularly pp. 20–21. Marxism still retains its influence in Asia and Africa. This is true, in part, because Marxist theory, with its stereotyped intellectual exercises, furnishes escape from trying to cope with the practical problems of underdeveloped countries which are so difficult of solution. The Marxist denial of the problem of pressure of population upon natural resources, except as this arises because of the evils of capitalism, is an example of the usefulness of Marxist theory as an escapist device.

versely the number of techniques required to fabricate, install and repair the elaborate kind of machines involved in the automation of production is increasing. The "horny-handed son of toil," the "bluenail" as the worker was called in medieval times, has within our generation largely ceased to typify the producer of goods and services under the current capitalistic system.[4] The previous image carries over nonetheless among intellectuals, and the attributes of this image are often ascribed to "labor" as though no changes had taken place. The blurring of class lines under the current form of capitalism, while it means that "the working class" as a revolutionary class in any sense has all but disappeared in the Western world, does not mean that workers have now become generally opposed to increasing the area of state control. Quite the contrary. They feel, and with realism, that the increased power of the state, through the extension of social security, through increasing the power of labor unions, through measures against economic depressions, through increasingly progressive taxation and the like, has been most advantageous to them. They consequently feel no inclination to oppose the extension of the area of state intervention and control. Indeed, they are likely to welcome almost any proposals for further extension. It is unreasonable to expect that concern lest personal liberties might be threatened would be likely to offset this feeling.

Nevertheless, this changing status of workers under capitalism has profoundly affected the economic programs of socialist parties, which formerly advocated nationalization of industries. Such programs of nationalization, rarely formally repudiated, lapse into abeyance so long as this improvement in standard of living of the workers continues, both absolutely and relatively.[5] Aside from the Communist parties, support

---

[4] Edward H. Chamberlin points out that there are indications that trade union members in the United States fall within the middle-income rather than the low-income sector of society. *The Economic Analysis of Labor Union Power*, American Enterprise Association, Washington, 1958, p. 4. Indeed, the *Federal Reserve Bulletin*, August 1957, p. 893, shows that of the lowest 20 per cent of all spending units, less than half received either wages or salaries.

[5] It is true that workers accustomed both to full employment and to so improved a standard of living would be likely to find any substantial worsening of either unendurable. Consequently, the advent

for which among the electorate was nowhere large enough to enable them to command a parliamentary majority, there currently is almost no country of the West where there is a socialist party seriously and actively advocating a program for further nationalization of the economic system. This is true in part because the socialist parties do not anywhere command parliamentary majorities of a size necessary for the enactment of the requisite legislation. But it is true for reasons of ideology as well. The Social Democratic Parties of Western Europe have almost totally abandoned even their "revisionist" Marxism of pre-World War II days. Now these "socialist" parties have become essentially "welfare state" parties, pushing for higher wages, shorter hours, more fringe benefits for workers, limitations upon profits, lower prices for consumer goods through state subsidies, more progressive taxes, more and higher social security payments and less restrictive monetary and credit policies. The only further modification of capitalism included in such programs is the advocacy, without great enthusiasm, as in the case of the Social Democratic Party of West Germany, of the expansion of codeterminism, which provides for representatives of labor to serve on the boards of directors of corporations. In the United Kingdom, the right and center of the British Labor Party have become disillusioned with the advantages to be gained by much further nationalization.[6] The left wing of the Labor Party, represented by Bevan, still favors some further nationalization of industry, but currently bases its campaign to win popular support largely upon foreign policy issues extraneous to the domestic economy. In the United States, of course, no political party of any significance proposes any basic departure from the existing form of capitalistic system. The Democratic Party, in contrast to the Republican Party, simply would accord greater power to organized labor, larger subsidies to farmers, more social security, greater expenditures for almost all public purposes, tax reductions for lower-income groups, the extension of publicly owned electric power, and a less restrictive mone-

---

of a serious economic depression would probably shake acceptance of the institutions of current capitalism even more seriously than in the past.

[6] See pp. 282–288.

tary and bank credit policy, in addition to deficit financing when necessary to meet higher costs of government and to guarantee the fullest possible employment.

The political situation in Western Europe would, of course, be radically altered if the avowedly socialist and Communist parties were to combine or even to collaborate. Under such circumstances it might not be impossible for a Communist-Socialist coalition after new elections to form a majority government in both France and Italy. The difficulties which have been encountered in Italy, where the most recent attempt at the reconstruction of a Socialist-Communist "Popular Front" has been made, indicate that there is little early prospect for coalition governments on this basis in the absence of an economic crisis.

The situation is quite otherwise in the underdeveloped and capital-poor countries of the world. The economic progress which has taken place in Soviet Russia is, by Asian and African standards, most impressive. Housing which by Western standards is appalling is not so by the standards of underdeveloped countries. The demonstration of accomplishments in science and industry afforded by space satellites and ballistic missiles is also bound to increase Soviet prestige enormously. The huge and costly sanatoria on the Black Sea coast, the Moscow and Leningrad subways and the like are impressive and lend themselves to Soviet showmanship on behalf of visitors from Asian and African lands. The contrast of income and perquisites of the ruling and managerial class in Soviet Russia with those of the working masses is consistent with the historical culture of these countries. Finally, limitations upon personal liberty which are shocking to Westerners are more tolerable for similar cultural reasons.

The Soviet type of economic and political system offers substantial and particular attractions to the emerging intellectuals of the underdeveloped countries. The prospect of belonging to the "New Class" which would plan and administer economic development is naturally alluring, even though this prospect would often not materialize. The perquisites which during the somewhat comparable period of development in Europe went to bourgeois enterprisers and suppliers of capital would under the Soviet system go to the "New Class." When capitalism was developing in Europe, the mechanism of profit making and interest earning operated simultaneously to keep income out of the hands and mouths of consumers and to concentrate it in the hands of private enterprisers. The capital accumulation for the industrialization of Japan at a later date was made possible through a governmental policy based upon the cultural structure of Japanese society which supplemented the normal processes of the early stages of capitalism. This policy prevented a rise in the low-cost standard of living of the peasants who became industrial workers.[7] It also maintained heavy taxation on agricultural income while keeping the taxation of income derived from industry low enough to facilitate the capital formation essential to rapid industrialization. While the mechanism for the accumulation of capital of the laissez-faire system did function very efficiently to insure the national accumulation of capital, it was, of course, inegalitarian. It did permit a substantial increase in the individual consumption of workers and peasants which in an authoritarian system might have been withheld as savings for capital investment.

In capital-scarce, underdeveloped countries, the combination of democratic institutions with socialist distributional policies confronts governments with a most difficult barrier to be overcome if capital accumulation is to take place. In India, for example, economic and political processes operating during the years before and since independence have allowed agricultural income which formerly had to be paid as land rent or as taxes to remain in the hands of the landholding peasantry. This has been of no benefit to the landless agricultural workers. The number of peasants with some sort of landholding is so large a proportion of the Indian population, however, that allowing the income of this class to rise without taxing substantial portions of it away has meant that, since little of it is saved, adequate funds for capital investment could not

[7] See the section on "The Pattern of Japanese Capitalism and the Industrialization Process" in "Competition and Monopoly in the Japanese Economy," by Gen-Ichi Abe and associates, in *Économic Systems of the West*, Rudolf Frei (ed.), Vol. I, List Gesellschaft, Kyklos-Verlag, Basel, 1957.

be obtained. Population growth has retarded a rise in the average income of this group while aggregate income has been increasing. The votes of the Indian peasantry are so important that an increase in agricultural taxes would be politically extremely difficult.[8]

Similarly, in countries like Egypt and Iran, when limited redistribution of landowners' properties to the actual cultivators has taken place, those responsible for the redistribution have often been surprised to find that the credit which the landlords formerly made available annually at high rates to their former tenants was no longer available. This was surprising because the annual credit advances had been less than the amount of the annual land rent formerly paid and from which the peasants were now free. The explanation is, of course, that the consumption of the former tenants had risen. The amount of the rent formerly paid was now being almost entirely consumed by the peasants, whose incomes, even after land rent no longer had to be paid, were not large. In consequence, the amount available to provide either fixed or circulating capital was less than had been available when the much higher individual consumption of the small number of landlords had been deducted from the rent which the peasants had formerly paid.

In Russia, the Soviet ruling class solved this problem, at great cost to the peasants, by collectivizing agriculture in such a way that income could be removed from the hands of the individual peasants who had previously been consuming it. A regime of the Soviet type, with a ruling class that does not have to fear the sanctions of a voting citizenry, can employ an extraordinary arsenal of weapons to keep consumption down and national investment up. Such a regime can hold wages down and prices up, since collective bargaining and strikes are not permitted. It can refrain from advertising con-

[8] See the article by Matthew J. Kust, "India: Deepening Crisis," *New Republic*, January 20, 1958, in which he makes some of these same points. Kust estimates that over the past century the governmental "take" has diminished from about one-third of gross income in agriculture to only a little more than one per cent of the value of agricultural output. Mr. Kust has been kind enough to allow the writer to see his privately published study on taxation for economic development in which this subject is most cogently analyzed.

sumer goods. It can deduct compulsory savings from wages if it prefers to do the bookkeeping in that way. Finally, it can simply not produce consumer goods.

Fired with the ambition of quickly attaining something approaching the standard of living of the industrialized countries, the intelligentsia of the underdeveloped countries have little patience with the prospect of accumulating capital through time-consuming historical capitalistic methods. Furthermore, withholding of income by the mechanism of the laissez-faire capitalistic system has come by dogma to be considered exploitative. Withholding of income from consumers by the state is not exploitative according to Marxist doctrine, which can conveniently be invoked at this point. The intellectuals assume that they, as a staff of planners and administrators of supposedly small size, can be furnished a satisfactory income without greatly diminishing the funds available for investment. This completes the rationalization by which the Soviet process of capital accumulation appears to offer advantages over the capitalistic process of accumulation. One cannot, of course, imagine the Communist Party in any country appealing to the electorate on the grounds of the greater effectiveness of a Soviet economic and political system in withholding incomes from consumers in order to increase capital investment. The appeal to the masses is always on other grounds. Not even to the intelligentsia is the Communist argument stated in this fashion. Nor do the intelligentsia ever admit to themselves that a conflict of goals exists between capital accumulation, democratic institutions, liberty and socialist egalitarianism. Yet in an unadmitted sense they recognize this. Once a Soviet type of regime is in power, the mechanism of withholding income from consumers for capital investment can be placed in operation without the limitations and inhibitions which are likely to be operative under a regime which attempts to be both democratic and socialist.

It is, however, the cumulative and partly unavoidable expansion of the area of state power, rather than any revolutionary change by ballots or bullets, that is likely to determine the fate of liberty in the countries of the West which still maintain a modified form of capitalism. That the increased complexities and interrelationships of modern life necessitate this extension of the power of the state is no less true because it is such a well-worn cliché. The need which arises for municipal ordinances against keeping pigs as soon as enough citizens are congregated in one place to constitute a municipality, hoary though the example may be, serves to illustrate an infinity of more complex cases. In this instance the curtailment of the liberties of the would-be swinekeepers is more than offset by the reduced exposure of other citizens to unpleasant odors, if indeed the respective liberties and exposures can somehow be weighed in the same scale. Because a more intricate economy has developed, the liberties of some citizens have had to be reduced in order to protect others. The problem would not have arisen in a simpler economy in which individuals had fewer unavoidable relationships to each other. It is illogical to deny that some liberty had to be sacrificed as the economy changed in character.

Apart from the infinity of cases where state power must increasingly be used in the public interest to limit the liberties of the individual, there are many other situations where certain functions can be performed with so much greater efficiency by the state that there can be little argument about its assumption of responsibility. This, of course, has been recognized since long before the days of Adam Smith. The list of the economic functions of the state steadily lengthens. Thus, it is now a commonplace that conditions in the modern economy render it inevitable that, through social security, protection will be available for the citizen which he cannot provide as an individual. The possibilities for expansion of this kind of protection beyond minimum necessity are almost unlimited.

The vulnerability of modern capitalistic economies to economic depressions and to inflationary movements in the absence of governmental controls and intervention adds a tremendous area into which hardly anyone any longer would deny the necessity for the entry of state power. In the United States this principle has been embodied in the Employment Act of 1946, but no government in a capitalistic country can any longer successfully avoid the assumption of this kind of responsibility.

The replacement of the individual enterpriser and the unorganized worker by the corporation and the labor union has created a new area from which the power of the state as referee, umpire or judge cannot be excluded, since it is out of the question to permit the uninhibited conflict of countervailing powers under circumstances which might result in unacceptable injury to the public. It may even become necessary in the future for the state to intervene in the process of election of corporate and labor union managements, and to regulate the internal and external affairs of these organizations.[9]

This does not, of course, exhaust the list of areas in which the expansion of state power has become necessary. A well-known result of the expansion of these functions of the state has been an increase in governmental expenditures. This trend seems to have been world-wide. In the United States total per capita expenditure by local, state and national government is now some nine times as great as it was forty years ago after allowance for changes in the purchasing power of money. The increase has been four times as great as the increase in national income. A major factor in this rise, of course, has been the cost of wars. But even apart from this, the ratio would have risen. When governmental expenditures amount to some one-fourth of gross national product, or to about one-third of national income, these expenditures themselves are a basic aspect of the power of the state over the economy. Changes in the level of governmental expenditures become a major factor in determining the level of industrial production, and in stimulating or inhibiting inflation. In addition, governmental agencies become the sought-after customers of corporate man-

---

[9] It is possible that the size and power of industrial corporations and labor unions may be diminished by legislation or court decisions such as that of the Supreme Court in June 1957 when the ownership by du Pont of a large block of stock in General Motors was held to be illegal. If this case were to constitute a precedent, the consequences might be epochal. Legislation regulating the managements of labor unions as a result of the disclosures of the McClellan Committee of the U.S. Senate might have a parallel result. However, it seems unlikely that the necessity for state intervention in contests involving countervailing power will be critically reduced. There is no indication as yet that the Supreme Court believes that the size and power of labor organizations should be limited.

agement. It becomes most important for sellers of goods and services to be on good terms with the appropriate echelons in the governmental bureaucracy. The political party in power may not follow an economic policy approved by corporate managers in general, but it may nevertheless be able to obtain substantial campaign contributions from actual or potential holders of governmental contracts.

The provision of resources to meet these increased governmental expenditures, whether from taxation or from deficit financing, represents an additional facet of the increased power of the state. As expenditures require an increasing proportion of national income, difficulty in finding additional resources out of which to meet them might constitute a possible source of economic crises, which in turn might render it difficult for a government of limited powers to carry out its functions.[10] There seems to be no closely calculated limit upon the proportion of the national income which may be taken to meet governmental expenditures, but serious difficulties would eventually arise if the proportion continued to grow.

Finally, a circumstance pushing towards the expansion of the state power into new areas is the relative ease with which a particular economic group can obtain a subsidy or an additional control by the state in its particular interest compared with the ability of the general public to resist such action. For example, it may well pay a particular corporation, a trade association, a labor union or a farm organization to hire lobbyists in order to get specific pieces of legislation passed. If the lobbyist fails to get his subsidy or his control measure enacted, he can hardly offer his employer the excuse that he had devoted his time to defeating the efforts of other lobbyists having realized that his employer would really be better off if no additional subsidies or controls were legislated for anyone!

Perhaps the greatest weakness of modern capitalism is its lack of support among a large part of the intelligentsia. Their failure to support it renders the system vulnerable to replacement by a substitute system through parliamentary or revolu-

[10] This problem would, of course, be temporarily greatly ameliorated if armament expenditures could be eliminated.

tionary means, or to continuous expansion of the role of the state to the point where drastic change might be required in order to keep the economy functioning. Lack of support from a large part of the intelligentsia is inherent in the original rationalization justifying the existence of the capitalistic system. Laissez-faire capitalism, together with the democratic parliamentary political system which developed alongside it, was based upon the assumption that the politico-economic system existed and functioned as it did because it best reflected the self-interest of the individuals who made up the population. Consequently, no defense of the system was necessary. The absence of governmentally organized propaganda in support of the capitalistic, democratic system, in contrast with the Soviet, Fascist or Nazi systems, reflected furthermore the feeling that of all the fields which a government dedicated to democracy and laissez faire should stay out of, that of interfering with and guiding men's minds headed the list. The essence of laissez faire and democracy was considered to be the freedom of citizens, not only from restraints, but from organized propaganda assaults upon their minds as well.

If propaganda in defense of capitalism was not the function of government, intellectuals could feel with a good deal of logic that it was not the responsibility of any individual intellectual either. Why should anyone who was not a capitalist defend the system by which each capitalist carried on production with the single-minded purpose of maximizing his profits? And why should any particular capitalist-industrialist take time out from maximizing his profits to defend the system as an entity? Even if he were to assume such a responsibility, it would be unlikely that a lifetime devoted to steelmaking, meat packing, banking or stockbroking would equip him to write or speak very effectively in behalf of the system. If the task were to be done efficiently, it obviously would have to be done by members of the non-capitalist intelligentsia hired or enlisted for the purpose rather than by the managers of capitalistic corporations.[11]

[11] Increased efforts to explain the way in which the modern form of capitalism serves the public interest are currently being undertaken under the slogan of "People's Capitalism." This term is being used by the Voice of America in its overseas broadcasts. As a fur-

The intellectual task of defending capitalism has always faced another major obstacle. Capitalism was never formally adopted at some sort of constitutional convention, where representatives of the people selected it as the most promising of alternative politico-economic systems. Instead, like the feudal-manorial system preceding it, it evolved and endured because it had survival value. It facilitated the more efficient organization of production during its historical epoch and permitted far greater personal liberty than did the feudal system. Like feudalism, the capitalistic system nevertheless required military coercive power to maintain its basic institutions against the, at best, latent hostility of the propertyless classes. It was partly because the capitalistic system was the heir of feudalism that an institution like private property could establish itself and be accorded such a high degree of popular acquiescence.[12] Here then was an economic system which had never been adopted by majority vote, which protected the vested rights of property owners and which depended upon the coercive power of the state for its continuance. How could such a system be defended as serving the public?

The defensive rationale, set forth by Adam Smith and developed by economists since his time, depended upon an intellectual model which proved that, under appropriate assumptions, the pursuit of self-interest by capitalists maximized the wealth of nations and simultaneously minimized the role of the state and hence the rule of men over men. This defensive rationale depended upon "the long run" for the attainment of its goal. The structure and mechanics of the economists' model, moreover, was not simple and the attainment of the goal of the greatest good for the greatest number depended upon, but was of doubtful reconcilability with, the institution of private property and inheritance. In the assumption of the existence of private property, the economist expositors had to recognize the payment of income to indi-

---

ther example, the Advertising Council, Inc. and Yale University in November 1956 jointly sponsored a round table at Yale University entitled "People's Capitalism." The participants were a number of professors from Yale, two business executives and two labor union executives.

[12] See pp. 12–14.

viduals which in the abstract was functionless.[13] The legal
status of private property did not depend upon a positive obligation of the owner to operate it in the public interest. To
the intellectual, therefore, it seemed hypocritical for anyone
to maintain that the institution of private property should be
protected against any conflicting group interest because private property contributed to the public good. Such an imputa-
tion appeared to the nonspecialist intellectual to depend upon
an assumed *noblesse oblige* on the part of the property owner,
since there was no legal obligation.

For all these reasons, the economists' efforts to present capitalism as an economic system operating in the public interest
have always remained, for many intellectuals, abortive. On
the contrary, the intellectual has come more and more to
think of the interests of the public and the capitalist as fundamentally in conflict, the capitalist being interested in the
highest price that he can get for goods and services out of
the consuming public. The intellectual is likely to think of
the state as prima facie representing "the public" and consequently tends to sympathize with any action by the state
which limits the power or the income of the capitalist, particularly the capitalist in corporate form. For example, in the
case of a governmentally regulated industry such as the railroads, a member of the Interstate Commerce Commission
who votes against an increase in freight or passenger rates is
considered to vote for the public interest, while a commissioner who votes for such an increase is considered to vote
against the public interest almost regardless of the reasons for
doing so. In the same way, any congressman who votes for
governmental construction and operation of electric power
dams, by common usage, votes in favor of "public power" and
against the private corporate alternative. Similarly, any legis-
lator who votes for rent controls, almost regardless of circumstances, is considered to vote in favor of the public; one who
votes against rent controls votes against the public. A rent

[13] The proportion of national income received by property owners
as such and the responsibility of private property for inequality in
income distribution are both smaller, however, than is probably generally believed. See pp. 320–321.

commissioner who permits a rent increase acts against the public, and vice versa.

The emergence of the large corporation as the dominant organizational form of private property in production greatly strengthened the tendency of the intellectual to think in terms of the conflict between "capital" and the public. He no longer thinks of this conflict, however, in terms of the interests of the individual capitalist-producer versus the public. To most intellectuals the conflict has become one between the public and the capitalistic corporation. There is little recognition that an even greater conflict of interest might exist between the public and the management of a nationalized industry or between the management and the workers in the industry. Any sympathy or admiration which in the past might have been felt for the capitalist as an individual owner-producer is not likely to be extended to the corporation. Indeed, as a growing proportion of the population become employees rather than individual producers, and as stockholders come to feel less and less identification with the corporation, the person who thinks of the corporation as "we" becomes rarer and rarer. To almost everyone the corporation becomes an anonymous "it" or "they."

This development coincides with a change in the model by means of which it is possible for the economist to explain how capitalism works in the public interest. While economists disagree widely about the extent to which competition still characterizes the modern corporate economy, no economist could seriously argue that the modern pricing system operates in just the way it did in the old-style, individual-enterprise economy. A case can nevertheless be made for the proposition that competition in the modern corporate economy is still not without effect and for the further proposition that the modern economy functions in the public interest to an even greater extent than did old-style capitalism. But if the previous model was not a convincing device to many intellectuals for proving the efficacy of capitalism as a system which functioned in the public interest, the more complicated model is even less effective for this purpose. Consequently, it becomes even more likely that the intellectual will consider the interests of "the public" or "the consumer" or "labor" or "the farmer" as on quite a different moral plane from those of the corporation.[14]

The fact that government officials or labor or farm leaders are intended to represent, and generally believe that they do represent, group interests rather than the legally and historically presumed profit maximization goal of the corporate executive is likely to be of decisive importance to the intellectual. Even the question of the source of power of the government official is seldom raised.[15] For the corporate executive, on the other hand, to claim to represent anyone other than corporate management or, at best, the stockholders of his company, the intellectual is likely to consider to be sheer hypocrisy or a form of woolly-mindedness even if well-intentioned. This assumption is indeed consistent with the purely legal situation. It is not easy to explain to an intellectual who is not a specialist that "the public" or "labor" or "the farmer" does not and cannot, in the mass, either carry on or control production any more than any mass of people can carry on the functions of government. Intellectuals generally do not accept the proposition that the alternative to capitalistic organization and direction of production through the market is administration of the economy by a hierarchical bureaucracy, accompanied by all the problems of how this bureaucracy can be induced or required to act in the public interest. This proposition is the more difficult to accept when it has to be

[14] It is this development which has been responsible to an important degree for the reversal in meaning of the term "liberal" in the United States. In the original European meaning of the term it stood, of course, for a policy of the elimination of restraints, governmental or other, upon trade and industry. It was also associated with the elimination of restraints upon personal liberty and with the development of political democracy. By a complete metamorphosis, the term "liberal" in the United States has come to mean the increase of governmental control or the increase in the power of other groups such as "labor" or "the farmers" over the corporation, which is not recognized as performing a social purpose.

[15] Thus, many intellectuals accept it as axiomatic that the Soviet Union is somehow a "workers' state," instead of an elite society created by a wing of the revolutionary intelligentsia which used the small working-class movement to engineer its capture of power. See R. H. S. Crossman, "Towards the Philosophy of Socialism," *New Fabian Essays*, Turnstile Press, London, 1952, p. 6.

recognized that in the modern capitalistic economy the market cannot be relied upon by itself to compel corporate management to act in the public interest, but that instead an expanding minimum of both countervailing power and of governmental regulation has now become unavoidable.

The intellectual who would undertake the defense of capitalism has to decide whether he is going to defend the ever-changing modern corporate capitalistic system as it has been modified by governmental intervention and controls, by measures to reduce inequality and by the development of the countervailing power of labor unions and whether he is going to regard these modifications of old-style capitalism as necessary reforms essential to capitalism's survival. Hardly any defender of capitalism could any longer, it is true, choose, as an alternative, to defend the economists' abstract model of pure and perfect competition. This rigorous and austere model never represented and could not represent actuality, however valuable it was as an analytical and expository device. The economic system in almost any capitalistic country departs even further from it now, of course, than it did during the past century. In consequence the defenders of capitalism must pick and choose among the modifications of capitalism which have taken place; they must choose among degrees of governmental control and intervention in the economy, stronger or weaker measures to equalize income distribution, and so on.[16] Thus the defense of the current capitalistic system has to be the defense of a moving, composite target, one of the most difficult of operations, as any officer responsible for air cover for naval vessels in World War II can testify.

---

[16] This is essentially the problem which has had to be grappled with by the advocates of the *soziale Marktwirtschaft* on the Continent and by American economists of like inclination who have wished to revive and restore the prestige of the competitive market as a mechanism operating in the public interest. This neoliberal movement represents one significant group of intellectuals who have tried both to explain the nature of the market economy and to study the problem of what governmental action is needed to make the market mechanism function more effectively in the public interest without impairing it. See Carl J. Friedrich, "The Political Thought of Neoliberalism," *American Political Science Review*, June 1955, pp. 509–525.

For all these reasons the intellectual defense of modern capitalism, in spite of the system's accomplishments, in spite of the extraordinary diminution of its traditionally criticized evils, presents inherently the most serious difficulties. These difficulties, as Schumpeter so brilliantly pointed out,[17] are compounded and intensified by the special character of a part of the intelligentsia who have great influence in shaping public attitudes towards political and economic institutions. To Schumpeter, "Intellectuals are in fact people who wield the power of the spoken and written word, and one of the touches that distinguish them from other people who do the same is the absence of direct responsibility for practical affairs." This statement recalls George Orwell's reference to the mentality of the English left-wing intelligentsia as reflected in their weeklies and monthlies, their "generally negative querulous attitude" and their "complete lack at all times of any constructive suggestion."[18]

It would, of course, be totally unfair to claim that intellectuals as a class are inevitably naive and irresponsible. When the evidence has become conclusive, serious-minded intellectuals can and often do cut through verbalisms, however ideologically consecrated, to reality. A number of the foremost intellectuals of the Labor Party in England, for example, have been willing to base their analysis of economic systems on the actual record and have shown an admirably clear understanding of the changed nature of modern capitalism, the limitations and difficulties involved in the nationalization of industry, and the illogic of considering the Soviet state a workers' society.[19]

Schumpeter attempted to distinguish between those who write and speak within the field of their specialized, professional competence and those who write and speak without special training or experience. Schumpeter found this distinction difficult to maintain since society requires the services of

[17] See Joseph Schumpeter, *Capitalism, Socialism and Democracy,* Harper, New York, 1942, particularly pp. 134–155.
[18] *The Lion and the Unicorn,* Secker & Warburg, London, 1941, p. 47.
[19] This is characteristic in substantial degree of the *New Fabian Essays,* which the writer has cited frequently, and also of various recent publications of the Labor Party, such as *Industry and Society.*

the non-specialist intellectual, not only to popularize but also to perform the functions of synthesis and integration of knowledge. The writer who performs these functions needs to be and often is of the highest intellectual type. Ill-equipped and irresponsible intellectuals, however, when they are also facile speakers and writers, says Schumpeter, come close to what the Duke of Wellington had in mind when he referred to "the scribbling set."[20] All special and group interests depend largely upon this "scribbling set" to state and to press their cases. They are the ghost writers for all men of affairs, from businessmen, labor leaders, farm leaders and politicians to cabinet ministers, court justices and heads of state.

It might be thought that capitalists would have the obvious means—the ability to pay for services rendered—to hire mercenaries from among these professional intellectuals to speak and write for the capitalistic system. In no other form of economic and political system has this type of intellectual fared so well and been so free, and these advantages also might be expected to facilitate the enlistment of the intellectual in the defense of capitalism. A corporate executive may, it is true, hire without much difficulty an intellectual to write advertising copy for cigarettes or automobiles. Intellectuals have, of course, been hired to write glowing articles and books in defense of capitalism as well. Yet, as has been pointed out, there appears something illogical about any one capitalist paying for a defense of capitalism in general. It has further been pointed out that the non-specialist intellectual naturally feels that if he takes on the assignment of defending capitalism he is working against "the public" or "labor" or "the farmer." His heart is not likely to be in it, and he is likely to be held in contempt—though perhaps envied too—by his fellows for accepting this kind of employment.

The intellectual strongly resents any restrictions upon his freedom of thought, expression or action. Naturally he finds attractive the prospect of having the power to direct other men to put his thoughts into action for their own good. The

---

[20] Schumpeter had a difficult struggle to separate, even in his own mind, "the scribbling set" from other intellectuals. It is indeed difficult to do so without using "scribbling set" simply to mean all those with whom one disagrees. Nevertheless, the concept is useful.

allurement of being able to direct others under a system which gives uninhibited power to men to rule over men is for most intellectuals immediately cancelled by the reflection that one may find himself among the ruled rather than the ruling. A small minority of intellectuals resolve this difficulty by joining the Communist Party, thus insuring that they will belong to the ruling class when capitalism is overthrown. A larger minority of intellectuals do not find the prospect of an authoritarian society necessarily repulsive if intellectuals are likely to be a favored class in such a society.

In the Soviet Union, engineers and physical scientists, industrial, agricultural and marketing executives, army officers and government officials belong to the elite who have a right to varying degrees of authority and prestige and to a higher standard of living. Authors and playwrights who benefit from large royalties on huge state-sponsored editions of their works also belong to this elite. The hierarchy of the Communist Party enjoy these privileges also, but they do not in the main form an additional category since almost everyone in the Party hierarchy holds a post also in the political, economic or cultural apparatus. Thus, in a sense, the intelligentsia might be said to be the ruling class in Soviet Russia. Indeed, higher compensation for the ruling class is reconciled with Marxist doctrine in terms of higher pay for "working intellectuals."[21]

For a sizable minority of intellectuals, therefore, it is not too difficult to see the Soviet system as rule by an elite in the pattern of Plato's *Republic*. Of course, by defining intelligentsia broadly enough to include economic and political executives of all types, under modern capitalism the upper-income classes and those who have positions of prestige and authority can also be said to belong to the intelligentsia. However, the power status of intellectuals under modern capitalism is not so categorically defined as under the Soviet system. Furthermore, under old-style capitalism, the favored status of intellectuals was largely dependent upon the decisions, preferences or whims of property owners. Under modern capital-

---

[21] See, for example, the leading editorial article in *Izvestia*, February 21, 1952 on the cultural educational work of the Soviet state, by M. Tiurin, in which Stalin's emphasis on the importance of the intelligentsia in any society is quoted.

ism the role of private property has greatly declined.[22] It has to some extent been superseded by corporate property, but the power of corporate property, as has been pointed out, is now much hedged about and limited.

A comparison of the role of the intellectual under the Soviet system as contrasted with modern capitalism makes it easy to understand why the Soviet system has a strong appeal for one who finds authority, prestige and a privileged standard of living more than adequate substitutes for personal liberty. This does not mean that most intellectuals have weighed the current capitalistic system and rejected it in favor of some form of statized economic system. It does not even imply complete neutralism, since most of these intellectuals, at least in the United States, would reject the alternative of a fully statized economy if it were presented to them as a clear-cut issue. It simply means that most intellectuals not only will accept increased intervention and control by the state when a strong case can be made for it but also will tolerate almost any piecemeal extension of the area of state power out of a feeling that the public interest is being served.

In part, the attitude of these intellectuals reflects only an admirable objectivity towards economic systems. In no other economic and political system is this kind of objectivity permitted. It is one of the most precious virtues of the current capitalistic system. To the extent that this attitude reflects objectivity it is a basic source of strength for the current economic system. Yet this strength is not easily mobilized against repeated extensions of the area of state power, no one of which seems directly to threaten the existence of the current capitalistic system.

The intellectual is naturally a critic. It is inherent in the development of ideas that the critic is not required to put forward a workable alternative to the economic or political institution he criticizes. It is natural for the intellectual to feel that to criticize existing institutions requires greater imagina-

[22] The declining role of private property in modern capitalism has been referred to again and again in this study. This concept is brilliantly developed by Crosland in "Part I—The Transformation of Capitalism" in his book *The Future of Socialism*. Indeed, Crosland in answering his own question "Is this still capitalism in Britain in 1956?" replies "No."

tion and courage than to defend them.[23] Within the cultural milieu of the West quite a successful career, even financially, can be made in this role, so the intellectual may enjoy the thrill of being a critic at little or no cost. Freedom of thought is fundamental to the economic and political system of modern capitalism. To restrict freedom of thought would be to restrict the whole complex of liberties which are essential to the system's operation. The risk of imprisonment, death and torture which has been a commonplace under the Soviet system for those suspected of critical thought and activity exists nowhere in the West. Yet because Communists have been the most violent critics of capitalism, the intellectual in the capitalistic West tends to feel a kinship with the Communist as a fellow critic, forgetting that the Communist in Russia who speaks against capitalism is not a critic of a regime in power and that the critic of the Soviet system has been allowed no voice at all.

To those intellectuals who were most unreservedly critical of capitalism, it seemed logical to feel that "All critics of capitalism are our friends." It was unthinkable to them that Soviet intellectuals who criticized the capitalistic economic system would continue to support the Soviet regime if it were guilty of really serious repression of the liberties of Soviet citizens. This fantastic naïveté was reflected by the small group of intellectuals in the United States and other countries of the West who joined the Communist Party. Their credulity would be unbelievable were it not for the evidence given by so many who at last broke with the Party.[24]

[23] His criticism need not be novel. Marxist criticisms of capitalism are now a century old and hardly anything in the intellectual world could be more stereotyped. Yet the feeling persists among many intellectuals that it is more exciting and courageous to repeat Marxist criticisms of capitalism than to defend an existing and presumably well-entrenched economic system.

[24] When Howard Fast broke with the Communist Party after the Hungarian revolt in 1956 his action was not mentioned in the Soviet press, but his flow of "fan mail" from the Soviet Union, where several of his plays were currently being produced, nevertheless ceased abruptly. It became evident to Fast that the Soviet censor had stopped this mail. His attempt at correspondence with a Russian friend at this time also showed signs of official interference. For the first time, apparently, Fast realized that such censorship existed!

Intellectuals who have been Communists or fellow travelers but have finally broken with the Party often show greater awareness than other intellectuals of the grotesquely repulsive characteristics of Soviet totalitarianism. Former Communists and some of the closer fellow travelers have naturally been in positions which enabled them to have intimate knowledge of these grotesqueries of a sort few non-Communist intellectuals have had.[25] For example, Alexander Fadeyev, the Russian writer who visited the United States in 1949 as head of the Soviet delegation to the Cultural and Scientific Conference for World Peace, was asked by Howard Fast and other Communist intellectuals about reports that a number of Russian intellectuals whom they mentioned by name had been arrested and in some cases executed. Fadeyev not only denied these reports but gave circumstantial accounts of having seen and talked with these men; he even recounted their amusement at the capitalistic lies about their "persecution." His listeners accepted his account with relief. Later, through the publication of Khrushchev's famous speech to the 20th Party Congress, Fast learned to his horror that all these people had been executed long before the conversation with Fadeyev. Not long after Khrushchev's speech, Fadeyev committed suicide. Similarly, Boris Polovoy, a Soviet writer, denied to Fast that

---

Only then did he recognize the significance of the fact that in the United States his mail had never been tampered with or censored, and that no American writer had been tortured or executed for his beliefs. Harrison Salisbury, "Writers in the Shadow of Communism," *New York Times Magazine,* June 9, 1957, p. 10. Fast gives this same account in *The Naked God,* Praeger, New York, 1957.

[25] The list of books by disillusioned former Communists and fellow travelers and of books showing this disillusionment which afford a particularly sharp insight into the nature of the Soviet authoritarian society includes *Verdict of Three Decades,* edited by Julien Steinberg; *The God That Failed,* under the joint authorship of Richard Wright, Arthur Koestler, Ignazio Silone, Louis Fisher, Stephen Spender and André Gide; *The Whole of Their Lives,* by Benjamin Gitlow; *The New Class,* by Milovan Djilas; and *The Naked God,* by Howard Fast. *Assignment in Utopia,* by Eugene Lyons, might be included, for Lyons, though not a member of the Party, was sympathetic to it until he became violently disillusioned after his experiences in Soviet Russia as a newspaper correspondent. In addition are the novels of disillusionment such as Koestler's *Darkness at Noon* and Gouzenko's *Fall of a Titan.*

anything had happened to the Jewish writer Kvitko. Kvitko, Polovoy said, was living in the same apartment with him and was finishing the translation of one book and planning to write another. After Khrushchev's speech it was learned that Kvitko had been arrested, had been beaten and had died long before the time of the conversation.[26]

This literature of disillusionment has had less impact upon most intellectuals than might have been expected. Such has been the habit of many intellectuals to believe that the Communist Party has in spite of everything somehow remained the vanguard of the proletariat in its revolutionary protest against capitalistic exploitation that Communists who have left the Party or have been expelled from its ranks are regarded with distaste, dislike or even revulsion.

In some respects the attitude of many intellectuals who never joined the Party but who nevertheless viewed the Soviet system with tolerance or even with some warmth is less comprehensible. These men could not by a formal act of faith and orthodoxy totally deny the fact that personal liberty was being crushed by the most atrocious means. Theirs was the more complex procedure of deprecation and excuse when such events could not be denied and of allowing the distasteful occurrences to slip into limbo as rapidly as possible. Since these intellectuals were accustomed to use words as symbols of reality, they simply could not believe that the steadfast and unblushing insistence of the Soviet regime that it *was* the dictatorship of the proletariat had no counterpart in reality. In the face of evidence which one would have thought to be overwhelming, many intellectuals found the bald reiteration of the Soviet claim to represent the government of the workers more convincing than the complex and involved reasoning, unsupported by the juristic status of private property, which was required to prove that modern capitalism operated in the public interest.

Yet the esteem in which the individual members of the "ruling class" of the economic and political system of modern capitalism are held by the public depends largely upon the way their activities and personalities are presented to the reading, listening and viewing population by this portion of the

[26] Fast, *The Naked God,* pp. 95–96 and pp. 133–134.

intelligentsia who are likely to view capitalism with reservations, skepticism and, occasionally, hostility.[27] Legislators, judges, cabinet members, heads of state and other members of the bureaucratic hierarchy, for most purposes, are successful or are failures depending upon what is said of them in newspapers, magazines and books and on radio and television. What is said and written about them determines in considerable measure whether they will become or remain part of the political ruling class. Whether they will be revered in history, live in infamy or simply be forgotten also depends largely upon what is said in these media.[28] It is fortunate that many intellectuals are nonconformists so that their strategic role as a class does not imply a monolithic attitude on the part of intellectuals towards men, institutions or events. Yet some tendency towards a generalized point of view is brought into being by the highly important secondary effect of the opinion of intellectuals in general upon individual intellectuals. For the influence of any particular intellectual is largely dependent upon what is written and said about him by other intellectuals.

Modern capitalism will be seriously vulnerable so long as the attitude of so important a segment of the intelligentsia remains negative. Fortunately, although totalitarian societies such as the Nazi and, particularly, the Soviet system have had a high degree of success in impressing their intellectuals into service—since the use of unlimited terror allowed them no other alternative—these intellectuals have greeted the overthrow of such a system with immense relief and unrestrained enthusiasm. It might well be that these liberated intellectuals will become the most effective expositors and protagonists of the virtues of modern capitalism.

[27] It might be thought that since newspapers, magazines and book publishing houses, as well as radio and television systems, are owned by capitalists, this would insure favorable treatment of individuals to the degree that they supported capitalism. But it would manifestly be quite unreal to expect such a result: effective motivation does not run in this direction.

[28] The historian who tries to supplement these sources by studying official documents to which government officials and prominent citizens have put their names will need to realize that these documents have generally been ghostwritten by anonymous intellectuals.

The attitude of the part of the intelligentsia which so largely molds public opinion is in contrast to that of the much larger class among which it lives and with which it shares a similar standard of living. This larger class, whose rising standard of living is reflected in the movement of population into the suburbs, is largely taking the place of the traditional "white-collar class." These junior and sub-sub-junior executives of corporations, managers of chain stores, engineers, technicians, salesmen, accountants and the like make up a growing proportion of the population. They naturally do not regard themselves as part of "the working class." Like the small merchants, real estate men, lawyers, physicians and others among whom they live, they have the tastes and the means to devote themselves to "gracious living." They certainly are not hostile to or even critical of the current capitalistic system. In the United States, for example, the major portion of this class seems to vote the Republican ticket. Yet most are employees and do not consider themselves to be responsible for corporate capitalism. In any event they are not part of the writing, teaching and speaking intelligentsia, any more than are the very top corporation executives, and for one of the same reasons: they work at their own jobs.

As the relative size of this class increases, its vote can usually be counted upon the conservative side in elections. Consequently, the growth of this class is a factor in limiting changes in the current capitalistic system. Nevertheless, even persons of this class are by no means entirely unaffected by the intellectuals who mold public opinion. Many of them, some of the time, and particularly their wives, wish to think of themselves as in favor of what they consider "liberal" and "modern" ideas. It is perhaps not to be wondered at that some of the wealthier members of society with whom this class sometimes associates find nothing repulsive or incongruous in the existence in the Soviet Union of a privileged class wielding unrestricted power.[29] Others of this class, by contrast, often

---

[29] It had become quite fashionable in England before World War II to be politically left, and something of the sort was true in the United States after the war, at least until the Hungarian revolution in 1956. Some of these "Turnstile Intelligentsia," as Richard Crossman has called them, continued to support the extreme left even

feel baffled in trying to express their conservatism through the ballot box. Should votes be cast for the politician who opposes all economic change and who might be thought to have small chance of election, or should votes be given to the candidate who has compromised? The voter who leans towards conservatism is likely to feel that he has no opportunity to express his attitudes and may end up not voting at all. In any event, the political weight of this group does not equal that of the intelligentsia as described above.

It has been pointed out that the possibility of the development of personal liberty and democracy in Soviet Russia at some time in the future depends in the economic realm upon some of the same factors which are likely to determine whether the countries that are still free and democratic will be able to remain so. Far fewer difficulties are, of course, involved in maintaining liberty and representative institutions under modern corporate capitalism than in developing free institutions out of the current Soviet political and economic system. Fortunately, the experience of Western countries with various modifications of capitalism strongly indicates that there exists a wide area for experimentation before net personal freedom is critically diminished.

The official admissions by the Soviet rulers of the real character of the regime under Stalin, the struggle for power among Stalin's henchmen after his death without even the pretense of a democratic election process within the Communist Party itself, and the uprisings in East Germany, Poland and Hungary, have finally made it intellectually impossible for anyone to believe that the Soviet regime is after all some sort of "People's Democracy." This final disillusionment with the Soviet regime may well be of strategic importance in convincing the minority of intellectuals who still cherish sympathy for eco-

---

after the Hungarian revolution. Howard Fast describes how at a party in a swank apartment on Park Avenue after his resignation from the Communist Party he was denounced as a renegade by his millionaire hostess, by a wealthy owner of a chain of restaurants, by a millionaire money lender, by a woman in a mink coat and by a businessman with a wife in ten thousand dollars worth of gown and gems. Fast, *The Naked God*, p. 65.

nomic and political reform through mass revolt under the leadership of a small self-chosen and self-proclaimed revolutionary elite that such a "People's Revolution" is simply the seizure of power by an oligarchy which inevitably becomes a personal tyranny. Concurrently, recognition has become widespread among intellectuals, particularly among those in the British Labor Party, that very limited advantages are to be attained through further nationalization of industry. There has also developed as a result of the experience with nationalized industries a recognition that neither governmental control nor governmental operation of industry automatically means that industry will be run by and for "the public" or "labor" or "the consumer." Instead it has now come to be realized that very difficult problems of organization and administration arise and that these must be gradually and painstakingly worked out before any further nationalization of industry would be justified. Disillusionment with the method of the seizure of power by a revolutionary junta as the road to economic reform and recognition of the limited advantages to be expected from the nationalization of industry and of the problems of social control of such industries provide the opportunity for serious study of other means by which the economic system can be made to function more efficiently and distribute its product more equitably.

Reference has been made to the great progress achieved through raising the floor of the standard of living for the lowest-income groups and through diminution of inequality in the distribution of income. There seems no doubt that the process of "raising the floor" will continue. Further diminution of inequality in income distribution also seems likely, although consideration of incentives associated with social costs and with differences in personal tastes may act as a brake on this development. The further extension of state control and intervention in the economy is no doubt inevitable, not only to facilitate this process of amelioration of the economic status of lower-income groups, but even to keep the modern complex economy functioning on a tolerable level. The maintenance of personal liberty will turn upon whether or not these extensions of the powers of the state can be restricted to those which are truly necessary. It will also depend upon whether, as the bureaucracy grows, political techniques can be evolved for continuing popular control over it through elected representatives. In turn, restriction of the powers of the state below the level critical to liberty will largely depend upon whether forms and processes of economic organization can be maintained or developed which will not themselves be inimical to personal liberty and which will relieve the state of the necessity for assuming complete responsibility.

We may conclude that the development of acceptable relations between the economy, liberty and the state clearly depends upon the evolution of the institutions of modern capitalism. Whether this evolution can be so guided that the role of the state remains below the critical level where the tyrant and his bureaucracy take over depends largely upon whether those who supply the guidance are endowed with the sometimes contradictory traits of tough-mindedness, goodwill and responsibleness.

EPILOGUE: THE CHANGING
ECONOMIC SYSTEMS
OF EASTERN EUROPE

After writing the foregoing chapters, I determined to take one more look at the economic and political systems of Soviet Russia and its current or former satellite states before sending the study to press. The Soviet sputniks had demonstrated to the world what I had already come to accept, that in the realm of production a centralized, ruthless, authoritarian economic and political system could compete successfully with the modern modified capitalistic systems of the West. I could no longer console myself with the belief that terror had not paid. I had, however, also confirmed by my visit to the Soviet Union in 1956 that some of the worst terrorist features of the Soviet system had been modified, at least temporarily, following the death of Stalin and his posthumous denunciation by Khrushchev at the 20th Party Congress. Moreover, Khrushchev had in 1957 proclaimed a grandiose program for the decentralization of control of industry and the development of a degree of local autonomy. Perhaps this was connected in some way with the relaxation of terror. Was it possible that a modification of the highly centralized, authoritarian Soviet system was under way which might eventually restore personal liberty in Russia or at least afford some compromise between state power and human freedom?

This question had been posed even more strongly by the developments in Yugoslavia and Poland. In both these countries, for somewhat different reasons and in different circumstances, claims had been made of an intention to diminish the direct power of the state over industry and agriculture and to give control to the workers themselves. Was there any substance to these claims? Had there been, in fact, any progress in "handing over the economy to the workers"? Was there any connection between what was happening in the Soviet Union and what was happening in Yugoslavia and Poland? If such a connection existed, had it manifested itself also in Czechoslovakia, where no break of any kind with Soviet domination had occurred?

In the late spring of 1958 I went first to Poland, then to Soviet Russia, to Czechoslovakia and finally to Yugoslavia in an effort to find the answers to these questions.[1]

POLAND

My stay in Poland left no doubt in my mind that the Polish revolution of October 1956 which had begun with the Poznan riots in July of the same year had greatly altered the situation in that country. It seems probable indeed that, if the Polish people had been entirely free to do so in 1956, they would have discarded Communist rule and tried to revert to some form of capitalism. This almost certainly would have happened in Hungary if the revolution had been successful there, and the feeling against the Soviet-dominated Communist Party was almost as strong in Poland as it evidently had been in Hungary. How capitalism in large-scale industry could have been restored in either country is not easy to visualize, but that is another matter.

Poland has undergone a wholesale reversion to individual peasant proprietorship in agriculture since the 1956 revolt. In

[1] During this tour I was accompanied by Mr. Harold Linder, formerly Assistant Secretary of State for Economic Affairs. The participation of Mr. Linder in conferences and in visits to factories and to state and collective farms was invaluable. I have particularly benefited by his careful and complete notes.

industry, a continuing effort has been made to give some effect to the seizure of industrial plants by the workers' councils which came into existence spontaneously at the time of the revolution. However, the threat of invasion by Soviet Russia, together with the deeply felt need for Soviet protection against a potentially remilitarized Germany, stopped the Polish revolution short of completion.

Soviet domination of Poland continually tends to reassert itself, although nothing like the status prior to the 1956 revolt has been restored. Polish dependence upon Soviet raw materials is substantial. Gomulka's compliance with Khrushchev's anti-Tito policy and his virtual condoning of the execution of former Hungarian Premier Nagy may reflect more than the realities of foreign policy, however. The Polish Communist Party may fear that its status as the ruling class in the country cannot be guaranteed independently of Soviet armed support in case of need. Consequently, it may be that the Polish Communist Party will find its domestic policies, like its foreign policy, subject to Soviet veto.

A great part of the force which overthrew the Stalinist type of government in Poland was furnished by violent and widespread discontent with the very low standard of living. By the spring of 1958 the standard of living had improved substantially. This was attributed largely to United States economic aid by a Polish cabinet member with whom I talked. Whatever its cause, the improvement in the standard of living has apparently gone a long way toward forestalling the danger of a violent overthrow of the Gomulka regime. Yet a revolution had taken place and the Gomulka regime has not been able, even if it wished to do so, simply to return to the near-replica of the Soviet economic and political system which existed previously.

To a significant degree the present Polish economic system resembles the model which has been much more fully developed in Yugoslavia and which will be described briefly later. It might be more exact to say that the Yugoslav system is a more clearly defined and recognized model towards which the Polish economic system is oriented, even though important differences do exist and the similarities are not admitted or even fully realized. As in Yugoslavia, but unlike the current situation in Czechoslovakia, the peasants of Poland have been allowed to escape from the collective farms. In industry, the escape from state authority through the control of industry by workers' councils has proved quite unworkable. Immediately after the 1956 revolution, the managers of industrial plants were elected by the workers' councils. At present, the workers' councils are supposed to have a veto power over the appointment of managers and to be able to obtain the dismissal of managers of whom they disapprove. However, they may not legally demand the replacement of a manager for acts which, even though unpopular with the workers, are required by law. Interviews with government officials and with management personnel of industrial plants indicated that there was a wide "no-man's land" of overlapping authority in this area, and that considerable confusion and conflict exist. While I was in Poland, Gomulka made a public statement designed to restore the authority of the manager and to set up a tripartite body with which he could work, consisting of representatives of the workers' councils, the trade unions and the Communist Party. Until this change was made the manager often found himself harassed by separate and often conflicting pressures from each of the three.

An effort is being made to break out of the embrace of the huge centralized, bureaucratic planning of the economy which permitted almost no autonomy or local initiative. The statement of economic policy approved by the Polish Communist Party, and published by the Economic Model Commission of the Economic Council,[2] expresses the intention of allowing market prices to reflect costs more closely and to play a greater role in the allocation of resources. Yet the yearning for something more like a free market economy is matched by a wish to retain centralized and authoritative planning. Conflicting

[2] "Theses Concerning Some Lines for the Change of the Economic Model." The mimeographed English translation was given to me in Warsaw in May 1958.

For an analytical discussion of the problems involved in combining a form of market price system with centralized planning, see Oskar Lange, "The Political Economy of Socialism," a lecture given November 18, 1957, published in mimeograph by the Polish Institute of International Affairs, and "Some Problems Relating to the Polish Road to Socialism," Polonia Publishing House, Warsaw, 1957.

statements—nearly schizophrenic—run throughout this statement of policy.

The "Theses" state: "Long-range planning, connected with the principle of continued correction of the assumption of long-range development of the economy, is considered a factor of special importance," and later, "The national long-range and annual plans constitute directive acts, binding for all authorities, which control the nation's economy." There is immediately added, however, the admonition that "The directive character of the national economic plans does not mean that their targets should necessarily be transmitted to enterprises as strictly obligatory plan-orders." On the one hand, "The operation of an enterprise is guided by the principle of profitability [but] with full concern to plan-orders, if any." A wide "sphere of independence of an enterprise" is set forth which includes "administration of capital resources," "the planning of production based upon estimated sales and supply possibilities [but] with the obligation, however, to conform the enterprise plan to plan-orders whenever they occur." A number of other main fields of action within this sphere of independence of an enterprise are also listed. Nevertheless, "The general manager of an enterprise is officially responsible for the fulfillment of the binding plan-orders." A somewhat similar conflict in principle with respect to the authority of the manager of the enterprise and the workers' councils is shown in the "Theses."

Poland is much more closely tied to the Soviet economic model and to Soviet political and military power than is Yugoslavia. Yet the very fact of the revolution of October 1956 has meant both that there is greater freedom to criticize the Gomulka regime and that greater criticism occurs than in the case of the Tito regime in Yugoslavia. This is true, paradoxically enough, in spite of the fact that there has recently been more overt governmental action to restrain published criticism in Poland than in Yugoslavia. While the strongest source of authority in Poland is the Communist Party, the governmental, economic and labor union bureaucracy is not virtually identical with it, as is true in Russia, Czechoslovakia and even in Yugoslavia.

It is not difficult at the present time to meet with Poles officially and unofficially. American officials meet with Polish officials in Warsaw just about as freely as they do with Yugoslav officials in Belgrade. This is in contrast with the situation in Moscow and in Prague. I attended several social occasions at which high-ranking Polish officials were present. One such official accepted my invitation to lunch. I had a long private conversation with a professor who had been in prison for years under the pre-Gomulka regime, as had his wife. He was not afraid to criticize the Gomulka government, although he undoubtedly depended upon me not to quote him. It was possible to arrange to visit Polish factories and to talk with Polish peasants in the countryside. All this represents a significant relaxation of the police state.

It was possible to discuss the problems of economic organization with some Polish officials, although not with complete freedom. They were a long way from accepting the doctrine stated to me later by several Yugoslav officials that the state is the natural enemy of socialism.

Thus Poland presented a picture of a country much more in ferment than I was to observe Yugoslavia to be, with considerable exercise of intellectual freedom to criticize in spite of renewed governmental restraints. Yet there has not been nearly so much positive intellectual achievement in the development of the theory and practice of the relationships among the economy, liberty and the state as I was later to find in Yugoslavia. This may, however, be primarily a matter of time lag, since the break between Stalin and Tito took place in 1948, eight years before the revolution in Poland.

With unimportant exceptions, the Polish Communists still maintain a one-party monopoly of political power although there are reported to be some conflicts between the responsibilities of government officials to the Polish state and to the Communist Party. Whether there is any democracy at all within the Polish Communist Party, I was no more able to ascertain than in the case of the Yugoslav Party. That no substantial degree of democracy exists in Russia or in Czechoslovakia is, of course, not in doubt. Recent measures taken by the government to prevent publication of critical comment show how far short of full intellectual freedom the present situation in Poland is. Yet the opportunity for oral criticism and discussion which does exist in substantial degree is a precious improvement over pre-Gomulka times. It afforded a favorable contrast to the situation in the other countries with collectivized economies which I visited in 1958.

Whether representative government and full personal liberty might gradually develop in Poland while state ownership of the means of production is retained is uncertain. So long as Poland is bound to Soviet Russia to the extent which is now true, this almost certainly will not happen. In the absence of this quasi-dependent relationship, much the same factors which operate in Yugoslavia would determine the outcome. Consequently, this problem will be considered more analytically in discussing the economic and political system of Yugoslavia.

THE U.S.S.R.

I found that there was very little parallel between the changes in the economic system which I had seen in Poland and was to observe in Yugoslavia and those which had taken place in Soviet Russia since my last visit in 1956. However, no one was quite sure what the decentralization of industrial controls proclaimed by Khrushchev had amounted to. Certainly it had not meant the dismantling of the central planning organ as had happened in Yugoslavia. Indeed, everyone was agreed that the elimination of 143 industrial ministries on the Union and Republican levels had meant the handing over of some of their functions to the central planning organization, with a concomitant expansion of its personnel and importance. A number of industrial institutes formerly attached to those ministries were still in existence, with their permanent status still undetermined. A hasty attempt had been made to set up a smaller number of sales and supply agencies to take the place of the complicated network that had operated under the defunct ministries, but here too the situation was still in flux.

Skeptics claimed that there had been almost no dispersal of the economic bureaucracy either to other occupations or to staff the *sovnarkhoz* in the 105 economic regions newly set up. It was clear, too, that adequate consideration had not been

given to the basic problems which inevitably arise if local
autonomy is to take the place of a centralized and authoritative
direction of an economy in the absence of individual or corporate ownership and a market price economy. If prices are
no longer to be set by a central authority, who is to set them?
Is competition between plants in the different areas supposed
to exist? If prices are set locally, may they be set to maximize
the returns to the particular region? Much the same question
arises with respect to wages. Are wages to be allowed to absorb
all the increased income due to higher prices, if these are permitted? Are regions to be required to compete with one another on a price basis? Are regions to be permitted to retain
additions to capital resources out of profits for their own purposes? May goods in short supply be retained in the region
where they are produced, regardless of the needs of other
regions? All these questions and a multitude of others have
already arisen since the decentralization program was put into
effect. Many of them have not yet been authoritatively answered. This situation was in sharp contrast with what I was
to find in Yugoslavia. There some of the same problems have
arisen but more consideration was given to the basic questions
and a number of remedial measures have been taken to solve
the problems or at least ameliorate the difficulties inherent in
them. It is only fair to say, however, that the changed economic system has been undergoing development in Yugoslavia
for some eight years instead of little more than a year as in
Soviet Russia.

While I was in Moscow a previously issued decree of the
Presidium of the Supreme Soviet was published, denouncing
some of the practices which had arisen by which local interests were being served instead of the interests of the whole
country. Dire punishment was threatened if these practices
did not cease.[3] The issuance of this order, while it indicated
that serious problems were arising in connection with the program of decentralization, did afford an answer to those who
argued that nothing had really been done to carry out decentralization. It became quite plain to me that the decentralization program had almost no resemblance to the partial control

[3] *Pravda*, May 19, 1958.

of industrial enterprises by the workers' councils which had come about by revolutionary action in Poland, or the turning over of industrial enterprises to be run, at least nominally, by workers' councils as had been done by formal action of the Yugoslav government. Although Khrushchev at one time talked of the appointment of trade union leaders to the councils of the newly formed economic regions, little of importance had apparently been done along this line and there was no apparent intention to provide for any direct worker control of industrial enterprises. The official line of the Soviet Communist Party has always been that since the Soviet state was set up as a dictatorship of the proletariat and since the Communist Party claims to be the leader of the working class, no possible conflict of interest between the state bureaucracy and the workers can exist. Consequently, it is still rigidly maintained that direct worker control over industry is unnecessary and would be disruptive of discipline now as it was when it was tried out in early revolutionary times. The changed Yugoslav system has been denounced as revisionist and syndicalist.

Quite apart, however, from any effort to provide for labor control of industry through the decentralization program, a decree of the Presidium of the Supreme Soviet of July 15, 1958 was published in the Soviet press which indicated an intention to restore the factory, plant and local trade union committees to a role which they had not played for some thirty years. Under Stalin, the primary role of the trade union committees had become that of assisting management in requiring the workers to increase production. Under this new decree, submitted to the Presidium by the Council of Trade Unions, the role of the trade union committees was redefined to include many of the protective functions relating to the interests of workers vis-à-vis those of plant managements which trade unions in capitalistic countries traditionally perform. The committees were also to continue to be consulted in connection with the production and capital construction plans of industrial plants and other economic enterprises. While the new decree does not appreciably increase the authority of labor union managements over industrial production, it tacitly recognizes the possible divergence of the interests of the workers and the managing bureaucracy of industry and, if put into effect, would represent a notable reversal of position. It is impossible, of course, to forecast how and to what extent this decree will be implemented.

In agriculture, compulsory deliveries of farm products from the individual plots of members of the collective farms have been abolished. The intention to abolish machine tractor stations and to permit collective farms to own their own tractors and other farm machinery has been announced and the process of transfer begun. In June 1958 the intention to discontinue compulsory deliveries at low prices to the state on the part of collective farms and the payment of higher prices for amounts above the compulsory quota was announced. Yet the exact meaning of the announcement remained unclear since there were still references to "guaranteed deliveries." In general these developments in agriculture, particularly the announced elimination of the machine tractor stations, seemed to represent some relaxation of outside control of collective farms by the state. At the same time, however, the output of collective farms continued to shrink in relation to that of state farms and it seemed that most collective farms might eventually be turned into state farms. This would mean that instead of "shares" agricultural workers would receive wages just as do workers in industry.[4] The change to the state farm type of organization would mean that the control of collective farms by the general meeting of the members and the election of the manager by the meeting, which in any case were always largely a matter of form, would altogether cease. The manager of a state farm now has the same authoritative status as the manager of an industrial plant.

The availability of consumer goods seemed to have improved somewhat since my previous visit in the summer of 1956. Prices were about the same. Minimum wages had been

---

[4] Benediktov, Minister of State Farms, in 1956 had commented to me upon the higher productivity of labor on state farms and the advantages of a known wage in the state farms over the uncertain "shares" of members of collective farms. He offered this as one of the reasons why the number of collective farms was diminishing in relation to the number of state farms.

increased somewhat, but the general level of wages had only increased very slightly. However, the standard of living in 1956 had represented a substantial improvement over that of the prewar period. An impressive number of apartment houses had been built in Moscow since 1956, although there was still a serious housing shortage and people lived in miserable circumstances in the older houses. There did not appear to have been so much housing construction outside of Moscow, but my opportunities for observation outside the capital on my most recent trip were limited. Maintenance of buildings continued to be bad but showed some signs of improvement. There were, moreover, significant exceptions to this poor maintenance, notably the Moscow and Leningrad subways and some of the Black Sea sanatoria. The "wedding cake" architecture of the postwar skyscrapers, government office buildings and hotels is neither functional nor graceful.

The Soviet success in building an industrialized society which operates under strict discipline and with large material rewards for individual productivity once more impressed me as it had in 1956. This is nowhere more evident than in the educational system. A regime in which the teachers are protected against potential or actual hostility of pupils and parents to the heavy work loads prescribed by higher authority, and one which is not responsible to either a national or a local electorate, can demand far more from its students than can a free society. The authoritative character of instruction in Soviet schools undoubtedly limits the development of new ideas, but the net result cannot be adequately weighed.

The remarkable skill demonstrated by the Moiseyev Dance Company on its visit to the United States is fully matched by the performances in Moscow of the Bolshoi Ballet and by the spectacular rendition of the Polovetzian dance in the opera "Prince Igor" or the Polish court dance in "Ivan Susanin." This near-perfection of technique is not entirely confined to Moscow; it is true of the Georgian Ballet in Tiflis as well. It apparently reflects incessant drill of personnel and refinement of technique rather than creativeness. Russian ballet, of course, was the best in the world in prerevolutionary times. Nevertheless, the impressiveness of the present-day ballet does seem to parallel developments in Soviet education, in athletics and to some extent in industry.

Thus the Soviet regime has succeeded to an impressive degree in transforming the illiterate, undisciplined and generally slovenly Russian masses into a people who no longer are characterized by the traditional *"nichevo"*—"nothing matters too much anyhow." Russian workers no longer spit out sunflower seed husks and drop cigarette butts in all public places. As a result Moscow is decidedly a cleaner city than New York. The demonstration effect of grandiose and extremely expensive public facilities such as the Moscow and Leningrad subways has been important in bringing about this change. Public facilities are kept immaculate not only by penalizing offenders but also by providing for unceasing maintenance. The respect for orders and regulations which the Stalinist terror instilled in the population undoubtedly has played a major role also.

The Russian people's fear of the secret police spread in Stalinist times to include a fear of the regular police as well. It is some measure of the relaxation of the terror in Russia since Stalin's death that there has apparently been a substantial increase in ordinary crime. Black market rubles were by no means unknown when I lived in Moscow in 1929–30 and later; but all Russians knew that it was mortally dangerous to engage in such transactions. The supply of cheap rubles which the newspaper correspondents depended upon in those days to keep their living costs within bounds was generally understood to come in in the diplomatic pouches of some of the small countries. During my most recent visit I was accosted in Moscow by two "students" who offered me rubles for dollars at a rate double the official rate for tourists—an offer which I did not, of course, accept. The black marketeers showed no great fear in approaching me to make the offer even though I was walking down one of the main streets. On another day, I observed just outside a well-known hotel in the center of Moscow a strapping young man, doubtless a black marketeer, pursued by a policeman through the crowded streets. The policeman was lustily blowing his whistle, but his quarry did not stop until he was trapped between his pursuer and another policeman. Perhaps this was only a negative coincidence, but I had never witnessed a similar incident during any of my previous stays in Moscow over the years.[5]

Finally, there has been a substantial tightening of the controls on discussion and on publication since the momentary relaxation following Khrushchev's denunciation of Stalin in early 1956. The tightening of these controls apparently reflects the renewed internal struggle for power which resulted in the downfall of Malenkov, Molotov, Shepilov, Kaganovich and, soon after, Zhukov. It also reflects the reaction to events in Hungary and Poland. As these lines are written the tragic news of the secret trial and execution of former Premier Nagy, General Pal Maleter and two associates as a long-delayed aftermath of the Hungarian revolution underlines the continuing violent character of the Soviet system.

Nevertheless, crosscurrents exist. The Legislative Proposals Committee of the Council of the Union and the Council of Nationalities of the Supreme Soviet published in June 1958 for public discussion and comment the drafts of proposed "Basic Principles of Criminal Legislation of the U.S.S.R. and the Union Republics" and "Principles of Criminal Trial Procedure of the U.S.S.R. and the Union Republics." They provide a number of important changes which would protect the individual against the arbitrary power of government.

These measures for the protection of civil rights seem designed to prevent arbitrary arrest, punishment for "crimes" which have no statutory existence and the like. If adopted by the Supreme Soviet and actually enforced, they would represent an almost immeasurable advance. However, it must be remembered that the present Soviet Constitution "guarantees" freedom of speech, of the press, of assembly and meetings, the inviolability of the person, the inviolability of the homes of citizens and the secrecy of correspondence. All these guarantees were meaningless in Stalin's day and to some degree still remain so. What effect adoption of the new drafts would have thus remains questionable.

[5] It is not meant to suggest that the ordinary crime rate is higher in the Soviet Union than in the United States; it may, in fact, be lower.

CZECHOSLOVAKIA

It was, of course, not surprising to find that there had been no developments in Czechoslovakia to match those in Poland and Yugoslavia. But it was a surprise to find the standard of living in Czechoslovakia considerably higher than in Russia. This was no doubt due largely to the fact that Czechoslovakia had been an industrialized country before the present Communist regime came to power. The far superior housing, particularly noticeable in the smaller cities, was a survival from pre-Communist times. The more attractive shop windows in Prague, the greatly superior restaurants, the better dress of the male population and the chic appearance of the women indicated only that Czechoslovakia had for generations been associated with the West. Nevertheless, it was a shock to find that a Communist country which was more Stalinist than Soviet Russia was not inevitably grayer and grimmer, but on the contrary seemed gayer and more lively.

It is doubtful whether the majority of the Czechoslovak people would agree with the description of themselves as gay and lively under present circumstances. The pressure upon the former bourgeoisie and the intelligentsia who have had connections with the West is very severe. Many of them are now working in steel mills as common laborers or have been sent to work in the forests.

Not all Czechs were willing to accept as signs of plenty the displays of pastries and other foods in bakeries and delicatessens or of consumer goods in department stores and specialty shops. Some complained that the products remained in the shop windows because prices were so high that people could not afford to buy them. Others complained that there was little on which money could be spent, and that this was the only reason why people could live on the current level of wages and salaries. These statements are hardly consistent. Moreover, people *were* buying the goods on display. On the basis of sample pricing of goods in shops and of estimates of average wages, the standard of living in Prague was definitely above that in Moscow.

Czechs were by no means free to discuss their real or exaggerated complaints about the standard of living with foreigners. At a little restaurant where we had been having lunch for several days, our waiter one day in a sort of desperate undertone claimed that the Czech people were only waiting for rescue by the West. "The West must come to our rescue! We live so badly and we live in such a state of fright. We have no freedom! The West will come, will it not?" The grave risk to the waiter in voicing these sentiments even in a whisper is well illustrated by my instinctive reaction as an economist. I was immediately tempted to argue that on the basis of statistics the Czech population could not be so badly off as he claimed. Fortunately for the waiter, long experience in Soviet Russia made me stop short of the ghastly absurdity of trying to carry on a statistical controversy in an undertone.

I found that there had been some very slight effort at increasing the autonomy of industrial plants in deference to Khrushchev's program of decentralization of industrial control in Soviet Russia. There was nothing, however, to indicate any movement whatever in the direction of greater direct control of industry by the workers of particular plants as had happened in Poland and Yugoslavia. Neither was there the slightest evidence of any recognition of the fundamental conflict between the liberty of the individual and the power of the state which I was to find freely acknowledged, at least on the theoretical level, when I arrived in Yugoslavia. It must be said, however, that in the one industrial plant in Prague which I was able to visit, working conditions appeared good, employees did not seem to be working under strain and relations with management seemed to be relaxed.

In sharp contrast with the situation in Poland and Yugoslavia, the collectivization of agriculture was being forcefully pushed by the Party-state authorities. During the past year the relative importance of collective farms had increased by some 50 per cent. At the present time something like 70 per cent of agriculture is carried on either on collective farms or on state farms. It is intended to reach at least 90 per cent by 1960. Collective farms are of much greater importance in the economy than state farms. While there is no doubt that severe pressure is being exerted upon the remaining individual peasants to force them to join collectives, it also appears to be true that the collective farms have been more successful than they were in Poland and Yugoslavia. Consequently, peasant resistance to collectivization does not seem to be so fierce. I cannot, however, be sure of the accuracy of this impression.

The usually far superior housing of Czech peasants compared with peasant housing in Soviet Russia, Poland or Yugoslavia has little to do with collectivization, of course, since it is a heritage from the past. The same is doubtless true of the superior tillage which characterizes Czech agriculture. Yet on the inadequate evidence afforded by a visit to two collective farms, both within a range of one hundred kilometers from Prague, collective farms appear to operate with considerable efficiency and to furnish a reasonably satisfactory income to the members. These two farms were probably more profitable than the average because of the relatively high fertility of their soil and their proximity to the Prague market. There was some evidence of more control by the peasant membership of the collectives than I had ever observed in Soviet Russia. In one of the collectives it was evident from the dress of the manager, from the calluses on his hands and from his manner that he was actually a working farmer. I found it possible to believe that he had really been freely elected by the membership of the collective farm.

YUGOSLAVIA

Before visiting Yugoslavia I was extremely doubtful whether the economic and political system of that country which had allegedly undergone fundamental change was in fact basically different from that of Soviet Russia. The recurring conflicts first between Stalin and Tito and more recently between Khrushchev and Tito had unquestionably been accompanied by the development of a Yugoslav economy no longer subsidiary to that of Soviet Russia. If, however, it had simply taken the form of a Yugoslav national soviet system, it would have had little interest for me, regardless of its significance in the international power struggle. After my stay in Yugoslavia I no longer doubted that the economic system had undergone changes, and that it now differs radically from that of Soviet Russia. These changes began with the setting up of workers' councils in 1948–49, following the break with Stalin. Further important changes were introduced in 1952–53, and others are still being made.

The break between Tito and Stalin was, indeed, an important factor in initiating changes in the Yugoslav economic system. It allowed Yugoslav Communists to personalize in the figure of Stalin those aspects of the Soviet system which had profoundly disturbed them, without repudiating Lenin and the October Revolution. Repudiation of the Soviet October Revolution was impossible for the Yugoslav Communist Party, since its own domination of the economic and political system was based upon similar revolutionary violence. The increasing bitterness of the current conflict between Tito and Khrushchev has gone far to remove the remaining inhibitions which Yugoslav Communists had felt about developing an economic system which deviated from Soviet Russia's. The virtual cancellation of Soviet loans to Yugoslavia while I was in Belgrade noticeably strengthened the decision to depart from the Soviet model.

Indeed, the Communist League of Yugoslavia (as the Communist Party now calls itself) has announced its determination to restore to the mass of the workers themselves the control of industrial plants and state farms which the state took over upon the successful seizure of power by Tito and his followers. The removal of the state from the control of industry and the substitution of worker control is visualized by Yugoslav Communists as that very process of the "withering away" of the temporarily necessary state after the dictatorship of the proletariat which was foreseen by Marx, Engels and Lenin. Whether this effort to have the mass of workers take over industry has any substantial chance of success is doubtful. It may even be that the readiness of Yugoslav Communist leaders to take this step is dependent upon the workers wanting to do no more than what the Communist leaders think they should. There can be no doubt, however, that the structural form of the economy has been basically altered by this effort to take industry out of the hands of the state and place it in the hands of the workers.

The conviction that state management of industry is not consistent with socialism was repeatedly stated to me by Yugoslav officials who were also Party members. As one official put it, "We came to the conclusion that the state is the enemy of socialism." Another said, "We had no doubt that a centrally planned and authoritatively directed economic system would work. We saw that it had worked in Russia. In a sense, it had worked with us. But we became convinced that it would only work at the greatest cost to personal freedom." The 1958 Program of the League of Communists expresses a similar view: "Our experience, as well as the experience of other socialist countries, has shown that the management of the economy and of the whole of social life by way of the state apparatus exclusively, leads perforce to greater centralization of power, to an ever closer merging of the state and party apparatus, to their further strengthening, whereby they tend to become independent and impose themselves as a force over and above society."[6] This is in complete conflict with the position of the Communist Party of Soviet Russia, which does not admit the possibility of conflict of interest between the workers and the state controlled by the Communist Party.

With the purpose of removing the state from the management of the economy, the Yugoslav government proceeded to jettison the whole system of a state planned and directed economy. Expressed in its simplest and most extreme form, the intent has been to set up a competitive, free market economy but with collective ownership instead of private ownership of the means of production—a sort of capitalism without individual stockholders. The institutional structure and working rules by which this end has been pursued are fascinating to an economist. There are even some theoretical resemblances to the *soziale Marktwirtschaft* of the neo-liberals of present-day Germany and Austria.

In line with this objective, individual industrial plants in Yugoslavia are organized as "working collectives." These are

---

[6] Draft Programme of the League of Communists of Yugoslavia, Belgrade, March 1958, p. 23 (mimeographed English translation given to me in Belgrade in June 1958). This Draft Programme of 176 pages is a most important document in the development of modern Marxist theory.

controlled, in principle, by the workers themselves, through elected workers' councils, which in turn elect a smaller management committee that works with the manager. The manager is hired by a committee representing both the workers' council and the local commune in which the plant is located. In principle, each workers' collective produces and sells its goods for the best prices it can get in competition with the workers' collectives of plants producing similar products. Total wages earned by the working collective depend upon the cost of production, the volume of production and the selling price. Wage rates within the plant are determined by the workers' councils, within the limits set by the national trade union organizations.

No sooner had the working collectives been set up than it became apparent that it would not be either feasible or equitable to allow the workers in a particular plant or a state farm to profit by the more productive capital equipment one plant might have as compared with another, or the more fertile land one state farm might have as compared with another. Consequently, an interest charge is made on the capital value of a plant's assets which is paid to the state. Similarly, a rental charge is made for the use of agricultural land by state farms and the use of mines by state mining enterprises. The theory is that the working collective of a particular plant or state farm is only the operator of the particular enterprise. Society as a whole "owns" the assets.

But what is to prevent the workers' collective of a particular plant from profiting by a monopoly position? First of all, there are anti-monopoly regulations which are supposed to prevent cartels and agreements in restraint of trade. In fact, some working collectives have tried to arrive at illegal "gentlemen's agreements" to prevent "capitalistic cutthroat competition." In spite of the regulations attempting to enforce competition, various "working collectives" have found themselves in a quasi-monopolistic position in being able to raise their incomes more easily than others. As a result, a whole series of measures, in addition to the payment of interest on assets and rent on land and mines, has been introduced to prevent "undue profits" or to prevent such profits from being paid out as wages. Some of these measures are intended primarily to prevent the workers in one factory from getting wages "unduly" higher than those paid for similar work in other factories, or to prevent the workers in marketing enterprises from benefiting at the expense of those who are producers in the more limited meaning of the term.[7] Such measures include the governmental fixing of prices on a limited list of basic industrial commodities, such as coal, steel, electric power and the most important food products. They include also the taxation of profits and the setting up of a whole series of reserve funds for the individual plant into which profits are paid instead of being disbursed as wages. There is also a regulation that prices of goods produced by any plant cannot be increased without obtaining a permit from the federal price office,[8] that the commune may refuse to allow profits to be disbursed as wage bonuses if these are due to price increases rather than to increased productivity and, finally, that annual additions to wages out of profits may not exceed two months' wages.

Some of these measures are a quite logical part of a competitive economic system, such as the requirement that interest be paid to the state upon the assets of industrial plants, that rent be paid for land held by state farms and that rental payments be made by the richer mines. Others, however, reflect a shrewd unwillingness to follow blindly a policy of depending upon uncontrolled competitive processes to govern prices, wages and investment in a modern industrial economy. Almost all of the measures which limit "undue" payments of wages out of profits limit the incentive effect of allowing wages in each plant to depend upon the valuation which a free market would place upon the productivity of that plant. Almost all these measures also constitute a form of compulsory savings and investment.

There are other means also designed for this purpose, such as the 10 per cent payroll tax which is set aside for housing

[7] Strikes among miners have occurred in protest against the payment of wage bonuses as high as 100 per cent in the agencies marketing coal. Such extravagant payments can no longer be made.

[8] The newspaper *Vjesnik* of Zagreb of May 23, 1958 carries an account of the trials of three industrial enterprises charged with illegal raising of prices. One enterprise was fined 400,000 dinars and the manager was fined 200,000 dinars. A second enterprise was fined 300,000 dinars and the case against the third was continued.

construction. In addition to the legally required withholding of profits from the wage fund of each working collective, the Communist leadership in the workers' councils continually tries to induce the workers' representatives to withhold as large an amount of profits as possible from the wages fund, even above the amounts legally required, in order that such withheld funds may be used for public purposes rather than for personal consumption by the workers.

Yugoslav government officials frankly claim that it is not possible at this time to have fully democratic control of the state and the economy in so poor a country. For economic growth and development, it is absolutely necessary to have much higher saving and investment than would be possible under full democracy. There can be no doubt that a high rate of saving and capital investment is taking place, accompanied by a high rate of economic growth. At the same time, there is some evidence that the profits withheld from wages are also going into the construction of unnecessarily elaborate administrative buildings in industry, on the state farms and at all levels of government.

With the development of the new type of partly autonomous, partly competitive industry the former system of centralized, authoritative planning was wiped out. No longer is there an elaborate central plan, with the various factories, mines, state farms and other economic enterprises assigned planned quotas to be fulfilled. No "plan orders" are issued. The state planning organization now only sets forth general objectives and lines of development. Monetary, fiscal and credit controls are primarily depended upon to implement this type of planning. However, a large measure of control over investment is provided by the state investment banking system, through which a large part of the funds withheld from wages by the state are disbursed.

The dismantling of the huge bureaucracy by which the state previously operated the economy has been largely superseded by another large bureaucracy needed under the new system of "operation of the economy by the workers themselves." There is a system of dual legislative bodies, starting with the communes and going up through the republics to the federal government. At each level of government there is a council elected by all citizens which legislates on political matters and a Council of Producers elected by producers only which legislates on economic matters. These are connected by a People's Committee representing both councils. Each of the councils is served by numerous committees designed to insure maximum popular participation in the actual process of governing. This insures that a large number of citizens devote a vast number of man-hours to the performance of such duties. The system of self-government in industry through the workers' councils and the Management Committee has a similar purpose and a similar result.

The situation is very different from that in Poland, where there have been serious and even bitter conflicts between the workers' councils and the managers of plants. Communist leaders in Yugoslavia say that their real problem has been to develop continued and serious worker interest in the workers' councils. Indeed, it may well prove as difficult to induce active participation of the majority of the workers of a plant in its affairs as it is to induce individual stockholders of American corporations to attend stockholders' meetings or to induce the membership of American trade unions to participate actively in union affairs.

That the Communist League dominates the whole economic and political structure of the country is beyond question. Although only some 25 per cent of industrial workers are Communists, about 50 per cent of the membership of the workers' councils are League members. Almost 100 per cent of plant managers are members of the League. The process by which the Communist League decides who is to be appointed or "elected" to what office in the economy or in the government is a closely held secret in Yugoslavia, just as it always has been in Soviet Russia. There is no way of knowing whether anything like democratic processes operate within the League itself. Communist leaders, government officials and industrial managers, largely overlapping categories, were sometimes reluctant to admit the role of the Communist League in the "control of industry by the workers." Under persistent questioning, the very important role of the League was admitted. However, it was insisted that there was no direction from above and that in the workers' councils, for example,

Communists voted simply as socially conscious individuals rather than as disciplined members of a Party cell. I frankly doubt that this is so.

The significance for the whole world of a Communist country in which the ruling class has come to recognize the state as at least the potential enemy of socialism cannot be overestimated. This significance is all the greater when a comprehensive economic system, fundamentally different from the Soviet system, has been set up with the purpose of removing the state from the operation of the economy. In my judgment the system functions with an impressive degree of success, measured both by the volume of production and by the success in preventing overt industrial conflict.

Paradoxically, what is not at all certain is whether the changed economic system really does what it was intended to do, that is, provide for the removal of state control and the implementation of industrial democracy through direct worker control of industrial plants. In the first place, as has been pointed out, industrial democracy may well be a utopian goal, impossible to make really effective. In the second place, control by the state may still exist through the Communist League's control of the economic and political apparatus. The Communist League in itself, like all other ruling Communist parties, constitutes a formidable state. One might say that the Communist League is now the state, which operates the economy through a new form of economic organization.

It may be that the whole system could not function without the monopoly of political power held by the Communist League or without at least the benevolent influence of the members of the Communist League exerted at all levels in the control and management of the economy. The explicit recognition by the Yugoslav Communist League of the dangers of permanent centralized management of the economy by the state, of the evils of bureaucracy and of the importance of personal liberty means, however, that an ideological foundation has been provided for those who would fight against these evils and dangers. Furthermore, the creation of actual machinery through which the protests of workers against managerial tyranny might be expressed appears to afford some protection against such tyranny developing.

I am limited in trying to make an appraisal of the new Yugo-slav economic system by the fact that Yugoslavia is still a po-lice state. True, these extraordinary police powers are primarily exercised against Yugoslav Stalinists and against those sus-pected of adherence to former Yugoslav governments. There is nothing in present-day Yugoslavia to correspond to the ter-ror of Stalin's day in Soviet Russia or to the terror in present-day Hungary. One can carry on most interesting and fruitful discussions of the relations among the economy, liberty and the state with Yugoslav Communist leaders and governmental officials. Contrary to the situation in Soviet Russia, these lead-ers and officials are accessible to foreigners for such discussions. Indeed, Yugoslav officials were so friendly and helpful that I found it difficult to maintain an appropriately objective at-titude.

Elections are not free in Yugoslavia. Neither is there free-dom to publish critical comment on governmental policy or with respect to important Communist leaders. The press and all means of publication are closely controlled. One hears only the most limited and guarded criticism of the government among the populace, though, in fact, I had little opportunity to hear such criticism if anyone had felt like giving expres-sion to it.

I could never forget that Yugoslavia is the country of the "New Class" about which Djilas wrote his book. Djilas is still in prison because of his criticism of the regime. His former high position and personal closeness to Tito did not protect him against the power of the state. Indeed, they seemed to aggravate the offenses with which he was charged. Dedier, who supported Djilas, is not in prison but is living in poverty, ex-cluded from all employment.

The "cult of personality," the term used by Khrushchev to account for the "mistakes" of Stalin, still flourishes in Yugo-slavia. A few days after I left Belgrade, Tito gave a public ad-dress in the mining town of Labin. In response, the crowd set up a rhythmic chant, in well-drilled unison, "Tito hero! We belong to Tito—Tito belongs to us!"[9] Tito has a number of residences at his disposal. Besides his well-known retreat on Brioni Island, he lives in one palace in Belgrade and has an-

[9] *New York Times*, June 16, 1958.

other which he uses principally as a guest house for distinguished visitors. Driving through the residential area once occupied by the wealthy and by officials of former governments, I asked a resident of Belgrade who it was that now lived in these villas. He gave me a wry look and replied, "Whom do you suppose? The New Class, of course!" Yet it is not a fact that all such villas are occupied by the New Class. There are too many circumstantial accounts of eight or ten families, often formerly poor peasants from Montenegro or Macedonia, living, to the detriment of the plumbing system, in one villa formerly occupied by a single bourgeois family. When I had lunch with a Yugoslav couple high in the councils of the state and the Communist League, I found the villa in which they lived comfortable and furnished in unusually good taste but not lavishly. There was apparently one house servant and a chauffeur. Since both my host and his wife had heavy official duties, it would appear that this was close to the minimum standard of living necessary for the most effective performance of their functions. Yet in a country as poor as Yugoslavia this level of living was far above the average.

Thus, to an important degree, the higher level of living of the New Class reflects no more than the standard which any ruling class must maintain in order to function efficiently. Its superiority to their own inevitably shocks industrial workers and peasants who were told by the former revolutionists now comprising the New Class that a higher living standard was the special perquisite of the capitalist exploiters and that it would disappear with the overthrow of capitalism. A regime which takes power under the name of socialism is thus likely to find that it cannot permit free elections, at least until the potential voters have become accustomed to the higher level of living of the New Class. Without free elections, the danger always exists that the New Class will abstract for itself out of the national income a higher standard of living than is functionally necessary.

Yugoslav salaries, both of state officials and of plant managers, are, by all accounts, kept quite low. The salary of a plant or state farm manager is claimed to be no more than three or three and a half times the average wage of workers. Indeed, it is claimed that some skilled workers on piece rates occasionally receive higher wages than the plant manager. Communist leaders commonly maintained that the differential between the salaries of managers and the wages of workers is too low. However, the greater part of the compensation of the ruling class in Yugoslavia consists of "fringe benefits." These usually include a car with chauffeur and sometimes living quarters and servants, plus other "expense account" items.

Evidently stung both by the publication of Milovan Djilas' book and by labor unrest, the Executive Committee of the Yugoslav League of Communists in early 1958 denounced the widespread abuse of power and the privileges of office by bureaucrats of state and industry. The Committee cited as instances the purchase of expensive motor cars by factory directors and their use for personal pleasure, lavish spending for entertainment, the bestowing of the most desirable living quarters—allegedly to stimulate production—on personal favorites who had performed no real service, and other similar practices. In many factories and other economic enterprises the wishes of the elected representatives of the workers were disregarded. Workers who criticized such arbitrary actions were often transferred or even fired.

The construction of luxury apartments was banned and the use of official cars for personal purposes was brought under regulation.[10] Thus the rulers of a totalitarian society may at times try to limit the power and privileges of the administrative ranks below them, just as the top management of corporations in a capitalistic society may try to limit the perquisites of corporation executives of lower rank.

My conclusion is that the "New Class" in Yugoslavia in setting up a new type of economic system is carrying out an experiment of profound importance to the whole world. This new economic system has already demonstrated its ability to carry on industrial production with substantial success. The "New Class" has declared through the 1958 Draft Programme of the League of Communists of Yugoslavia that "Legal order in Yugoslavia protects, and must protect, any citizen from the arbitrary action of any social factor or any state body."[11] The

[10] See dispatches from Belgrade in the *New York Times,* January 25, March 1 and March 16, *et passim.*
[11] Draft Programme, p. 125.

League of Communists also considers ". . . proclamation of an absolute monopoly of the Communist Party to political power as a universal and 'perpetual' principle of dictatorship of the proletariat and of socialist development as an untenable dogma."[12]

Whether the new Yugoslav economic system can be operated without intolerable interference with the liberties of individuals will depend in large degree upon whether the Communist League can and will carry out these expressed principles. The Communist League still expresses its devotion to the doctrine of the "withering away of the state," and believes that the new economic system is a giant step in this direction. Personally, I do not believe that the new system can bring about the withering away of the state. That is impossible for any modern industrialized economy.

The results of the Yugoslav attempt, and to a lesser extent that of the present Polish government, to reduce the power of centralized autocratic bureaucracies over the economy are still inconclusive. If either should demonstrate that a state which came into existence by revolutionary violence, dedicated to the establishment of a collectivist economy, can operate such an economy without an intolerable degree of limitation of personal liberty while developing a form of government which is workably representative, it would be an immense service to mankind.

Until now there seemed little hope that a totalitarian economic and political system could ever evolve through internal processes into a system with the kind of personal liberty which exists in the quasi-capitalistic countries of the West. This hope may not be fulfilled, since trends in Yugoslavia and Poland may be reversed by events. Moreover, with the best of will on the part of the leaders of any form of economic and political system, it is not going to be easy to preserve personal liberties when, owing to the nature of modern industrial society, the power of the state must be great and widespread. Yet the recognition of the problem by the leaders of states which were previously totalitarian and the actual setting up of new forms of economic systems in an effort to solve the problem represent a most important step.

[12] *Ibid.*, p. 113.

In a real sense the countries which have modern forms of modified capitalism face the same basic problem of how to reconcile the increased power of the state with liberty. The experience of France, for example, shows that the minimum authority needed to carry on the functions of the state may require limitations upon traditional forms of representative government. While the crisis which brought de Gaulle to power was not primarily economic, developments in France illustrate the kind of alternatives which might have to be faced in an economic crisis in other countries of the West. The 1957–58 economic recession in the United States, reflecting the need to control inflation while preventing economic depression, gives point to this observation. Yet it does not appear that any such powers of the state over the economy and over the individual as exist in totalitarian states would be required to deal with such a situation. The recollection that democratic and parliamentary institutions were adequate in most countries of the West to win through the far worse economic depression of the thirties offers substantial hope that these institutions can be adapted to solve the complex problems associated with the necessary growth of the power of the state over the economy. The high level of productivity which has been attained by the quasi-capitalistic economies of the West should mitigate the fierceness of the struggle for distributional shares among alternative recipient groups and thus facilitate the solution of these problems.

If the Yugoslav type of economic system, with production carried on by semi-competitive corporations, should some day come to be accompanied by a free political system, it would afford a striking comparison with the kind of economic and political system which would exist if the present trends in the countries of the West continue. There would still be differences in form between corporations of the Yugoslav type and the "privately owned" but managerially operated corporations which, for example, would still presumably operate under a Labor government in the United Kingdom. If the distribution of real income, including perquisites and fringe benefits, were essentially the same, the difference between the two systems would not be great. Indeed, there would not have to be much further evolutionary development of corporations in the

United States or much further redistribution of income before the differences between the so-called capitalistic systems and the so-called socialist systems of the Yugoslav type would lose their sharpness.

There is evidence that the kinds of constitutional systems such as characterized the Third and Fourth Republic in France or the Weimar Republic in pre-Hitler Germany which gave rise to a multiplicity of parties may not during periods of economic or political crisis permit the functioning of the state at a level of minimum efficiency. Other countries that have political systems in which the more conservative and the more radical parties must try to outbid each other for popular votes by offering special advantages to particular economic classes or groups may also find difficulty in carrying on the functions of government at a level of minimum efficiency. When such situations arise, the danger of the appearance of the tyrant is always great. He typically comes to power by revolution. His removal and the restoration of liberty are likely to prove extremely difficult, for one tyrant is likely to be followed by another, and the restoration of representative government may require generations.

The avoidance of tyranny has through history depended upon the prevention of intolerable social injustice by a governing class which remains open to accretion from outside its ranks, chosen by as popular a form of that "virtual representation" described by Burke as will still permit the effective functioning of the state. Such a governing class, of diverse social origins, with its top echelons responsible to and periodically replaceable at the will of the whole body of citizens, but with sufficient authority to resist irresponsible pressure groups, remains the best guarantee against revolution and tyranny. This balance between popular control and effective state power is now being worked out under new and difficult circumstances in a number of countries which have not yet definitely fallen under the rule of the tyrant. Out of the tyrannies which now govern in so large an area of the globe over huge populations, development of this fortunate but precarious balance may also some day take place. Only faint signs of such a development have so far appeared, but these afford some grounds for hope.

Finally, the evolution of new institutional relations among the economy, liberty and the state depends upon the avoidance of armed conflict between states with varying economic systems. So long as the economic and political systems of the Soviet type of totalitarian state appeared immutable, war between the Soviet state and the free societies of the West seemed inevitable. Though as yet inconclusive, the evidence that free societies might develop out of collectivist states of revolutionary origin affords the best hope that the catastrophe which now menaces mankind can be averted.

BIBLIOGRAPHY

Abramovitz, Moses. "Resources and Output Trends in the United States since 1870," Occasional Paper 52, National Bureau of Economic Research, New York, 1956

Adelman, M. A. "The Measurement of Industrial Concentration," *Review of Economics and Statistics*, November 1951, pp. 269–296

Badayev, A. *The Bolsheviks in the Tsarist Duma*, International Publishers, New York, 1932

Bauer, P. T., and Yamey, B. S. *The Economics of Underdeveloped Countries*, University of Chicago Press, Chicago, 1957

Benedict, Murray R. *Farm Policies of the United States, 1790–1950*, Twentieth Century Fund, 1953

Bergson, Abram. "On Inequality of Incomes in the U.S.S.R.," *American Slavic and East European Review*, April 1951, pp. 95–99

———— (ed.). *Soviet Economic Growth*, Row, Peterson and Company, Evanston, Ill., 1953

————. *The Structure of Soviet Wages: A Study in Socialist Economics*, Harvard University Press, Cambridge, 1944

Berle, Adolf A., Jr. *The Twentieth Century Capitalist Revolution*, Harcourt, Brace, New York, 1954

Blair, John M. "The Measurement of Industrial Concentration: A Reply," and M. A. Adelman, "Rejoinder," *Review of Economics and Statistics*, November 1952

————. "Statistical Measures of Concentration in Business, Problems of Compiling and Interpretation," American Statistical Association, December 29, 1950 (mimeo.)

Blough, Roger M. "Statement before the Subcommittee on Antitrust and Monopoly of the Senate Committee on the Judiciary," Washington, August 8, 1957

Boulding, Kenneth E. *The Organizational Revolution*, Harper, New York, 1953

Cartter, Allan M. "Income Shares of Upper Income Groups in Great Britain and the United States," *American Economic Review*, December 1954, pp. 877–883

————. *The Redistribution of Income in Postwar Britain*, Yale University Press, New Haven, 1955

Chamberlin, Edward H. *The Economic Analysis of Labor Union Power*, American Enterprise Association, Washington, 1958

————. "On the Origin of 'Oligopoly,'" *Towards a More General Theory of Value*, Oxford University Press, New York, 1957

Chamberlin, William Henry. *The Russian Revolution*, Vols. I and II, Macmillan, New York, 1935

Chapman, Janet. "Real Wages in the Soviet Union, 1928–1952," *Review of Economics and Statistics*, May 1954, pp. 134–156

Clark, J. M. "Competition: Static Models and Dynamic Aspects," *Papers and Proceedings of the American Economic Association*, May 1955, pp. 450–462

————. "Criteria of Sound Wage Adjustment with Emphasis on the Question of Inflationary Effects," *Impact of the Union*, edited by David McCord Wright, Harcourt, Brace, New York, 1951, pp. 1–33

————. *Economic Institutions and Human Welfare*, Knopf, New York, 1957

————. "Toward a Concept of Workable Competition," *American Economic Review*, June 1940, pp. 241–256

Commons, John R. *The Legal Foundations of Capitalism*, Macmillan, New York, 1924

Crosland, C. A. R. *The Future of Socialism*, J. Cape, London, 1956

————. "The Transition from Capitalism," *New Fabian Essays*, Turnstile Press, London, 1952, pp. 33–68

Crossman, R. H. S. "Towards the Philosophy of Socialism," *New Fabian Essays*, Turnstile Press, London, 1952, pp. 1–32

Current Digest of the Soviet Press (weekly published by the Joint Committee on Slavic Studies, New York)

de Tocqueville, Alexis. *The Old Regime and the French Revolution*, translated by Stuart Gilbert, Doubleday, Garden City, 1955

Dewhurst, J. Frederic, and associates. *America's Needs and Resources: A New Survey*, Twentieth Century Fund, 1955

Djilas, Milovan. *The New Class*, Praeger, New York, 1957

Dudintsev, Vladimir. *Not by Bread Alone,* translated by Edith Bone, Dutton, New York, 1957

Dulles, Allen W. *Germany's Underground,* Macmillan, New York, 1947

Dun & Bradstreet. *Commercial Failures in an Era of Business Progress, 1900–1952,* New York

———. *The First Five Years Are the Hardest,* New York

Economic Model Commission of the Economic Council (Poland). "Theses Concerning Some Lines for the Change of the Economic Model," Warsaw, May 1958 (mimeo.)

Economic Systems of the West, Rudolf Frei (ed.), List Gesellschaft, Kyklos-Verlag, Basel, Vol. I, 1957; Vol. II, 1958

Edwards, Corwin D.; Stocking, George W.; George, Edwin B.; Berle, A. A., Jr. "Four Comments on 'The Measurement of Industrial Concentration' with a Rejoinder by Professor Adelman," *Review of Economics and Statistics,* May 1952, pp. 156–178

Eisenhower, Dwight D. *Crusade in Europe,* Doubleday, Garden City, 1952

Fainsod, Merle. *How Russia Is Ruled,* Harvard University Press, Cambridge, 1953

Fast, Howard. *The Naked God,* Praeger, New York, 1957

Federal Reserve Bulletin, August 1957, p. 893

Federal Trade Commission. *The Concentration of Productive Facilities,* 1947

———. *Report on Changes in Concentration in Manufacturing, 1935 to 1947 and 1950,* 1954

———. *Report on Corporate Mergers and Acquisitions,* May 1955

Fellner, William. *Competition among the Few,* Knopf, New York, 1949

———. *Trends and Cycles in Economic Activity,* Holt, New York, 1956

Frane, Lenore, and Klein, L. R. "The Estimation of Disposable Income by Distributive Shares," *Review of Economics and Statistics,* November 1953, pp. 333–337

Friedman, Milton. "Significance of Labor Unions for Economic Policy," *Impact of the Union,* Harcourt, Brace, New York, 1951, pp. 204–234

Friedrich, Carl J. "The Political Thought of Neoliberalism," *American Political Science Review,* June 1955, pp. 509–525

Gaitskell, Hugh. "Public Ownership and Equality," *Socialist Commentary,* July 1955, pp. 165–167

Galbraith, J. K. *American Capitalism: The Concept of Countervailing Power,* Houghton Mifflin, Boston, 1952

———. "Economic Preconceptions and Farm Policy," *American Economic Review*, March 1953, pp. 40–52

Galenson, Walter. *Labor Productivity in Soviet and American Industry*, Columbia University Press, New York, 1955

George, Edwin B. "How Big Is Business?" *Dun's Review*, March 1939, pp. 18–31

———. "How Did Big Business Get Big?" *Dun's Review*, September 1939, pp. 21–36

———. "Is Big Business Getting Bigger?" *Dun's Review*, May 1939, pp. 28–36

Gervin, Spencer. *The Delegation of Legislative Power* (doctoral dissertation), Duke University, Durham, 1957

Gitlow, Benjamin. *The Whole of Their Lives*, Scribner's, New York, 1948

Goldsmith, Selma F. "Changes in the Size Distribution of Income," *American Economic Review*, May 1957, pp. 508–509

Gouzenko, Igor. *Fall of a Titan*, translated by Mervyn Black, Norton, New York, 1954

Hamburger, Ludwig. *How Nazi Germany Has Controlled Business*, Brookings Institution, Washington, 1943

Harberger, A. C. "Monopoly and Resource Allocation," *Papers and Proceedings of the American Economic Association*, May 1954, pp. 77–87

Hazard, John N. "Laws and Men in Soviet Society," *Foreign Affairs*, January 1958, pp. 267–277

Heflebower, Richard B. "Toward a Theory of Industrial Markets and Prices," *Papers and Proceedings of the American Economic Association*, May 1954, pp. 121–151

Hicks, J. R. "Economic Foundations of Wage Policy," *Economic Journal*, September 1955, pp. 389–404

Hodgman, Donald R. *Soviet Industrial Production, 1928–1951*, Harvard University Press, Cambridge, 1954

Homan, Paul T. "Socialist Thought in Great Britain," *American Economic Review*, June 1957, pp. 350–362

Hoover, Calvin B. "The American Organizational Economy," *Perspectives U.S.A.*, Winter 1955, pp. 105–118

———. *The Economic Life of Soviet Russia*, Macmillan, New York, 1931

———. *Germany Enters the Third Reich*, Macmillan, New York, 1933

———. "Institutional and Theoretical Implications of Economic Change," *American Economic Review*, March 1954, pp. 1–14

International Monetary Fund, *International Financial News Survey*, March 8, 1957, p. 270

Izvestia (daily newspaper of the Soviet government)

Jasny, Naum. "The Rates of Soviet Economic Growth," *American Statistician*, June 1958, pp. 21–24

Jenkins, Roy. "Equality," *New Fabian Essays,* Turnstile Press, London, 1952, pp. 69–90

Johnson, Gale. "Agricultural Price Policy and International Trade," *Essays in International Finance*, Princeton University Press, Princeton, June 1954

———. "Competition in Agriculture: Fact or Fiction," *Papers and Proceedings of the American Economic Association,* May 1954, pp. 107–115

———. "The Functional Distribution of Income in the United States, 1850–1952," *Review of Economics and Statistics*, May 1954, pp. 175–182

Joint Economic Committee, *Productivity, Prices and Incomes,* Materials Prepared for the Joint Economic Committee, 1957

Kaplan, Abraham. *Big Enterprise in a Competitive System*, Brookings Institution, Washington, 1954

———. "The Current Merger Movement Analyzed," *Harvard Business Review*, May–June 1955, pp. 91–98

Kautsky, Karl. *The Dictatorship of the Proletariat*, National Labour Press, London, 1919

Kerensky, Alexander. *The Crucifixion of Liberty*, John Day, New York, 1934

Kerr, Clark. "Labor's Share and the Labor Movement," Reprint No. 93, Institute of Industrial Relations, Berkeley, California, 1957

Keynes, John M. *General Theory of Employment, Interest and Money*, Macmillan, London, 1936

Koestler, Arthur. *Darkness at Noon*, translated by Daphne Hardy, Macmillan, New York, 1941

Korol, Alexander G. *Soviet Education for Science and Technology*, Technology Press, Cambridge, 1957

Kropotkin, Peter. *The Great French Revolution, 1789–1793*, Vanguard, New York, 1927

Kulev, I. A. "O Dallneishem Sovershenstvovanii Planirovania i Rukovodstva Narodnym Khoziaistvom," Seriia III, No. 11, *Izdatelstvo-Znanie*, Moscow, 1957

Kust, Matthew J. "India: Deepening Crisis," *New Republic*, January 20, 1958, pp. 9–11

Kuznets, Simon. "Economic Growth and Income Inequality," *American Economic Review*, March 1955, pp. 1–28

———. *Shares of Upper Income Groups in Income and Savings*, National Bureau of Economic Research, New York, 1953

Labour Party. *Industry and Society: Labour's Policy on Future Public Ownership*, Transport House, London, 1957

———. *Public Enterprise: Labour's Review of the Nationalized Industries*, Transport House, London, July 1957

Lange, Oskar. "The Political Economy of Socialism" (a lecture given November 18, 1957), Polish Institute of International Affairs (mimeo.)

———. "Some Problems Relating to the Polish Road to Socialism," Polonia Publishing House, Warsaw, 1957

League of Communists of Yugoslavia. Draft Programme, Belgrade, March 1958 (mimeo.)

Legislative Reference Service of the Library of Congress. *Soviet Economic Growth: A Comparison with the United States*, 1957

Lenin, Vladimir. *Collected Works of Lenin*, Vol. XVII, International Publishers, New York, 1927

———. *State and Revolution*, Vanguard, New York, 1929

Levinson, H. M. *Unionism, Wage Trends and Income Distribution, 1914–1947*, University of Michigan Press, Ann Arbor, 1951

Lewis, Arthur. "A Socialist Economic Policy," *Socialist Commentary*, June 1955, pp. 171–174

Lewis, Ben W. *British Planning and Nationalization*, Twentieth Century Fund, 1952

Lilienthal, David E. *Big Business: A New Era*, Harper, New York, 1953

Lindblom, Charles E. *Unions and Capitalism*, Yale University Press, New Haven, 1949

Lipset, Seymour M. "The Political Process in Trade Unions: A Theoretical Statement," Reprint No. 171, Bureau of Applied Social Research, Columbia University, New York, 1954

Lurie, Samuel. *Private Investment in a Controlled Economy: Germany, 1933–1939*, Columbia University Press, New York, 1947

Lyons, Eugene. *Assignment in Utopia*, Harcourt, Brace, New York, 1937

Machlup, Fritz. *The Political Economy of Monopoly*, Johns Hopkins Press, Baltimore, 1952

Mack, Ruth P. "Discussion of 'Monopoly and Resource Allocation' by A. C. Harberger," *Papers and Proceedings of the American Economic Association*, May 1954, pp. 88–92

Markham, Jesse W. "Merger Policy under the New Section 7: A Six-Year Appraisal," *Virginia Law Review*, May 1957, pp. 489–528

Marx, Karl. *Capital*, Charles H. Kerr and Co., Chicago, 1906, Vol. I

————. *A Contribution to the Critique of Political Economy,* Charles H. Kerr and Co., Chicago, 1934

————, and Engels, Friedrich. *Communist Manifesto,* New York Labor News Co., New York, 1948

Mason, Edward S. "The Apologetics of 'Managerialism,'" *Journal of Business of the University of Chicago,* January 1958, pp. 1–11

————. *Economic Concentration and the Monopoly Problem,* Harvard University Press, Cambridge, 1957, pp. 196–223

————. *The History of the Paris Commune,* Macmillan, New York, 1930

Massachusetts Institute of Technology, School of Industrial Management. "The Evolving Role of the Corporate Director," *Adventures in Thought and Action,* M.I.T. Press, Cambridge, 1957, pp. 46–56

Means, Gardiner. "Industrial Prices and Their Relative Flexibility," 74th Cong., 1st sess., S. Doc. 13, 1935

————, and Ware, Caroline F. *The Modern Economy in Action,* Harcourt, Brace, New York, 1936

Morrison, Herbert. "Election Afterthoughts: Some Lessons of 1955," *Socialist Commentary,* July 1955, pp. 201–204

Mosca, Gaetano. *The Ruling Class,* translated by Hannah D. Kohn, McGraw-Hill, New York, 1939

Narodnoe Khoziaistvo SSSR (The National Economy of the U.S.S.R.), Central Statistical Administration, Moscow, 1956

Nathan, Otto. *The Nazi Economic System,* Duke University Press, Durham, 1944

The New Leader, January 21, 1957

Nourse, Edwin G. *Economics in the Public Service,* Harcourt, Brace, New York, 1953

Nove, A. "The Pace of Soviet Economic Development," *Lloyd's Bank Review,* April 1956, pp. 1–23

Nutter, Warren G. *The Extent of Enterprise Monopoly in the United States, 1899–1939,* University of Chicago Press, Chicago, 1951

————. "Industrial Growth in the Soviet Union," *Papers and Proceedings of the American Economic Association,* May 1958, pp. 398–411

————. "Some Observations on Soviet Industrial Growth," *Papers and Proceedings of the American Economic Association,* May 1957, pp. 618–630

Organization for European Economic Co-operation, *Europe Today and in 1960,* 8th Report, Paris, 1957, 2 vols.

Orwell, George. *The Lion and the Unicorn,* Secker & Warburg, London, 1941

————. *Such, Such Were the Joys*, Doubleday, Garden City, N.Y.

Panov, D. "Science and Socialism," *Kommunist*, No. 1, pp. 11–25

Papers and Proceedings of the Meetings of the American Economic Association, May 1954, 1955, 1956, 1957 and 1958

Pechtel, Rudolf. *Deutscher Widerstand*, Erlenbach, Zurich, 1947

Perlman, Selig. *A Theory of the Labor Movement*, Macmillan, New York, 1928

Perlo, Victor. " 'People's Capitalism' and Stock-Ownership," *American Economic Review*, June 1958, pp. 333–347

Pravda (daily news organ of the Central Committee of the Communist Party of the U.S.S.R.)

Promyshlennost' SSSR, Central Statistical Administration, Moscow, 1957

Quarterly Review Amsterdamsche Bank, No. 117, Second Quarter, 1957

Rauschning, Hermann. *The Revolution of Nihilism: Warning to the West*, Longmans, Green, New York, 1939

Report of the Attorney General's National Committee to Study the Anti-Trust Laws, March 31, 1955

Reynolds, Lloyd G., and Taft, Cynthia H. *The Evolution of Wage Structure*, Yale University Press, New Haven, 1956

Robinson, Geroid T. *Rural Russia under the Old Regime*, Macmillan, New York, 1932

Ross, A. M. *Trade Union Policy*, University of California Press, Berkeley, 1948

Rothfels, Hans. *Die Deutsche Opposition Gegen Hitler*, Im Scherpe-Verlag, Krefeld, 1951

Russian Institute of Columbia University (ed.). *The Anti-Stalin Campaign and International Communism*, Columbia University Press, New York, 1956

Salisbury, Harrison. "Writers in the Shadow of Communism," *New York Times Magazine*, June 9, 1957, p. 10

Schlabrendorff, Fabian von. *Offiziere Gegen Hitler*, Europa Verlag, Zurich, 1951

Schumpeter, Joseph. *Capitalism, Socialism and Democracy*, Harper, New York and London, 1942

Schwartz, Harry. *Russia's Soviet Economy*, Prentice-Hall, New York, 1954

Seton, F. *The Tempo of Soviet Industrial Expansion*, Manchester Statistical Society, Manchester, 1957

Shub, David. *Lenin: A Biography*, Doubleday, Garden City, 1948

Slichter, Sumner. "Do the Wage-Fixing Arrangements in the American Labor Market Have an Inflationary Bias?" *Papers and Pro-*

ceedings of the American Economic Association, May 1954, pp. 322–346

———. "Government Expansion in a Dynamic Society," *Commercial and Financial Chronicle,* April 25, 1957, pp. 3, 30–33

———. "The Growth of Competition," *Atlantic Monthly,* November 1953, pp. 56–70

———. "How Stable Is the American Economy?" *Yale Review,* June 1950, pp. 577–590

Souvarine, Boris. "October: Myths and Realities," *The New Leader,* November 4, 1957

Spulber, Nicholas. *The Economics of Communist Eastern Europe,* Wiley and Technology Press, New York, 1957

Steinberg, Julien (ed.). *Verdict of Three Decades,* Duell, Sloan and Pearce, New York, 1950

Stigler, George J. *Five Lectures on Economic Problems,* Longmans, Green, London, 1949

———. "Mergers and Preventive Antitrust Policy," *University of Pennsylvania Law Review,* November 1955, pp. 176–184

———. "Monopoly and Concentration," *Journal of Political Economy,* February 1956, pp. 33–40

Stocking, George W., and Watkins, Myron W. *Monopoly and Free Enterprise,* Twentieth Century Fund, 1951

———, and Mueller, W. P. "The Cellophane Case and the New Competition," *American Economic Review,* March 1955, pp. 29–63

Suetonius (Caius Suetonius Tranquillus). *Lives of the Twelve Caesars,* Modern Library, New York, 1931

Sukhanov, N. N. *The Russian Revolution, 1917,* translated by Joel Carmichael, Oxford University Press, London, 1955

Survey of Current Business, July 1958, pp. 4–5

Tacitus, Cornelius. *The Annals,* Ginn and Company, Boston and London, 1890

Tinbergen, Jan. "The Netherlands Social and Economic Council," *National Planning Association Bulletin,* October 1957

Trotsky, Leon. *History of the Russian Revolution,* Vol. III, Simon & Schuster, New York, 1937

———. *My Life,* Scribner's, New York, 1930

United Nations. *World Economic Survey, 1955,* New York, 1956

U.S. Department of Health, Education and Welfare, Office of Education. *Education in the U.S.S.R.,* 1957

Viner, Jacob. "International Trade Theory and Its Present-Day Relevance," *Economic and Public Policy,* Brookings Institution, Washington, 1954

Vjesnik (Zagreb), May 23, 1958

Vneshnyaya Torgovlya (Ministry of Foreign Trade, Moscow), November 1957

"Wage Determination in the American Economy" (three papers by Clark Kerr, Martin Bronfenbrenner and Harold M. Levinson), *Papers and Proceedings of the American Economic Association*, May 1954, pp. 279–316

Wall Street Journal, March 16, 1955

Weber, Wilhelm. "Österreichs Wirtschaftsverfassung und Wirtschaftsordnung im Lichte moderner Wirtschaftstheorie und Wirtschaftspolitik," *Zeitschrift für Nationalokonomie*, Band XVII, Heft 1, 1957, pp. 55–101

Weintraub, Sidney. "Revised Doctrines of Competition," *Papers and Proceedings of the American Economic Association*, May 1955, pp. 463–479

Wheeler-Bennett, John. *Wooden Titan*, Morrow, New York, 1936

Wilcox, Clair. "On the Alleged Ubiquity of Oligopoly," *Papers and Proceedings of the American Economic Association*, May 1950, pp. 67–73

Wolfe, Bertram. *Three Who Made a Revolution*, Dial Press, New York, 1948

Wright, Richard, and others. *The God That Failed*, Richard Crossman (ed.), Bantam Books, New York, 1952

INDEX

Abramovitz, Moses, 269 n.
Academic freedom in Soviet education, 147–48
Adair v. U.S., 180 n., 183 n.
Adelman, M. A., 247 n., 257 n.
"Administered prices" in U.S. industry, 191, 213–17, 240
Agricultural Adjustment Act, 192, 195
Agricultural Adjustment Administration, 191 n.
Agriculture: collectivized, 65–71, 140–41; in Czechoslovakia, 392–93; in Denmark, 304; in Great Britain, 275; in Nazi Germany, 168; in Poland, 379, 381; in Sweden, 300–1; in U.S., 191 n., 192, 195, 196, 200, 219–21, 223, 224–27, 232; in U.S.S.R., 59–60, 65–71, 102, 126, 127, 138–41, 387
Allen, G. C., 274, 280
Amana, 12
American Economic Association, 203 n., 222 n., 243, 243 n., 244 n., 247 n., 249 n., 339 n.
American Economic Review, 205 n., 221 n., 229 n., 230 n., 247 n., 285 n., 339 n.
American Federation of Labor, 211
Anarchism, 15, 310–11
Antitrust laws, 181–82, 183 n., 247–48; in Great Britain, 277
Antonov-Ovseenko, V.A., 33 n., 84
Argentina, Peronista regime, 161, 341 n.

Arrest, immunity from: under capitalism, 15; under Nazi and Soviet systems, 15
Artel (collective farm unit), 70
Arzumanyan, A., 153 n.
Austria: Soviet withdrawal from, 103; state-owned industry in, 292

Badayev, A., 51 n.
Bain, Joe S., 247 n.
Bakers Union, 210
Banking and Currency, Senate Committee on, 189
Barras, 108 n.
Bauer, P. T., 130 n.
Belgian economic system, 297–98
Bell, Daniel, 115
Benedict, Murray R., 223 n.
Benediktov, Ivan A., 387 n.
Bergson, Abram, 80 n., 124 n., 279 n.
Beria, Lavrenti, 51, 91–92, 93
Berle, Adolf A., Jr., 243, 257 n.
Berlin blockade, 82
Bernstein, Eduard, 29, 40, 93
Bezsmertnyi Garnison (Soviet film), 107
Bill of Rights, 14
Black markets, 214, 389
Blair, John M., 191 n., 257 n.
Blanqui, Louis Auguste, 43 n.
Bloody Sunday, 95
Blough, Roger N., 213
Bolshevik coup in October revolution, 32–35